THE BIOLOGY
AND EVOLUTION
OF LANGUAGE

THE BIOLOGY
AND EVOLUTION
OF LANGUAGE

Philip Lieberman

Harvard University Press
Cambridge, Massachusetts
London, England
1984

Library of Congress Cataloging in Publication Data

Lieberman, Philip
   The biology and evolution of language.

   Bibliography: p.
   Includes index.
   1. Biolinguistics.   2. Language and languages — Origin.
3. Evolution.   I. Title.
P132.L53   1984   401   83-22582
ISBN 0-674-07412-2 (alk. paper)

To
Erik and Diane Lund
and to
Arend Bouhuys (1925 – 1979)

But we may go further, and affirm most truly that it is a mere and miserable solitude to want true friends, without which the world is but a wilderness.　—FRANCIS BACON

PREFACE

HUMAN LANGUAGE AND COGNITIVE ability are so linked to the question of human uniqueness that we often implicitly accept the premise that these abilities are unique. The thesis I shall develop is that our present place in the scheme of things and the manifest differences between human beings and all other living animals regarding language and cognition follow from a sequence of small structural changes that together yield a unique pattern of linguistic and cognitive behavior. The total pattern of human behavior and human culture is unique, but to understand how it evolved we must differentiate between the biological "devices" that underlie human cognitive and linguistic ability and these behavioral patterns. The distinction is similar to that which we must draw between the electronic circuits and devices that make up a digital computer and the computer's programmed behavior.

The evolution of human linguistic and cognitive ability, like other aspects of human evolution, is probably the result of Darwinian natural selection acting to retain structural variations that, though they may seem small and trivial, made profound changes in human behavior and culture possible. The anatomical development of the opposable thumb, for example, facilitated the development of tool culture. The development of the ability to produce sounds like the vowel [i] (the vowel of the word *bee*) likewise facilitated the development of human speech, which in turn facilitated the rapid interchange of information in humanlike animals who already had their hands occupied using tools and carrying objects because of the previous sequences of small anatomical changes that yielded upright bipedal locomotion. The evolution of human linguistic and cognitive ability, to me, thus is part of the general process of human evolution. The data I discuss in connection with the evolution of human speech again bear on the general question of the processes that were and are operant in human evolution—these data refute the theory of neoteny.

The framework of this book is thus biological and differs from that of most linguistic studies. A biological approach to the study of language has as its goal the development of theories that can account for the greatest range of data. A biological approach also takes into account the genetic variation that is inherent in any human population. We should not expect to find a uniform "universal" grammar that is based on identical biological mechanisms throughout the total population. We again do not expect to find anatomical, physiologic, or neural mechanisms that necessarily are "logically" designed. Biological systems have an evolutionary logic that may, or may not, conform to present-day notions of what constitutes an elegant or simple solution to a problem. The human respiratory system, as we shall see, looks like a Rube Goldberg system, but it works and has a logic based on its particular evolutionary history. The transformational, generative school of linguistics has resulted in a period of intense linguistic speculation on what the properties of human linguistic and cognitive ability might be. The principal intellectual tools of the linguists engaged in this endeavor have been their introspection and some logical analysis. The range of acceptable data for linguistic theories has, moreover, become ever more constrained and arbitrary for many theoretical linguists continuing the trend established with Saussure's langue-parole distinction. The Chomskyian competence-performance distinction imposes arbitrary limits on the range of behavior and data that a linguistic theory should account for. We simply do not know how we are put together. We do not know that the biological mechanisms that structure linguistic ability also do not play a role in structuring other aspects of human cognitive behavior. Indeed, we are only beginning to understand how the brain may function. We likewise have been able to identify only some of the innate, genetically transmitted anatomical and neural mechanisms that structure human speech and syntax. The path toward understanding the nature of these mechanisms is to study them. My hope is that this book will provide a useful starting point.

I would like to thank my friends and colleagues for their patience in discussing, reading, and commenting on many aspects of this study. I would especially like to thank Professors Sheila Blumstein, Henry Kučera, Pauline Jacobson, Peter Eimas, James Anderson, Walter Quevedo, Leon Cooper, and Robert Meskill of Brown University, as well as Marcia Lieberman, Terrance Nearey, Robert Buhr, Karen Landahl, Carol Chapin, and Jack Ryalls. John Mertus's elegant computer programs made much of my research possible. Again I am indebted to the many conversations I had with Franklin Cooper, Alvin Liberman, and Katherine Harris at Haskins Laboratories; to Eric Wanner at Harvard University Press; and to Jeffrey Laitman, Edmund Crelin, and Alan and Beatrix Gardner. Moira Russo's heroic work with an obstinate word-processing system gave form to this book, and the generous support of the National Institute of Child Health and Human Development made possible research on the development of speech in infants and young children.

CONTENTS

THE BIOLOGY
AND EVOLUTION
OF LANGUAGE

Introduction: The Biological Framework

THE ISSUES THAT ARE CENTRAL to this book are the biological bases of human language, language in relation to cognition, the evolution of modern *Homo sapiens*, and the nature of some of the mechanisms that structure evolution. I will discuss the possible nature of the biological substrate of human language and how some of the anatomical and neural mechanisms that underlie human linguistic ability may have evolved. I will also discuss some aspects of the relation, that holds between human linguistic ability and other aspects of cognition. The central premise of this book is that human linguistic ability is based on rather general neural mechanisms that structure the cognitive behavior of human beings as well as that of other animals, plus a limited set of language-specific mechanisms that differentiate the particular manner in which we transmit information. Thus I propose that many aspects of the syntactic structure and semantic interpretation of human language derive from neural mechanisms which also structure all other aspects of human cognitive behavior, and which derive from homologous mechanisms that structure the cognitive behavior of other animals. The language-specific aspects of human language, in my view, are the anatomical and neural input-output mechanisms for the production of speech and some of the neural mechanisms that structure rule-governed syntax. The present form of human language is the result of how these particular biological systems mesh with more general neural substrates for cognition.

I shall attempt to present data that are consistent with the theory that these specialized biological mechanisms evolved by the process of Darwinian natural selection from similar, homologous mechanisms in other animals. I do not claim that any other living species has a communication system with the capabilities of human language. However, I do not view human language as outside the domain of the

1

general evolutionary processes that resulted in the present form and behavior of other living species. Human language, in my view, is different from the communication systems of other animals in the same sense that the communication system of a dog differs from that of a frog. It is more complex; it can express concepts that probably are not relevant or possible to frogs and involves different anatomical and neural mechanisms. But these mechanisms are related in a biological and evolutionary sense. The apparent discontinuity between the language and cognitive ability of human beings and that of other living species follows from the extinction of earlier humanlike, hominid species.

I will present the view that the present form of human language and human culture follows from the evolution of the biological substrate for human speech in the past 500,000 to 250,000 years or so. Human speech has special properties that make rapid vocal communication possible. Human language followed from adding the specialized anatomical and neural mechanisms that structure human speech to the neural structures that had been evolving over millions of years to enhance general cognitive ability and rule-governed, syntactic behavior. Thus I claim that the particular form of human language follows from comparatively recent adaptations in the course of homonoid evolution. The language-specific mechanisms that are peculiar to human vocal communication are furthermore analogous to communicative specializations that can be found in other animals, such as crickets, frogs, and monkeys. The evolution of human language is therefore analogous to the evolution of behavioral patterns that are "unique" to other species. The unique mating calls of bullfrogs follow from their supralaryngeal airways and auditory system. The unique aspects of human speech likewise follow from the anatomical structure of our airways and the properties of our central nervous system. Though the functional properties of bullfrog calls are quite different, their evolution follows from the same principles.

My theory is in opposition to that held by many linguists. The opposing theory, which is perhaps best exemplified by Chomsky's work (1980a, 1980b), claims that human language is unique because of a hypothetical neural "language organ," which can be localized in the human brain and which embodies a constellation of innate, genetically transmitted neural devices that determine the syntactic and semantic properties of all human languages. According to Chomsky (1980a, p. 182), these neural devices are language-specific: that is, they are disjoint from the neural mechanisms that structure other aspects of human cognitive behavior or the neural mechanisms that are involved in the social communications of other animals. This theory, like other aspects of Chomsky's linguistic theories (Chomsky, 1966), appears to derive from the philosophical system of Descartes, who in his letter of 1646 to the Marquis of Newcastle claims that language "belongs to man alone." Implicit in this neo-Cartesian position is the uniqueness of *Homo sapiens* in an evolutionary sense. Indeed, the extreme position as expressed by Chomsky is that human capacities like the ability to use language or the capacity to deal with the number system could not have evolved by means of Darwinian natural selection. Chomsky notes that "the capacity to deal with the number system . . . is not specifically 'selected' through evolution, one must assume — even the existence of the number faculty could have not been known, or the capacity exercised until human evolution had essentially reached its current stage" (1980b, p. 3). Chomsky essentially proposes that these capacities are the result of events that are unique to human evolution, perhaps sudden mutations that abruptly yielded the "current stage" of human evolution.

Throughout this book I will discuss data gathered from a number of areas in terms of a model derived from the biological sciences. These data refute the neo-Cartesian position of Chomsky, which precludes any connection between the intelligent behavior or social communications of any other living species and the "special" characteristics of human language. Though Chomsky compares the study of language to the study of an organ of the body, such as the heart or the liver, it is clear that his hypothetical language organ has unique properties. Every other organ of the human body — the heart, the liver, the foot — can be related to similar organs in other living animals. We are quite close to some of these animals in terms of geological time. Only ten to twenty million years have elapsed since we and chimpanzees, gorillas, and orangutans had a common ancestor (Sarich, 1974; Pilbeam, 1972; Yunis and Prakash, 1982). The similarities that characterize our external and internal organs have been a constant feature of all studies in comparative anatomy since Tyson's first study of the chimpanzee at the close of the seventeenth century (1699). Though chimpanzees and human beings do not have exactly the same anatomical structures, there are similar, homologous structures. Much of the evidence that supports the Darwinian theory of evolution by means of natural selection rests on the overwhelming evidence for homologous organs throughout a large range of species. Human beings and chimpanzees, for example, do not walk in the same way. The anatomy of the bones of the leg and feet as well as the pelvis reflects these differences and differs for human beings and chimpanzees. There are, however, many similarities, and we can see that the morphology of nonhuman primates is related to that of human beings.

THE DARWINIAN MODEL OF EVOLUTION

The Darwinian model of evolution has furnished a coherent frame-work for the study of human evolution ever since the publication in 1859 of *On the Origin of Species by Means of Natural Selection*. The Darwinian model essentially involves three elements: (1) the "struggle for existence," (2) genetic variation in a population, and (3) natural selection. The struggle for existence is essentially recognition of the fact that life is precarious. For most species, and that included most human beings until comparatively recent times, life is chancy. The average human lifespan was about thirty years throughout the world until the beginning of the nineteenth century — about the lifespan of chimpanzees living in the wild (Goodall, 1968). We tend to forget, with our grain surpluses, what life was, and is, for other people. Families with large numbers of offspring, of whom only a few survived, were typical for our ancestors, as they are today in the many "underdeveloped" parts of the world. The "struggle for existence" is evident in that most species are extinct. As Jacob (1977) notes, the number of living species in the animal kingdom can be estimated to be about a few million, whereas the number of extinct ones since life existed on earth probably is about five hundred million.

The struggle for existence is linked to the process of natural selection, "filtering" the effects of genetic variation:

> Owing to this struggle for life, any variation, however slight and from whatever cause proceeding, if it be in any degree profitable to an individual of any species, in its infinitely complex relations to other organic beings and to external nature, will tend to the preservation of that individual, and will generally be inherited by its offspring. The offspring, also, will thus have a better chance of surviving, for of the many individuals of a species which are periodically born but a small number can survive. I have called this principle, by which each small variation if useful is preserved by the term of Natural Selection.
>
> (Darwin, 1859, p. 61)

The Darwinian struggle for existence is *not* Tennyson's vision of "Nature red in tooth and claw" or the neo-Darwinian views of "Captains of Industry" justifying their control of wealth and power. In Darwin's words, "I should premise that I use the term Struggle for Existence in a large and metaphorical sense, including dependence of one being on another, and including (which is more important) not only the life of the individual, but success in leaving progeny" (1859, p. 62). Darwin's view of life in relation to "organic nature," though phrased in a different manner, is the ecological model we are still debating:

> A struggle for existence inevitably follows from the high rate at which all organic beings tend to increase. Every being, which during its natural lifetime produces several eggs or seeds, must suffer destruction during some period of its life, and during some season or occasional year, otherwise, on the principle of geometrical increase, its numbers would quickly become so inordinately great that no country could support the product. Hence, as more individuals are produced than can possibly survive, there must in every case be a struggle for existence, either one individual with another of the same species, or with the individuals of distinct species, or the physical conditions of life. It is the doctrine of Malthus applied with manifold force to the whole animal and vegetable kingdoms; for in this case there can be no artificial increase of food, and no prudential restraint from marriage. There is no exception to the rule that every organic being naturally increases at so high a rate, that if not destroyed, the earth would be soon covered by the progeny of a single pair. Even slow-breeding man has doubled in twenty-five years, and at this rate, in a few thousand years, there would literally not be standing room for his progeny.
>
> (1859, p. 63)

THE "SYNTHETIC" THEORY OF EVOLUTION: ALLETIC VARIATION

Darwin clearly recognized the relevance of genetic variation to his theory: "all organs and instincts are, in ever so slight a degree, variable" (1859, p. 459). Darwin did not understand the genetic basis of transmission of inherited characteristics; he had no knowledge of Mendel's genetic theory. The "synthetic theory" of evolution (Simpson, 1944; Mayr, 1942) represents the successful merging of the insights derived from genetic theory with the Darwinian model. The modern synthetic theory of evolution claims that natural selection operates, for the most part, on the variations in the *population* that defines a species. The individuals that constitute the population that we may call a species differ from one another genetically to some degree. Indeed, the data of "artificial selection," the breeding of horses, pigeons, and plants that Darwin reviewed all point to the presence of alleles, or variant genes, within the population that defines any species. As Ayala (1978, p. 61) notes, "The fact that artificial selection works almost every time it is attempted indicates that there is genetic variation in populations for virtually every characteristic of the organism." An agronomist thus does not have to wait for a random mutation to occur in order to develop a drought-resistant variety of corn. Within the population of corn plants there are already alletic variations that are more resistant to drought. Large amounts of genetic variation have been found in recent years in many species. The degree of genetic variation that is typical of human beings is at least 6.7 percent. This estimate probably is too low, owing to the procedures for estimating variation (Ayala, 1978). There is always a large pool of variation within the population that defines a species which can allow the species as a *population* to adapt to changing circumstances. The *potential* for selection therefore can be viewed as a mechanism for the survival of the species in the struggle for existence. Specialized species may do better in a restricted environment, but a species that has the genetic potential for changes that will allow survival in a variety of circumstances can survive changes in the environment that would lead to the extinction of a specialized population lacking the range of alletic variation.

THE MOSAIC PRINCIPLE AND GRADUALISM

There is a general "mosaic" principle that appears to govern the process of evolution that is consistent with alletic variation. We are put together in bits and pieces that evolved separately. When we look at the genetic mechanisms that govern the development of even simple anatomical systems like the upper and lower jaws, it is apparent that the development of the lower jaw, the mandible, is not keyed to that of the upper jaw. Though the upper and lower jaws must work together so that we can chew, they did not evolve and do not develop ontogenetically in concert. This is true even for animals like dogs, whose lives literally are structured about their jaws and teeth. Some people, and some dogs, have undershot or overshot jaws because the upper and lower jaws are each under independent genetic regulation (Stockard, 1941). Though the upper and lower jaws are functionally related when we use our teeth, there is no master gene that evolved to control their form. If we were to make a genetic survey of a population of dogs, we would find a great deal of alletic variation in the genes that regulate the form and growth of the upper and lower jaws. Mismatches commonly occur in individuals. The structural harmony that we see in the population of dogs as a whole reflects the filtering effects of natural selection. Dogs whose upper and lower jaws are mismatched will not be able to feed as effectively as ones who have more functional jaws. In a state of nature the struggle for existence that is the key element in Darwin's theory of evolution by means of natural selection would select for functional jaws. These animals would be better adapted and would leave more progeny. Two *structures,* the upper and lower jaws, that are under independent genetic regulation thus are matched in the population of dogs to yield a *functional* system that has a selective advantage. The distinction between *structure* and *function* is important. It is central to Darwin's theory, and I will discuss its significance later on.

Darwin, in the *Origin of Species,* continually stresses the selective value of small *structural* changes that yield the continuity of evolution. The general principle of mosaic evolution explains why "big" mutations, which affect the central, life-supporting systems of an organism, are not likely to be viable. A big mutation that yielded an animal with two hearts would, for example, seem to be a very useful mutation in terms of the struggle for existence. However, we do not find any animal that has two hearts. All animals are similar in that they have one heart, though it logically would be a great advantage to have two hearts. If one heart were weakened we could still survive. Individuals who had two hearts would be more likely to live longer and thus would be more likely to leave more progeny who also had two hearts. However, the unfortunate individuals who have two hearts rarely survive the late fetal stages and are to be found in the glass jars in which "monsters" traditionally are exhibited in the corridors of schools of anatomy. A big mutation that yielded an animal with two hearts could be viable if, and only if, it occurred together with a set of correlated changes in the circulatory system of veins and arteries and the receptors and neural mechanisms that regulate the flow of blood throughout the body. The principle of mosaic evolution, which follows from the accumulated data of more than a hundred years, precludes a master gene that regulates all of these independent biological systems—the heart, circulatory system, and neural control mechanisms. In contrast, a small peripheral change that involves the addition of a sixth digit to the hand is viable because it is limited, does not need an elaborate support system, and will not interfere with other basic systems. The small peripheral mutations are the ones that are viable and the ones that are retained when they are "useful" in the struggle for existence. Thus, as Darwin noted, various species of birds differ in the length of their beaks. No bird has two hearts.

"PUNCTUATED EQUILIBRIA" AND NEOTENY

Darwin, in Chapter 14, the recapitulation of his theory, noted that "nothing at first can appear more difficult to believe than that the more complex organs and instincts should have been perfected, not

by means superior to, though analogous with, human reason, but by
the accumulation of innumerable slight variations" (1859, p. 459). The
theory of "punctuated equilibria" proposed by Eldridge and Gould
(1972; Gould, 1977) claims that the tempo of evolution is not even.
Gould and Eldridge claim that longer periods of stasis or slight change
occur, punctuated by periods of rapid changes that yield "new"
species. In the Gould-Eldridge model the small gradual changes that
Darwin stressed mark the slight gradual changes within a species in the
static periods. The changes that yield new species, in contrast, are
supposed to be rapid and profound. Gould (1977), for example,
proposes that the recent stages of human evolution involve rapid
changes in the genetically transmitted mechanisms that regulate ontogenetic development. Gould thus claims that modern human adults
retain anatomical features that are associated with newborn nonhuman primates. The theory of neoteny, which Gould (1977) has revived, explicitly claims that there is a master regulatory gene that
governs the expression of the structural or protein genes that determine the form of our bones, hair, brains, and the like. Structural
genes are ones that directly determine the form of some element; for
example, a structural gene determines whether your eyes are blue or
brown. Regulatory genes determine the rate or pattern in which the
structural genes are expressed in the growth of a plant or animal.
According to Gould, the anatomical changes that differentiate human
beings from other, nonhuman primates reflect the putative fact that
we retain the anatomical structures and the "plasticity" of the brain
that mark the infantile forms of our pongid cousins.

    Much of the detailed discussion of the evolution of human speech
in Chapters 11 and 12 necessarily will involve testing the theory of
punctuated equilibria and other models that have been developed to
account for the tempo of evolution. The anatomical data that I will
present show that Gould's theory of neoteny is wrong. Adult human
beings differ profoundly from newborn human infants. Normal
human adults in fact differ more profoundly from the general newborn morphology that is typical of all primates than do all other living,
nonhuman primates. The only human adults who sometimes do
retain the newborn morphology are the victims of Down's syndrome
—"mongoloid idiots" (Benda, 1969). Down's syndrome interferes
with the regulatory processes that govern normal development.

    The mechanisms of evolution that yield new species are not
entirely clear at this point. As Mayr notes, "The discovery of molecular biology that there are regulatory genes as well as structural ones
poses new evolutionary questions. Is the rate of evolution of the two

kinds of genes the same? Are they equally susceptible to natural selection? Is one kind of gene more important than the other in speciation or in the origin of higher taxa?" (1979, p. 54). Although the process of neoteny is not a likely agent in hominid evolution, other genetically controlled regulatory mechanisms may have been involved. The structural genes of humans and chimpanzees, for example, are quite similar (Sarich, 1974). However, chimpanzees and human beings differ greatly with respect to their morphology and behavior; it is possible that regulatory genes account for these differences.

The problems of viability that I have noted in connection with big changes involving structural genes will also limit the success of "experiments of nature" that involve big changes in genetic regulatory mechanisms. Profound craniofacial anomalies that involve changes in the expression of structural genes are not usually viable (Pruzansky, 1973). The interrelationships among the "components" of a higher mammal are usually too complex to allow very rapid changes in one system. The neotenous victims of Down's syndrome, for example, often have lungs that are too small to provide enough oxygen for their body weight. They therefore do not have the same resistance to respiratory infections as normal children, and they have a higher death rate (Bouhuys, 1974).

FUNCTIONAL BRANCH-POINTS

One of the curious aspects of the current controversy regarding the tempo of evolution — whether it is always gradual or instead is uneven — is that the Darwinian model does *not* preclude abrupt changes. In discussing the evolution of the lung, for example, Darwin states that an "organ might be modified for some other and quite distinct purpose . . . The illustration of the swimbladder in fishes is a good one, because it shows us clearly the highly important fact that an organ originally constructed for one purpose, namely flotation, may be converted into one for a wholly different purpose, namely respiration" (1859, p. 190). The pace of evolution can change as the result of sudden changes in *function*. A series of small, gradual *structural* changes in, for example, the anatomy of the swim bladder can lead to an abrupt change in behavior that opens up a new set of selective forces. As Mayr notes:

> behavior often — perhaps invariably — serves as a pacemaker in evolution. A change in behavior, such as the selection of a new habitat or food source, sets up new selective pressures and may

lead to important adaptive shifts. There is little doubt that some
of the most important events in the history of life, such as the
conquest of land or of the air, were initiated by shifts in behavior.
(1978, p. 55)

The detailed comparative studies of Negus that I will discuss in
Chapter 11, for example, demonstrate that there were a number of
what I shall term *functional branch-points* in the evolution of the larynx
and upper respiratory system — points at which the course of evolution could be channeled into different directions through selective
forces that would enhance different *functional* behavioral modes. At
one point in the evolution of the larynx, natural selection could result
in the survival of animals whose larynges were better adapted for
either respiration or phonation. The ancestors of animals like modern
horses followed the pathway of adaptation for efficient respiration;
our ancesters were among the animals who retained changes that
favored sound production at the expense of efficient respiration.
There is no contradiction in the claim that a series of small, gradual
structural changes can yield at some point an abrupt functional
change.

Changes in *behavior* can be abrupt. This again follows from the
principle of mosaic evolution. If the biological components of an
organism are under separate genetic regulation, then the change of
one *key* element can result in an abrupt, qualitatively different mode of
behavior. To use a mechanical analogy, the basic engines and chassis
of all cars are, in principle, very similar. What differentiates various
models of cars is the peripheral elements. Some cars have automatic
transmissions. Others have four-speed manual transmissions; others,
five-speed close-ratio "racing" transmissions. Some cars have suspen-
sions designed for smooth rides; others have transmissions designed
for high-speed stability. Tires differ too — some are designed for long
wear, others for high speeds. If the peripheral elements are gradually
modified, step by step, changes can be made that will appear to be
gradual in the short term. If the changes are small, such as the
substitution of one type of tire for another, they can be made without
considering the interaction of too many other components. Over the
long term one model may evolve for high-speed road racing from the
basic family car. Both cars, however, may share the same basic engine
design, drive train, and chassis. An abrupt change in function can in
some instances be traced to the addition of a key element, such as
high-speed rated tires that, added to a long list of other, small,
peripheral changes, yield a vehicle suitable for 150-mile-per-hour
racing. However, the racing tires *in themselves* would not yield a
road-racing car if they were added to the family car. A long series of

gradual changes that preceded the "functional branch-point" would be necessary.

The "sudden" invention of the motion picture camera is another example of a functional break-point. Improvements in the technology of film making from glass plates, to celluloid sheet film, to roll film gradually made still cameras more convenient than before and yielded the *potential* of developing the motion picture camera at the point when long rolls of flexible film could be manufactured. Film cameras opened a *funtional* prospect that was different in kind from that of still cameras. A functional branch-point occurred with the potential for the production of the first motion picture camera. Thereafter the development of motion picture cameras necessarily diverged from that of still cameras because different "selective" forces were operant. Still cameras, for example, are better if they have shutters that can open and close in a short interval. Motion picture cameras, in contrast, operate perfectly well with a relatively slow shutter speed but keep the frame of film that is being exposed still while maintaining the movement of exposed and unexposed film. After a century of divergent development, still and motion picture cameras are quite different, though they have a common "ancestor." The divergence follows from functional differences that result in different selective forces.

ON STATIC PERIODS AND PARALLELISM IN EVOLUTION

The development of still and motion picture cameras illustrates another point. Though still cameras of the 1870s are ancestral to modern movie cameras, still cameras are not "extinct." Still cameras have their place in the world; they cannot be replaced by movie cameras. Similarly fishes have not become extinct, though some fishes were the ancestors of terrestrial animals. Sponges likewise still exist, though they are more primitive than fishes. The fossil record shows that more primitive hominids like the australopithecines coexisted for at least one million years with more advanced *Homo erectus.* Though similar species will compete for the same resources, factors like population density, geographical separation, and the abundance of resources obviously result in similar, related species surviving for long periods.

The persistence of a particular species, with little modification for a long period of time, likewise can be viewed as the natural result of a successful "experiment" of nature. If a species represents an optimal adaptation to a particular environment, then natural selection should act to filter out deviations from this optimal solution.

POPULATION ISOLATES AND CHANGES IN THE ENVIRONMENT

One of the predictions of the synthetic theory of evolution regarding the tempo of evolution and the mechanisms of speciation involves the role of population isolates and environmental change. Mayr (1959) suggests that "new" species can arise in small peripheral populations that are isolated and under environmental stress. Recent paleontological data in which there are no "gaps in the fossil record" show that under these conditions the morphological variation of the species does increase markedly (Williamson, 1981). Some sort of buffering mechanism that normally limits variation in the population breaks down. Changes in the environment can make the previous optimal solution that a species presents less than optimal. The isolate adapts to the new environment. In Mayr's model, the sudden appearance of an apparently new species in the fossil record coincides with the invasion of the ancestral range by the modified isolate when the environmental conditions that formerly were restricted to the isolate, which was living on the periphery of the range, extend to the entire range. Mayr's model predicts, conversely, that the "new" species will disappear if the environmental conditions on the periphery return to the previous conditions that prevailed throughout the range. Williamson's (1981) data are consistent with this model, though he interprets them in terms of the Gould and Eldridge model. The fossil mollusks that Williamson traces in a lake bed change to new species when the water level of the lake falls. The new species, however, become extinct when the water level of the lake returns to its former level.

BIOLOGICAL VARIATION AND LINGUISTIC ANALYSIS

The biological framework of this book leads to a perspective on the biological bases of human language and the goals of linguistic research that is rather different from either the langue-parole dichotomy of Saussure or the competence-performance distinction of Chomsky. Saussure, in his lectures on general linguistics at the University of Geneva between 1906 and 1911, essentially defined the primary goal of linguistic research as the discovery of the principles of language (*langue*). Language to Saussure "is a well-defined object in the heterogeneous mass of speech facts . . . Whereas speech is heterogeneous, language, as defined, is homogeneous" (1959, pp. 14–15). Saussure's model of human linguistic communication assumes that there is an invariant, common, underlying object, the language that all speakers of a particular dialect know at some internal level of mental representation. It is the task of linguistics to discover the principles of the common language that somehow underlies the varied speech acts of individuals. Saussure's model is essentially a Platonic, typological model. There is a fixed *eidos* (idea) — language — that underlies the observed variability of the speech patterns of a population of speakers who share a common dialect. The *eidos* to Saussure is the only thing that is fixed and real; the goal of linguistics therefore is to discover the property of the *eidos,* the language, which to Saussure is "a self-contained whole" (1959, p. 2).

The competence-performance distribution that pervades recent studies in the transformational school of linguistics is essentially a restatement of Saussure's position. As Chomsky notes, "Linguistic theory is concerned primarily with an ideal speaker-listener, in a completely homogeneous speech-community, who knows its language perfectly . . . we thus make a fundamental distinction between *competence* (the speaker-hearer's knowledge of his language) and *performance* (the actual use of language in concrete situations) . . . the distinction I am noting here is related to the *langue-parole* distinction of Saussure" (1965, pp. 3–4). Chomsky differs from Saussure insofar as he claims that linguistic competence derives from innate, biological mechanisms, but Chomsky's view of the competence-performance distinction with its hypothetical ideal speaker-listener is simply a restatement of the Platonic concept of *idealization* as a psychological reality. Thus to Chomsky the goal of linguistic research is to derive the properties of the "competence" grammar.

The goal set forth by Chomsky and Saussure is inherently impossible in light of the data on biological variation that are the basis of evolution by means of natural selection. These data have been replicated time after time and have been found to be typical of all living organisms in the course of biological studies since Darwin's time. As Mayr points out,

> Darwin introduced a new way of thinking, that of "population thinking." The populationist stresses the uniqueness of everything in the organic world. What is true for the human species — that no two individuals are alike — is equally true for all other species and plants . . . All organisms and organic phenomena are composed of unique features and can be described collectively only in statistical terms. Individuals, or any kind of organic entities, form populations of which we can determine the arithmetic mean and the statistics of variation. Averages are merely statistical abstractions, only the individuals, of which the populations are composed have reality. The ultimate conclusions of the

population thinker and the typologist are precisely the opposite. For the typologist, the type (*eidos*) is real and the variation is an illusion, while for the populationist, the type (average) is an abstraction and only the variation is real.

(1959, p. 2)

The trend of modern molecular biology in recent years has been to stress the genetic variations that make up natural populations. Human linguistic ability, insofar as it is based on innate information, must be subject to the same variation as other genetically transmitted biological traits. Thus there cannot be any speaker or hearer in a population who has the grammar of Chomsky's ideal speaker-hearer. The properties of the abstract average, if that is what we mean by the competence grammar or *langue,* can be determined only by studying the *variations* that typify the linguistic behavior of individual members of a population. Some biological properties of language may indeed be present in almost all "normal" human beings, but we can determine what these central properties are only if we study the total range of variation in linguistic behavior. Greenberg's (1963) studies of linguistic universals are therefore convincing since they are derived from the study of actual variations between different languages. Jakobson's (1940) discussion of the hierarchy of phonological universals again was convincing because it attempted to account for variations in linguistic behavior. The details of Jakobson's theory probably are not correct, but the basic premises are in accord with the principles of modern biology.

Variations always occur in the population that constitutes a species. We can derive some insights into the functional—hence selective—value of particular biological attributes of a species by studying the pattern of variation. The morphology of the pelvis and foot that has a functional value for upright bipedal locomotion is, for example, similar for all normal human beings. Variations that interfere with upright bipedal locomotion have for millions of years been filtered out by the process of natural selection. In contrast, the external shape of the human nose has little functional value and varies across the species. Biological traits that are more uniformly distributed across a species thus inferentially may be more important in a functional sense. However, in order to study variations we first must accept the fact that we are in what Mayr terms the population thinking mode.

CHAPTER 1

Neurophysiology, Neural Models, and Language

ONE OBVIOUS WAY OF approaching the different theories that attempt to account for the neural basis of language and its relation to other aspects of cognitive behavior is to study the brain. Chomsky's position is, as I noted, that language is a neural "organ" whose site is "that little part of the left hemisphere that is responsible for the very specific structures of human language" (1980a, p. 182). Chomsky here makes two explicit claims concerning the nature of the human brain: (1) that discrete functions can be isolated in a specific part of the brain, and (2) that the function that is isolated in the left hemisphere is "responsible for" and specific to language.

Throughout history people have tended to compare the human brain to the most complex piece of machinery available. The model most often cited these days is the digital computer, or at least the architecture of the programs that are run on digital computers. Chomsky appears to be following this trend. The digital computer–brain analogy follows a long series of models in this tradition. In the eighteenth century the brain was compared to a clockwork automaton. In the late nineteenth and twentieth centuries, until the 1950s, it usually was compared to a telephone exchange. It then became a digital computer. All of these devices have one common attribute: the computing or active elements are discrete. If you destroy one of the discrete elements that make up the machine, some function will cease, or some stored memory will be lost. Different parts of the machine perform different functions that are all essential to the machine's functional output. The clock's spring, for example, provides the clock's power. If the center of power of the clock — the spring — is removed, the clock will stop. The telephone exchange likewise has discrete circuits. If you cut the wire to Mr. Descartes' house, he will not be able to use the system. If the central switchboard, the interconnection center, is destroyed, the entire telephone system will fail. The

15

digital computer model of the brain is a little more complex, but it is fundamentally a discrete system in which particular parts each perform a discrete function or store the memory of some event in a discrete location.

The model that I think best accounts for the data we have on the neural bases of language is structured in terms of the modern synthetic theory of evolution. I think that there are two components to the neural bases of human language. One component, which is very conservative in regard to its evolutionary history, is a distributed neural "computer," which is the biological basis of cognition. The neural substrates that provide the bases for cognitive behavior in human beings and other animals have, as Changeux (1980) points out, a long evolutionary history. Recent experimental data, for example, demonstrate that very simple animals, which have no central nervous system, much less a cortex, can learn to associate stimuli that are presented in the classic Pavlovian paradigm. Other data and theoretical studies indicate that memory and associative learning are best modeled by using a distributed rather than a locationist neural model. In a distributed neural model the memory of an event is stored in a "trace" that extends throughout the entire neural circuitry or a significant portion of it. In a distributed model of human memory we would not store our memory of someone's face in a neural circuit that occupied a specific location. The memory would be stored by modifying synaptic pathways throughout the neural memory. The distributed model accounts for the fact that we usually do not suddenly lose a specific memory as we age and lose the neurons that make up the computational elements of our brain. Our memory gradually becomes noisier and access slower, but we do not completely lose the memory of specific events. I will discuss distributed neural models in some detail in this chapter; the discussions that follow should explicate these comments.

The view I present claims that the central, distributed human neural computer is the result of the gradual elaboration of the central nervous system. It appears to be built up of the same neural components as the brains of other animals, and its structure is probably not qualitatively different from the brains of other "higher" mammals. In contrast to Chomsky, I do not think that there are any data consistent with the claim that species-specific and language-specific neural "devices" exist that determine a hypothetical fixed nucleus, the possible form of syntax and semantic representation, for human language.

The neural component that I think is language-specific and species-specific — that is, specific to the *particular* form that human language has happened to take—is the set of peripheral neural mechanisms that structure the input-output levels of human language—speech, gesture, facial expression. These neural mechanisms are peripheral in two senses. First they are peripheral in a functional sense, since they structure the manner in which we communicate rather than the quality or nature of the concepts that language captures and communicates. They are also peripheral in a structural and evolutionary sense. I view them as comparatively recent specializations in an evolutionary sense—add-ons to the basic, distributed cognitive computer. I am using the term *computer* here in its broader sense. The computer that is a reasonable model of the distributed cognitive brain is quite different in its architecture from any computer that has yet been built by human beings. The peripheral language-specific neural mechanisms can be regarded as discrete transducers that are interposed between the central computer and the mechanisms that human beings have available to transmit and receive information —the motor "output" systems that control the vocal apparatus, gestures, and facial expression and the visual and auditory "input" systems.

Distributed versus Discrete Neural Mechanisms

The distinction between a distributed, central cognitive computer and discrete, peripheral neural mechanisms is probably difficult to follow because most of the devices with which we are familiar are discrete. However, the electrical power grid that supplies power to your home is a reasonable, though simplified, example of a distributed system. The electrical appliances that you can install in your home, moreover, are usually discrete devices. My use of the terms *central* and *peripheral* in regard to distributed and discrete neural mechanisms may also be unclear. The distinction I want to draw in this regard is functional rather than anatomical; the central distributed cognitive computer is not necessarily physically central with respect to the peripheral discrete mechanisms. The central electrical power grid and peripheral appliances, respectively, also illustrate some aspects of this functional distinction.

The properties that make an electrical supply grid a distributed system are *the interconnections and the fact that no single generator is necessary for the functioning of the system.* The task of the system is distributed among hundreds of generators. No single generator in an operating system need supply all the electrical power that is flowing into the light bulb in your lamp. The system is redundant. A properly designed electrical grid system will continue to provide power when individual generators are out of service because there is sufficient excess generating power. The system also will continue to operate as transmission lines between generators are cut; there are parallel, redundant lines and switching points that can direct the flow of power through alternative pathways. The supply of electrical power can be interrupted by single cuts only at the periphery of the system where single lines go to individual subscribers.

The distributed system can adapt to different conditions by setting up new pathways through its switching points. In the hypothetical and simplified system diagram in Figure 1-1, the electrical grid will continue to supply power to Springfield, Massachusetts, even if the supply line from Pittsfield is cut. The grid's switching points can be rearranged to take up the Springfield load by using all the alternative interconnections that feed into Springfield. The rearrangement of the network is not confined to the immediate vicinity of Springfield. The changes in the vicinity of Springfield occasion changes distant from Springfield as the system distributes the perturbations in the load. The circled nodes in Figure 1-1, for example, show the switching points that assumed new values after the failure of the Springfield-to-Pittsfield feed transmission line. The switching points are junctions at which the current flow can be changed in the lines or branches that meet at that node. These switches have to send more current through the lines into Springfield that remain after the failure of the Pittsfield feed line. Changes in the values of the switching points throughout the distributed system can also follow from changes in the electrical demand at a particular point. They do not occur only when a line falls down. On a hot summer night, the distributed power grid's "synapses" — its switching points — continually rearrange the flow of electrical power as air-conditioning systems in city offices turn down and home air conditioners turn on. Power from the cool regions of Canada streams toward the hot, humid cities of the east. Additional generators come onto the power grid. As the night cools, the pattern changes and the distributed system takes on new synaptic conditions.

The key to the distributed system is the activity of the "synapses," the electrical switching points that connect the lines between the "generator-neurons." In other words, the *coupling between the cells* of the model (or the brain) is the key. Let me designate the array of cells represented by the loads of cities of southeastern Massachusetts and Providence, Rhode Island, the input to the model. The input is a set of numbers that represents an observation of the "behavior" of these cities, how much electricity each is using at a given moment. The

The human brain is a complex, interconnected structure that has a long evolutionary history. It was not designed by a team of engineers who were aiming to produce a device that would operate by using discrete modules that each independently carried out the computations for some cognitive act. The data that have been acquired by neurophysiologists are not consistent with the assumption that the human brain functions by using discrete "modules" — that is, neural devices like a language module, a space perception module, a number system module — that abruptly evolved as Chomsky (1980b) proposes, fully developed at different stages of human evolution. As the neurophysiologist Changeux notes,

> Apparently simple operations of behavior, such as the movements of the eye or the killing of a mouse by a cat, in fact involves the recruitment of a large number of neurons (thousands, even millions) from many different areas of the brain. In addition, no simple rule appears to exist in the macroscopic and histological organization of such centers in the brain. Why should there be any logic, for instance, in the presence and the role of subcortical structures in highly "corticalized" mammals, except for the very fact that these structures existed in the brain of more primitive animals from which they evolved? A given behavioral act may indeed engage, *simultaneously* and *necessarily,* groups of neurons which appeared at different periods in the evolution of vertebrates. The stabilization or selection of these centers had its own logic at the time they were formed. But this logic becomes masked by millions of years of history that followed under the influence of eminently variable ecological conditions. To some extent, the "arbitrary nature" of the anatomy reflects the historical variability of the environment. Anatomy cannot be inferred from anything other than its direct investigation.
>
> (1980, p. 188)

The arbitrary nature of anatomy that follows from the changing course of natural selection is a biological constant. We have two lungs that are elastic sacs that inflate by means of a very indirect process that makes us susceptible to a wide range of disease-induced trauma (collapsed lungs, pleuresy, emphysema). Our lungs evolved from the swim bladders of fish. There was a selective advantage in a fish's having two elastic sacs that could gradually expand or contract to hold more or less air. Two balanced sacs kept a fish from spinning around on its long axis and allowed it to stop. "Advanced" fish can stop to rest, hide, or feed. Earlier, more primitive fish like sharks lack balance mechanisms and must constantly move or else they sink. Swim bladders are logically designed devices for swimming — they constitute a

Rube Goldberg system for breathing. The brain's organization may be just as illogical. As the ecological conditions that faced different organisms changed, the course of natural selection changed. We have brains that obviously work, but they do not necessarily work in a "logical" way.

Aphasia: The Experiments of Nature

Many of the data that bear on the relation of the brain to language have been derived from the study of aphasia. These data have yielded important insights on the nature of the brain and its possible "wiring diagram." However, certain implicit assumptions underlie many of the theories that interpret these data. Perhaps the most direct approach to the study of aphasia is first to consider the general procedure for investigating an unknown functional wiring diagram by using data that are similar to the data of aphasia. All interpretations of aphasia necessarily involve a correlation between a break in a hypothetical neural circuit and some aspect of linguistic or nonlinguistic behavior. To illustrate, I will start with a simpler, similar problem. When I first went to Providence, Rhode Island, I had the problem of determining the functional wiring diagram of a fifty-year-old house that had been rewired a few years before I moved in. Most of the original wiring had been replaced; there was a new circuit-breaker box, but nothing was labeled! The former owners had not replaced any of the lights throughout the house, and I wanted to install new ones without being electrocuted. I therefore had to determine the circuits that each of the breakers in the circuit-breaker controlled. The solution was elementary; though the circuit-breakers were not labeled, the function of each breaker was soon determined by turning all the lights on. I then determined the functional wiring diagram of the house by sequentially switching off each breaker and seeing which lights went out. If the human brain were a discrete computer, a similar technique could, in principle, be used to determine the "functional wiring" of the human brain and the locations of the discrete devices that might be the neural correlates of various aspects of human linguistic ability. Various parts of the brain could be switched off while we observed the linguistic responses of the subject. Although techniques like this have been used in experiments with other animals, such as dogs, cats, and pigeons, we obviously cannot study the human brain and human language by using this technique. However, accidents frequently happen that destroy parts of the brain. The study of the linguistic effects of aphasia, organic brain damage that results from accident or disease, can be regarded as the study of the "experiments of nature." The data of aphasia have been studied since Paul Broca in 1861 first identified some of the linguistic deficits that can occur when a person's brain is damaged.

The study of aphasia is quite complex. The literature is enormous, and no two patients exhibit exactly the same symptoms. There is no general agreement among "aphasiologists" on the different "types" of aphasia or even on the appropriate categories for the classification of aphasia; either anatomical or functional criteria can be used. The traditional characterization of the different types of aphasia, however, is in terms of the site of the trauma to the patient's brain. The data of aphasia constitute the principal evidence for the view expressed by Chomsky that the specific structures of human language involve the neural activity of specific sites or locations in the human brain. Although many aphasiologists have rejected locationist models (See Blumstein, 1981, for a comprehensive review of recent data and theories of aphasia), the dominant view appears to be a "loose" locationist model in which certain linguistic deficits can usually be correlated with lesions in specific regions of the brain. The pattern that emerges from these data, however, is that the peripheral input-output aspects of human language, rather than the central cognitive functions, are the ones that are affected by lesions that are confined to discrete sites in the brain. Unfortunately, much of the discussion of aphasia is still colored by a strict locationist model, which is often implicit and is ultimately derived from the nineteenth-century theory of phrenology.

The historical framework for the study of aphasia probably derives from the theory of phrenology. Although phrenology often comes to mind today as a quack science, it was in the mainstream of scientific endeavor in the early part of the nineteenth century. The theory, proposed by Gall (1809) and revised by Spurzheim (1815, 1826), claimed that human character and cognitive ability can be factored into a number of independent "faculties." Each faculty has its "seat," its neural embodiment, in a distinct region of the surface of the brain. A typical phrenological map of the brain in Figure 1-2 shows the various parts of the brain that control various "sentiments" and "faculties."

The partitioning of the surface of the brain into "regions" is rather like the partitioning of the world's continents, oceans, seas, and nations on a globe. Phrenologists believed that the size of each region was innately determined in a given individual and determined the character or cognitive ability of that individual. Thus a larger area 14,

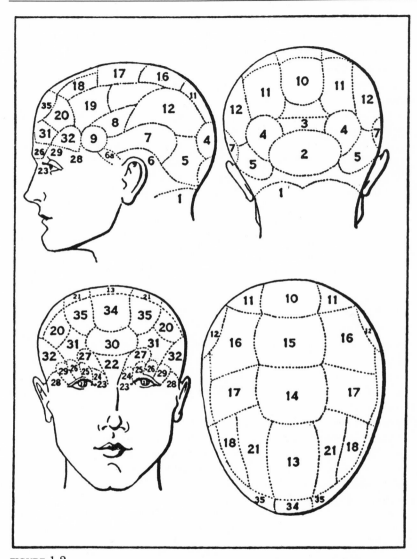

FIGURE 1-2.
Phrenological map of faculties of the human mind. (After Spurz-heim, 1826.)

the seat of "veneration," in a person's brain would result in a greater degree of veneration in that person's conduct. Phrenologists also believed that the outer surface of the skull corresponded with the underlying region of the brain. Thus empirical studies could, in theory, determine whether people whose skulls had a larger expanse in area 14 in fact manifested a greater degree of veneration in their daily life than people whose skulls had a smaller area 14. Gall conducted many investigations in such places as prisons and lunatic asylums, correlating qualities with the skulls and conduct of the inmates. Other correlations involved clerics, scholars, poets, and the like. There are skulls in the collection of the Musée de l'Homme in Paris that served as museum exhibits and pedagogic aids and were carefully engraved to exhibit various qualities. Phrenology fell into disfavor as anatomical studies of cranial development showed that the surface of the skull does not necessarily correlate with the surface of the brain. However, the locationist aspect of phrenological studies was retained in Paul Broca's announcement in 1861 of the seat of articulate speech in the left side of the frontal region of the brain.

THE LINGUISTIC DEFICITS OF APHASIA

In 1861 Broca demonstrated that lesions in the anterior region of the left dominant hemisphere of the brain resulted in a linguistic deficit, the absence of articulate speech. The left lateral cortex of the brain (see Figure 1-3) is dominant for language in most people. This is especially true for right-handed people, in whom damage to the left hemisphere will result in "aphasia" — linguistic deficits — almost 99 percent of the time (Zangwell, 1962). The linguistic deficits of patients who have suffered brain damage in Broca's "area" are often characterized as expressive: their speech is slow, labored, and slurred; phonetic and phonemic errors occur; and phonation is irregular and hoarse (dysarthric). The third frontal convolution where Broca localized the lesions in his patients' brains after post mortems is an "association" area adjacent to the part of the brain that controls motor activity — the coordinated movements of a person's arms, lips, and so on. The concept of association is psychological: Pavlov's classic experiments with dogs established an association between the sound of a bell and the dogs' behavioral responses to food. However, as Lenneberg (1967) notes, the neurological correlate of the association is still unknown. Pavlov proposed that the neurological basis of these associations must be cortical, but recent data that I will review later show that this is not necessarily the case. What is certain is that the motor

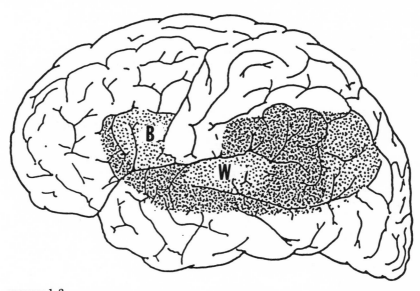

FIGURE 1-3.
Schematic of locations of language zones of the left cerebral cortex
showing Broca's and Wernicke's areas. The frontal, parietal, and
temporal lobes are also indicated.

association area is near the motor area of the brain. Lesions in the
motor area of the brain can result in paralysis or profound weakness
and are among the most disabling consequences of strokes. It is thus
not too surprising that lesions near the motor area result in difficulties
in speech production.

The victims of Broca's aphasia, however, have linguistic and
cognitive deficiencies that go beyond articulatory coordination and
phonemic errors. Their speech is agrammatic. They frequently drop
grammatical endings like the plural and past tense markers of English
as well as grammatical markers like *the, a, is.* Their comprehension of
spoken sentences is also impaired. While they can follow a conversation that consists of simple sentences, they may have difficulties with
syntactically embedded sentences in which two prepositions are embedded in a single syntactic frame. In an experiment (Goodglass et al.,
1979) in which spoken sentences were presented to Broca's aphasics,
they, for example, understood the sentence *The man was greeted by his
wife, and he was smoking a pipe,* but had difficulties with the embedded
sentence *The man greeted by his wife was smoking a pipe.* Broca's aphasics
also have difficulty when they deal with written sentences. Given a

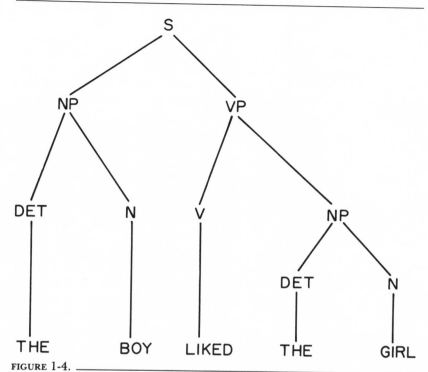

FIGURE 1-4.

Syntatic structure of the sentence *The boy liked the girl: S*, sentence;
NP, noun phrase; *VP*, verb phrase; *Det*, determiner; *N*, noun; *V*, verb.

written sentence, normal subjects will consistently "parse," or group
words together in a manner that is not very different from a formal
linguistic analysis. The sentence *The boy liked the girl* in Figure 1-4 is
parsed by normal subjects in terms of its phrase structure. In contrast,
Broca's aphasics will randomly cluster grammatical particles together,
violating the normal phrase structure of the sentence (Zurif, Caramazza, and Myerson, 1972).

The linguistic deficits of victims of Broca's aphasia present a
curious cluster. The effects seem, to a first approximation, to be
consistent with a discrete, localized model of the brain. The damage to
the patient's brain is near the area of the brain connected with motor
control; thus speech production deficits are to be expected. However,
if all that is involved is motor control for linguistic tasks, why should
there also be grammatical deficits?

Lesions in other parts of the left dominant hemisphere of the brain can result in different problems. Wernicke's aphasia involves lesions in the second temporal gyrus in the posterior left hemisphere (see Figure 1-3). This area of the brain is an auditory association area; it is involved in the perception of speech since it connects with the auditory system (Heschel's gyrus), which is deep in the temporal lobe. Wernicke in 1874 first noted that patients with lesions in this area have difficulty understanding words; that is, they have "receptive" difficulties. Their speech is fluently articulated compared with that of Broca's aphasics, but it is often devoid of real content. The patient will often substitute sounds, such as *bin* for *pin*, or will substitute inappropriate words or neologisms. The linguistic deficits of Wernicke's patients are not simply limited to the perceptual level as we might expect, considering the site of the damage to the brain. Wernicke aphasics who are anomic—that is, who cannot recall particular words—also appear to have difficulty with the semantic relations that these words convey. These difficulties occur even when anomics are asked to characterize pictures of cups and bowls in terms of the semantic relations that normal subjects use (Labov, 1973; Whitehouse, Caramazza, and Zurif, 1978): cups, for example, are used to drink coffee; bowls are usually used for soup and breakfast cereal. The anomics lack these distinctons. The Wernicke's aphasics are not able to integrate the semantic information that normally is associated with the words *cup* or *bowl* even when they deal with pictures.

The pattern of linguistic deficits associated with Wernicke's aphasia, like that of Broca's aphasia, is not consistent with a strict locationist model like that proposed by Geschwind (1965). Geschwind's model stresses the role of cortical organization. In the locationist model, as in the phrenological model, particular behavioral functions are related to the neural activity of certain areas of the cortex. Particular parts of the cortex perform discrete linguistic functions and are connected by a limited number of major "pathways." Breaks in the neural pathways or destruction of the cortical areas in a locationist model result in a particular linguistic deficit. The expressive speech production difficulties of Broca's aphasia and the receptive deficits of Wernicke's aphasia fit into a locationist model. However, the linguistic deficits of Wernicke's aphasia like those of Broca's aphasia go far beyond what we would predict from a strict locationist model in which the behavioral consequences of lesions in the auditory association area would be limited to perceptual difficulties. Why should the victims of Wernicke's aphasia be unable to integrate semantic information? Why should they be anomic? There is yet another aspect of the behavior of aphasics that is often overlooked. Their performance on virtually all linguistic, cognitive, and perceptual tasks is generally poorer than that of normal subjects. This is true for Wernicke's and Broca's aphasia as well as for other types of aphasia. The aphasics' performance in a controlled behavioral task deteriorates and becomes "noisier." Higher error rates, for example, occur in simple speech perception tasks for Broca's aphasics (Blumstein, 1981).

THE CORTEX, COGNITION, AND LANGUAGE

One of the legacies of phrenology probably is an overemphasis of the role of the cortex in higher cognitive and linguistic activity. The cortex is the most recent part of the brain in a phylogenetic sense. The brain is like an onion in that it is organized in layers. The most primitive parts — the parts that are found in animals that appear to be similar to animals that first evolved a hundred million years or so ago — are in the center of the brain. The most recent part of the brain, the cortex, is the outer layer of the onion.

Some aphasiologists — for example, Brown (1975, 1976) — have claimed that these older and more primitive parts function in concert with the cortex. Brown's thesis is that the function and morphology of the motor and auditory association areas of the human brain reflect their phylogenetic evolution. Thus the old portions of the brain stem that are present in the most primitive animals function in concert with the most recent additions to the cortex that evolved in the last ten million years. Brown's theory and observations are consistent with Changeux's comment that the simplest act involves the activity of both primitive, phylogenetically old parts of the brain and the most advanced recent parts. However, the cortex until recently was thought to be essential for all associative learning in higher animals. Recent data show that this is not necessarily the case.

Some of the most interesting data on cognitive activity in the absence or diminution of the cortex come from the study of hydrocephalic human beings. Hydrocephalus, or water on the brain, occurs when the circulation of cerebrospinal fluid through the brain is disturbed. Hydraulic pressure builds up, which typically enlarges the soft skulls of infants and young children (Crelin, 1969). Internally brain tissue is pressed against the cranium, reducing the size of the brain, the outer cortical areas in particular. In severe cases the cerebral hemispheres are virtually absent. The behavior of individuals who have hydrocephalic brains is another experiment of nature that allows us to assess the relative role of the cortex and the gross architecture of the normal brain in various cognitive tasks.

As I noted earlier, the precise role of cortical association areas is unknown. In theory, cross-modal stimuli are supposed to be associated in these regions of the brain as, for example, in a traditional Pavlovian conditioning paradigm. Pavlov's dogs learned to associate an auditory stimulus, the sound of a bell, with the presentation of food and responded with a motor act, salivation. The cortex was supposed to be essential for associative learning in higher animals, particularly for cross-modal stimuli. Although simpler animals can function in the absence of cortical structures, the behavioral capacity of higher animals whose brains have relatively large cerebral hemispheres diminishes when they are decerebrated (Lenneberg, 1967, p. 211). It thus is reasonable to assume that associative learning would not be possible in human beings in the absence of a cortex. A recent behavioral experiment with premature hydrocephalic and normal infants, however, demonstrates that cross-modal associative learning can take place in a human infant in whom the cerebral hemispheres of the brain are virtually absent.

The subjects of the experiment were dizygotic twins who were born two months prematurely. One twin, a male, was normal but the other twin, a female, was hydrocephalic. Air encephalography and computer axial tomography (CAT scan) showed the "virtual absence of the cerebral hemispheres" (Tuber et al., 1980, p. 1035). The learning task involved two stimuli, a 1 kHz tone that lasted 1.5 seconds and a light from a reflector type of flashlight directed toward the infant's face. Both stimuli were relatively weak (the loudness, sound pressure level of the tone was 76 db, and the illuminance of the light was 90 foot-candles) and were presented to the infants in a dimly lighted and quiet room in tests that were conducted 40, 50, 57, and 62 days after birth. The two stimuli, controlled by a programming apparatus, were presented to the infants one after the other; the tone was presented first and was stopped as the light was turned on for 0.5 seconds. The heart rate of both infants was monitored throughout the experiment. The heart rate data show that both the normal and the hydrocephalic infant learned to associate the tone and the light. The infants first heard isolated tones to establish their cardiac response pattern to an isolated tone. They then were presented paired tone-light patterns. Each infant heard 162 paired stimulus trials in which the tone was followed by the light. The heart rate responses of the infants to these paired stimuli showed consistent patterns for each infant over the four experimental sessions after they heard the first two tone-light pairs. The presentation of the tone without the light produced a statistically significant marked change in the cardiac pattern after the initial associative "training." This pattern was different from the responses of the infants to isolated tones presented prior to the tone-light pairings.

The study of hydrocephalic human beings has reopened the question of the role of the cerebral cortex and the phylogenetically deeper structures of the brain in cognitive tasks. In a report in the "Research News" section of *Science*, December 12, 1980, the observations of John Lorber are discussed. Lorber, a pediatrician, has compiled a series of over 600 CAT scans of hydrocephalic patients. Computer axial tomography provides relatively safe, noninvasive data on the brains of these patients. Lorber divides his subjects into four categories according to the degree of hydrocephalus. About 10 percent of his subjects fall into the fourth, most severely affected population, in which 95 percent of the subject's cranium is filled with fluid. Although many of these subjects are severely disabled, half have IQs greater than 100. Lorber notes:

> There's a young student at this university [Sheffield University, England] who has an IQ of 126, has gained a first-class honors degree in mathematics, and is socially completely normal. And yet the boy has virtually no brain. We did a brain scan on him; we saw that instead of the normal 4.5 centimeter thickness of brain tissue between the ventricles and the cortical surface, there was just a thin layer of mantle measuring a millimeter or so. His cranium is filled mainly with cerebrospinal fluid.
>
> (1980, p. 1232)

Lorber's work is, of course, controversial since it challenges many of the standard theories of neurology — that the cortex is the primary and indeed the essential neural component of intelligence, that brain size and weight correlate in a rough way with intelligence (Jerison, 1973) (an animal with a 1000-gram brain should be more intelligent than one with a 50-gram brain, all other things being equal), and that we can make some inferences regarding the function of the brain from its external architecture. Lorber notes that a number of uncertainties are inherent in his data. It is not possible to determine the exact weight or structure of a person's brain from CAT scans. However, the deviations from normal brains are so extreme that it is obvious that traditional locationist models that limit the neural "seats" of cognitive activity and language to particular areas of the cortex must be wrong. Thus he points out, "I can't say whether the mathematics student has a brain weighing 50 grams or 150 grams, but it's clear that it is nowhere near the normal 1.5 kilograms, and much of the brain he does have is in the more primitive deep structures that are relatively spared in hydrocephalus" (1980, p. 1233). Lorber concludes that "there must be a tremendous amount of redundancy or spare capacity in the brain" and that "the cortex probably is responsible for a great deal less than most people imagine." Lorber's observations do not necessarily bear on the normal functioning of the brain. It is possible that the redundant structure of the brain and its plasticity can result in its functioning "normally" though in a manner different from that of an intact brain. Children, for example, frequently recover normal functions after massive brain damage (Lenneberg, 1967). Lorber's observations, however, indicate the probable role of subcortical as well as cortical neural structures in cognition.

Associative learning apparently can occur in very simple animals. Aversive associative learning has been demonstrated in *Aplysia californica*, a gastropod mollusk (Carew, Walters, and Kandel, 1981; Walters, Carew, and Kandel, 1981). These invertebrates, of course, lack a cortex or anything that approaches the complexity of the brains of even simple mammals like mice. The animals learned to associate a conditioning stimulus, shrimp extract, with an aversive unconditioned stimulus, an electric shock, using the classic Pavlovian paradigm. The training sessions involved first presenting the shrimp extract to the animals for 90 seconds. Six seconds after the start of the presentation of the conditioning shrimp extract stimulus, an electric shock was applied to the head of the animal. Twenty mollusks were trained in this manner and received six to nine paired stimuli. Twenty mollusks served as a control group and received unpaired electric shocks and shrimp extract stimuli that were presented at 90-minute intervals.

The animals were then tested 18 hours after the training sessions. Shrimp extract was applied to the heads of all the animals for one minute, and weak electric shock was then applied to the tail of each mollusk. The animals that had been exposed to the paired stimuli in the training sessions reacted more forcefully than the animals that had not been exposed to paired stimuli. The behavior of the animals was monitored both by observing the number of steps that they took to move away from the weak electric shock and by observing the electrical activity of the motor systems of escape locomotion, inking, and siphon withdrawal by means of intracellular recording from identified motor neurons for each response.

Significant correlates of learning were found in the trained mollusks in all three separate motor systems. The application of the conditioning stimulus (shrimp extract) to trained mollusks, moreover, produces a depression in feeding. Electrophysiologic data furthermore demonstrate that the conditioning stimulus acts to enhance synaptic input to the motor neurons produced by stimuli that trigger defensive responses. The correlate of learning in the mollusks' central nervous system thus is synaptic modification. The trained mollusks act in the same manner as higher animals do when they are afraid. What is startling is that the mollusks quickly learn to associate a stimulus that ordinarily would be benign, shrimp extract, with an unpleasant stimulus, a strong electrical shock to their heads. The mollusks have learned to adapt to a new "environment"; furthermore, they are able to do this in the absence of any neural structures that remotely resemble the mammalian cortex. Associative learning obviously has a selective value to any animal since it allows rapid phenotypical changes to new environmental conditions. These experiments are therefore significant in demonstrating that the neural bases of "cognitive" acts may be found in very simple animals. Either we must accept the proposition that these animals "think" to some degree, or we must arbitrarily decide that associative learning is not really a cognitive act.

Clearly mollusks do not think in the same sense that human beings do. Mollusks also do not walk in the same way that people do, but probably no one would be upset to read a discussion of the neural bases of "walking" in mollusks. There clearly are different patterns of locomotion that map into the concept conveyed by the word *walking*. If we want to restrict the range of concepts that map into the word *thinking* to the full range and extent of cognitive activity typical of modern *Homo sapiens,* then there is no problem — mollusks clearly do not think. The problem with this approach is that it inherently leads to an arbitrary partition between human beings and other animals in one restricted domain, that of mental activity. If we want to maintain the traditional separation between human beings and all other living animals, this distinction is necessary. Though mollusks could easily be excluded from the category of thinking animals by setting up some particular cognitive act as the crucial factor that makes "thinkinglike" behavior thinking, the danger exists that we would admit such animals as dogs, cats, and apes into the thinking category by making the crucial act too simple. On the other hand, we would exclude many people if we made the crucial factor too difficult in order to exclude animals like chimpanzees. If we are not concerned with the "special" status of human beings, there is no problem. Mollusks thus can share some of the biological, neural mechanisms that are involved in human thought. Mollusks could "think" by using these neural mechanisms, though they could handle neither the range nor the complexity of the problems that human beings usually think about.

The mollusk experiments are also extremely significant in that they are consistent with Hebb's (1949) theory relating synaptic modification to learning and memory. The distributed models of the brain that I think are the most powerful and plausible models all follow from Hebb. The mollusk preparation makes direct access to the synaptic level possible in association with behavior that involves learning and memory. The dual approach of basic electrophysiologic and histological study of neuroanatomy and theoretical modeling of large neural nets based on these data has yielded, and will yield, some knowledge of how we think.

A DISTRIBUTED-DISCRETE MODEL OF THE BRAIN

The data noted by Lorber, many of the data of aphasia, and the lesion studies cited by Lenneberg (1967) can be explained by distributed models of the brain. In 1967 Lenneberg presciently noted that distributed models probably would be developed that would "explain" the phenomena that just do not make sense if we assume that *all* aspects of neural activity are localized. Lenneberg came to this conclusion after reviewing studies in which animals retained normal modes of behavior after massive lesions in the cortical centers that hypothetically were regulating these behaviors. The model of the brain that makes most sense to me is one in which the specialized peripheral input-output functions are localized but "feed into" a central, general-purpose distributed computer. I should stress that the model I shall propose is *not* "logical," "economical," or "elegant." As I noted earlier, biological systems are not necessarily logical, economical, or elegant; they reflect the chances of evolution. For a start — and we must remember that when addressing the question of *how* the brain works, we are still at the start — some of the bits and pieces of neural hardware that may go together to structure human language and cognition are:

1. Innate specialized mechanisms that structure the perception and production of speech signals. These mechanisms are analogous to similar mechanisms that exist in other animals and that structure their calls, displays, and the like — the input-output stages of communication. They are species-specific insofar as human beings use a particular set of communicative signals and appear to confer certain selective advantages in the particular framework of human speech and language. Though these mechanisms are innate, they still need exposure

to the environment and can be regarded as mechanisms that facilitate the acquisition of a communication system or language.

2. Innate specialized neural mechanisms that also play a part in structuring other aspects of behavior, such as the motor control involved in locomotion. The motor control of locomotion is not part of the complex that we usually associate with cognitive behavior. However, I shall argue that the neural mechanisms that first evolved to facilitate motor control now also structure language and cognition. The rules of syntax, for example, may reflect a generalization of the automatized schema that first evolved in animals for motor control in tasks like respiration and walking. In other words, I shall argue that the formal rules of Chomsky's "fixed nucleus" are ultimately related to the way that lizards wiggle their tails.

3. Generalized neural mechanisms that are adaptive and that form the substrate that structures other aspects of human cognitive behavior and the intelligent behavior of other animals. These mechanisms are plastic and associative; they enable animals to classify and respond to the changing properties of their external environment. These neural mechanisms constitute a central distributed computer that has gradually evolved and become more powerful in the course of the evolution of the higher mammals, of which human beings constitute one branch.

Note that these proposals are diametrically opposite to Chomsky's views on the neural basis of human language. The species-specific neural mechanisms would be, in Chomsky's view, trivial insofar as they pertain to the input-output stages of human speech and perhaps the "production" constraints of short-term memory. In my view, the abstract, logical aspects of human language that are formalized by linguists in the rules of a grammar and the metatheory of "universal" grammar share a common neural base with the cognitive behavior of other animals. In this model the language and cognition of human beings may be more complex than that of other animals, but it is based on similar neural mechanisms and has similar formal properties.

CHAPTER 2

Distributed Neural Computers and Feature Detectors

ALTHOUGH MANY NEUROLOGISTS still favor brain models that make use of localized, discrete "devices" that correspond on a one-to-one basis with all linguistic and cognitive processes, another model has been developed by neuroscientists. This model proposes that the brain is a distributed associative computer. The computations that go on in the brain take place in many units in a distributed model. The traces of memory are stored in thousands, if not millions, of units, no one of which bears a complete representation of the whole event. Furthermore no single unit is essential for the preservation of the stored memory or computation. This may seem vague and mysterious, but I will attempt to convey some of the properties of distributed models of the brain.

First, consider the data derived from studies of aphasia that are often interpreted in terms of strict locationist models, such as that implicit in the work of Falk (1980). A lesion occurs in a particular site and can be correlated with a behavioral deficit. The site of the lesion then is considered to be the seat of the particular aspect of behavior being studied. As Lenneberg (1967) notes, these interpretations of lesion studies are not necessarily valid; the classic neurologists (such as Head, 1926) did not accept strict locationist models nor do most aphasiologists (Blumstein, 1981). The data of aphasia can instead be interpreted in terms of the distributed localized model that I propose. The following armchair experiment points out some of the difficulties that can occur when a strict locationist model is used to interpret the data of experiments in which behavior is disrupted by a lesion. The object is to determine the center of light for Times Square, New York. The methodology of the experiment is simple. The inhabitants of Times Square will be instructed to turn on all their lights. The lighting pattern of the normal intact system will be recorded. We then will systematically begin to drill 6-inch-diameter holes to a depth of 50 feet into the pavement of Times Square. At the bottom of each hole we will detonate a 2-pound charge of high explosive, "ablating" the subsurface region of the hole. If we were interpreting the data of this experiment using a strict locationist model, we would identify the places where the dynamite charges were exploded as the centers of light for various buildings.

The Times Square light experiment would doubtless result in a variety of "behavioral" consequences — burst water mains, flooded subways, gas main explosions, and interruptions of electrical service that would follow either from cutting the circuits or from the circuit-breakers' tripping in the *distributed* electrical supply system. But there is no light center under Times Square. There is in fact no central source of electricity for the electrical grid that supplies power for the northeastern part of the United States and Canada. We can interrupt the electrical service at a given location either by severing the wires that lead to that peripheral location or by disrupting some part of the distributed system. The great Northeast power blackout of 1966, which turned the lights off in Times Square, was the result of a power surge in Canada that propagated through the distributed system, disconnecting hundreds of generators as overload relays tripped. The lights went out in Times Square because the distributed system went into an unstable mode.

NEURONS AND SYNAPSES

A short digression on neuroanatomy may be helpful. The elementary units that make up the nervous system are neurons. A neuron is a cell that is isolated from other neurons by a cell membrane. Neurons interconnect by means of dendrites and axons. Input signals from other neurons are transmitted into a neuron's cell body through its dendrites. The output signal of the neuron is transmitted through its axon. The connections between neurons are made through synapses. Figure 2-1 shows a diagram of a hypothetical neuron and some synaptic connections to this neuron. Note that the synapses do not cross the cell membrane boundary of the neuron. Synapses can occur on the cell body or on its dendritic connections. The concept of the synapse of a connecting, modifiable element is comparatively new (Sherrington, 1947), though the discussion and description of the neuron goes back to the end of the nineteenth century. The synapse acts as a coupling device in the transfer of a signal from a dendrite to the neuron.

The electrophysiologic studies of the nineteenth century had

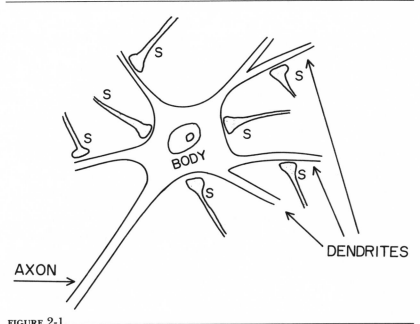

FIGURE 2-1.
Diagram of a neuron. Synapses (S) can occur on the cell body or on
the dendrites.

shown that electrical nerve impulses are transmitted through the
system of neurons, dendrites, and axons in the nerve "trunks" that
control various muscles, the spinal column, and the brain. These
nerve impulses carry information that trigger an all-or-nothing response in the cell body of the neuron. The all-or-nothing response of
the neuron is an electrical discharge that in turn is transmitted along
the nerve trunk through the axon to another neuron.

The activity of neurons in nerve trunks may become clearer if we
compare them with telegraph repeater amplifiers. The telegraph
system in its early days was called the electric telegraph to differentiate
it from the first telegraph systems in which messages were transmitted
visually through a chain of stations by means of semaphore machines.
The operator placed the arms of the semaphore into a configuration
that signified a letter of the alphabet or a number. The observer at the
next station would look at the semaphore machine and take down the
sequence of letters that each corresponded to a particular configuration of the arms of the semaphore machine. Flags held at arm's length

FIGURE 2-2a.

Telegraph system using semaphore machines. Operators would
repeat the position of the semaphore arms on the previous machine.

also could be used in place of a machine. The operator then would
repeat the message on his machine so that the next observer would be
able to read the message and pass it down the line. Figure 2-2a
illustrates the process. Telegraph systems were in place in European
nations in the early nineteenth century. Napoleon's return to France,
for example, is noted in a telegram on display in the Musée de l'Armée
in Paris.

The electric telegraph that replaced these systems transmitted
electrical signals through wires. In the earliest electric telegraphs the
distance between stations was limited by the attenuation of the electrical signal by the resistance of the telegraph wire. The electrical signal
became weaker and weaker to the point where it would not reach the
threshold voltage necessary to trip the telegraph receiver and make a
click that the operator could hear. The solution, at first, was to divide
the telegraph line into sections. An operator would listen to the
telegraph receiver sited at a distance where the input signals would
reliably exceed the threshold voltage. The operator, sketched in
Figure 2-2b, would then repeat the message, generating a new, strong
signal that would be transmitted down the telegraph line to the next
repeater operator. The repeater operators were soon replaced by
electrical devices that would automatically repeat the input signal.
Note that the input signal cannot physically move across the junction
in Figure 2-2b. Note also that the input signal in an electric telegraph
system has to exceed a threshold in order to be heard by the operator
and repeated.

A similar situation seems to occur in peripheral nerve trunks.

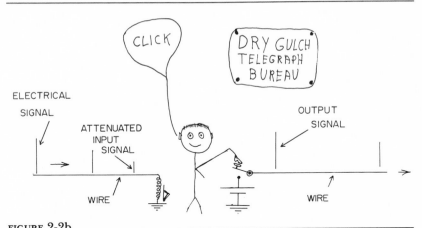

FIGURE 2-2b. ————————————————————————————————
Early version of an electric telegraph. The operator repeats the
signals that have been attenuated. The signals that are to be
repeated must, however, exceed the threshold amplitude that is
necessary to operate the device that produces an audible click.

The electrical impulses transmitted along the long axons of a cell
gradually are attenuated and lose their amplitude. The attenuated
signal, however, triggers a response in the neuron that it connects to
through a synapse. The synapses in the trunks may act simply as
devices to facilitate the triggering process (Pribram, 1971). In effect,
synaptic modification changes the threshold level of the input signal at
which a response will be triggered in the neuron. The anatomical
structure and function of neurons vary, and the function of synapses
in the neurons of the brain is probably quite different from that of
synapses of peripheral neurons in nerve trunks (Hebb, 1949). However, synaptic modification is the key element of the distributed
neural models of memory and cognition that I will discuss.

DISTRIBUTED NEURAL NETS

The diagram in Figure 2-3 indicates some of the complexity of a
neural network (there are about 10^{10} neurons in the human brain).
Close inspection of this spaghetti-like drawing will reveal that every
neuron in set α projects to (that is, has a synapse with) every neuron in
set β. Since this drawing, where $N = 6$, understates the size and
connectivity of the nervous system by several orders of magnitude, it
can be seen that single neurons and single synapses may have little
effect on the discharge patterns of the group as a whole.

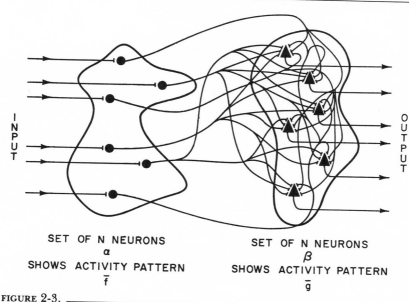

SET OF N NEURONS
α
SHOWS ACTIVITY PATTERN
f̄

SET OF N NEURONS
β
SHOWS ACTIVITY PATTERN
ḡ

FIGURE 2-3.

Diagram of interconnections of two sets of six neurons. (After J. A. Anderson, J. W. Silverstein, S. A. Ritz, and R. S. Jones, Distinctive features, categorical perception, and probability learning: some applications of a neural model, *Psychological Review* 84[1977]:413–451, figure 1. Copyright 1977 by the American Psychological Association. Adapted by permission of the author.)

Models of distributed systems have been implemented on digital computers (for example, Anderson, 1972; Anderson et al., 1977; Kohenen, 1972; Kohenen et al., 1977) in which the model incorporates synaptic modification rules. Hebb (1949) suggested that learning in adult animals involves modification of the synapses of the brain. He proposed that the activity of cells in the brain will tend to become correlated when the cells continually respond to stimuli that share some similar properties. Hebb's suggestion was that when "cell A is near enough to excite a cell B and repeatedly or persistently takes part in firing it, some growth or metabolic change takes place in one or both cells such that A's efficiency as one of the cells firing B, is increased" (1949, p. 62). This theory is, of course, consistent with the studies of associative learning in mollusks that I discussed earlier (Carew, Walters, and Kandel, 1981; Walters, Carew, and Kandel, 1981). Conduction across the synaptic boundary is enhanced when the animal "learns" to associate the two paired stimuli.

In the development of neural models it is important to see whether the model "explains" at least some of the known properties of human thought. A plausible scientific explanation of neural activity must satisfy at least two criteria. The model must be based on assumptions that are anatomically and physiologically feasible. Given these constraints that mirror the real world, the model must then simulate an aspect of human cognitive behavior. The best explanation is the one that is most constrained in terms of our knowledge of the real world and that simulates the widest range of phenomena. Thus Newton's laws of motion are a better explanation of the physical world than Ptolomey's laws, since they are more constrained and account for some aspects of the motion of objects on the earth as well as the motions of the planets. Ptolomey accounted for the motions of the planets by postulating ad hoc devices, rotating spheres on which the stars were located. His theory could account for the motion of the stars, but it could not account for the trajectories of cannon balls. In contrast, Newton's theory accounts for the details of planetary motion by using general principles that apply to a wide range of terrestrial phenomena — cannon balls, carts, automobile pistons, and so on. Kohonen and his colleagues in Finland have, over the past ten years, developed a neural model for distributed memory that meets some of these criteria. It probably is not the optimal model; neither was Newton's model. No scientific theory is ever the optimal solution. Kohonen's model, however, does show that we can account for some of the known properties of human associative memory by using assumptions that are anatomically and physiologically possible.

In the Kohonen model the computer takes account of the columnar organization of the cortex and lateral inhibition. Recent anatomical and electrophysiologic studies show that the neural tissue of the cortex is functionally organized in macroscopic units that resemble columns — vertical cylinders oriented perpendicular to the surface of the cortex (Asanuma, 1975). The cells within a column respond together to external stimuli and are tightly connected to the other cells within the column. The columns can be regarded as links between the external signal that is the input to the cortex and the output signal. The input to the top of the column thus is the primary determinant of the output at the bottom of the column. However, every column also receives axons that originate in adjacent columns and in other areas of the brain. In particular, subcortical association fibers interconnect all the columns. Lateral inhibition involves the suppression of activity in the area surrounding a signal.

The key to the Kohonen model is synaptic modification. Like the

Anderson distributed neural model, small changes take place in the synaptic connections between many neurons when something is stored in the memory. The details of the algorithms that the Kohonen model uses (Kohonen, 1972, 1977) differ from those of Anderson's model, but the net effect is similar. The synaptic connections between columns are enhanced following Hebb's (1949) general principle that the excitatory synapses are strengthened in proportion to their synchronous presynaptic and postsynaptic activities. In other words, if the activity in two adjacent columns is similar, then the synaptic connections will be strengthened. A simplified hydraulic example may make this aspect of a distributed neural model clearer.

Suppose that we trace a pattern of pathways in a sloping surface covered with sand to a depth of 4 or 5 inches. All the pathways initially have the same depth and width and are sketched in Figure 2-4(*a*). If we then slowly pour a bucket of water into a pool at the top of the sloping table, the water will begin to run down the surface through the channels; the channels that carry the most water will become wider and deeper. The pathways between adjacent channels that are interconnected and have high flow rates will also deepen. The pathways throughout the entire network of water channels on the tilt-board of this distributed system follow from the "input" pool of water. The memory trace of the input is thus represented by the total pattern of the water channels in Figure 2-4(*b*) that is the consequence of the input.

A different input will yield a different pattern throughout this same distributed system. Suppose that we start with the same traced pattern of channels in the sand on the tilt-board but instead apply a different input, such as the bar-shaped pond of water in Figure 2-5. The distributed system will take on a different pattern as a consequence of this input. Note that the pattern of waterways differs for the two inputs within the part of the tilt-board pattern within the dashed lines for the circle and bar inputs. We could differentiate between these two inputs by looking at the partial pattern. Further, we could use this distributed system to differentiate between circle and bar inputs even if we could not access the tilt-board pattern outside the dashed lines. Distributed systems typically will operate when part of the system is not available or is destroyed.

Distributed systems can be connected to discrete peripheral devices. If we connected a water-measuring device at node D in Figure 2-5, we could trigger a bell that would ring for a bar input. A "lesion" of the channel monitored by the peripheral bell ringer would, of course, destroy the bell-ringing response. The specific speech produc-

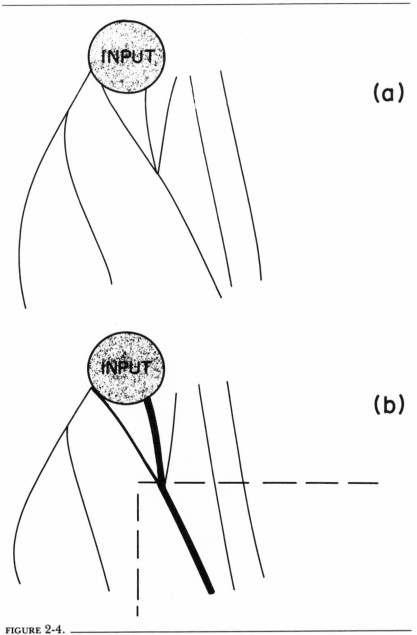

(a)

(b)

FIGURE 2-4.
Distributed system illustrated on a "tiltboard." Channels are traced
on the sand of the tilt-board (a). The "memory trace" is represented by the pattern formed after pouring a bucket of water into
the circle-shaped input (b).

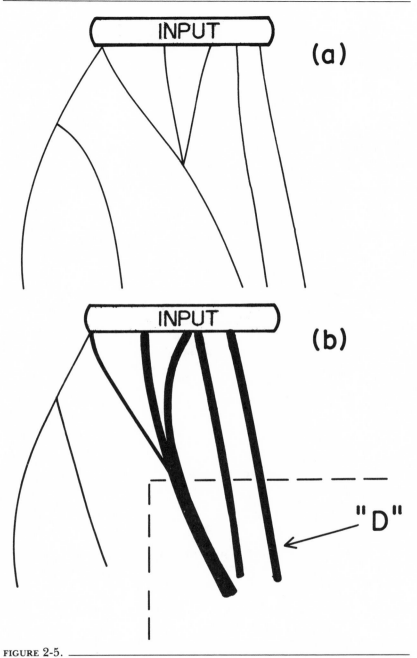

FIGURE 2-5.
Same set of channels traced on the sand of the tilt-board with
bar-shaped input (a). Pattern after pouring a bucket of water into
the bar-shaped input (b). D marks the location of a peripheral
transducer.

tion and perception deficits that follow from Broca's and Wernicke's aphasia can be interpreted in light of the lesions that affect the peripheral motor control and auditory systems as they interface the central distributed cognitive neural computer.

TESTING A DISTRIBUTED MODEL

The computer-implemented model of Kohonen is quite realistic compared with the sand-covered tilt-board model. The tilt-board model is at best a crude analog of some of the properties of a distributed memory system. The Kohonen computer model, if we are to take it seriously, should be able to perform a task in which its performance can be compared with that of human beings or other intelligent animals. Recognizing human faces is a reasonably difficult task. Some people are better than others in recollecting the image of a person's face, but we all can recognize faces. The test of the associative properties of the Kohonen distributed memory model reported in the work of Kohonen and his colleagues (1977) was carried out with photographs of human faces. Photographs were scanned with a television camera; the camera's output signal was represented in digital form and was presented to a computer system that modeled the distributed memory (Kohonen et al., 1977). Different configurations of the distributed model were used to test for the effects of "noise" and the absence of lateral inhibition. In different trials the distributed memory model stored 16, 160, and 500 different faces. The associative task involved the computer model's "remembering" the picture of a person's face when it was presented with a picture of one-half of the person's face. The recollections of the machine—that is, the machine output—when it was asked to associate this image with the images stored in its memory were almost perfect when 16 and 160 different faces were stored in the distributed memory; there was only slight deterioration when 500 different faces were stored.

The test of the Kohonen distributed model also showed two more parallels between the human ability to remember faces and the inherent properties of a distributed system. First, the process is very resistant to noise. The computer system's recollection when its resolution was cut in quarters and a randomly interconnected network was used was equivalent to that of a slightly out-of-focus photograph. The effect of cutting the resolution is roughly equivalent to storing the same images in fewer memory locations, or reducing the number of neurons in the brain while keeping the number of stored memory traces constant. That is essentially what happens as we age, since we constantly lose neurons each day. The recollection is not "lost," though its quality deteriorates.

The second additional characteristic that the computer model of distributed memory shares with human memory is the lack of any "addressing" problem. In the Kohonen model the input pictures and the associational key all are presented to the same set of input locations in the computer program that correspond to the input locations of an array of neuronal columns in the cortex. The transmitted patterns in the computer model that correspond to the outputs of the neuronal columns are accessed by a digitally controlled typesetting machine which forms the "recollections." The 500 input photographs and the "associational key" all feed into the same location. The computer simulation automatically yields the appropriate recollection at its output. We do not have to keep track of specific locations when we store the 500-picture input library as we would have to *if* we were using a discrete locationist model of the brain. In a discrete library we have to note *where* we store each image. In a conventional library we have to keep track of the location of every book if we want to access the books. The books are worthless if we cannot find them. In the distributed system the appropriate output automatically is produced when we present the key to the input. A fragment of the image that we want to recall is itself the address of the complete picture of a specific face.

A linguistic dictionary that was implemented as a distributed memory could capture one of the basic properties of a concrete or "psychological" dictionary. The phonetic representation of a word always serves as its "address" in a dictionary; for example, *bat* comes after *add* and comes after *bag*. The phonetic representation of a word could likewise serve as its address in the dictionary of an associative, distributed neural memory. The memory would yield the semantic associations of a word whenever the dictionary was addressed with the phonetic specification of the word. A partial semantic "reading" of a word could also yield a complete semantic and phonetic output. The data of Wernicke's aphasia, where lesions in or near the auditory association area of the brain result in semantic deficits and anomia, point to a connection between phonetic and semantic representation. Traditional printed dictionaries are also usually arranged on phonetic orthographic principles, which approximate phonetic representations. There appear to be psychologically valid reasons for organizing a dictionary along phonetic lines. We can capture these intuitions and solve the addressing problem, which otherwise is in itself a formidable problem, by constructing dictionaries based on associative distributed neural models.

LANGUAGE LEARNING AND DISTRIBUTED MODELS OF THE BRAIN

There has been a certain degree of confusion regarding the linguistic implication of distributed neural models in the linguistic literature. Models like those of Anderson (1972) and Kohonen fall under the rubric of AI, artificial intelligence, studies. Some of the claims that were made in the earliest period of AI studies were not justified by the performance of the AI models, which at that period were variations of the perceptron model (Rosenblatt, 1958). The perceptron model makes use of associative random connections that mediate between an input and an output stage. There is little in common between the perceptron model and models like those of Anderson and Kohonen. Random connections are *not* part of these models. Indeed, as I noted, one of the demonstrations of the power of the Kohonen model was that it could overcome random, noisy conditions (Kohonen et al., 1977). The perceptron model is furthermore not consistent with anatomical or physiologic data and stands in contrast to these recent distributed neural models. However, critiques of AI models by linguists (Dresher and Hornstein, 1976) continue to put all models since the perceptron into the same conceptual basket.

The deficiencies of the perceptron make it an easy target for a critique, but recent AI models have demonstrated interesting "cognitive" and "linguistic" behavior. The Kohonen model, for example, has been used for word and phoneme recognition (Kohonen et al., 1979; Kohonen et al., 1980) drawing on an inventory of 1000 words. The most interesting linguistic application of distributed neural models is perhaps that demonstrated by Schrier (1977) and Liberman (1979), in which modifications of the Anderson (et al., 1977) neural model were used as grammar induction machines.

One of the strongest arguments for the presence of a "fixed nucleus" of innately determined linguistic "rules" is the supposed ability of children to learn the correct grammar of their first, native language without any tutelage and from a very "noisy" input. Many discussions of the acquisition of language by linguists trained in the transformational model of Chomsky (1957, 1965) contain the claim that children learn the grammatical rules of their native language even though the utterances that they hear are supposedly almost always ungrammatical (as proposed by Chomsky, 1980). This claim is, however, not consistent with the data of studies of language development in normal children (Snow, 1977; Bates, 1976; Fernald, 1982). These studies show that parents modify their speech when they address young children who are in the early stages of language development. The speech directed to these children tends to be simpler and closer to grammatical norms than that used in conversations with adults and older children.

The grammar induction experiments of Schrier and Liberman used an algorithm that operated with two "machines," a parent machine and a child machine. The two machines were implemented by means of software rather than by any distinct physical devices. The parent machine mirrored the role of a human adult who actually knows a language; the child machine, that of the child learning a first language. The parent machine was programmed to know all the relevant aspects of a grammar. The child machine at the start of the learning process knows only a set of terminal symbols — the words of the language that it was attempting to learn. The child machine did not know the grammatical functions of any of those words.

The learning process, which is described in a clear manner in Kucera's work (1981), involved a three-part interaction between the child and parent machines: (1) The parent machine produced a set of well-formed sentences. The child machine "listened" to those sentences. (2) The child machine attempted to "speak" and produced strings of words that were sentences as well as some that were not. (3) The parent machine either accepted strings that were sentences or rejected strings that were not. The child machine used these data and the process of "abduction" to discover both the rules of the grammar and the selectional restrictions that were appropriate for each word in its vocabulary. The concept of abduction, derived from the works of Charles Pierce (1955), involves the process of hypothesis making and hypothesis testing. As Kucera notes, "speech occurs. The learner makes a preliminary hypothesis about this observed fact. That is the process of abduction. The hypothesis is then tested deductively, by speaking. But the result needs to be tested inductively — it will elicit some response: positive, negative, or perhaps indifferent. Depending on the response, the initial hypothesis may need to be revised, in which case the entire cycle of inference is resumed" (1981, p. 34).

The implementation of the grammar abduction program by Schrier (1977) had a finite-state grammar with 18 states and 52 words arranged into 23 grammatical classes. The grammar was equivalent to 87 different rules. The child machine learned 18 of these classes after 70 trial sentences; 22 classes were learned after 852 sentences. Although finite-state grammars are recursive, they clearly lack the power of the transformational grammars that many linguists believe are necessary to capture the power of human languages. The Liberman (1979) study, however, used a "matrix grammar" that, though it is not an exact equivalent of an ATN, (augmented transition network) grammar (see Chapter 3), approximates the power of an ATN grammar. ATN grammars actually have more generative capacity than most transformational grammars. The model of Liberman (1979) also incorporated a "forgetting factor" into the learning process. Erroneous assumptions learned by the child were eventually discarded using this procedure. The child machine in the Liberman study discovered 22 of the grammatical word classes after only 250 trial sentences.

Continuing work with this model (Kucera, 1981) is perfecting the grammar. What is interesting is that the child machine's discovery of the grammatical classes for words and the syntactic rules of the grammar follows from the application of cognitive processes whose scope clearly is not language-specific. The principles of the induction model could just as well be used to derive the street map of a city, using as input data the "child's" experience of walks with its parent. The corrections furnished by the parent machine are somewhat artificial. Parents do not continually provide yes-no responses to the sentences that their children produce. Children, however, have a much richer input than that of the child machine. They can learn the grammatical classes of words by observing how words relate to the external world. The nouns that occur in speech directed to young children usually refer to people, animals, or things. Many of the verbs refer to activities, such as run, eat, sit. Parents, furthermore, interact with their children in language-play games from at least the sixth week of life (Lock, 1980). Objects and pictures are named as the child's parent points out things in the immediate environment or names the pictures in books. The input of human parents is also tailored to the child (Bates, 1976; Snow, 1977; Fernald, 1982). Human children thus probably have *more* corrective feedback than is the case in the Kucera, Schrier, and Liberman studies.

The computer programs used in these experiments have no built-in, special knowledge of the linguistic rules that might describe the corpus of sentences that served as an input. They instead use the general associative ability of the distributed neural model to deduce the rules of grammar that underlie the input sentences. The differences between the induction model's ability to discover a grammar and that of normal children bear on three issues:

1. What are the limits of the particular distributed neural model? Is it a reasonable characterization of the general associative ability of human beings? Can human beings deduce the rules of grammar by using their biological general associative neural "computer"?

2. What are the differences between the linguistic input to the

induction model and the linguistic and pragmatic input to children? Do children have more information that helps them to deduce the linguistic structure of sentences? Are children sometimes given explicit instructions—are they told what they should say and what they should not say?

3. Do any deficiencies of the grammar derived by the induction algorithm reflect the absence of "innate" special linguistic knowledge that children might have?

The differences between the induction model's "behavior" and that of children has not yet been studied in detail, but the performance of the induction model and present data on the development of language in children point to a mixed system in which the general associative ability of our human cognitive computer is active in the acquisition of language. The acquisition of some aspects of grammar may, however, be facilitated by innate knowledge. These innate constraints, which structure the possible form of linguistic rules, may not be restricted to the domain of language. I will return to this topic later on.

NEURAL FEATURE DETECTORS

The input to the Kohonen distributed memory model consisted of a visual representation of a picture. A great deal of experimental data, however, indicate that specialized "feature detectors" exist in the visual system that structure perception (Hubel and Weisel, 1962, 1970). In the experiments of Hubel and Weisel the visual systems of cats and monkeys were explored at the level of the retina through the striate cortex by means of electrophysiologic techniques. In these experiments a microelectrode is inserted in the near vicinity of a cell in an anesthetized animal while visual stimuli are presented to the immobilized animal's visual system. By systematically presenting visual stimuli to the cat's eyes, it is possible to determine some of the signals that will cause a cell to respond. The cell's response will show up as a series of electrical pulses or spikes when the signal recorded by the microelectrode is amplified and monitored on an oscilloscope.

Recordings from cells at the retinal level show that a cell will respond when a small circle of light is projected onto the cat's retina. At the retinal level, the "atomic" units of the cat's visual system are similar to a photograph. All black-and-white photographs are composed of small clumps of silver that make up a dotlike grain pattern. The grain pattern sometimes shows when a negative is enlarged, but at a distance the grain pattern is not obvious and we are not aware of the quantized dots. As in a photograph, there is a one-to-one relationship in the visual system at the retinal level between points on the retina and cells that respond when particular points are stimulated.

The situation is radically different at the level of the visual cortex. Hubel and Weisel (1962) found that cells in the visual (striate) cortex did not respond in the same manner as cells closer to the periphery of the visual system. Instead of a one-to-one relationship between points on the retina and neural cells, certain cells responded to particular shapes at particular orientations placed *anywhere* in the cat's visual field. Figure 2-6 shows the responses of a cell in the visual cortex to black horizontal bars. Hubel and Weisel have systematically demonstrated the presence of a variety of cortical cells that are "tuned" to different elementary shapes, the orientation of these shapes, the speed at which the shapes move across the retina, and binocular vision.

At the level of the striate cortex the visual system of cats and monkeys thus appears to analyze the retinal image in terms of elementary "features." Large sections of the striate cortex of an animal can be removed without affecting the animal's ability to discriminate patterns. Lashley (1950), for example, reports removing 80–90 percent of the striate cortex of cats without impairing their discrimination of visual patterns. The visual system at this level, which is still very close to the periphery, is not a simple photographic mapping of the visual world. The external world is already being interpreted in terms of basic form classes.[1]

I will return to the discussion of the Hubel and Weisel data in Chapter 9 since they also are germane to the discussion of "critical periods" and the issue of innateness. In brief, the response of neural cells in the striate cortex depend on the animal's exposure to visual stimuli before a certain critical period. Kittens and monkeys raised in darkness or in diffuse, nonfocused light fields do not show these responses in the striate cortex. If they are raised under these conditions for more than eight weeks to a year (the period varies for particular response patterns), they never develop these patterns. The visual behavior of these animals also shows deficits: they stumble about and do not see normally. Similar visual deficits occur in human children who are born with cataracts of the eyes that are surgically removed several years after birth.

These specific feature detectors are *peripheral* in the sense that they form the *input* to any cognitive model for visual memory or association. The striate cortex is only four or five synapses "into" the visual system. Whatever we do in associating or putting together the

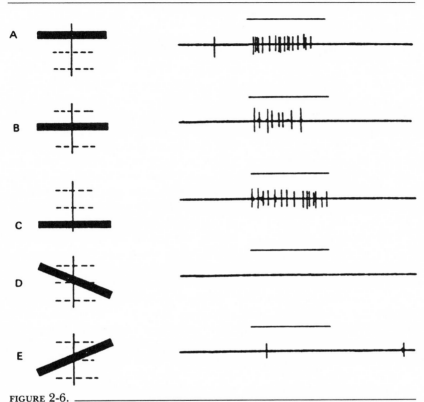

FIGURE 2-6.
Responses of a cell in the visual cortex of a cat to black bars
presented at various orientations to the cat's eye (A – E). The spikes
at the right of each bar represent the electrical response of the cell
recorded by a microelectrode. Note that there is no response when
the bar is tilted. (After Hubel and Wiesel, 1962.)

output of the cells of the striate cortex—the elementary feature
detectors—into "memories" of faces, houses, streets, and the like
must be at higher levels of the brain. The input level of Kohonen's
distributed model, for example, should consist of the outputs of
specialized, peripheral feature detectors. Kohonen and his colleagues
(1977) note that their model would work with an input array of feature
detectors; they avoided modeling feature detector outputs because of
the technical difficulties involved in computer simulation.

Innate "Tuned" Neural Devices and Rule-Governed Behavior

The peripheral systems of other animals besides cats and monkeys are also structured in terms of innately determined feature detectors that extract aspects of the signal that have behavioral importance to the animal in the external world. In "simple" animals like frogs (frogs are simple if compared with people, complex if compared with fruit flies), some of the most important aspects of behavior are structured by innate "hard-wired" feature detectors. I once watched a frog catching insects. It was at night near the lights outside an isolated Michelin one-star hotel restaurant in the French Pyrenees. I had just eaten my way through the "Menu Gastronomique" and was feeling stuffed as I watched the frog eating insect after insect. The frog sat almost motionless until his (or her) tongue shot out to intercept an insect. The frog's ability was impressive; the intercepts augmented the frog's dinner, insect after insect, though the light was dim and the bugs flew fast. I tried to catch a few insects (not to augment the Menu Gastronomique, but as a comparative experiment) and failed. I did not really expect to catch any insects, but it was an opportunity to see just how good frogs are at catching flies. Frogs are adapted to fly catching. In a series of electrophysiologic experiments, Lettvin and his colleagues (1959) showed that five different types of cells which act as feature detectors are distributed throughout the frog's retina. These innately determined cells at the periphery of the nervous system structure the ability of frogs to catch flying insects and to avoid being eaten.

These electrophysiologic data were obtained by recording the electrical output of cells from the optic nerve of *Rana pipiens* (an American species, but the data probably apply to French frogs as well). The response of cells was recorded as the experimenters systematically placed various objects in the visual field of the frog. Five basic types of cells were identified: edge detectors, bug detectors, change detectors, light-dimming detectors, and blue-light color detectors. All these cell types are distributed throughout the frog retina, so that visual events that reach any part of the retina will be analyzed by all five. The first type of cell, the edge detector, produces an image in which the boundaries of objects are preserved. Thus the frog can discern trees, bodies of water, and the like. The second type of cell, the bug detector, responds only when a small object that has a convex shape moves toward the center of the frog's visual field. It does not respond to any other moving objects, to stationary small convex objects, or to objects moving out of the visual field. The third type of cell, the event detector, responds to any movement or to a rapid change in light level. Event detectors signal a change in the visual field. The fourth cell type, the dimming detector, responds when the light intensity falls, while the fifth cell type is a color detector that responds to "watery blue" light.

The frog's bug detectors fired in the Lettvin experiments only when small buglike objects were moved across a color photograph of natural frog environments. The bug detector response will, however, be interrupted by signals from the dimming and event detectors. In the frog's normal environment birds swooping down to eat frogs will cast a shadow as they dive with the sun at their backs, triggering the dimming detector. Nearby snakes, rodents, or people gathering frogs for the Menu Gastronomique will trigger the event detector. The frog's bug detector output will stop, and the frog will, in an optimal situation, jump to the safety of the place signaled by a watery-blue detector response somewhere in his or her visual field. In the case of frogs, it thus is appropriate to speak of the neural sites of frog behavior, since the behavior is largely determined by these specialized detectors at the periphery of the visual system. No comparable electrophysiologic data have yet been derived which show that the "fixed nucleus" of the grammar of human language can be related to similar, specific neural feature detectors.

HUMAN UNIQUENESS

In the chapters that follow I shall discuss data which indicate that human beings have peripheral neural devices that are tuned to some of the acoustic attributes of human speech. Some of these devices appear to be species-specific in that they are tuned to particular sound contracts that only human beings can make. However, the uniqueness of these feature detectors is the ordinary uniqueness that typifies any species. Elephants have unique trunks, crocodiles unique skins, monarch butterflies unique wings. We appear to have neural devices that respond to some of the unique sounds that we can use for speech communication. Neural feature detectors tuned to salient, species-specific acoustic parameters of signals used for communication have been found in other animals. Crickets, for example, have neural units that code the rhythmic elements of their mating songs. The calling song of male crickets consists of pulses produced at stereotyped rhythmic intervals; female crickets respond to conspecific males by means of their songs (Hoy and Paul, 1973). Electrophysiologic studies of squirrel monkeys *(Saimiri sciureus)* show "tuned" peripheral units.

Wollberg and Newman (1972) recorded the electrical activity of single cells in the auditory cortex of awake monkeys during the presentation of recorded monkey calls and other sounds. Eleven calls, representing the major classes of this species' vocal repertoire, were presented, as well as tone bursts, clicks, and a variety of acoustic signals designed to explore the total auditory range of the monkeys. One cell responded with a high probability to only one specific acoustic signal, the "isolation peep" call.

The neural bases for speech production and speech perception may constitute the species-specific aspects of human speech at the peripheral neural level. At this level the specific aspects of the human speech-producing anatomy appear to be structured into the neural system in the form of innate neural devices that facilitate the acquisition of speech. The particular form of these devices is species-specific in the sense that they conform to the particular morphology of *Homo sapiens,* but they are related to similar mechanisms in other species.

CHAPTER 3
Automatization and Syntax

ROBERT HUTCHINS, FORMER chancellor of the University of Chicago, in his 1960s Zuckerkandel lectures related the life and philosophy of Albert Zuckerkandel, the putative sage of the village of Adel. The central thesis of Zuckerkandelism is that we should eliminate conscious thought from our lives. As conscious thoughts are replaced by "automatized" patterns of behavior, life becomes less painful. Hutchins cited many examples of Zuckerkandelistic behavior, such as the absence of conscious memories by commuters on the Long Island Railroad, the orations of statesmen, the learned papers of scholars. As is the case in successful parodies, most of the story could have been true: we do, in fact, systematically eliminate patterns of conscious thought in everyday life by the process of automatization.

I would like to begin this discussion of some of the possible biological mechanisms that structure human language at the syntactic level with the process of automatization. Through this process animals perform complex motor acts precisely and quickly. The hypothesis I shall develop is that the neural mechanisms that evolved to facilitate the automatization of motor control were preadapted for rule-governed behavior, in particular for the syntax of human language (Kimura, 1979). Preadaptation involves the use of a biological structure or system for a new function. It is important to note that this hypothesis does not entail a downgrading of the role of syntax in modern human languages. The evolutionary antecedents of an organ or a biological mechanism do not necessarily bear on its functional significance in living species. The lungs, for example, evolved by the process of preadaptation from the swim bladders of fish. Lungs nevertheless are absolutely essential for respiration in terrestrial animals. Rule-governed syntax likewise is an essential element of human linguistic competence, though the neural mechanisms that underlie syntax may have first evolved to govern limbic activity.

The general process of automatization is not restricted to the facility of human language or to communication. Though we rarely think specifically about automatization, it is a process that is essential to everything that we do or want to do. One of the best descriptions of automatization that I know of is that of Howie Mitchell, who builds and plays hammered dulcimers, a traditional folk instrument that usually has twenty-seven strings that are divided by two bridges into at least thirty or so notes. Mitchell, writing about learning to play the hammered dulcimer, states:

> At first I played almost every note deliberately and hesitatingly. A bit later I found that I was able to play short groups of 3 or 4 notes rapidly, before hesitating for the next group. Thus, learning seemed to involve increasing the number of notes in each grouping and reducing the times of hesitation . . . The first experience of being able to play the Irish Washerwoman fairly rapidly all the way through was one of the most curious sensations I can remember. By then my speed was perhaps 5-or-so notes per second, much too fast for me to be consciously aware of the details of each hammer blow. Along with this inability to follow motions consciously, I became aware of a sense of *physical separation* from the hands doing the playing. I would look down at these rapidly-moving hands, and would sheepishly have to remind myself that they were *mine!*
>
> I have wondered quite a bit at this feeling of physical separateness, which was strongly noticeable off and on for the first month or two and then became less pronounced as I became used to the instrument. I suspect that my learning of a new skill made me unusually aware of a common but marvelous mechanism of the mind, whose function is to learn and control repetitive, routine tasks. I imagine this mechanism is what makes it possible to speak, write, drive a car, play the piano, ride a bicycle, or perform any of the multitude of other muscular actions one is accustomed to doing without conscious thought. Thus learning to play the hammered dulcimer probably does not make much demand upon any rare or unusual ability.
>
> (1971, pp. 5, 6)

Automatization is the essential element in many traditional training manuals for the martial arts. Both the elaborate manuals of eighteenth- and nineteenth-century European armies and the traditional Japanese theory of Zen swordsmanship stress the formation of automatized response patterns to facilitate immediate action without any conscious thought. Automatization yields quick responses to external stimuli in the absence of specific innate mechanisms shaped to every possible contingency, such as the innate mechanisms that determine the response patterns of bullfrogs. Automatization also allows an animal to focus on the "creative," higher-level aspects of a task, whether it be driving a car, playing a piano concerto, ballet dancing, speaking a word, producing a sentence, or cutting wood. The basic "atomic" elements that we manipulate in all these activities would otherwise occupy our conscious thought and limit our creative output. We may use conscious visual feedback, for example, to monitor the positions of our fingers when we *learn* to type or to play the piano. As we automatize the process, we set up "preprogrammed" sequences that allow us to focus on the higher levels of the problem. It is significant that once a sequence of events has been automatized, the *sequence* becomes the primary unit at the psychological level. Behavioral studies like those of Goodman and Kelso (1980) demonstrate that human beings program the sequence of muscular maneuvers that underlie an automatized movement as a whole entity. In other words, once a movement is automatized, we mentally effect the movement by invoking the neural equivalent of a subroutine of a computer program. Automatization seems to me to be one of the essential elements of human language, not only at the level of motor control but at the higher syntactic levels of the grammar of human language. The formal model of the grammar of human language captured by the ATNs (augmented transition networks) that have been developed for syntactic comprehension (Wanner and Maratsos, 1978) makes use of subroutines. To me these subroutines appear equivalent to sets of automatized syntactic subroutines.

FEEDBACK SYSTEMS

Feedback systems are part of the process whereby we initiate and regulate automatized action. Human beings use feedback systems to regulate the activity of many of their muscles while speaking, singing, walking, and so on. In a feedback control system, the output is continually monitored in order to apply any changes necessary to achieve a particular goal. In a deep space probe that is under feedback control, the position of the spacecraft is continually radioed back to ground control. The present position of the spacecraft that has been telemetered back by the feedback system enters into the computations that determine the thrust and direction of the firings of the spacecraft's engines. The instructions of ground control are then telemetered back to the spacecraft. Feedback-regulated systems do not have to involve electrical signals and computers. The production of cakes in a bakery, for example, can be regulated by a feedback system in which the customers' comments — the cakes are too sweet, too dry, perfect — constitute the feedback signals that the bakers take into account in regulating the mixing and baking.

FEEDBACK REGULATION OF MOTOR ACTIVITY

All feedback systems must have sensors that monitor the state of the system or its output. The feedback system also has to transmit this information back to some place where corrections can be made. In Figure 3-1 a schematic diagram of the intercostal muscles of the chest and a segment of the spinal cord illustrates some of the components of the feedback system that operates in the muscle systems of primates and other mammals. Similar mechanisms function in the muscles of the hand and arm, but it is convenient to illustrate the feedback system for the respiratory system since we will be discussing respiration in some detail. The muscle spindle, the middle fiber in the diagram, transmits the state of the muscle's contraction through the afferent pathway back to the spinal cord. Muscle spindles indicate the relative state of a muscle's contraction. This information is integrated in the spinal cord with information that has traveled down from the motor control centers of the brain and brainstem. The efferent signals that travel down from the brain and the afferent, feedback control signals from the spindles together control the contraction of a muscle. The regulatory mechanisms in the spinal cord, which generate electrical signals that are transmitted to the muscle by the efferent pathways, can be regarded as local control stations that take into account the control signal from the brain as well as the state of contraction of the muscle.

The motor cortex of the primate brain, the source of the efferent control signals, also receives afferent signals from the muscles that it controls (Asanuma, 1975). Various parts of the motor cortex control various parts of the body through the transmission of electrical signals. Maps of the motor cortex can be derived by experiments in which parts of the exposed motor cortex are stimulated by electrical signals. These experiments show the relative complexity of function of the peripheral organs, which are mapped by proportionately larger areas in the brains of various animals, as well as the minimum time delay between cortical activity and the response of the controlled muscle. Evarts (1973) shows time delays of 5 to 7 msec between cortical activity in the leg and arm areas of the primate cortex and the muscle response monitored by electromyographic (EMG) techniques which record the electrical signals that control muscles.

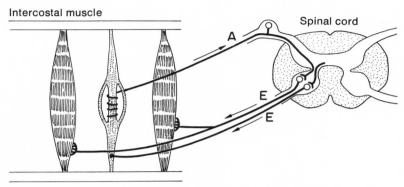

FIGURE 3-1.
Schematic diagram of intercostal muscle and a segment of the spinal cord. The muscle spindle transmits an afferent signal through pathway A to the spinal cord. The regulatory mechanisms in the spinal cord generate efferent signals that travel back to the muscle through the pathways E.

THE NEURAL BASES OF AUTOMATIZATION

Recent years have seen the development of techniques for experiments on the neural bases of automatization. In experiments with monkeys, Evarts, for example, has monitored both the activity in the neurons of the motor cortex using microelectrode techniques and EMG efferent signals to, as well as afferent signals from, the muscles of the monkey's arm under the control of these neurons. Evarts (1973) trained a monkey to grasp a movable handle and position it in a particular area on a target. The correct position was signaled by a lamp's lighting up. After a 2-to-6-second period, an external force abruptly moved the handle out of the correct area. The monkey could then gain a reward by promptly returning the handle to the correct area. Using microelectrode techniques, recordings were made of muscles from the hand area of the monkey's motor cortex after the task had been learned. Electromyographic recordings were also made of the electrical control signals to the muscles of the monkey's arms. Electromyographic recordings of muscles, in contrast to recordings of the activity of neurons in the brain, are quite safe if performed by competent people and can be used with human subjects. EMG techniques, for example, have been used for years in the study of respiration (Bouhuys, 1974) and speech (Harris, 1953). It thus is possible to get comparative data on human subjects performing a similar task. In this instance Hammond (1954), in an earlier study, derived EMG data for human subjects who flexed their forearms and were instructed to either resist or let go in response to a sudden pull.

For both the monkeys in the Evarts (1973) study and the human subjects in the Hammond (1954) study, the EMG signals showed responses in the muscles of the arm 12 and 18 msec after the abrupt motion of the handle or the sudden pull. These responses were involuntary stretch reflexes mediated by the muscle spindle afferents; they occurred for the human subjects regardless of whether they had been instructed to resist or to let go. Muscular responses at less than 100 msec in human beings usually are considered to be reflexes that are not under volitional control. The responses that occur when a neurologist taps our knees fall into this class of reflex responses. It thus was not surprising to find similar reflex activity in human beings and monkeys performing similar tasks. A second phase of muscular activity, however, monitored by Hammond and by Evarts, was not consistent with the usual pattern of reflex activity. Hammond found EMG responses at about 50 msec in his human subjects that were always present when the subjects had been instructed to resist. These responses were usually absent when the subjects were instructed to let go. Evarts found similar EMG responses in a trained monkey at 30 to 40 msec. These EMG responses were absent in a naive monkey. The monkey gradually acquired these 30-to-40-msec EMG responses as he learned the task.

The microelectrode recordings from the trained monkey's motor cortex found neurons that responded 24 msec after the perturbation of the handle while the monkey performed the task. The delay between stimulation of this area of the monkey's motor cortex and EMG response in the monkey's forearm was about 7 msec. The conclusion reached by Evarts is that the trained monkey's motor responses in this task were controlled by a pathway through the motor cortex that was under voluntary control. The 24-msec delay between the response of the neurons of the motor cortex to the perturbation of the handle, plus the 7-msec delay between motor cortex activity and EMG response, is equal to 31 msec, which is consistent with the 30-to-40-msec delay between perturbation of the handle and EMG responses in the monkey's forearm muscles. The time delay is too short to involve other areas of the monkey's cortex. The time delay between motor cortex activity and response triggered by a visual stimulus, for example, is about 100 msec. The monkey thus could not have been using visual feedback.

The data of Evarts (1973) and Hammond (1954) have been replicated and refined (for example, by Polit and Bizzi, 1978; Miles and Evarts, 1979). They point to a model for the acquisition of patterns of automatized behavior in which an animal first learns to perform a motor task, perhaps using visual or auditory feedback (for speech). As the task is learned, the animal gradually forms a direct, reflexlike control loop in the motor cortex in which afferent input from muscle spindles directly initiates a response in neurons that control the motor activity. The animal, in effect, forms subroutines for various motor acts relying on motor feedback alone. The subroutines are carried out within the peripheral motor cortex, leaving the distributed, general-purpose computer or computers of the brain free for higher, cognitive activity.

Thus the lesions of Broca's aphasia probably produce "expressive" deficits in which a person has difficulty producing the sounds of speech because they involve the motor association area of the cortex and prevent access to the automatized motor subroutines of human language. It appears, for example, that the dominant hemisphere of the human brain is not specialized so much for the motor control patterns necessary for speech as it is for patterns of motor activity that are sequential and temporally ordered (Kimura, 1979; Bradshaw and Nettleton, 1981). Lesions in the dominant hemisphere in Broca's area thus can interfere with the expression of the serially ordered, automatized motor patterns that are necessary for the production of human speech.

The results of many recent experiments in which the activity of the jaws, tongues, and lips of human speakers is monitored while they produce speech are consistent with this model of automatized behavior. Speech production involves the close patterning of complex articulatory maneuvers. Normal adult human speakers act as though they were equipped with articulatory schema that will yield the acoustic patterns of meaningful speech. The production of speech does *not* involve a continual process of trial and error in which we tentatively move our lips, tongue, jaw, larynx, and so on, and start to make a sound that we monitor, correcting the sound as we listen to ourselves. Human speakers are immediately "on target" and produce the appropriate acoustic signals (Lieberman, 1967; Nearey, 1978; Lindblom, Lubker, and Gay, 1979). The fundamental frequency of phonation, for example, generally is within 5 Hz of a fixed "anchor frequency" 10 to 20 msec after the onset of phonation during the course of a sentence (Lieberman, Landahl, and Ryalls, 1982). The muscles of the larynx and respiratory system are adjusted by the speaker to produce the appropriate pitch each time that phonation begins. The only model that can account for the behavior of human speakers is one that hypothesizes the presence of automatized motor patterns for the various sounds of speech. Adult speakers indeed can immediately compensate when external events interfere with the normal activity of their speech articulators. It is apparent, for example, that people can talk with a pipe or cigarette in their mouth. Formal experiments in which subjects talk while their jaws are propped open by bite blocks demonstrate that the speech produced under these conditions is perceptually good. The speaker compensates for the interfering bite block.

Recent data (Folkins and Zimmerman, 1981) show that the muscular activity of speakers producing utterances while their jaws were constrained by bite blocks appears to involve fixed, automatized "central" motor patterns. The electrical activity of the muscles that close the jaw, as well as the motion of the speaker's jaws, was monitored in these experiments. Four normal adult subjects were monitored during the production of repeated sequences of the syllable [pae] and [pI] under a normal condition and in two instances in which their jaws were locked into a fixed position. The speaker's jaws were fixed by placing special bite blocks between their upper and lower molar teeth. The bite blocks were adjusted so that in one experimental condition there were 5 mm between the speakers' central incisor teeth. A second fixed-jaw condition used bite blocks that yielded a 15-mm separation. The speakers compensated for the bite blocks by appropriate adjustments in their tongue and lip movements. They, for example, had to move their lips further in the bite block condition when they produced the syllable [pI]. However, there was no difference in the timing or magnitude of the muscles that they would have used to close their jaws when their jaws were fixed by the bite blocks. The automatized articulatory subroutine for the production of these syllables resulted in the speakers' tensing of these muscles, although they knew and could feel that their jaws could not move. Their jaw movements were automatized. Folkins and Zimmerman (1981) conclude that lower-level neural control systems interact with central control programs in these bite block experiments.

The degree to which the automatized motor programs that are the basis of speech production in human beings are learned or are innately specified is not known. Certainly exposure to speech is necessary. Children appear to learn gradually the motor subroutines that are necessary to speak a particular dialect with a native accent (Buhr, 1980; Lieberman, 1980). Auditory feedback is necessary to set up the automatized motor subroutines of human speech production. Proprioceptive feedback may also be useful. However, the automatized motor subroutines of speech production, once established, do not appear to involve either auditory or proprioceptive feedback. People deafened after the acquisition of speech, for example, retain almost normal speech patterns. The automatized patterns that underlie speech production persist when people lose their hearing (Hamlet, Stone, and McCarty, 1976). Similar comments apply to communicative vocal signals in other animals. Like human speech, the purring of cats involves the coordinated activity of many muscles. Purring in cats persists after the afferent feedback pathways from these muscles are cut (Remmers and Gautier, 1972); purring thus seems to be an automatized behavior. However, there appears to be a species-specific neural basis for the ability of human beings to master the complex automatized subroutines of speech production. Chimpanzees, for example, cannot learn to produce speech sounds that they anatomically could produce (Hayes and Hayes, 1951).

SYNTAX AND AUTOMATIZED MOTOR ACTS

As I noted earlier, the grammatical deficits associated with Broca's aphasia are one of its more puzzling symptoms. The grammatical deficits include expressive ones. Grammatical endings are dropped and verbs are expressed as nominals: for example, *writing* in English or infinitives in other languages in the speech of Broca's aphasics. Grammatical function words, such as determiners and prepositions *(the, by)* and verb modals *(may, will)*, are dropped (Goodglass, 1976; Zurif, Caramazza, and Myerson, 1972). Broca's aphasics do not consistently lose all of these words, nor does a particular subject consistently drop a particular word or grammatical ending. Only the severest cases are marked by the loss of all grammatical endings; in most cases the pattern of grammatical endings is inconsistent. Complex grammatical structures are more likely to be distorted (Goodglass, 1968, 1976; Devilliers, 1974).

Although clinical observations do not show deficiencies in the comprehension of either speech or written sentences by Broca's aphasics, psycholinguistic techniques have revealed syntactic comprehension deficits. The context of normal conversation is so rich in pragmatic and semantic cues that agrammatic aphasics probably are able to piece together the meaning of sentences though they have syntactic deficits. A series of experiments in which agrammatic aphasics were asked to choose which of two pictures correctly captured the meaning of tape-recorded sentences showed that comprehension was poor when only syntactic cues were present (Zurif and Caramazza, 1976; Zurif and Blumstein, 1978). Comprehension of a sentence like *The apple the boy is eating is red* was good because apples are often red, and apples do not usually eat boys. Comprehension of the sentence *The boy that the girl is chasing is tall* was poor since boys can also chase tall girls and girls can also chase boys.

The syntactic deficits of Broca's aphasics are not restricted to speech signals that they hear. They also have difficulties with written sentences. Normal speakers of English, for example, are able to group the words of a written sentence in a way that closely approximates the phrase structure of the sentence. The traditional parsing exercises that at one time constituted part of the school curriculum were aimed at grouping words in terms of a sentence's phrase structure. Broca's aphasics, when they are asked to group the words of a written sentence, instead cluster content words and group other words on a random basis (Zurif, Caramazza, and Myerson, 1972). The words of the sentence *The dog chases a cat*, for example, might be grouped by an aphasic as follows:

(The) (dog chases) (a) (cat).

Normal speakers of English, in contrast, would group the same words as follows:

(The dog) ((chases) (a cat)).

The dramatic linguistic deficiencies associated with isolation aphasia are also consistent with the premise that the neural structures which first evolved to facilitate the automatized motor control of speech were preadapted for rule-governed syntax. Geschwind, Quadfasel, and Segarro (1968) documented a case of isolation aphasia in which the intact Broca's and motor association areas of the brain were isolated from other areas of the brain by a lesion. The patient readily produced well-articulated speech and could even correct the syntax of incoming speech; but he was completely at a loss concerning the meaning of speech. The peripheral neural mechanisms responsible for automatized, rule-governed speech production and rule-governed syntax were isolated from other regions of the brain, and the patient was unable to connect his unimpaired ability to produce speech and handle syntax with the productive, cognitive aspects of language.

The Neural Bases of Syntax

We could account for the normal grouping of the words of the sentence *The dog chases a cat* with the following set of phrase structure rules:

> Sentence ⟶ Noun Phrase + Verb Phrase
> Noun Phrase ⟶ Article + Noun
> Verb Phrase ⟶ Verb + Noun Phrase

In a phrase structure grammar, a given rule rewrites one item at a time. Many of the arguments that have been advanced for the necessity of transformational grammars claim that phrase structure grammars cannot account for the sentences of any natural language (Chomsky, 1957; Bresnan, 1978, pp. 35–40). Recent versions of phrase structure grammar meet these objections; the phrase structure grammar proposed by Gazdar (1981), for example, makes use of indices on rules to capture the problems of agreement that are difficult to handle with traditional phrase structure grammars (Bresnan, 1978, pp. 36–40). However, phrase structure grammars are part of the syntactic component of virtually all theories of grammar. The "psychological" claim — that is, the only valid basis for taking any of these theories seriously in a biological context — is that phrase structure rules capture some aspects of the linguistic behavior of normal human beings. People thus "know" that a sentence can be divided into a noun phrase and a verb phrase, that a noun phrase can be divided into an article plus a noun, and that a verb phrase can be divided into a verb plus a noun phrase. Other phrase structure rules would be necessary to account for the full range of English sentences, but these three rules will do for this example and for the question I would like to raise — and will attempt to answer: Where did the neural "equipment" for these syntactic rules come from? How did it evolve?

What I propose is, in essence, that the rules of syntax derive from a generalization of neural mechanisms that gradually evolved in the motor cortex to facilitate the automatization of motor activity. Human syntactic ability, in this view, is a product of the Darwinian mechanism of preadaptation, the channeling of a facility that has evolved for one function toward a different one. Darwin's comments on the evolution of lungs from swim bladders explicate this principle: "The illustration of the swim bladder in fish is a good one, because it shows us clearly the highly important fact that an organ originally constructed for one purpose, namely flotation, may be converted into one for a wholly different purpose, namely respiration" (1859, p. 190). Note that I am *not* claiming that there have not been any specializations for syntactic abilities in the neural structures of the motor cortex and motor association areas of the brain. I instead propose that there is an evolutionary and morphological link between the neural bases of structured, automatized motor activity and syntax. The syntactic deficits of Broca's aphasia that involve lesions in or near the motor association area of the cortex are consistent with this linkage, as are the data cited by Kimura (1979); so are the observations of Piaget (1980) and his colleagues, which demonstrate a consistent developmental pattern in normal children in which sensorimotor development usually progresses in concert with linguistic achievement. In Piaget's words, "in the sensorimotor period preceding language one sees the establishment of a logic of actions (relations of order, interlocking of schemes, intersections, establishments of relationships, and so on) rich in discoveries and even in inventions (recognition of permanent objects, organization of space, of causality)" (1980, p. 25). A wide range of data are consistent with a link between the neural bases of motor control and abstract, cognitive behavior. Many of the factors involved in this possible link are discussed, for example, by Kimura (1979). In reviewing the data of aphasia, Kimura claims that motoric speech deficits always occur in concert with other motoric deficits. She proposes that the evolution of the neural mechanisms that are the biological substrate for the production of speech in human beings followed from evolutionary adaptations for the neural control of sequential, time-ordered motor commands. As Kimura (1979, p. 210) notes, the system appears to depend on "internal representation of moving body parts . . . somewhat akin to a system that has been suggested for the control of 'preprogrammed' movements (Polit and Bizzi, 1978)."

Kimura (1979) proposes that the evolution of the lateralized neural mechanisms involved in the control of human speech follows from adaptations of motor tasks that involve the division of labor between the hands, so that one hand holds an object while the other effects some operation on that object. We can see these operations in the behavior of chimpanzees when they make tools like "termite sticks" (Goodall, 1968). The cultural record that is the indirect evidence of hominid evolution also supports Kimura's thesis, since we see a progression from simple tools whose manufacture can be described by fairly simple "rules" to tools whose manufacture can be described only by means of fairly complex rules (Lieberman, 1975a). The tools that have simple grammars are rather easy to make; people can learn to make them after only a few lessons. The tools that have complex grammars are, in contrast, quite difficult to make, and people need years of training. Kimura (1979) and Bradshaw and Nettleton (1981), who review much of the data relevant to left-hemispheric brain lateralization in human beings, suggest that the *functional* assymetry of the human brain and the speech deficits of aphasia follow from adaptations for the neural control of precise, sequential patterns of motor control in *Homo sapiens.*

The alletic basis for the evolution of lateralized and specialized neural control of speech thus may rest in similar, though more limited, tendencies for lateralized control of various patterns of behavior in other animals. Denenberg (1981), for example, reviews data that demonstrate such behavior as functional lateralization of running-wheel activity, taste aversion, and left-right spatial choices in rats; pawedness in mice; and singing in birds. As Geschwind notes, "failures to find assymetry in animals in the past have resulted from concentrating on features that are very noticeable in humans, such as speech or handedness, rather than on features that are obviously important for the survival of nonverbal species" (1981, p. 26).

Anatomical studies of the brains of other species also demonstrate that human beings are not the only animals whose brains are assymetric. LeMay and Geschwind (1975) showed that apes have the same assymetry of the Sylvian fissure as humans: the right Sylvian fissure climbs higher than the left. There furthermore appears to be an evolutionary trend in regard to this particular assymetrical feature of the primate brain. In chimpanzees the longer left-sized Sylvian fissure is seen in about 80 percent of individuals, which is about the same as in human populations (Yeni-Komshian and Benson, 1976). The percentage is only 44 percent in rhesus monkeys (Witelson, 1977). Behavioral data derived from lesion studies in monkeys again suggest an evolutionary precursor to Wernicke's area of the human brain in the auditory association area of the monkey brain (Dewson, 1978). One caution in interpreting the results of lesion studies directly is that they do not necessarily indicate the *localization* of a discrete part of the brain in the performance of a specific function. As Denenberg notes in regard to hemispheric dominance:

> a conclusion that the right hemisphere (or left) is more active than the left (right) cannot be construed as implying that the function is located in the right (left) hemisphere. This may be indeed the case, but lesions also tend to interrupt cortical-subcortical connections as well as damaging a hemisphere. Thus the locus of a function may be in a subcortical region, or may involve a network containing both cortical and subcortical pathways.
>
> (1981, p. 4)

The evolution of the biological bases of human syntax probably has its beginnings in the neural mechanisms that structure the behavior of simple animals like mollusks (Walters, Carew, and Kendell, 1981; Carew, Walters, and Kandel, 1981; Lukowiak and Sahley, 1981). In more complex animals the degree of organization of these neural mechanisms elaborates. However, the responses of animals like frogs to various stimuli that are relevant to frogs (Frishkopf and Goldstein, 1963; Lettvin et al., 1959) still demonstrate a close link between a particular stimulus and a particular response pattern, coded at the neural motor control level. The evolution of thought and of cognitive processes like the syntax of language, which are closely linked if not equivalent to the elements of thought, may follow from a process in which these "logical" neural mechanisms are dissociated from the direct link between a stimulus and a motor act. In Rozin's (1976) terms, intelligence evolves as access to the logic of the cognitive unconscious develops. In other words, over the course of evolution two things happened: (1) animals evolved neural mechanisms that involved more and more complex patterns of rule-governed behavior; and (2) some of these neural mechanisms became available as logical devices for thought and as devices for the transmission of conceptual information. Human beings still retain neural mechanisms that mediate automatic, physiologic responses to various stimuli. We, however, also make use of the internal logic of the mechanisms that have evolved in these neural response-and-control systems for abstract, rule-governed thought and logic. Some of the examples that follow may make this connection clearer.

GRAMMARS FOR MOTOR ACTIVITY

The "rules" for a motor act like picking up a water tumbler constitute at the simplest level of representation a finite-state grammar in which particular muscle instructions are contingent on the previous steps.

You cannot pick up the water tumbler unless you are already holding it. You cannot hold it unless you have already opened your hand around the tumbler. You cannot do that until you have reached out for the glass, and so on. The rules for picking up a water tumbler could be written as shown below, in a "macro" language in which we are specifying the general muscular maneuver. Machine languages, to continue the digital computer analogy, would have to translate these macro instructions into instructions to the individual muscles of the arm and hand.

Rule 1.   Extend arm toward tumbler.
Rule 2.   Open hand and place fingers about tumbler.
Rule 3.   Close hand on tumbler.

Rule 4.   Raise hand and arm.
Rule 5.   Move forearm back toward body.
Rule 6.   Raise tumbler toward mouth.
Rule 7.   Drink from tumbler.
Rule 8.   Lower tumbler back to initial position on table.
Rule 9.   Open hand and release tumbler.
Rule 10.   Return arm to rest position, state 1.

The output of the rules can be represented by the finite-state automaton sketched here:

$$(1) \rightarrow (2) \rightarrow (3) \rightarrow (4) \rightarrow (5) \rightarrow (6) \rightarrow (7) \rightarrow (8) \rightarrow (9) \rightarrow (10)$$

The rules must be executed in sequence. They constitute a subroutine that can be used whenever you pick up a water tumbler. Rule schema like the one above appear to be automatized in the primate motor cortex (Polit and Bizzi, 1978). Once you learn the subroutine, you do not have to think about the individual steps; you simply call out the whole routine as an entity. Once a task is automatized, it functions as an indivisible entity in which you do not access or program the individual steps (Goodman and Kelso, 1980).

Automatized behavior in human beings clearly is not restricted to simple acts like picking up a tumbler. We do not, for example, consciously think of the many operations involved in eating dinner or driving a car. How many times is it apparent that you have no recollection of the last twenty miles that you have been driving your car? These higher-order levels of automatized behavior can be represented in terms of finite-state or phrase structure grammars in which simple subroutines like picking up a tumbler are the elementary operations. Thus some of the rules that would generate appropriate behavior in a dinner-eating automation could take this form:

1. Dine → Eat + Drink + Dine
2. Eat → Cut Food + Fork Act
3. Drink → Water from Tumbler
4. Water from Tumbler → Subroutine GT
5. Cut Food → Hold Food + Cut

Note that rule 1 is recursive in that dine yields eat, drink, and dine. Subroutine GT in this example consists of the sequence of rules 1 – 10 noted above.

RULE-GOVERNED BEHAVIOR AND GRAMMARS

A phrase structure rule can apply to any line of a derivation on which an appropriate symbol appears. Thus if we write a fragment of a phrase structure grammar of English, we could have these rules:

6. S → NP + VP
7. NP → T + N
8. VP → V + NP
9. T → the
10. T → a
11. N → man
12. N → house
13. N → ball
14. N → ship
15. V → hit
16. V → saw

Each rule of this fragment of the phrase structure rules that presumably would form part of a grammar of English, $X \rightarrow Y$, is interpreted as the instruction rewrite X as Y. The sequence of operations that describes the application of these rules to form a sentence of English can be called the derivation. Thus the derivation of the sentence *The man saw the ship* is as follows:

Structural Elements and Words	Rule Applied
S	
NP + VP	6
T + N + VP	7
T + N + V + NP	8
T + N + V + T + N	7
the + N + V + T + N	9
the + man + V + T + N	11
the + man + saw + T + N	16
the + man + saw + the + N	9
the + man + saw + the + ship	14

Each line of the derivation is formed by applying one of the rewrite rules to the string of symbols. The sequence of operations can also be represented by the "tree" diagram in Figure 3-2, which has the advantage of presenting the syntactic relationships of the various elements in a convenient form.

The formal property of phrase structure rules that limits their explanatory power superficially appears trivial. A phrase structure rule can be applied in a derivation whenever the alphabetic symbol on the left of the rule appears in the line of the derivation being considered. *A phrase structure rule thus can apply to a line of a derivation regardless of its past history.* Phrase structure grammars constituted the

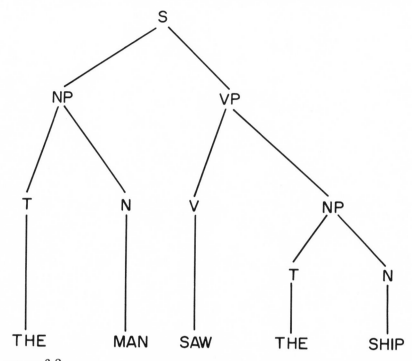

FIGURE 3-2.

"Tree" showing syntactic relationship of words of the sentence *The man saw the ship.*

primary devices for morphophonemic and syntactic analysis in the "taxonomic" theories of the 1950s that were the starting point of transformational theory. Much of the early work in the development of transformational grammars from Chomsky (1957) onward involved demonstrating the empirical inadequacies of phrase structure grammars. This view persists to the present day; Bresnan, for example, repeats the familiar claim that "the cross-phrasal regularities in natural languages cannot be adequately described within these grammars" (1978, p. 37). Bresnan notes that in English, the agreement in number between the subject noun phrase and the verb *were* (plural) or *was* (singular) operates not only when these constituents are proximate to each other, as in the sentences:

The problem was unsolvable
The problems were unsolvable

but also when the verb is some distance from the noun phrase, as in the following sentence:

Which problem did you say your professor said she thought was unsolvable?

These deficiencies of traditional phrase structure grammars, however, can be solved by introducing a memory component into a phrase structure grammar that allows rules to consider the past history of a derivation as well as the last line of the derivation. In essence, this is the difference between traditional phrase structure grammars and transformational grammars (Lieberman, 1975a). A transformational grammar achieves its descriptive power — its ability to generate strings of words that are restricted to the grammatical sentences of a natural human language — by virtue of its *memory*. A transformational grammar's memory resides in the global nature of the structural description of each transformational rule, which restricts its operation to particular classes of phrase markers. The structural description takes into account the entire derivation rather than a single line. A transformational grammar can thus keep track of the fact that the noun phrase and verb must agree in number though they are not proximate to each other on the last line of the derivation.[1] In the examples that Bresnan cites, the formal devices of a transformational grammar (Chomsky, 1957, 1965; Bresnan, 1978) can "remember" that the noun phrase at the head of a sentence is singular and match it with a singular verb that occurs later in the sentence. Recent modified versions of phrase structure grammars like that of Gazdar (1981) implement this memory component, as well as the descriptive adequacy, of transformational grammars by means of indices on rules. These indices remember the fact that a noun phrase early in a derivation is singular and that it goes with, that is, selects, a singular verb. Gazdar's system appears to be as descriptively powerful as a transformational grammar, and it makes some interesting claims about what sorts of sentences are not psychologically plausible.

ATN Approaches to Grammar and Comprehension

Augmented transition network (ATN) models of grammar provide another way of modeling the grammars of human languages with a formal mechanism that incorporates a memory. The recent modification of transformational grammar proposed by Bresnan (1978) in fact makes use of an ATN component plus some transformational rules. However, there is no reason for incorporating transformational rules at all. An ATN grammar has the descriptive power of a Turing machine; that is to say, it has the generative capacity of any transformational grammar (Wall, 1972, p. 274; Charniak, personal communication). ATN grammars, moreover, have two advantages with respect to conventional transformational models if we are operating in a biological framework. First, they provide a psychologically motivated formal model that predicts some aspects of the comprehension of sentences by human beings (Wanner and Maratsos, 1978). Second, they formally embody the concept of automatization in the operation of their subroutine networks. Matrix grammars that are formally similar to ATNs have already been implemented using Anderson's (1972) distributed neural model.

The elementary ATN grammar in Figure 3-3 illustrates the way in which an ATN grammar functions to comprehend a sentence. In the course of many attempts to devise automata that would comprehend a sentence, it has become evident that methods that directly apply the rules of a transformational grammar simply will not work. Various ad hoc devices can be used to interfere with a transformational model, but they do not yield a general solution (for example, see the work of Fodor, Bever, and Garrett, 1974). ATN grammars have evolved in the course of the development of computer systems that can provide a syntactic analysis of a sentence. A concise discussion of the properties of ATN grammars, as well as of the psychologically relevant predictions of sentence comprehension that are yielded by ATN grammars, is contained in the work of Wanner and Maratsos (1978). The simplified ATN grammar that will be described is drawn from that study. As Wanner and Maratsos note:

> The grammar is organized as a pair of separate networks. Each network is composed of a set of states represented as circles. The symbols inside the circles provide a unique name for each state. The arrows that connect the states are called arcs. If an arc connects two states, it is possible to make a transition between those states in the direction indicated by the arc. The labels on each arc specify the conditions that must be satisfied before a transition can be made. In addition, certain actions must be performed whenever a transition over an arc is made . . . A sentence is analyzed as the processor works its way through the grammar, state by state, examining the input sentence, word by word, to see whether it meets the conditions stated on the arcs. Wherever the conditions are satisfied, the processor executes the actions associated with the current arc, makes the indicated transition, and turns its attention to the next word in the sentence.

> (1978, p. 125)

Sentence Network:

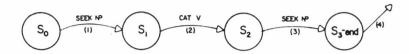

Noun Phrase Network:

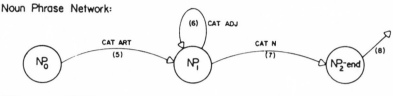

ARC	ACTION
1	ASSIGN SUBJECT to current phrase
2	ASSIGN ACTION to current word
3	ASSIGN OBJECT to current phrase
4	ASSEMBLE CLAUSE
	SEND current clause
5	ASSIGN DET to current word
6	ASSIGN MOD to current word
7	ASSIGN HEAD to current word
8	ASSEMBLE NOUN PHRASE
	SEND current phrase

FIGURE 3-3. _____

A simplified ATN grammar. (After Wanner and Maratsos, 1978.)

In the analysis of a sentence like *The old train left the station,* the processor would start with *S.* The only arc leaving *S* instructs the processor to *SEEK NP.* It stores in its memory any partial results that may have been obtained (in this instance, none), stores the identity of the arc that prompted the *SEEK* action, and transfers to the noun phrase network. Operating in the noun phrase network, the processor successfully packages together the string of words *the old train* under the name *NOUN PHRASE* and keeps track of the associations between these words and the function labels that are stored in traversing the *NP* network. In this example the bundle of associations is:

NOUN PHRASE
   DET = the
   MOD = old
   HEAD = train

Note that the ATN assigns the functional label *SUBJECT* to this noun phrase. The ATN then returns back to the sentence network. The ATN will switch back to the *NP* network on arc 3, which will assign the functional label *OBJECT* to the noun phrase *the station.*

As Wanner and Maratsos (1978) note, the ATN network analysis yields a prediction of psychological "complexity of comprehension" that is consistent with experimental data. The ATN model analyzes the words of a sentence, one at a time, from left to right. In many sentences it is impossible to decide the function of a group of words until the ATN works its way through a long string of words. As the ATN model progresses through a string of words in which it has to defer the functional labeling, it in effect is storing in its short-term memory a string of unintegrated verbal material. Experimental psychoacoustic and written experiments show that the human memory can more successfully keep track of semantically meaningful verbal material than of unintegrated verbal material (Miller, 1951). Thus if human beings process sentences like an ATN model and defer assigning a functional label until they reach the point at which the ATN model would assign a label, we should be able to measure the relative comprehensibility of sentences that differ with respect to the number of words that must be stored unlabeled. A series of careful experiments demonstrates that the relative comprehensibility and transient memory load that is placed on human beings in the comprehension of sentences is reasonably consistent with the predictions of ATN models (Wanner and Maratsos, 1978; Wanner and Shiner, 1976). We are only beginning to gain some insight into the mechanism of comprehension. It is probable that ATN models in their present form will not suffice; however, they provide a reasonable starting point for systematic experiments that test psychologically relevant formal models.

SUBROUTINES AND AUTOMATIZATION

ATN networks yield a direct formalization of my proposal regarding the evolutionary connection between the subroutines of automatized neural control for sequential motor activity and the rules of syntax. A network like the noun phrase network is analogous to the subroutines that are operant in motor control (Polit and Bizzi, 1978). The ATN networks, furthermore, act as whole entities; this is again similar to the neural control of motor activity (Goodman and Kelso, 1980). Since complete grammars for the control of movement or for any language do not exist, it is at present impossible to see how far the parallel between ATN networks and motoric subroutines goes. The states of an ATN network and the local constraints on arcs, however, appear to be at least a good first approximation for the formal description of motor activity.

SUMMARY

Human beings and other animals learn to perform complex, structured motor acts through the process of automatization. Neurophysiologic and behavioral data show that mechanisms that act like reflex arcs are set up in the motor cortex when a pattern of motor activity is learned. These neural mechanisms are the neural correlates of rules that structure motor activity, such as playing a musical instrument, driving a car, using a Samurai sword, or talking. Automatization yields quick responses to external stimuli and thus is a process that has a higher selective value. Automatization also allows an animal to focus on the higher-level, cognitive aspects of a task; it allows human beings, for example, to focus on the interpretation of a violin sonata rather than on the bowing of the violin. The neural bases for syntax may reside in the preadaptation of neural structures that originally evolved to facilitate the automatization of motor activity. The neural structures that first evolved for the automatization of motor control may have been generalized to other aspects of rule-governed behavior, including human language. The evolution of rule-governed syntax thus may follow from Darwin's theory of preadaptation, wherein an organ that evolved for one purpose happens to facilitate a new pattern of activity. The data of Broca's aphasia and isolation aphasia that associate expressive and receptive syntactic deficits with lesions in or near the motor association area of the cortex are consistent with this hypothesis, as are the Piagetian observations that link sensorimotor and language development.

ATN (augmented transition network) grammars appear to be equivalent in generative capacity to phrase structure grammars that make use of indices and transformational grammars. ATN grammars, however, formally capture the concept of automatized subroutines in their networks. ATN grammars also are consistent with psychologically significant data on the comprehension of sentences by human listeners and offer at least a starting point for further psychologically relevant formal models.

CHAPTER 4

Syntax, Words, and Meaning

THE PREMISE OF THIS CHAPTER is that human language is inherently ambiguous and that rule-governed syntax perhaps initially evolved as a device to supplement context in inferring the meaning of a message. We derive the meaning of a linguistic message by means of the total context in which the message occurs, as well as by formal procedures that take into account the rule-governed syntax of a language. The selective value of syntax may rest, in part, in its role in reducing the inherent ambiguity of linguistic communication. Syntactic rules thus may have been rapidly introduced into human language, making use of the preadapted neural substrate that had evolved for automatized motor control. Syntax undoubtedly has other functional attributes in human language. It is an important component in the creative power of human language: it enables people to construct new sentences that can convey concepts that previously did not exist. There indeed are data which suggest that enhanced linguistic ability in the form of bilingualness enhances cognitive ability. The syntax of human language also may be a factor in increasing the rate at which we can transmit information (Lieberman, 1975a, p. 14). It is faster to transmit the "complex" sentence *Joe saw the dirty old man who was wearing the hat* than to transmit the set of simpler sentences that convey the same information: *Joe saw the man; The man was old; The man was dirty; The man was wearing a hat*. However, the data that have been derived from the study of the acquisition of language by young children and the comparative ethological study of animal behavior and communication suggest that the *initial*, primary function of syntax is to facilitate communication by limiting ambiguity.

WORDS AND SIGNALS

Part of the recent controversy regarding the linguistic ability of chimpanzees and gorillas concerns their ability to use words as symbols for things. Both those who believe that apes do not display any linguistic ability and those who believe that apes do display some measure of linguistic ability have focused on experiments in which apes have been asked to name objects or photographs of objects (Gardner and Gardner, 1969, 1980; Fouts, 1975; Rumbaugh, Gill, and Von Glasserfeld, 1973; Sebeok, 1981; Terrace, 1979a; Premack, 1972). I shall discuss these experiments in Chapter 10; the point that I would like to make here is that the experiments and the critiques usually ignore one of the salient characteristics of the *words* of human language: words are *not* tokens for things; they instead convey concepts. The meaning of a word never is precisely equivalent to a thing, a set of things, or even a property of a set of things. The identification of a word with a specific thing or action is traditional. It pervades the philosophic literature. Jonathan Swift, for example, captured the essence of the presumed equivalence between words and objects when he parodied Leibnitz's concerns regarding the "exact signification of words" (Leibnitz, 1949, p. 387) in *Gulliver's Travels.* The learned scholars of the Academy of Laputa were concerned about the inherent imprecision of words. The meaning of a word never is precisely the same to any two people. The philosopher's solution thus was, as Swift noted,

> a Scheme for abolishing all Words whatsoever . . . since Words are only names for *Things,* it would be more convenient for all Men to carry about them, such *Things* as were necessary to express the particular Business they are to discourse on . . . many of the most Learned and Wise adhere to the new Scheme of expressing themselves by *Things,* which hath only this Inconvenience attending it; that if a Man's Business be very great, and of various Kinds, he must be obliged in Proportion to carry a greater Bundle of *Things* upon his Back, unless he can afford one or two strong Servants to attend him. I have often beheld two of these Sages almost sinking under the Weight of their Packs, like Peddlers among us, who when they meet in the Streets, would lay down their Loads, open their Sacks, and hold Conversation for an Hour together; then put up their Implements, help each other to resume their Burthens, and take their Leave.
>
> (1726; 1970, p. 158)

Words are not simply convenient labels for things; the difficulties of the learned sages of the Academy of Laputa would not have ended even if they had semitrailers following them loaded with things. Futile attempts to define words in terms of the properties of things have persisted to the present day. Bertrand Russell, for example, spent a good part of his productive life in a vain attempt to refine the Laputan position. Russell's autobiography (1967) notes the problems that beset him through the years 1900 and 1901, when he was attempting to show that words can be defined in terms of straightforward logical operations that ultimately refer to things. The problem is that words, even "simple" words that we "know" refer to material objects, cannot be defined by reference to material objects.

Consider a simple word like *table*. By introspection we of course know that *table* does not refer to a particular table. But if we think about the way in which we can use *table* in even a few sentences, it is apparent that we cannot define it, as Russell attempted to do, in terms of some set-theoretical procedure through which we try to capture the meaning of *table* by partitioning the universe into a set of objects that are tables and a set of objects that are not tables. The problem is inherent in the attempt to relate words directly to things. As Jacob Bronowski notes,

> you cannot make a single general statement about anything in the world which really is wholly delimited, wholly unambiguous, and divides the world into two pieces.
> You cannot say anything about gravitation which excludes it from the space-time in which it is now embedded; you cannot say anything about a table or chair which does not leave you open to the challenge, "Well I am using this chair as a table." Kids do it all the time, "I am using this chair as a table, it is now a table or chair." . . . the world does not consist simply of an endless array of objects and the word "table" was not invented in order to bisect the universe into tables and non-tables. And if that is true of "table," it is true of "honor" and it is true of "gravitation," and it is true, of course, of "mass" and "energy" and everything else.
>
> (1978, p. 107)

We all know when we are talking about a real table. A table has legs; we sit down before it, put things on it, occasionally sit on it, and can generally recognize one when we see one. We can, moreover, generally tell when something is not a table. It should therefore be possible to devise a simple definition of a table. We could adopt Russell's solution and simply state that the word *table* refers to the class of things that people consider to be tables and does not refer to the class of things that are not considered to be tables. Suppose we did this and enumerated a long list of the objects that were tables and the objects that were not tables. The list could refer to the meaning of the word *table* only in a particular setting. If we are sitting and eating dinner at a table, the set of possible tables does not include chairs. The set of objects that are tables must include chairs if the setting is a buffet dinner at which I say, "I'll use this chair as a table." Your thought may be that this is a silly discussion; we all know what we mean when we use the word *table*. We know that the word *table* has a fuzzy, floating set of references; but we also know that there is some precise limit to the range of references. The trouble comes in attempting to capture formally the precision and the fuzziness. We can use the word *table* to refer to all manner of things that have some property of tableness in a particular setting. The degree to which we all ascribe the property of tableness to something in any setting will vary. And the quality of tableness will change for each of us. What seems to be a table at some time in some place may not be a table to us at another time in another place.

Language is inherently ambiguous and uncertain. That is the problem and the power of the system. The ambiguity and uncertainty of the linguistic system probably matches the richness of our inner, psychological conceptual framework. As Bronowski points out, the concept conveyed by the word *atom*, for example, is different to a nuclear physicist and to a taxi driver in 1982. The concept, moreover, was different to a nuclear physicist in 1922. The context of a word always plays a part in specifying its meaning. Words and sentences are almost always ambiguous; they are never precise unless we take into account the context of a communication. This lack of precision is not a deficiency of language; it rather is an aspect of language that mirrors human thought. As Cassirer (1944) and Bronowski (1971) note, the inherent imprecision of any linguistic statement keeps the frontier of human language open. We *must* always creatively interpret an utterance: the new interpretation always has the potential of achieving a new insight. Thought is not static; language mirrors thought, whether artfully in the brilliant word games of Nabokov or crudely in the rhetoric of the advertising world. A linguistic communication always is inherently ambiguous to some degree and must be interpreted.

The inherent ambiguity of human language is furthermore shared by all systems of mathematical logic that involve self-reference and arithmetic enumeration. Bronowski (1971) demonstrates that the theorems of Godel and Tarski show that all systems of mathematical logic that approach the power of human language are inherently ambiguous. The attempts of logicians, including Russell, Chomsky, and Montague (1974), to develop formal systems of logic that are unambiguous probably are inherently flawed.

Animal Communication

The communication systems of simpler animals appear to make use of signals that have fixed references, are never ambiguous, and lack syntax. The alarm call of a frog (Bogert, 1960) or the mating signal of a cricket (Hoy and Paul, 1973) always has the same meaning independent of the context in which it occurs.[1] The focus in ethological studies of communication — for example, the work of Smith (1977) — is decidedly on signals that elicit consistent responses in one animal or group of animals when they are produced by another animal. Indeed the underlying, though usually implicit, model in ethological studies is that of an animal as an automaton that is "hard wired" to produce signals whenever the appropriate stimulus occurs:

> in natural circumstances it often appears as if most animals perform their displays whenever an appropriate set of circumstances arises, whether or not the displays appear to be necessary or effective — as if the displays were more or less automatic responses. Further, in natural circumstances each participant does not usually appear to perceive itself as the target of another's signalling, as conversing humans do.
>
> (Smith, 1977, p. 265)

The ethological model thus seems to suggest that an animal is a pinball machine. External stimuli trigger fixed responses that are automatically broadcast. The communication system is a set of primary or unconditioned reflexes that are triggered by particular events or classes of events. In the ethological framework, a clear, invariant relation must be demonstrated between a signal and a particular behavioral pattern. There must be a "common knowledge of a display's referents held by both communicator and recipient" (Smith, 1977, p. 264). The signal's unitary, invariant meaning is demonstrated when it consistently appears in a *particular* context and elicits a *constant* behavioral response. Smith thus notes that a particular call produced by the Venezuelan *Cebus nigrivittatus* monkey that sounds like a "huh-yip" to human observers is not a food-sharing call, because the call can occur both when the monkeys feed and when they do not feed. Smith concludes that the call's referent must be something *common* to both situations. Thus, in Smith's view, its "functions probably have to do with group cohesion" (1977, p. 311).

In Smith's ethological framework the call can be either a food-sharing call or a group cohesion call. It cannot have both functions. The monkey call would be a food-sharing call in the ethological model if, and only if, it were produced only when the monkeys fed. Although the communication systems of invertebrates, birds, and perhaps

simpler mammals may consist of ensembles of signals, Smith's examples indicate that this may not be the case for dogs, monkeys, or apes.
The ethological, primary reflex, "pinball machine" model of animal
communication does not consider the possibility that the "huh-yip"
vocalization that the Venezuelan monkeys produce while they feed
probably does *not* have a single meaning. Like a human word, it occurs
in different contexts and can elicit different behavioral responses on
the part of the monkeys who hear it. In some contexts it apparently
serves to keep a group of monkeys in touch with each other and to
maintain the group. It may serve the same function as the words *Hey,*
or *Hey guys,* or *Keep together* would in a large group of human beings
hiking through dense woods. In the context where one group of
monkeys discovers a food source, it again might serve the same
function as the words *Hey, Hey guys,* or *Come here* would if two of the
hikers suddenly discovered a patch of ripe, sweet blueberries in the
woods.

　　There obviously is a profound difference between the communicative power of human language and the hypothetical function that I
have proposed for the monkey call in these situations. However,
greater similarities exist in situations involving a restricted pragmatic
context. We can make use of either very explicit or general linguistic
communications. If the party of human beings was deliberately going
through the woods in search of blueberries, the less explicit *Hey* or *Hey*
guys would, in most situations, convey the same meaning as the explicit
Hey guys, come here or the even more explicit *Hey guys, come here. We've*
found some sweet, delicious blueberries. The less explicit version will
suffice because the restricted pragmatic context in which the message
is transmitted restricts the range of meanings of the words *Hey guys.* In
the world of the Venezuelan *Cebus Nigrivittatus* monkey, the pragmatic context is probably even more restricted. The monkeys may not
have the option of producing either expanded and explicit or con-
densed and general linguistic communications. In their range of
relevant linguistic output, the "huh-yip" call could be regarded as a
primitive word that does not have an invariant unitary meaning. In
the context of a moving band of monkeys, it may serve to maintain
group cohesion; in the context of a subgroup of monkeys feeding, it
serves to attract the other monkeys to the food source.

　　The basic limitations of the ethological model of animal communication that Smith proposes probably derive from Darwin's pioneering work *The Expression of the Emotions in Man and Animals.* Darwin
(1872, p. 48) clearly states one of the underlying premises of Smith's
ethological model, namely, that the communicative signals of animals

"differ little from reflex actions" and are triggered by specific stimuli. Put in other terms, the signals that animals use for communication follow from "the principles of actions due to the constitution of the Nervous System, independently from the first of the Will, and independently to a certain extent of Habit" (Darwin, 1872, p. 29). The premise of most current ethological models of animal communication, that each signal has a specific, "invariant" meaning, is implicit throughout Darwin's descriptions of animal communication. In the introduction and Chapters 1 through 5 of *Expression of the Emotions*, Darwin's one-to-one mapping between a call or gesture and its meaning extends to his theory for the expression of emotion in human beings. On page 189, for example, he discusses the "grief muscles" of the eye.

The discussion of the possible use of "metaphorical displays" by animals in Smith (1977) essentially points out the continuity from Darwin to contemporary ethological models. Smith defines communication by metaphor and poses a question:

> In a situation in which no display in the repertoire has a set of referents that fits, does an animal ever try to communicate by pressing into service a display whose referents have something in common with the message he needs to convey? For the attempt to be successful, a recipient individual would have to be able to recognize that the circumstance is one in which the established referents of the display apply only in part. Such a recipient would respond on the basis of only some of the information made available by the display — that portion which fits appropriately with the pertinent information available from sources contextual to the display. Humans do this regularly, and it can be a powerful procedure when the recipient grasps the relevance of the metaphor. It is at the same time a risky procedure because the common knowledge of a display's referents held by both communication communicator and recipient must be partially set aside.
>
> (1977, p. 264)

What Smith fails to note is that virtually *all* human linguistic communication involves the process of *restricting* the range of concepts that the words of an utterance *could* convey. Both the formal linguistic mechanisms of morphology and syntax[2] and the pragmatic context of a message play a part in setting aside the inappropriate semantic interpretation of a word or string of words. The rules of syntax have a functional purpose: they limit some of the semantic referents of words. In the sentence *It's important to bank your money,* the syntax of English limits the semantic referents of the word *bank* to the range of concepts relevant to its functioning as a verb. The semantic referents of the word *object* in the sentence *I object to your proposal,* where it functions as a verb, are quite different from its semantic referents in the sentence *A spoon is an object,* where the concept that we want to refer to is conveyed by the noun *object.*

CONTEXT AND AMBIGUITY

Syntax in itself, however, is not sufficient to restrict the range of semantic referents of a word. Consider the sentences *The boat drifted to the bank* and *The businessman walked to the bank.* We will in most instances select the appropriate semantic referent of *bank* in these two sentences by making use of the pragmatic context furnished in the "frame" of the sentence. There is nothing that is strictly linguistic in this formation. Boats usually drift on water; hence the semantic referent of the noun *bank* in the first sentence is the interface between water and land, that is, the *bank* of an implied river, stream, or lake. A businessman is more likely to be walking to the *bank* that is concerned with finance; hence we would not see the ambiguity of the second sentence. A businessman, however, could walk to the river bank; hence our initial failure to see the ambiguity of the sentence *The businessman walked to the bank* reflects an internal statistical process that must weigh real-world, pragmatic probabilities to determine the un-marked case, when we have to determine the semantic interpretation of a sentence by using only the information that is conveyed in the frame of the sentence.

For example, the only reason we do not see the inherent ambigu-ity of a sentence like *He pulled the dog home* is that the semantic referents of the noun *dog* to most people do not include the following:

> 12. *Mach.* a. any of various mechanical devices, as for gripping or holding something.
> (*Random House Dictionary of the English Language,* 1966, p. 422)

Nor do most people usually think of the nautical semantic referent of *home:*

> 18. *Naut.* a. into the position desired, perfectly or to the greatest extent.
> (*Random House Dictionary,* p. 679)

If we were to read the sentence *He pulled the dog home* in the context of a Conradian account of a storm at sea, we might derive the intended semantic interpretation if we had some knowledge of the real world of late-nineteenth-century steamers in which watertight bulkhead doors were secured by things called "dogs." To the degree that there are many real worlds, words and sentences are almost always ambiguous.

Context versus Syntax: Language in Children

Studies of the development of language in children show that the process of communication in a linguistic mode from its inception depends on the use of context to convey the intent of the speaker's message (Bates, 1976; Lock, 1980). The study of the development of language in children, however, also shows development of syntax as the child's range of words and concepts expands. Children do not use words simply as tokens for things. Even in the one-word stage of language acquisition, words convey concepts rather than discrete things or actions.

The initial one-word utterances of children — that is, the sounds that adults can recognize as words — gradually emerge from strings of unrecognizable babble and gestures with which children start to communicate from at least the time that they are 6 or 7 months old. Children at this age typically pick things up and show them to adults. By about 10 months or so children begin to point to objects. These pointing gestures serve as a form of communication between parents and children (Freedle and Lewis, 1977; Stern, 1974; Lock, 1980). Gestural communication by pointing in children raised in a normal environment seems to follow from the model furnished by the infants' caretakers, who start to pick things up and name and talk about them to the infant from about the time that the infant is 3 or 4 months old (Escalona, 1973; Lock, 1980). Adults consistently point to things from about the time that infants are 7 or 8 months old.

The gestural systems that normal children use for communication are fairly elaborate by the time they reach their first birthday. The systems also develop gradually and appear to be learned rather than innate. Pointing gestures are, for example, used as intentional communicative signals. A child will, at this age, point to an object and look at his mother to see if she followed his point. If she did not, he will tug at her hand or clothes to attract her attention and will point again (Bates, 1976). Children at this age also follow the pointing gestures of other people. They look in the direction of the gesture. Younger children look at a person's hand or face rather than in the direction that the pointing gesture signals.

Grasping gestures and iconic representations of particular activities or things are also used by children at this age. Open-handed

reaching or grasping gestures are used to signal that they want
something. A fairly elaborate communication system is already in
place in the late sensorimotor period of development before the
child's first words can be identified (Carter, 1974; Bates, 1976; Bruner,
1975). Gestures and speech in the early stages of language development function together. It is usually difficult to establish precisely
when a word appears in the repertoire of a child in the one-word stage
of language acquisition. The child's phonetic output is usually somewhat idiosyncratic. A child's utterances are often at first incomprehensible; the child's gestures carry the primary communicative load.
The balance gradually shifts to the speech signal as the child's words
become comprehensible (Landahl, 1982). The gestural component of
communication, however, never quite vanishes and is part of the adult
communication system (Birdwhistell, 1970; McNeil, 1980).

Given the interactive gestural communication system established
during the early stages of development, it is not surprising to find that
deaf children develop structured communication systems based on
pointing, grasping, and "motoriconic" gestures. One school of educa-
tion for deaf children in the United States, the "oral" school, opposes
the use of formal sign languages. Parents who elect to have their deaf
children trained by the methods of the oral school are sometimes
cautioned not to use formal sign languages when they communicate
with their children. Deaf children raised in these circumstances nevertheless appear to develop sign language communication that is similar
to that of normal, hearing children. Goldin-Meadow and Feldman
(1977) observed six deaf children of hearing parents who had decided
not to expose their children to manual sign languages in order to
concentrate on oral communication. The children, whose ages ranged
from 17 to 49 weeks at the start of these observations, were videotaped while they were playing with toys and interacting with the
experimenters and mothers. An analysis of the videotapes found that
the children developed a lexicon of signs and that they combined
these signs into phrases that expressed semantic relations in a systematic way. Slightly over 50 percent of the signs that the children used
were pointing gestures that allowed the child to refer to particular
persons or objects. The remaining signs were motoriconic gestures
that referred to objects or to activities involving objects. Thus, "a
closed fist bobbed in and out near the mouth referred to a banana or
to the act of eating a banana. Two hands flapped up and down at
shoulder height referred to a bird or to the act of flying" (Goldin-
Meadow and Feldman, 1977, p. 402). The children concatenated their
signs into multisign phrases that conveyed relationships between ob-

jects and activities. For example, "one child pointed at a shoe and then pointed at a table to request that the shoe . . . be put on the table" (Goldin-Meadow and Feldman, 1977, p. 402). The children throughout the period of observation, which varied from 4 months to 2 years for different children, continued to set the pace for the communication process. Their mothers reciprocally communicated back to their children with these gestural signals, but they followed the children's lead as new signs were introduced.

Goldin-Meadow and Feldman claim that these data demonstrate that human children have a "natural inclination to develop a structured communication system" that is independent of their parents' actions. However, the development of these children's sign systems probably follows their parents' normal use of pointing gestures and object displays in the earlier stages of language development (ages 3 to 9 months), which were not monitored by Goldin-Meadow and Feldman. The syntactic rules that the children used in combining their signs, moreover, appear to reflect the *semantic* real-world sequential iconic relations between the constructs that they were attempting to communicate. Thus all three communicative sign sequences noted by Goldin-Meadow and Feldman mirror the real-world strategies by which shoes are put on tables, jars are opened, and people are given things. In the description of the shoe-on-table message that was cited, the child first pointed at the shoe and then pointed at the table. If a person were to place the shoe on the table, that sequence of events would necessarily be followed. In the second example cited, "the child pointed at a jar and then produced a twisting motion in the air to comment on the mother's having twisted open . . . the jar" (Goldin-Meadow and Feldman, 1977, p. 402). The third example cited also follows real-world strategies. The "child opened his hand with his palm facing upward and then followed this 'give' sign with a point towards his chest, to request that an object be given . . . to him" (Goldin-Meadow and Feldman, 1977, p. 402).

However, the relationship that probably holds between real-world, pragmatic relationships that are inherent in opening jars, placing a shoe on a table, and so on and the children's sign sequences should not obscure the fact that *the children established and used rule-governed, that is, syntactic, communication.* Thus in contrast to the communication systems of simple animals, the communications of these deaf children clearly were linguistic. The children demonstrated that they could abstract the principle of using rule-governed relationships as a communicative device in the absence of overt linguistic instruction. The Goldin-Meadow and Feldman studies are therefore consistent with the hypothesis that human beings have a neural substrate that is predisposed toward using syntax as a device in communication. Most of the gestural communications reported in these studies probably would be incomprehensible in the absence of context. However, this does not diminish the significance of these data. The early linguistic communications of hearing children raised in normal environments are also often incomprehensible in the absence of context (Landahl, 1982). Normal, hearing children, moreover, typically mix gestures and words in their earlier "linguistic" communication. Neither the communications of normal children nor those of deaf children can be interpreted without making use of the total context of the communication through the method of "rich interpretation" (Bloom, 1970; Brown, 1973): the context includes *everything* that is known about the children — their adult companions, toys, games, habits, and daily routine.

Children's Words

Children never appear to use *signals,* as I have defined the hypothetical elements of communication that figure in ethological studies. The one-word utterances of children typically have an ensemble of semantic referents, whether the "words" are signaled vocally or by gestures. As Clark and Clark note, "children use words not just to name objects, then, but also to pick out the roles those objects play in whatever event is being described" (1977, p. 30). In a study of the earliest one-word utterances, Greenfield and Smith (1976) note, for example, that the utterance *Down* marks the action of sitting down in the context of sitting down or stepping down from somewhere. *Down,* however, also signifies the state of an object affected by an action, as when the child uses it in the context of shutting a cabinet door.

Single words have multiple semantic referents well into the two- and three-word stages of language acquisition. In an ongoing study at Brown University, we have been tape recording the speech of children at two-week intervals from birth to about age 5. We record the children's speech and the speech directed to them by adults, using high-quality tape recorders and microphones while we simultaneously enter notes on the context of the communications on synchronized cassette recordings (Buhr, 1980; Lieberman, 1980; Landahl, 1982). A typical transcript of a "conversation" with subject JRS at age 86 weeks shows that she uses one-word utterances that have different semantic references depending on the context in which they occur. The word *sour* in this transcript thus refers to the taste of a lemon in one context. In a different context a few minutes later, JRS uses the word *sour* to request a hard "sour candy." She probably derived the referent to sour candy from one of the members of the tape-recording crew who habitually had these candies with her. The referents of the word *sour*, however, also referred to what she experienced when she sucked a lemon. The two semantic references — the sugary sour candy and the sour lemon taste — were attached to the same word *sour* by speaker JRS prior to age 86 weeks.

The data derived from the study of these children show different styles in the development of language. In a study of three children from the late babbling stage through the one-word, two-word, and later stages of language development to age 3, one child at age 86 weeks was still producing single words while the other two were already producing two-word utterances (Landahl, 1982). By age 2 these two children had highly developed sentence structures, whereas the other child was still chaining together two- and three-word sequences. Two samples from these children's speech at their second birthdays show the difference (Landahl, 1982, p. 7):

JRS
Who's coming?
Take it off.
He needs a plate.
I wanna get it myself.
He's lying down.

JD
Books.
The kitty in there.
Bunny go?
Piggy.
Cow hops.
He walking.

However, though these children differ with respect to the rate at which they have acquired speech (JRS appears to be somewhat precocious; JD, normal), their use, or rather disuse, of syntax in the two-word stage is consistent with earlier studies (Bloom, 1970; Brown 1973; Bowerman, 1973).

A Functional View of Syntax

Though it is clear that linguistic communication can take place at a presyntactic level, all human languages that have so far been encountered make use of syntax. Syntactic and morphologic processes, which can be viewed as syntactic operations that modify the phonetic shape of words, have a functional role in communication. They limit the possible range of conceptual referents that a word can be transmitting in a particular utterance. For example, one of the processes that can be observed in the earliest stages of language development, both in human children and in chimpanzees trained in sign language, is the extension of "verbal," that is, motoric, referents to words that may initially refer to objects. The earliest one-word utterances of children involve reference to a pattern of activity as well as to an object. Thus the child's utterance *Sour*, which I noted earlier, means *give me a sour candy* in a particular context. It does not simply refer to an abstract class of sour candies. In multiword utterances, syntax allows the listener to eliminate some of the possible semantic referents of each word in the message. In the sentence *I want to table the bill*, we know that the word *table* is being used as a verb. We still do not know what the word means in the sentence. In the context of a conversation about a meal in a restaurant, *table* could refer to my desire to place on the table the bill that the waiter has just presented. In the context of a debate governed by *Robert's Rules of Order* in the United States, I probably would like to postpone a resolution indefinitely. In the context of a parliamentary debate in the United Kingdom, I would be communicating my intention to have the bill brought up immediately. The syntactic rules of English, however, eliminate the assorted semantic concepts that *table* can invoke as a noun, including an article of furniture, a group of people who convene together, a plateau, a part of a printing press, a flat bone of the body, or the flat surface of a faceted jewel.

The process of syntax is an inherent, functional part of human language, since it allows us to attach families of semantic referents to particular words and facilitates the recovery of a particular referent. The propensity of human languages to attach different classes of referents to words seems to me to manifest the sensorimotor genesis of gestural and verbal communication. Children in their natural gesture systems make use of rule-governed motoriconic gestures that serve to convey the pattern of activity involving an object or a person that is important to the child. By means of their general cognitive facilities, they observe events, extract the salient activities, and imitate these activities. Children thus appear to abstract the gestural elements of human communication (Goldin-Meadow and Feldman, 1977; Lock, 1980). As the range of words and concepts expands, syntactic devices come into play. Syntax makes it possible to extend the semantic referents attached to words by providing a framework for the recovery of the speaker's intent. Words can take on the "natural" sensori-motoric referent-word scheme whereby concepts pertaining to things and persons (nouns) assume the verbal concepts germane or related to some of the real-world referents of these nouns.

The advantages of syntactic rules are more apparent as the number of words and the number of concepts that are the semantic referents of each word increase. Nelson (1973) found that the age at which children achieved a fifty-word vocabulary varied from 14 to 24 months, with a mean of 20 months, for a sample of eighteen English-speaking children. A fifty-word vocabulary really does not need an elaborate syntactic rule system to sort out the different referents of words. These ages fall roughly into the later part of Brown's (1973) Stage I. As Brown notes, the expansion of the semantic range of individual words also does not appear to start until the end of the two-word Stage I phase of language development. Brown, moreover, notes that the semantic expansion of the referents of words continues gradually in Stage II, when children begin to make use of grammatical morphemes in their multiword utterances:

> In Stage II we shall see that, for instance, the first past-tense verbs are limited to the immediate past and future forms to present intentions and immediate actions. We shall find the prepositions *in* and *on* limited to their spatial senses, and not applied in such abstract senses as *an idea in the air* or *a train on time*. Indeed all prepositions are at first used in only a narrow part of their semantic range, generally in their spatial relationship or part-whole senses. Adjectives like *big, little, warm, cool,* and the like are used in their physicalistic senses before they are applied to personality.
>
> (1973, p. 196)

The major semantic relations that children appear to intend to express in the one- and two-word stages of language development—that is, through Brown's Stage I—are usually limited to situations within the child's immediate context. Bloom (1970), for example, lists the following major semantic relations (Brown, 1973, p. 119):

Subject and predicate
Verb and object
Subject and object
Attributive
Genitive
Recurrence

Nonexistence
Rejection
Denial
Demonstratives with predicate nominatives
Subject and locative
Verb and locative
Noticing reaction

There is no necessity for fixed word order or any other syntactic devices in the two-word stage of language development. The immediate context of a child's conversation will generally "disambiguate" the utterance. As the child progresses to longer utterances and greater semantic complexity, formal grammatical devices begin to be used. Brown's claim (1973, pp. 118–119) that fixed word order functioned as a syntactic device in Stage I of language development, which includes the two-word stage, probably follows from the comparatively advanced language development of the children in his study at the start of Stage I. A general reappraisal of the data on the early stages of language acquisition shows that there is no clear evidence that children consistently use word order as a syntactic device in the two-word stage (Clark and Clark, 1977, pp. 311–312).

Since children and apes in the one- and two-word stages of language development do not usually engage in discussions of situations beyond their immediate environment, context is a sufficient element to make the speaker's intent clear. The earliest stages of hominid language probably resembled the early stages of child language in that words served to transmit messages that had as their focus the immediate environment, and the speakers used a comparatively small vocabulary of words that each conveyed a range of semantic concepts linked by sensorimotor constraints. Syntax probably was not necessary in a functional sense because the immediate, pragmatic context of an utterance restricted the range of semantic concepts associated with each word. The speaker's intent thus could be conveyed without a rule-governed syntax. As both vocabulary size and the range of concepts linked to each word increased, the communicative value of syntactic constraints increased. Finally, utterances that referred to situations beyond the immediate environmental surroundings lessened the filtering role of context and enhanced the value of formal syntactic operations. As Clark and Clark note,

Once past the two-word stage, children begin to elaborate both in the structure and function of their first language . . . Children also elaborate language function. They extend their repertoire of speech acts beyond representation, representatives and directives to commissives and expressives. They also add to their repertoire for conveying each speech act . . . Children have to build up structure and function at the same time.

(1977, p. 372)

The acquisition of the formal devices of syntax goes hand in hand with the elaboration of the child's conceptual framework, vocabulary, and range of topics that are communicated. Whether the possible forms for syntactic rules are innately determined in human beings is at present an open question. However, there obviously is a neural substrate that makes it possible for human beings to readily learn syntactic rules.

LINGUISTIC ABILITY AND COGNITIVE ABILITY

One of the debates on the nature of human language concerns the relation between linguistic and cognitive ability. To many philosophers and logicians human language is the key to cognition. Bronowski, for example, notes:

> The gift of humanity is precisely that, unlike the animals, we form concepts; and we express that gift in our thinking language. Man constantly invents ideas to express what seems to him to lie behind the appearances of nature and to hold them together. The invention of these ideas and their interplay in language is imagination — the making of images inside our heads. Man has out-distanced the other animals because he has not one but two languages: a thinking language for manipulating concepts inside his head, as well as a speaking language (such as animals have) for communicating them with others.
>
> (1971, p. 50)

Bronowski's position is actually not the extreme one in the philosophical debate, since he in essence argues that there is a cognitive base present in human beings, and possibly in other animals, which language builds on and enhances. A more extreme view is that of Humboldt (1836), who essentially claims that thought is not possible without language and that the particular expression of human thought itself is constrained by the particular language that we use. Humboldt's view, which takes expression in recent theories like that of Whorf (1956), is that "man lives with his objects chiefly — in fact, since his feeling and acting depends on his perceptions, one might say exclusively — as language presents them to him. By the same process whereby he spins language out of his own being, he ensnares himself in it; and each language draws a magic circle round the people to which it belongs, a circle from which there is no escape save by stepping out of it into another" (as translated by Cassirer, 1944, p. 9).

In this view, which Cassirer develops in a richer manner than either Humboldt or Whorf, human thought, culture, and language all form a matrix that defines the quality of the human condition. However, the deepest level of this matrix is linguistic. Cassirer thus claims that reason and logic follow from language: "logic springs from language when that greatest of symbolic modes is mature" (1946, p. ix). Recent experimental data point to a possible link between syntactic and semantic facility and cognition. These data are preliminary and do not isolate specific syntactic skills. However, studies like those of Ben-Zeev (1977a, 1977b) find that bilingual children show more advanced processing of verbal material, more discriminating perceptual distinctions, and more propensity to search for structure in perceptual situations than is the case with monolingual children. Hebrew-English bilingual children, who have to master different syntactic and semantic systems, appear to develop strategies that accelerate cognitive development. These differences were apparent when groups of bilingual Hebrew-English children, whose ages ranged from 5 to 8 years, were compared with ethnically and socially balanced groups of monolingual children whose native language was Hebrew or English. The test groups were also balanced with respect to the children's intelligence. Similar results were noted by Bain and Yu (1980) in experiments that were run in Alsace, Alberta, and Hong Kong with bilingual and monolingual children whose ages ranged from 22 to 48 months. The bilingual speakers of German and French, English and French, and English and Chinese performed better than monolingual speakers in both verbal and nonverbal cognitive tests. These recent data replicate the experiments of Peal and Lambert (1962), who studied bilingual French-English children in Montreal. Bilingualism may not yield an absolute cognitive advantage to the adult; the data of Ianco-Worrall (1972) indicate that monolingual children catch up with matched bilingual children in cognitive tests. However, a clear connection between linguistic and cognitive skill is evident. These data on human children are, moreover, consistent with those of chimpanzee experiments (Premack and Woodruff, 1978; Premack, 1980). Language-trained chimpanzees performed better than other chimpanzees in cognitive tests.

Summary

The semantic referents of *words* cannot be equated to unitary objects or to unitary referents; they are concepts that are "fuzzy" but also have definite limits. The ethological model of animal communication derives from Darwin's attempts to find *signals*, that is, units that stand in a one-to-one correspondence with some particular object or action. While the communication systems of simple animals like frogs and fish may rely on signals that have fixed referents, this is probably not the case for "advanced" animals like dogs and monkeys. Human linguistic communication involves strings of words that do not have fixed referents—words that are always inherently ambiguous to some degree. The initial functional value of syntax may rest in the limitation of semantic interpretation. Children use both the context of an utterance and syntactic devices to reduce the ambiguity of a communication. Gestural communication is an important element in the early communications of children. The balance between "linguistic" word order and morphology on the one hand and gestural and pragmatic information on the other hand shifts in the communications of children. The functional value of rule-governed syntax is to reduce role reliance on context for disambiguation of a communication. The relation of human language to cognition has been the focus of many philosophical debates. Human cognitive ability is enhanced by means of the linguistic aspects of thought.

CHAPTER 5
Respiration, Speech, and Meaning

ONE OF THE POINTS OF AGREEMENT among virtually all theories of grammar is that the sentence is the minimal unit of speech for a complete semantic interpretation (Jesperson, 1909; Trager and Smith, 1951; Chomsky, 1957). The traditional description of a sentence is that it expresses a complete thought. The primary function of the traditional punctuation marks of orthographic notation is to indicate the scope of a sentence. It is easy to perform a simple experiment that will test these claims. Take a short account of some event from a newspaper and move the final periods and initial capitalization of sentences one word to the right. The modified strings of words will usually be incomprehensible. It is actually quite difficult to read these strings of words with normal sentence intonation.

The articulatory maneuvers that we use to produce the intonation, or "melody," that can group a series of words together demonstrate the psychological reality of the sentence. Before a person utters a sound, complex patterns of muscular activity are "preprogrammed" that take into account the length of the sentence that *will* be spoken. These muscular maneuvers are complex because our lungs evolved from the swim bladders of fish. It is therefore not a simple matter to produce the controlled patterns of pitch and loudness that segment the flow of speech into sentences. The basic "vegetative"—that is, life-sustaining—aspects of respiration structure the way in which we produce these intonational signals. This is, of course, consistent with the long evolutionary history of the respiratory system, which evolved primarily to sustain life. Like other species, we are equipped with neural control mechanisms that adjust our breathing to take account of greater or lesser levels of physical exertion, the oxygen content of the air we breathe, and so on. However, human beings, when they talk, override some of the most basic vegetative patterns of respiratory activity. The production of intonation by human beings thus appears to involve an interaction between physiologic mechanisms that are similar to those of less vocal terrestrial animals and physiologic mechanisms that may have evolved to facilitate our segmenting speech into sentences. In other words, the evolution of the physiologic mechanisms that we use to regulate respiration may reflect the presence of the rule-governed syntax that generates sentences.

The Anatomy and Physiology of Respiration

The schematic diagram of the human respiratory system in Figure 5-1 shows the lungs, the larynx, and the upper supralaryngeal airways. The function of the respiratory system can be divided into three components: the larynx, the supralaryngeal airways, and the subglottal trachea and lungs. The term *glottal* refers to the opening that can be formed in the larynx. The larynx thus is the reference point in this traditional description of the anatomy of speech production (Müller, 1848). The primary function of the respiratory system is to pump air into and out of the lungs to provide oxygen to the bloodstream. The topology of the respiratory system reflects its evolutionary history. The lungs developed from the swim bladders of fish (Darwin, 1859). The larynx first evolved as a device to protect the lungs from the influx of water and foreign objects (Negus, 1949). The basic physiologic factors that structure the way in which human beings produce intonational signals follow from these phylogenetic events.

The lungs essentially are two elastic sacs that are suspended in an enclosure that can change its volume. The enclosure is sealed, but the lungs connect to the atmosphere via a tube, the trachea, that can be closed by a valve, the larynx. We have two lungs because it was probably a selective advantage for fishes to have two swim bladders. In a primitive fish, such as a shark, there is no swim bladder. A shark must constantly swim, or else it will sink. The swim bladder evolved in fishes that could pump internal bladders full of air that had been filtered out of the water by their gills. As the fish pumped air into its swim bladders, it could match its buoyancy to that of the water and float, essentially in the same manner as a Zeppelin can float in the air by matching its total weight to that of the air it displaces. A fish equipped with swim bladders thus could swim slowly or could hover by matching its total weight to that of the water its body displaced. Two swim bladders probably evolved because fishes have two gills; a symmetrical arrangement of two swim bladders may yield a more stable floating position than one bladder — the fish is less likely to spin on its long axis.

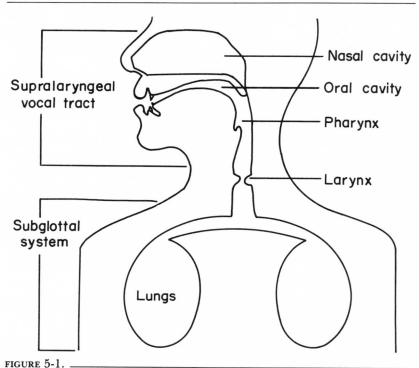

FIGURE 5-1.
Schematic of the human respiratory system.

Figure 5-2 shows the basic mechanical arrangement for pumping air into and out of the lungs. The sketch shows only one lung, to keep matters simpler. The two side walls of the model can move inward or outward as the rib cage is moved by the intercostal muscles. The volume inside the box formed by the rib walls, abdomen, and diaphragm thus can increase or decrease as the intercostal muscles move the rib walls outward or inward. The abdominal muscles can also change the box's volume, as can the diaphragm, which in this diagram moves in the vertical plane. The lung sac in the model is like an elastic balloon. Note that the lung balloon is open to the outside and is not attached to the moving walls of the box. The space between the lung and the box, the pleural space, is sealed.

Inspiration involves filling the lung with air. It takes place in this model in an indirect manner. The walls of the chest can move outward or the diaphragm can move downward. Either or both maneuvers will

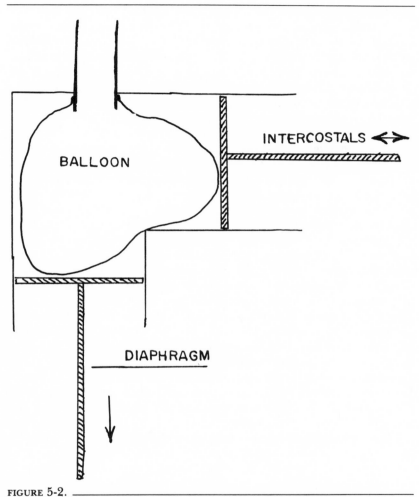

FIGURE 5-2.
Schematic diagram of one lung. The two pistons can change the
volume of the lung balloon through the action of the intercostal
muscles or the diaphragm muscle. Air and recoil energy are stored
in the elastic lung balloon.

increase the volume of the box. The pressure within the sealed pleural
volume, P_p, of the model will tend to fall as the volume of the pleural
space, V_p, increases because $V_p(P_p) = K$, where K is a constant. Since
the inside of the lung balloon is open to the outside air, it will expand
as the pleural air pressure falls. because the higher atmospheric air
pressure pushes against the inside wall of the lung balloon. As the box

expands, the lung balloon will stretch and expand. As the lung expands, it stores air and energy in the "elastic recoil force" of the lung. If you think of a rubber balloon, it is clear that you store energy when you blow it up as you stretch the elastic walls of the balloon. The energy stored in the stretched elastic walls of the balloon will force the air out of the balloon if you release your hold on its open end.

The lungs of "adultlike" human beings and some other animals operate in a manner similar to the balloon-and-box model. The external intercostal and part of the internal intercostal muscles of the chest can move outward to inflate the lungs. These muscles can inflate the lungs because the ribs are slanted downward from the spinal column in human beings after the third month of life. As Langlois and his colleagues (1980) note, the almost perpendicular orientation of the ribs to the spine in early infancy makes it impossible to use these muscles to inflate the lungs.

Although the respiratory pattern that human neonates use in cry and noncry vocalizations departs from the pattern that they use for quiet vegetative breathing, the difference between these two patterns of respiratory activity becomes more extreme after the third month of life, when the ribs restructure toward the adult configuration. The diaphragm can also move downward to inflate the lungs. The energy for inspiration is applied through the intercostal muscles and diaphragm. However, these muscles also store energy for expiration in the elastic recoil force of the lungs. During expiration the elastic recoil forces air out of the lungs. Part of the internal intercostal muscles and the abdominal muscles can also act to force air out of the lungs. The forces that act in inspiration thus are the chest muscles and diaphragm; those that can act in expiration are the elastic recoil force of the lungs plus other muscles of the chest and abdomen.

REGULATORY MECHANISMS

A number of "layered" feedback mechanisms monitor breathing in humans and other animals to ensure that the respiratory system meets the physiologic demands of both normal and strenuous activities. One layer of control involves feedback systems similar to those we have already discussed. Mechanical stretch receptors in the lung tissue feed afferent signals back via the vagus, or tenth cranial, nerve to the brain. The vagus nerve is composed of both efferent and afferent pathways to and from the larynx, pharynx, esophagus, stomach, and heart. These stretch receptors monitor the degree of inflation of the lungs and activate a control system that limits the depth, that is, the magnitude, of inspiration. Herring and Breuer first described this feedback control system over 100 years ago. Recent data derived from experiments with cats and human beings show that it may function to limit the depth of inspiration in strenuous activity, but its importance in regulating normal breathing is not clear (Bouhuys, 1974). There are, however, two additional layers of feedback control that make use of chemoreceptors that monitor the levels of dissolved CO_2 (carbon dioxide) and oxygen as well as the pH (the degree of acidity or alkalinity) of our blood and cerebrospinal fluid. These feedback mechanisms are basic in that they sustain the ventilatory conditions that are necessary to support life. They are probably layered to maintain redundancy in the life support system. However, we routinely override these regulatory systems when we talk, sing, or play wind instruments.

The two layers of chemoreceptor-actuated feedback are central and peripheral with respect to the brain. The central chemoreceptors are located near the ventrolateral surface of the medulla, or spinal bulb of the brain. The medulla is continuous with the spinal cord and is one of the primitive parts of the brain. The chemoreceptors are located in a part of the medulla that is relatively far from the traditional respiratory centers that regulate respiration. They monitor the CO_2 and pH of both the cerebrospinal fluid and the blood that perfuse the medulla. Peripheral chemoreceptors are located in two places: in the carotid bodies, near the bifurcation of the common carotid artery in the neck, and in the aortic bodies, near the arch of the aorta. The aorta is the main artery that carries oxygenated blood from the heart. The peripheral chemoreceptors monitor pH and oxygen in the arterial blood (Bouhuys, 1974).

The central and peripheral chemoreceptor feedback systems complement each other. The peripheral system acts rapidly to make small changes in respiration. The central system operates slowly, but it can effect large changes in respiration. When healthy people breathe low concentrations of CO_2 in air (3 to 7 percent), their breathing rate, the depth of their breathing, and the volume of air that passes through their respiratory system per minute all increase. The chemoreceptors are quite sensitive. For example, they initiate increased respiratory activity when you breathe in a closed room with a number of other people, because the oxygen content of the stale room air is lower than it should be. The chemoreceptor feedback systems can operate rapidly; when you are breathing stale air, a single breath of pure oxygen will lead to a temporary reduction of ventilation (Dejours, 1963).

SPEECH PRODUCTION AND RESPIRATORY REGULATION

Despite these regulatory systems, human beings typically override the
control pattern that prevails during quiet respiration when they talk.
When you breathe room air and talk, ventilation per minute increases.
The ventilation rate can become quite high when you produce high-
flow sounds like the consonant [h], the first sound of the word *hat*
(Klatt, Stevens, and Mead, 1968). A significant decrease from normal
blood CO_2 levels thus can occur during sustained speech during
normal activity. In contrast, speech production decreases the flow rate
when it is necessary to transfer more air through the lungs to meet
basic vegetative constraints during strenuous activities. Though
speakers in some cases adopt patterns of respiration that maintain
optimum air transfer with flow rates compatible with intelligible
speech, they usually give priority to the flow rates that are necessary
for speech production and override the regulatory mechanisms. The
graphs in Figure 5-3 show two instances of breathing patterns for
subjects breathing a 3% CO_2 in air gas mixture. The plot shows the
volume of air in the speaker's lungs for quiet breathing and speech.
The "proper" flow rate for oxygen transfer is in each case 18 L/min,
which is met by the nonspeech pattern in both trials. The respiratory
pattern for speech in the trial plotted in the uppermost graph, however, is *not* compatible with gas exchange requirements because the
flow rate is only 7.6 L/min. In the trial plotted in the lower graph, the
speaker has increased his flow rate during speech to 18 L/min by
increasing the mean expiratory flow rate during speech, which is
apparent in the increased slope of the expiratory phases, and by
superimposing deep inspirations and expirations on the speech pattern. Speech quality, however, deteriorates because the speaker's
voice becomes "breathy." Note in both graphs the typical speech
pattern of short inspirations followed by expirations that can be quite
long since they are keyed to the syntactic structure of the speech.

RESPIRATORY CONTROL AND LINGUISTIC ANALYSIS

The pattern of breathing during speech is quite different from that
typical of quiet respiration with respect to both the relative duration
of the inspiratory and expiratory phases of respiration and the control
of air pressure (Bouhuys, 1974; Mead, Bouhuys, and Proctor, 1968;
Draper, Ladefoged, and Whitteridge, 1960; Klatt, Stevens, and Mead, 1968;
Lieberman, 1967; Lieberman and Lieberman, 1973). During speech pro-

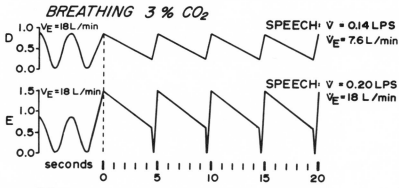

FIGURE 5-3. _____

Lung volume as a function of time for subjects breathing at an average flow rate, V_E of 18 liters per minute (L/min) during quiet respiration, which is plotted to the left of the vertical dashed line. Note that the inspiratory and expiratory phases of respiration have about the same duration during quiet respiration. The plots to the right of the dotted vertical line show lung volume during speech for two flow rates: D at 7.6 L/min and E at 18 L/min. Note the long linear fall in lung volume during expiration, which is typical of respiratory activity during speech. (After A. Bouhuys, *Breathing* [New York: Grune and Stratton, 1974], pp. 210, 253; figures 10-4, 11-2. Adapted by permission.)

duction short inspirations are followed by expirations whose lengths are generally keyed to the phrase structure of the utterance. The length of the expiration usually is determined by the span of a sentence both when speakers read material (Lieberman, 1967; Maeda, 1976) and when they speak spontaneously (Tseng, 1981; Landahl, 1981, 1982). A speaker can further subdivide a sentence in terms of its phrase structure by segmenting it with expirations (Armstrong and Ward, 1926; Lieberman, 1967; Atkinson, 1973; Tseng, 1981). Speakers usually indicate that the sentence is not over by means of prosodic signals at the end of the first expiration (Armstrong and Ward, 1926; Pike, 1945; Lieberman, 1967; Tseng, 1981). Much of the discussion of phonemic pitch and juncture of the "taxonomic" school of linguistics involves instances in which speakers map out the phrase structure of a sentence by clustering words into expirations. As Trager and Smith note (1951, p. 77), the utterance's prosodic structure can indicate "what goes with what."

The Trager-Smith notation consists of a string of phonemic pitch and stress levels. The Trager-Smith system makes use of a set of four phonemic pitch levels. The pitch levels are relative pitches. A person who has a higher average fundamental frequency of phonation, F_0, would thus generate a higher F_0 for level 2 than a person who has a lower average F_0. However, for a given speaker the fundamental frequency associated with level 4 is supposed to be higher than that associated with level 3, and so on. The Trager-Smith system also uses three main terminal junctural symbols. The terminal juncture denoted by the symbol # had as its hypothetical correlate a rapid fall in F_0; the terminal juncture / / had a hypothetical rapid rise in F_0, while the terminal juncture / had a somewhat smaller F_0 rise. The Trager-Smith phonemic pitch levels are quite similar to Pike's (1945) phonetic pitch levels and junctures, though the ordering of the two systems of notation is, for some reason, almost reversed. Pike's pitch level 1 is thus the highest pitch that a speaker produces; 4, the lowest.

The Emperor's Old Clothes

It is interesting to note that the "generative" school of phonology has from its start (Chomsky, Halle, and Lukoff, 1956) accepted as a given the prosodic "facts" of the taxonomic Trager-Smith descriptions of sentences. This perhaps follows from the common deficiency of both taxonomic and generative analyses of sentence-level ambiguity. Both schools of thought assume that linguistic information expressed or conveyed within the frame of a sentence always can resolve a sentence's ambiguity. In taxonomic analyses that lacked a "deep" level, some phonetic, physical events had to convey the different semantic interpretations of a sentence like *They decorated the girl with the flowers.* There are at least two semantic readings of this sentence, which loosely can be paraphrased as *A girl who had flowers was decorated* or *They decorated a girl by giving her flowers.* Since only one set of words occurs in this crucial example (Stockwell, 1961), something else had to be physically present in order for people to derive one or the other semantic interpretation. Ambiguous sentences like this example usually are perfectly clear when they are heard or read in context. People usually are not even aware that the sentence is ambiguous, because the context conveys the semantic interpretation that is appropriate. Linguists operating in the taxonomic school apparently did not want to admit the possibility that a sentence could inherently be ambiguous when it occurred in isolation. They instead invented prosodic morphemes that, in turn, consisted of strings of phonemic pitch levels and stress levels that would lead a hearer to an unambiguous interpretation of the sentence.

The arguments of taxonomic prosodic phonology concerning the necessity for these prosodic morphemes have always seemed somewhat circular to me. Trager and Smith argue that a listener *always needs* these prosodic morphemes in order to interpret correctly the meaning of a sentence. However, the orthography of English (and all other languages) usually does not transcribe these prosodic morphemes or their constituent pitch and stress phonemes. Thus a person reading a sentence aloud has to arrive mentally at the "correct" semantic interpretation of the sentence from its context in order to enunciate the "correct" pitch phonemes. If the prosodic morphemes presumably "necessary to indicate what goes with what," (Trager and Smith, 1951, p. 77) are always deduced from the semantic interpretation that is consistent with the sentence's context, they are not necessary in the first place.

Early "generative" phonologic analyses simply borrowed wholesale the hypothetical phonemic pitch and stress levels of taxonomic studies. Chomsky, Halle, and Lukoff (1954), for example, generate the four Trager-Smith stress levels of English compound words, such as *lighthouse keeper*, by using a binary stress symbol and a set of rules. The object of their paper apparently is to show that an underlying binary stress distinction can be mapped into a four-level (or n-level) surface form. To Chomsky and Halle (1968) this solution is a better phonological statement than the four-level Trager-Smith transcription because it meets a "simplicity" metric that they apparently believe has some psychological merit. Their simplicity metric notes that the underlying level of Chomsky, Halle, and Lukoff (1954) has only a one-binary stress symbol for each word string in place of the Trager-Smith surface sequence involving four-level stress symbols.

Chomsky and Halle's (1968) analysis of stress levels is an elaboration of the earlier paper. The underlying forms that it posits, which often are rather odd, appear to have been derived in order to make the rules apply to as many words as possible, with the fewest binary stress levels noted in the hypothetical underlying forms. Some linguists and phoneticians apparently learn to memorize the complex sequences of hypothetical pitch and stress phonemes that specify the crucial examples that are in the taxonomic and generative literature (Lisker, Personal Communication). Acoustic analysis and psychoacoustic experiments (Lieberman, 1965) demonstrate that phoneticians trained in the Trager-Smith system in fact cannot reliably make prosodic transcriptions using four-pitch and four-stress phonemes. However, generative phonologic studies continue to specify sentence-level prosody in terms of fine distinctions of pitch and stress.

The basic motivation for incorporating pitch and stress morphemes in taxonomic studies never seems to have been examined by generative phonologists. Taxonomic grammarians had no underlying or deep level of syntax. They therefore were unable to describe formally the fact that a string of words can be bracketed in two different ways at the surface level, corresponding to two different deep structures that each have a different semantic interpretation. The power, and the immediate acceptance, of Chomsky's (1957) model was that it explained in simple, clear terms how a single surface form, such as the sequence of words *Flying planes can be dangerous,* can have two meanings: *The act of flying planes can be dangerous* or *Planes in flight can be dangerous.* Chomsky provided a formal model for paraphrase. The ideal speaker-listener presumably would be able to derive the different underlying structures that conveyed the different meanings of *Flying planes can be dangerous* when he or she "saw" the ambiguity. The underlying deep structures thus appeared to have a psychological reality. The excitement that followed the publication of *Syntactic Structures* was that it appeared to present a testable psychological model. Chomsky's theory explained how a reader could see the ambiguity of a sentence like *They decorated the girl with flowers* and group the words together into the two surface forms that corresponded to the different underlying, deep structures when the sentence was read using standard English orthography. In other words, the Trager-Smith pitch and stress phonemes were not needed in generative phonology. They were superfluous since a reader could derive them, as Chomsky and Halle (1968) imply, by means of internal computations.

Recent generative studies, in which the status of the deep level has been restricted, place more emphasis on the surface structure. Detailed prosodic information has again apparently become, as it was to Trager and Smith (1951), "necessary to indicate what goes with what"; thus the recent focus of generative phonologists, such as Pierrehumbert (1981), on prosodic phenomena that supposedly are *necessary* for people to derive the appropriate semantic interpretation of a sentence. These recent claims of generative phonologists seem as misguided as those of taxonomic phonologists. If detailed prosodic information, which is not transcribed by normal orthography, is *necessary* to derive the meaning of a sentence, how can we read? Generative studies, like earlier taxonomic studies, are again making the mistake of ignoring context in resolving the ambiguity of sentences.

BREATHING PATTERN AND STRUCTURE

As already noted, there seems to be no acoustic, physiologic, or phonetic basis for the hypothetical strings of phonemic pitch and stress levels that constitute Trager-Smith or Chomsky-Halle prosodic transcriptions. Phoneticians trained in the use of Trager-Smith notation consistently produce random results when they have to identify phonemic stress or pitch levels in controlled experiments (Lieberman, 1965). The linguists in these experiments, however, used *patterns* of pitch levels and junctures that correspond to the expiratory breath pattern. The sequence of so-called phonemic pitch levels and "junctures" 2 3 1 #, for example, was used to note the occurrence of all expirations in which the perceived pitch of the speech ended with a falling contour. This sequence could *not* be divided into smaller units. The pitch level 2 from one pattern, for example, might correspond to a fundamental frequency of 150 Hz and in another pattern to 260 Hz. The pitch levels indicated only the relative F_o within a particular pattern. The basic patterns of the Trager-Smith system correspond in their simplest form to complete expirations (Lieberman, 1967). The point I would like to note here is that the length of an expiration is conditioned by the "higher-level" syntactic analysis of the utterance.

The same patterns for respiration, wherein the duration of an expiration is determined by higher-level structure, holds for respiration during wind instrument playing and during singing (Bouhuys, 1974). The duration of the expiratory phase of respiration is keyed to the length of a musical phrase. The duration of expiration is not merely keyed to the simple constraints of vegetative breathing, that is, maintaining particular oxygen and carbon dioxide levels in the bloodstream. It instead is influenced by seemingly abstract cognitive events — the duration of a sentence or a syntactic constituent or the duration of a musical phrase. The intuitive relation between breathing and cognitive structure has been incorporated into a theory of poetic structure and practice. The American poet Charles Olson regarded breath control as an inherent structural element in poetry: "The line comes (I swear it) from the breath, from the breathing of the man who writes it, at the moment that he writes . . . for only he, the man who writes, can declare at every moment, the line, its metric and its ending — where its breathings shall come to termination" (1959, p. 2).

Figure 5-4 shows the breathing pattern of a poet (a member of Olson's circle) while reading. Olson did not devise a notation that would indicate the breathing points in his poems; the readings thus depend on an "oral" tradition, which is, of course, consistent with the oral tradition of poetry that has been interrupted only in the past few

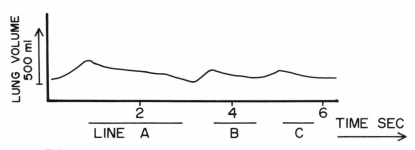

FIGURE 5-4.
Lung volume for a poet reading one of Charles Olsen's poems. The
individual lines of this part of the poem, A, B, and C, are each
produced on an individual expiration. Note that the magnitude of
inspiration is greater for the line that has a longer duration.
(Adapted from Lieberman and Lieberman, 1973.)

hundred years. The points at which expiration ends do not always
coincide with sentences, sentencelike intervals, or major elements of
the phrase structure. The poem achieves a rhythmic structure
through the interplay of the breathing pattern and the meaning
derived from the strings of words. Words and breathing points that
are syntactically anomalous achieve emphasis, and we become aware
of the poet's breath. The Olson poems "work" because they violate
the usually close relation between syntax and respiration (Lieberman
and Lieberman, 1973).

PREPROGRAMMING

One last point needs some emphasis: the respiratory maneuvers that a
speaker uses during normal discourse appear to be "preprogrammed." Before beginning a long sentence, the speaker draws
more air into the lungs so that there is more air (and a greater elastic
recoil force) for the sentence than would be the case if the sentence
were going to be short. Speakers, of course, occasionally make mis-
takes in this regard and do not take enough air into their lungs before
they start a long sentence. They "run out of air" when this happens.
Small children occasionally can be heard doing this, such as when they
are excited and enumerate the animals at the zoo or the good things to
eat at a party. Adults obviously also make "production errors," but
even in these instances they tend to stop, as Armstrong and Ward
(1926) note, where the words of the sentence indicate that the sentence probably is not over.

Speakers also interrupt their expiratory pattern as they pause to think or as the degree of involvement with the topic of a conversation changes (Goldman-Eisler, 1958). The pattern of interruption, however, varies with different speakers; we cannot conclude that someone thinks a lot because he frequently pauses. The pattern of respiration also changes for some speakers with their emotional state (Lieberman and Michaels, 1962), but we really do not know how these phenomena intersect with the linguistic aspects of respiratory control. Information is indeed still lacking on how we balance the conflicting requirements of air flow and speech when we run or walk uphill, as well as on the limits of this interaction (Bouhuys, 1974).

THE REGULATION OF EXPIRATORY DURATION AND AIR PRESSURE

Lenneberg claims that human beings are "endowed with special physiological adaptions which allow us to sustain speech driven by expired air" (1967, p. 81). Lenneberg is correct: compared with many other animals, we clearly have anatomical specializations that allow us to maintain a steady subglottal air pressure throughout the course of a long expiration. We probably have "matching" innate neural motor control programs that allow us to execute the complex muscular maneuvers that are necessary. However, other primates, such as chimpanzees and gorillas, also have some of the same anatomical specializations that allow us to regulate subglottal air pressure during a long expiration.

Human speech probably takes place on the expiratory phase of respiration because of the elastic recoil force of the lungs. The air pressure in a speaker's lungs gradually falls during expiration in the absence of speech. This gradual decrease of air pressure follows from the gradual decrease of the elastic recoil force of the lungs during expiration (Mead, Bouhuys, and Proctor, 1968). The elastic recoil force is greatest when the lung is stretched to hold more air at the start of the expiration. As air flows out, lung volume decreases; the lung is stretched less and less, so the elastic recoil force gradually decreases. The situation again is similar to the elastic recoil force generated in a rubber balloon: it is maximum when the balloon is blown up and decreases as the balloon empties.

The situation is quite different during speech production. The speaker can maintain a steady air pressure throughout a long expiration until its end, where the air pressure abruptly falls. Figure 5-5 shows lung volume and air pressure during the production of a sentence. Electromyographic recordings of the activity of the intercostal and abdominal muscles show that human speakers maintain a

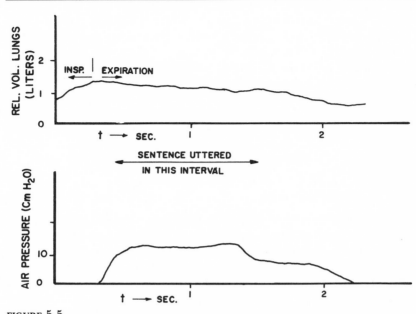

FIGURE 5-5. _____

Lung volume and air pressure in the lungs during the production of
a sentence. Note the long length of the expiratory phase relative to
inspiration. Note also the air pressure function, which does not
gradually decrease following the decrease in lung volume.

steady subglottal air pressure throughout an expiration by setting up a
preprogrammed pattern of muscular activity. They first use their
"inspiratory" intercostal muscles to oppose the force developed by the
elastic recoil force of the lungs and then gradually bring their "expiratory" intercostal and abdominal muscles into play to supplement the
elastic recoil force as it gradually falls (Draper, Ladefoged, and Whitteridge, 1960; Mead, Bouhuys, and Proctor, 1968). The diaphragm is inac-
tive in this process, probably because it lacks proprioceptive muscle
spindles (Bouhuys, 1974). The balance of forces and muscles that are
available in the hominoid (human and ape) respiratory system makes it
possible to maintain a steady subglottal air pressure by working
against the elastic recoil force. The diagram in Figure 5-6 sketches the
process. The vertical axis plots lung volume and air pressure; the
horizontal axis, time. The interrupted line shows the linear air pressure function that would result from the gradual decrease of the

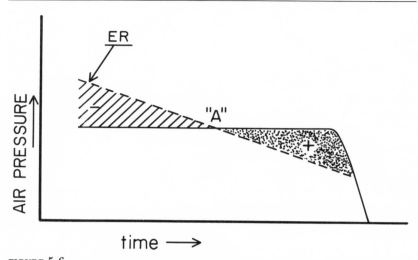

FIGURE 5-6. _____
Regulation of alveolar air pressure during speech. The elastic recoil
(*ER*) of the lungs generates the linear falling air pressure indicated
by the interrupted line. At the start of a long expiration, this air
pressure exceeds the level suitable for phonation. The speaker
opposes the elastic recoil, generating a force indicated by the
diagonally lined area. When the elastic recoil force reaches point *A*,
the speaker starts to supplement it with the force indicated in the
stippled area. The net result is the steady air pressure indicated by
the solid line throughout the nonterminal portion of the breath-
group.

elastic recoil force as the volume of air in the lungs gradually fell
during expiration. (Note the almost linear decrease of lung volume
during speech production in the graphs of Figure 5-3, 5-4, and 5-5.)
The solid line in Figure 5-6 shows the level subglottal air pressure that
a speaker usually produces in the nonterminal portion of an expiration (Lieberman, 1967). The elastic recoil function intersects this air
pressure line at point *A*. The speaker initially produces the steady air
pressure function by opposing the elastic recoil force by pulling
outward on the rib cage with the inspiratory intercostal muscles until
point *A*. The speaker has to reduce gradually the force generated by
these inspiratory muscles, as the diagonally lined area indicates. After
point *A* is reached, the speaker must supplement the elastic recoil
force by compressing the lungs with the expiratory intercostal and

abdominal muscles. The stippled area indicates the gradual increase of expiratory muscle activity that supplements the falling elastic recoil force.

The connection between anatomy, human uniqueness, and motor control on the one hand and the regulation of subglottal air pressure on the other rests on the fact that the system that we use could not work unless our ribs slanted downward from our spine. The geometry of the downward slant and the insertion of the intercostal muscles into the ribs allow the inspiratory intercostals to expand the chest and oppose the elastic recoil force to effect a steady subglottal air pressure at the start of an expiration. Newborn humans, whose ribs are almost perpendicular to the spine, cannot do this. They do not start to use the control pattern that adults use for expiration during speech until the third month of life, when their ribs have assumed the adultlike configuration. The ribs of adult chimpanzees and gorillas slant downward, so they too have the anatomy necessary to regulate subglottal air pressure during expiration. Computer-implemented analyses of the vocalizations of chimpanzees in the Gombe Stream Reservation suggest that they regulate subglottal air pressure during expiration. Some of the chimpanzee vocalizations involve long sequences in which the pitch of their voices rapidly alternates between fixed fundamental frequencies. It would be virtually impossible for human beings to achieve similar patterns unless they regulated the subglottal air pressure throughout the utterance. Human beings continually generate relatively even subglottal air pressures during expirations keyed to the length of their sentences, and they continually override the chemoreceptors that regulate vegetative breathing. This fact suggests that natural selection has occurred for speech communication at this level. Comparative studies that determined whether apes also override the chemoreceptors that regulate vegetative breathing would indicate whether these adaptations occurred in the course of hominoid evolution or instead are characteristic of hominid evolution.

THE LARYNX

Lenneberg (1967), in commenting on the physiologic adaptations for speech, also states that the human larynx is particularly well adapted for "phonation upon expired air, in contrast to the vocal cords of certain other primates which are so constructed that they can phonate upon inspiration as well as expiration" (1967, p. 81). This claim is not consistent with the data of experiments in which the effects of various physiologic parameters on phonation are studied by exciting an excised larynx. These experiments date back to the time of Johannes Müller, who developed the myoelastic theory of phonation as well as the source-filter theory of speech production.

The larynges of baboons, sheep, and dogs all behave functionally in much the same manner as the human larynx (Negus, 1949, pp. 142, 143; Van den Berg, 1962). The larynges of all animals have a common phylogenetic origin, and those of mammals are very similar (Negus, 1949). The larynx evolved from a valve that protected the lungs in such fish as the modern lung fish protopterus, neoceratodus, and lepidosiren. The larynx in these fish is a longitudinal slit in the floor of the pharynx, with muscle fibers lying on either side of the slit that close it in a sphincteric manner (Negus, 1949, pp. 1-7). The function of this primitive larynx, which looks like a small set of human lips (another sphincteric organ), is simply to protect the fish's lungs from the intrusion of water. Victor Negus, in his monumental comparative studies of the phylogenetic development of the larynx, *The Mechanism of the Larynx* (1929) and *The Comparative Anatomy and Physiology of the Larynx* (1949), shows the series of adaptations from the simple larynx of the lung fish to the mammalian larynx. In brief, a series of adaptations added cartilages that initially served to facilitate the closing of the larynx's opening, the glottis. These adaptations resulted in the arytenoid and thyroid cartilages, which can be seen in such animals as the alligator. Further adaptations facilitated breathing or phonation. Negus (1949, pp. 31-41), for example, shows that the larynges of ungulates are better adapted for respiration than the larynges of human beings.

The vocal cords are not really cords. The term derives from a theory proposed by Ferrein (1741), who thought that the larynx worked like a stringed instrument in which strings (hence *cordes*, in French) vibrate to produce sound. This is not the case; Müller (1848) showed that the larynx instead works like a woodwind instrument, in which reeds flap to interrupt the flow of air through the instrument. The larynx during phonation essentially converts the steady flow of air from the lungs into a series of rapid puffs of air. The cartilages and muscles of the larynx, in preparation for phonation, first gradually close the glottis by pulling the vocal cords together. Figure 5-7a shows a sequence of photographs of the larynx closing for phonation. The photographs are frames from a high-speed motion picture sequence that was exposed at a frame rate of 10,000 frames per second (Lieberman, 1967). The closing gesture took about 0.6 second.

The sequence of photographs in Figure 5-7b is from the same

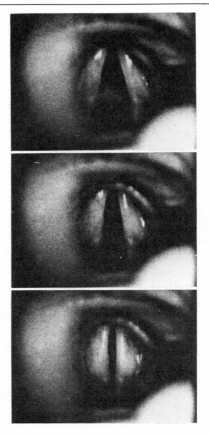

FIGURE 5-7a.

Frames from a high-speed motion picture of the human larynx. The camera is looking downward on the vocal cords. The posterior part of the vocal cords is oriented toward the bottom of each frame. The uppermost frame shows the vocal cords at the start of the closing gesture. The lower frames were exposed 50 and 100 msec later.

high-speed movie during phonation. The interaction of the forces developed by the airstream from the lungs and the tension of the tissue of the vocal cords causes the vocal cords to open and close rapidly. Phonation cannot take place without a person's blowing air through the closed or partially closed vocal cords. For phonation, a speaker must first move the vocal cords inward from the open position that they hold for inspiration. The vocal cords thus reach a "phona-

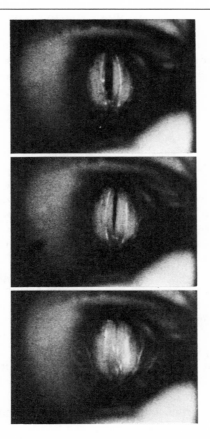

FIGURE 5-7b.
Three frames from the same high-speed movie during phonation.
The uppermost frame shows the maximum opening of the vocal
cords. The bottom frame, which was exposed 7 msec later, shows
the vocal cords closed. Note the rapidity of vocal cord motion
during phonation compared with the closing gesture of Figure 5-7a.

tion neutral position." Phonation then takes place when the flow of air
impinges against the closed or partially closed vocal cords. As the
vocal cords open and close the glottis, they interrupt the expiratory
airflow and generate a sequence of puffs of air. These puffs of air
contain acoustic energy at the "puff rate" and at harmonics of the rate
at which the puffs occur. The fundamental frequency of phonation is
the rate at which the puffs of air from the larynx occur. Our percep-

tual response to this fundamental frequency is the pitch of a person's voice. The faster the rate at which the puffs occur, the higher the pitch that we hear. The fundamental frequency of phonation of the larynx and the amplitude of the laryngeal output are sensitive to variations in the air pressure that "drives" the vocal cords. Hence the subglottal air pressure—that is, the air pressure developed by the lungs, which impinges on the vocal cords of the larynx—has to be regulated during the production of speech.

The larynges of all primates can inherently generate sound on the inspiratory as well as the expiratory phase of respiration. The cries of newborn human infants, for example, typically are phonated during part of the inspiratory phase (Lieberman et al., 1972). However, because phonation cannot take place until the glottis closes, it cannot be sustained throughout inspiration since the glottis *must* be open to admit air into the lungs during the short time interval of an inspiration. As I noted earlier, human beings and hominoids like chimpanzees and gorillas have an anatomical specialization, their downward-slanting ribs, that allows them to regulate subglottal air pressure during expiration. We initially oppose the elastic recoil force of the lungs with our intercostal muscles to effect a steady subglottal air pressure function. Acoustic analyses of the vocalizations of chimpanzees and gorillas show that they also tend to produce most of their sounds during expiration. Though the "quality" of their phonation differs from that of normal human speakers, tending to be breathy, it would have little effect on their phonetic ability (Lieberman, 1968). Our vocal quality probably sounds as "unnatural" to chimpanzees as theirs does to our ears. In short, the larynges of nonhuman primates appear to be as well adapted for speech production as ours.

THE BREATH-GROUP

The breath-group is a phonological construct that hypothetically has perceptual, physiologic, and linguistic reality (Lieberman, 1967, 1970, 1976c). The breath-group's primary characteristics are structured by the vegetative constraints of the respiratory system. The breath-group theory proposes that human speakers usually segment the flow of speech into sentences, or other syntactic units, by grouping words in complete expirations. The breath-group theory further proposes that the acoustic cues that delimit the end of a sentence usually follow from articulatory gestures that represent the minimal departure from the articulatory maneuvers that would occur during quiet respiration. The explanation for why we produce speech on the expiratory phase of respiration follows from the fact that we can generate a steady subglottal air pressure function throughout most of the expiration. This ability, in turn, follows from the anatomy of our ribs and from our ability to schedule a complex pattern of inspiratory and expiratory muscle activity acting in a coordinated way with the elastic recoil force of the lungs. Newborn human infants do not do this in their birth cries (Lieberman et al., 1972; Truby, Bosma, and Lind, 1965), and their fundamental frequency of phonation tends to vary throughout their cry. The subglottal air pressure frequently rises to levels that are too high to sustain phonation during newborn cry; the vocal cords blow open and phonation is interrupted by breathy noise excitation of the supralaryngeal airways (Truby, Bosma, and Lind, 1965).

The fundamental frequency and amplitude of phonation are functions of the subglottal air pressure (Van den Berg, 1958, 1962; Lieberman 1967, 1968b; Atkinson, 1973; Ohala, 1970). It thus is necessary to stabilize the subglottal air pressure to avoid uncontrolled variations in perceived pitch and amplitude. Normal children are able to control their subglottal air pressure function throughout the duration of the expiratory phase from about the third month of life (Langlois, Baken, and Wilder, 1980) before they begin to produce meaningful words. They start to imitate the intonation of their mothers between the sixth week (Lieberman, Ryalls, and Rabson, 1982) and the third month of life (Sandner, 1981).

Most human languages for which phonetic data exist signal the end of a simple declarative sentence with a fundamental frequency contour that abruptly falls, with a concomitant fall in amplitude (Lieberman, 1967). This pattern occurs at the end of an expiration and is probably derived from the inherent vegetative constraints of respiration. A positive air pressure must be generated in the lungs during expiration in order to force air out of the lungs. During inspiration a negative air pressure must be generated in the lungs in order to pull air into the lungs. If speech and phonation are prolonged until the end of expiration, as is the case in the newborn cry, there has to be an abrupt fall in the subglottal air pressure function. If the speaker either maintains a uniform pattern of laryngeal control or opens the larynx in preparation for inspiration, the fundamental frequency of phonation must fall at the end of the expiration together with the amplitude of the speech signal. A speaker *must* open the larynx and *must* develop a negative air pressure in the lungs in order to breathe. If a speaker effects these maneuvers, the fundamental frequency of phonation and amplitude of the speech signal at the end of a breath-group must fall, unless the speaker executes a set of additional muscular maneuvers that are not necessary for breathing. *The state of minimum control thus yields the pattern of fundamental frequency and amplitude that defines the "unmarked," or normal, breath-group.*

Although some controversy exists regarding the degree to which the fundamental frequency of phonation will vary with respect to subglottal air pressure (Ohala, 1970; Lieberman, 1967, 1968a, 1976c), there is general agreement concerning the fall in amplitude and fundamental frequency at the end of a normal breath-group. It is possible to counteract a fall in subglottal air pressure by tensing certain laryngeal muscles (Müller, 1848; Van den Berg, 1958, 1960; Ohala, 1970; Atkinson, 1973). In many languages this forms the basis for a phonetic opposition with the normal breath-group, and some sentences can end with a "marked" + breath-group that has a rising or level fundamental frequency of phonation, such as English yes-no questions. The breath-group theory derives from Stetson's work (1951) and was developed by Lieberman (1967), but the concept is implicit in phonetic analyses like those of Armstrong and Ward (1926) and the phonemic analyses of Pike (1945) and Trager and Smith (1951).

The salient acoustic features of the breath-group that signal the end of a sentence are the terminal falls in fundamental frequency and amplitude. There is also a concomitant decrease in the energy of higher harmonics of the glottal source. All of these acoustic parameters follow from the basic vegetative constraints involved in going from the expiratory to the inspiratory phase of respiration. The vocal cords are detensioned as the lateral cricoarytenoid and vocalis muscles relax. The mean opening of the glottis increases, reducing both the aerostatic and aerodynamic forces generated by the airflow from the lungs. The vibrating mass of the vocal cords also increases as the posterior section of glottis opens, putting the arytenoid cartilages into motion. All of these factors lower the fundamental frequency and amplitude of phonation (Van den Berg, 1958, 1960, 1962; Atkinson, 1973).

Adult speakers of English appear to supplement these acoustic cues by increasing the duration of the last word or syllable of a sentence (Klatt, 1976). This cue appears to be learned by children who are raised in an English-speaking environment. They gradually learn to shorten the duration of words that do *not* occur in a breath-group terminal position (Kubaska and Keating, 1981). Whether children innately have or gradually learn the control patterns that maintain a steady nonterminal subglottal air pressure function is another open question. Recent data that I will discuss later suggest that some aspects of the human control pattern are innate.

Summary

The syntactic component of human language generates sentences that are the minimum units of speech that normally express complete thoughts. Sentences are signaled during normal discourse by the intonation of speech. The psychological reality of the sentence is evident in the preprogrammed pattern of articulatory maneuvers necessary to generate the intonation patterns, the breath-groups, that segment the flow of speech into sentences. Human speech is produced on the expiratory phase of respiration. The pattern of respiration during speaking, singing, and wind instrument playing departs from that of quiet breathing. During quiet breathing the expiratory and inspiratory phases of respiration have about the same duration. During structured activities like speaking, the length of the expiratory phase is variable and is "keyed" to the higher-level syntax. The duration of an expiration during speech is that of a sentence and sometimes of a smaller unit of the phrase structure. Human speakers, during the production of speech, continually override the layered feedback systems that make use of central and peripheral chemoreceptors to monitor the level of CO_2, O_2, and the pH of the cerebrospinal fluid and blood. The fact that we are able to override these chemoreceptors suggests that natural selection for speech communication has occurred at this level in the course of hominid or hominoid evolution.

Despite the claims often cited in linguistic literature — for example, in Lenneberg's work (1967) — the anatomy of the human respiratory system and larynx is quite similar to that of some other animals which also produce their vocalizations on the expiratory phase of respiration. The anatomy of the lungs, which evolved from the swim bladder by means of Darwinian preadaptation, yields a system in which it is possible to store energy for expiration in the elastic recoil force of the lungs. Human beings set up complex patterns of motor activity involving their inspiratory and expiratory muscles and the elastic recoil force. The anatomy of the human rib cage, which is similar to that of adult apes like chimpanzees and gorillas, allows us to regulate subglottal air pressure during expiration by using our intercostal muscles to oppose the elastic recoil force of the lungs. These maneuvers, which are preprogrammed in terms of the length of the sentence that the speaker is about to produce, structure the basic form of the breath-group. The breath-group as a phonetic event accounts for the ensemble of acoustic cues that speakers use to segment speech into sentences and elements of the phrase structure. The acoustic cues of the normal breath-group are terminal falling fundamental frequencies of phonation and amplitude. These acoustic events follow from the physiology of the larynx and the segmenting of speech into episodes of expiration. At the end of an expiration the physiologic conditions that are necessary to initiate inspiration, the opening and detensioning of the vocal cords and the switch from positive to negative air pressure in the lungs, automatically generate the salient acoustic cues of the breath-group.

CHAPTER 6

Elephant Ears, Frogs, and Human Speech

THE MAY 2, 1980 ISSUE OF *Science* reports that elephants can hear sounds whose frequencies range between 17 hertz and 10.5 kHz (Heffner and Heffner, 1980). The relevance of the report is that it is set in the context of a comparative study of the factors that might determine the upper frequency limit of the range of sounds that a mammal can hear. The upper, high-frequency limit of auditory perception was related to the distance between a mammal's ears. Elephants were included in the study since they have widely set ears. Mice were also included since they have closely set ears. The authors of the study conclude that the upper limit of audition is related to the distance between an animal's ears and appears to have a functional explanation: it enhances the ability of animals to localize the source of a sound. The process of Darwinian natural selection appears to have operated to match a central mechanism, audition, to a peripheral anatomical constraint, the distance between an animal's ears. Animals whose ears are set closely together, such as mice, must be able to perceive sound frequencies that are high enough to be shadowed by their heads and ears. Thus, "given the ecological importance of an animal's localizing the sound of a stealthy intruder, animals with functionally close-set ears are subjected to more selective pressure to hear high frequencies than animals with more widely set ears . . . when the selective pressure for high frequency hearing is reduced as a consequence of evolving a large inter-aural distance, the upper limit of hearing is reduced" (Heffner and Heffner, 1980). In other words, if your ears are farther apart, you do not have to hear sounds at very high frequencies in order to localize their source. The term *hertz* simply specifies the frequency of a "pure" sound. A low note on a violin, for example, has a low frequency; a high note, a high frequency. The range of human hearing is about 20 hertz to 15 kHz. A kHz is simply shorthand for a thousand hertz.

Why should animals localize by using the lowest frequency that will work, given the distance between their ears? The answer again appears to be functional. Darwinian natural selection seems to be operating to optimize the process of sound localization. All things being equal, the high-frequency components of a sound are attenuated more readily than low-frequency components. Thus your neighbor's hi-fi set usually produces a series of low-frequency thuds through the wall when it is turned up. The low-frequency thuds propagate through the wall; the higher-frequency components are fortunately attenuated by the wall. The same effects would occur in the primeval forest. The low-frequency components of the padding tiger would propagate a longer distance than higher-frequency components. We therefore see evidence of an evolutionary *match* between an animal's ears and an animal's hearing. Neural mechanisms that have been matched with the anatomical constraints of human speech production will be discussed in detail here. As these prefatory examples demonstrate, similar matches effected by the mechanism of natural selection occur between peripheral, anatomical mechanisms and central, neural mechanisms in other species.

RESPIRATION AND SWALLOWING

That neural-peripheral systems are matched should not be surprising. What use would a specialized anatomical structure have without the requisite neural control mechanism? The respiratory systems of air-breathing animals thus have layered control systems whose function is to maintain sufficient oxygen in the bloodstream to sustain life. These neural systems are built in. We do not, for example, have to learn to take air into our lungs when we come to the end of a breath. The reflex mechanisms discussed earlier monitor the level of carbon dioxide gas in our bloodstream and initiate inspiration if the amount of CO_2 exceeds a certain critical level. The reflex systems are all built-in and constitute part of our innately determined neural endowment (Bouhuys, 1974).

Both the pattern of morphological restructuring of the upper respiratory system and the matching neural control of this system are innate, that is, genetically transmitted, and are present in human infants. The larynx of a newborn is positioned high relative to the base of its skull (Crelin, 1969). This yields a supralaryngeal airway that is quite different from that of a normal adult human being, in whom the larynx's position is low (Negus, 1949). The larynx's high position in the newborn allows it to lock into the nasopharynx during respiration.

The epiglottis and soft palate form a double seal, and the infant can breathe while it feeds since there is a closed, sealed airway from the nose into the lungs. Food can pass to either side of the raised larynx into the pharynx, which is positioned behind the larynx.[1] Newborn humans, as well as monkeys, who have this configuration thus can feed without danger of ingesting foreign material into their lungs (Laitman, Crelin, and Conlogue, 1977). Matching this respiratory anatomy is a neural control system that prevents infants from breathing through their mouths. Newborn infants are obligate nose breathers. They will almost suffocate if their nasal airway is obstructed. In the course of normal development, the supralaryngeal airways of infants usually change toward the configuration typical of adult human beings. By the third month of life the larynx has descended to the point where it can no longer effect a seal with the nasopharynx (Laitman, Crelin, and Conlogue, 1977; George, 1978; Grosmangin, 1979). Infants, after their third month of life, no longer can simultaneously breathe and feed because they cannot form a sealed airway from the nose to the lungs. The neural systems that regulate breathing also change in normal infants to match the "new," restructured supralaryngeal airway. Infants after the age of three months *can* breathe through their mouths.

The match between the anatomy of the supralaryngeal airways and the neural control of respiration that does not allow, or does allow, mouth breathing is thus dynamic and genetically programmed. Mothers do not teach infants how to breathe. Laitman, Crelin, and Conlogue (1977) indeed suggest that "sudden infant death syndrome," which is the sudden death by asphyxiation of otherwise normal infants, may reflect some anomalies in the neural control mechanisms involved in the changeover from obligate nose breathing. The change in the pattern from obligate nose breathing to voluntary mouth breathing probably reflects the mechanism of natural selection operating in terms of the selective advantages that accrue to the total population of maturing human infants. At birth there is a selective advantage in an infant's not breathing through the mouth since this would allow foreign matter to lodge in the infant's larynx, with a high probability of asphyxiation. If the infant breathes through the nose, the sealed supralaryngeal airway will guarantee that foreign matter will not lodge in the larynx. Infants thus are programmed to breathe only through their noses. Though some infants undoubtedly will die because their nasal airway becomes obstructed, the total population of newborn infants benefits from the retention of obligate nose breathing. After the age of three months, when the larynx has descended, there no longer is any selective advantage for obligate nose breathing with regard to protecting the larynx. Foreign matter is just as likely to lodge in the larynx during nose breathing as it is during mouth breathing; the larynx has descended down into the neck and can no longer effect a seal against the nasopharynx (Negus, 1949.) In these conditions, there is a selective advantage for voluntary mouth breathing for the population of human beings older than three months, since they will not asphyxiate when their nasal airway is blocked.

WALKING

Breathing is, of course, a basic function that all animals maintain. We might expect it to be structured in terms of innately determined mechanisms matched to the peripheral anatomy, since we know that the behavior of simple animals like frogs is almost entirely controlled by innately determined reflexes. The responses of frogs to visual events, for example, are structured by means of a small set of innately determined neural "devices" that are built into the frog's visual system (Lettvin et al., 1959). It is, however, apparent that matched neural-peripheral systems are part of the innately determined biological endowment that allows human beings to walk upright. Human upright, bipedal locomotion is a comparatively recent specialization. It probably is no more than five million years old, perhaps ten million years old at most (Campbell, 1966). Human bipedal locomotion clearly involves a number of anatomical specializations involving the feet, pelvic region, legs, and spine. The evolution of these anatomical specializations has been studied in detail by means of comparative and paleontological studies. Comparative studies of related living animals, such as chimpanzees, who cannot walk as we do show what is similar and what is different between our anatomy and that of the nonwalking living animal. Comparative studies thus establish the *functional* anatomical aspects of the specializations for human walking. Paleontological studies chart the appearance of these anatomical specializations in the fossil record. Comparative and paleontological studies are complementary. Thus when Mary Leakey (1979) found footsteps of hominids walking upright, preserved in a mudflat that they had walked across 4.5 million years ago, it was not too surprising: comparative and paleontological data and analyses had already indicated that Australopithecine hominids were walking upright in that epoch (Campbell, 1966; Pilbeam, 1972).

The point of this discussion of walking is that human beings have specialized anatomical structures that have evolved for walking in an upright, bipedal manner; they also have matching neural mechanisms that, without much learning, enable them to control these peripheral, anatomical structures and walk. In other words, human beings have a built-in, innately determined walking "reflex." If you lift a normal newborn human infant, holding him under his armpits in front of you, he will start to move his legs and "walk."

Infants, of course, do not normally start to walk by themselves until they are about 11 or 12 months old. Newborn infants in fact lack the necessary anatomy for walking. Their bones, muscles, and so on, could not support their weight. The newborn's spine (vertebral column) has no fixed curves at birth and is so flexible that when "dissected free from the body [it] can easily be bent into a perfect half circle" (Crelin, 1973). The lower-limb musculature is relatively underdeveloped in the newborn infant, though it constitutes as much as 55 percent of a normal adult's total muscle weight. If you released a newborn infant when you were holding him in front of you to elicit the walking reflex, he would collapse in a heap. Infants normally "lose" the walking reflex in the months after birth in which they cannot support their own weight. However, if a child's parents systematically hold their child upright for a few minutes each day, the child will retain the newborn walking reflex throughout the months in which the lower limbs and spine develop. Infants who are exercised in this manner will start to walk on their own about two months earlier than the age at which they otherwise would start to walk (Zelazo, Zelazo, and Kolb, 1972).

Is the newborn walking reflex ever really lost in infants who are not exercised in the period between birth and the onset of spontaneous walking? Probably not; we do not really "learn" to walk in the sense that we learn arithmetic or the rules of chess. Children start to walk with virtually no instruction. All normal children in fact learn to walk, just as they learn to talk, without any formal instruction.

If we were building a walking robot, we would have to build in complex control circuits that would take into account the effects of gravity, length of step, inclination of the surface that it would be walking on, speed, and the like. The total human "walking system" has been optimized over a long period so that the central neural walking "computer" matches the constraints of the peripheral walking anatomy and the external environment. When we change the environment and substitute a zero gravity field, such as outside a space satellite, we have to relearn the walking process, and walking becomes more difficult and more strenuous. The human walking computer (the term *computer* is used loosely here since, as I have noted before, I do not think that the human brain functions in the same manner as any electronic or mechanical computer that has yet been built) is one of the species-specific attributes of anatomically modern *Homo sapiens* that differentiates us from all other living animals.

COMMUNICATION

Comparative studies of other species demonstrate the presence of innate perceptual mechanisms that apparently are "designed" to facilitate the recognition of meaningful communicative signals. These systems are matched or tuned in the sense that they respond to communicative signals that the species can generate. The modality of these signals can be chemical, visual, acoustic, or electrical (Smith, 1977; Hopkins and Bass, 1981). The point is that animals have perceptual systems that respond to the particular signals that they *can* produce. These matched systems are found at all phylogenetic levels. Thus crickets have species-specific response patterns to the acoustic signals, the "songs," that they can generate by rubbing their legs together (Hoy and Paul, 1973). Electric fish in the African family Mormyridae recognize members of their own species by "listening" to a temporal pattern of electrical signals. These electrical signals are generated by specialized electric organs that are found only in electrical fish. Experiments with normal and computer-modified electric patterns demonstrate that the fish take account of the waveform properties of the electrical signals that these specialized organs generate (Hopkins and Bass, 1981). Birds appear to have innate devices that allow them to respond to their vocal calls. Laughing gull chicks between 6 and 13 days respond to the vocal characteristics of their own parents' calls (Beer, 1969). The social canids appear to have innate stereotyped display patterns that involve their total body posture. The "play bow" in infant coyotes, wolves, wolf-dog hybrids, beagles, and adult free-ranging dogs shows marked stereotypy (Bekoff, 1977). Human infants are able to imitate the facial expressions of adults from between 12 and 21 days of life (Meltzoff and Moore, 1977).

The presence of a matched system for communication in which an animal makes use of signals that have species-specific qualities involves two factors. Production devices must have evolved to produce the particular signal — chemical, acoustic, kinesthetic, electrical, and so on. Perceptual devices likewise must have evolved that can respond to these particular signals. Although human beings clearly make use of visual signals in their linguistic communication (Hewes, 1973), the primary modality of human language is speech.

HUMAN SPEECH AND BULLFROG CALLS

Two related hypotheses are central to this discussion of human speech. First, human speech communication works because we have a neural, perceptual mechanism that is matched to the physiologic constraints of our peripheral speech-producing anatomy. Second, though the particular system that we use is probably unique to anatomically modern *Homo sapiens,* similar though simpler systems can be found in other animals. Later on I will argue for the gradual evolution of this matched system as part of the total mosaic pattern of evolution of linguistic and cognitive ability in hominids.

I will start the discussion of human speech by considering sustained vowels—sounds that are fairly simple to describe. These sounds are also simple in another sense: some of the sounds that very simple animals like bullfrogs make are really short, isolated vowels. As I shall point out, the acoustic properties and physiology of human sustained vowels and bullfrog mating calls are similar.

Human vowels are produced in a manner analogous to the way that different notes are produced on a woodwind instrument like a clarinet. The larynx acts as a source of acoustic energy, rather like the reed of a woodwind. When we produce a *voiced* sound, such as a normal English vowel, we blow air through the larynx. The larynx has meanwhile been adjusted so that it tends to open and close rapidly, interrupting the flow of air. Thus what comes out of the larynx is a very rapid sequence of puffs of air, from under 100 puffs per second for adult males to over 1000 puffs per second for young children (Keating and Buhr, 1978). Human beings can control the rate at which the larynx produces this sequence. The perceived pitch of a person's voice is related to the rate at which these puffs occur. The process by which the larynx produces the sequences of puffs is known as *phonation;* the rate at which the puffs occur is the *frequency.* If 100 puffs occur in a second, we can formally note that the *fundamental frequency of phonation* is 100 hertz.

Contrary to what we often hear and read, the process of speech production is not complete after we have specified the output of the larynx. If we had only a larynx, we could only change the fundamental frequency of phonation, the pitch of our voice. We could not convey information by means of differences in vowel quality. Johannes Müller (1848) noted this in his studies with larynges excised from human cadavers. Müller's experiments have a very modern quality. He tested a functional theory of phonation by modeling the activity of the larynx and varying several physical parameters that his theory claimed were significant. Müller's experiments were replicated over a century later (Van den Berg, 1958, 1960, 1962) in studies that modified his procedures to take advantage of recent technology. Müller's method is modern because he tested his theory by generating a physical output and comparing this output with the actual event. In contrast to Müller's work there are many purely descriptive studies of how the larynx looks. Unsupported speculations on how it functions still typify many studies.

Modeling the Larynx

Müller's modeling was quite straightforward. He placed a larynx that had been excised from a cadaver over a hole on a board. A tube was placed under the hole so that air could be blown through the excised larynx (which consists of a complex set of cartilages, muscles, and ligaments). Cartilage is a stiff, bonelike material that resists deformation; ligaments are similar to nylon strings or monofilament fishline. I will not go into a detailed description of the larynx — you can find such descriptions in works like Negus's (1949) *Comparative Anatomy and Physiology of the Larynx.*

   Though Müller did not use electronic instruments or high-speed photography to monitor the output of the larynx, he did get quantitative data that were consistent with his theory of phonation. Müller used a mechanical system of strings, weights, and pulleys to apply different forces to the thyroid cartilage while he blew air through the larynx. This allowed him to simulate the effects of changing the tension of the cricothyroid muscle during phonation. As the thyroid cartilage moved, it produced the tension that the cricothyroid muscle would have placed on the vocal cords in real life. Müller listened to the pitch of the laryngeal output as he varied the simulated muscle tension. He found that increasing the simulated tension placed on the vocal cords by the cricothyroid muscle raised the fundamental frequency of phonation.

   Müller also discovered that the fundamental frequency of phonation would increase if he blew air through the vocal cords with greater force. These findings have since been replicated in experiments with excised larynges (Van den Berg, 1960) and in experiments in which the tension of the laryngeal muscles in living human beings is monitored during actual phonation by means of electromyographic techniques (Ohala, 1970; Atkinson, 1973). Other experiments have monitored the force of the air against the vocal cords (the subglottal air pressure) during actual phonation (Lieberman, 1967; Ohala, 1970; Atkinson, 1973).

The Source-Filter Theory

Müller, in his experiments, noticed that the sound that came directly from the larynx differed from the sounds of human speech. Speech-like quality could be achieved only when he placed over the vibrating vocal cords a tube whose length was roughly equal to the length of the airways that normally intervene between the larynx and a person's lips. The sound then resembled the vowel [ʌ], the first vowel in the word *about*. The symbol within the brackets, [ʌ], is part of the phonetic alphabet that we can use to specify particular sounds. The square brackets show that we are specifying a phonetically defined sound (Phonetic Association, 1949). Müller probably was not surprised to find that the sound produced by the larynx had to be passed through a tube in order to sound natural. Kratzenstein (1780) had won a prize offered by the Academy of Sciences of St. Petersburg to the first person who could artificially produce the vowel sounds of Russian. Kratzenstein synthesized, that is, mechanically produced, the vowels [a], [i], and [u], the vowels of the English words *mama, meat,* and *boot,* by using tubes that had different shapes and lengths, which he "excited" by similar reeds. The acoustic properties of the tubes determined the synthesized vowel. The tubes acted as acoustic filters; the reeds, as sources of acoustic energy. Müller found that the larynx bore the same relation to the airways of the human supralaryngeal tract as the reeds bore to the tubes of Kratzenstein's mechanical model. The larynx provides the *source* of acoustic energy, while the supralaryngeal airways act as an acoustic filter that determines the phonetic quality of the vowel sound. A given supralaryngeal airway shape will let more or less acoustic energy through at different frequencies. The frequencies at which relative energy maxima can pass through the acoustic filter are called the *formant* frequencies (Hermann, 1894, introduced the term). The formant frequencies determine the perceptual quality or color of a vowel sound. The situation is quite similar to the way that optical filters, such as those of a stained glass window, work. The daylight that illuminates the stained glass window is the source of light energy. The stained glass lets relatively more or less electromagnetic, or light, energy through at different frequencies; the different balance of electromagnetic energy at different frequencies is perceived as differences in color. More energy at high frequencies yields blues; more at low frequencies, reds.

It would be perfectly feasible to continue to synthesize speech signals by using tubes and mechanical reeds. We could, for example, synthesize the vowel [i] by first determining the shape of the human supralaryngeal airways that is necessary to produce this vowel by examining x rays and then making a brass tube that had the appropriate shape. If we then excited this tube with a source of acoustic energy, such as a reed or, better still, an artificial larynx, we would have energy at the correct formant frequencies and would hear the vowel [i]. However, it is more convenient and more accurate to make use of the technology of the last quarter of the twentieth century. Many different types of speech-synthesizing devices have been developed in the course of modern research on the source-filter theory of speech production (Fant, 1960; Rabiner and Shafter, 1979). Unlike the devices of the eighteenth and nineteenth centuries, which used reeds and pipes, modern speech synthesizers are either electrical or computer-implemented systems.

Bullfrog Calls

Returning now to bullfrogs, the graph in Figure 6-1 shows a frequency analysis of the acoustic output of a synthesizer generating a bullfrog's mating call. The synthesizer was actually designed for generating human vowel sounds, but it serves equally well for some bullfrog sounds. The speech synthesizer, a POVO system (Stevens, Bastide, and Smith, 1955), is generating a sustained vowellike sound that has a fundamental frequency of phonation of 100 Hz. In Figure 6-1 the fundamental frequency of phonation shows up in the lines that occur at 100 Hz intervals. When bullfrog or human vocal cords open and close at a rate of 100 times a second, they generate an acoustic signal that has energy present at 100 Hz and at integral multiples of 100 Hz. The bullfrog call thus has acoustic energy present every 100 Hz — that is, 100, 200, 300, 400, . . . , 900 Hz, and so on. The supralaryngeal airways of the bullfrog (*Rana catesbeiana*) consist of a mouth, a pharynx, and a vocal sac that opens into the floor of the mouth in the male. The formant frequencies that follow from these supralaryngeal airways acting as an acoustic filter show up in Figure 6-1 as the relative peaks in the graph, which occur at 200 Hz and at 1.4 kHz.

Bullfrogs produce their vocalizations in the same manner as we produce the vowels of English. The vocal cords of the larynx open and close rapidly, emitting puffs of air into the supralaryngeal vocal tract, which acts as an acoustic filter. Frogs can make a number of different calls (Bogert, 1960), including mating calls, territorial calls that serve as warnings to intruding frogs, rain calls, distress calls, and warning calls. The different calls have distinct acoustic properties, and there are some obvious differences in the manner in which frogs produce some

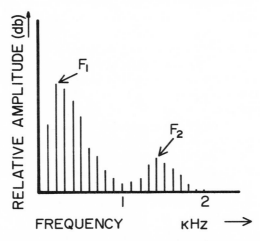

FIGURE 6-1.
Spectrum of bullfrog mating call produced on a POVO synthesizer.
F, denotes the first formant frequency at 0.2 kHz (or 200 Hz); F_2,
the second formant frequency at 1.4 kHz (or 1400 Hz).

calls. For example, the distress call is made with the frog's mouth wide open, whereas all other calls are made with the mouth closed.

The articulatory distinctions that underlie the other calls are not so obvious, and acoustic analyses of all the calls are not available. Capranica (1965), however, analyzed the acoustic properties of the bullfrog mating call in detail. In behavioral experiments Capranica used a POVO speech synthesizer to synthesize the mating call and presented the synthesized stimuli to bullfrogs. The bullfrogs responded by joining in a mating call chorus, as long as the synthesized mating call had acoustic energy concentrations at either F_1 or F_2, or both. The presence of energy concentrations at other frequencies inhibited the bullfrogs' responses.

Studies of the neuropsychology of human beings are always limited by the indirect techniques that have to be used. Direct techniques that record the electrical activity of the brain at the single-cell level involve using electrodes that ultimately destroy parts of the animal's brain. These direct techniques, however, can selectively record the electrical responses of cells to stimuli that are presented to an anesthetized animal. Frishkopf and Goldstein (1963), in their electrophysiologic study of the bullfrog's auditory system, found two types of auditory units in the anesthetized animal. They found units of the eighth cranial nerve whose cells had maximum sensitivity to frequencies between 1.0 and 2.0 kHz and other units whose cells had maximum sensitivity to frequencies between 0.2 and 0.7 kHz. Maximum response occurred when the frogs were presented with acoustic signals that had energy concentrations at or near the two formant frequencies of bullfrog mating calls, at rates of 50 to 100 pulses per second. The fundamental frequency of phonation of natural bullfrog calls falls into the range of 50 to 100 pulses per second. Adding acoustic energy between the two formant frequencies at 0.5 kHz inhibited the response of the low-frequency units.

The electrophysiologic, acoustic, and behavioral data thus all complement each other. Bullfrogs appear to have a neural mechanism that specifically responds to the bullfrog mating call. Capranica tested his bullfrogs with the mating calls of thirty-four other species of frogs, and they ignored them all, responding only to bullfrog mating calls. Bullfrogs do not respond to just any sort of acoustic signal as though it were a mating call; they respond to acoustic signals that have energy at the formant frequencies of the bullfrog's supralaryngeal airways. The best stimuli, furthermore, must have the appropriate fundamental frequency of the natural bullfrog mating call. The bullfrog's neural perceptual apparatus is demonstrably matched to the constraints of its peripheral sound-making apparatus.

Human Speech

Although electrophysiologic data similar in kind to that derived from frogs is obviously not available for human beings, other, indirect data that I will discuss later on are consistent with the theory that we have a vocal communication system that makes use of neural mechanisms matched to speech-producing capabilities. There are, of course, many differences between people and frogs, but there are also some striking similarities. The basic acoustic parameters that describe the speech signals of human beings and frog vocalizations, the fundamental frequency of phonation and formant frequencies, are similar. This similarity seems to follow from the continuity of evolution. Negus, in the classic anatomical studies that resulted in his *Comparative Anatomy and Physiology of the Larynx* (1949), demonstrated that there was a continual and gradual elaboration of the larynx from the simplest terrestrial air-breathing animals (except insects) to the higher animals, that is, mammals. Birds have diverged on their separate pathway, but the vocal signals of animals as far apart as frogs, rats, cats, horses, dogs, apes, and humans are inherently structured in terms of their formant frequencies and the fundamental frequency of phonation because they all can produce sounds by exciting their supralaryngeal airways with a laryngeal output—a laryngeal source and a supralaryngeal filter.

The few comparative electrophysiologic studies that we have (no one has yet attempted a monumental comparative anatomical study like that of Negus) indicate that these animals also are equipped with neural devices that match the laryngeal source and the supralaryngeal filter. Studies of cats (Whitfield, 1967), for example, show that cats are equipped with a neural device that tracks the fundamental frequency of phonation. This is no mean achievement, since we have yet to make an electronic device that will track fundamental frequency, though hundreds of attempts have been submitted to the U.S. Patent Office since 1936. Digital computer programs, while somewhat more accurate, still cannot track a fundamental frequency contour with the accuracy and speed of the "device" in the cat's brain. Systems for the early detection of cancer of the larynx that depend on accurate measurements of the fundamental frequency of phonation (Lieberman, 1963) have not proved practical because the basic measures of the fundamental frequency derived by computer are inaccurate and must be manually checked.

The computer systems that have been devised for measuring formant frequencies and the fundamental frequency of phonation of human speech make use of computer programs that are structured in terms of the constraints of speech production. Formant frequencies, for example, can be derived by using an analysis-by-synthesis procedure (Bell et al., 1961), in which the computer program "knows" the possible combinations of formant frequencies that specify vowels. The analysis-by-synthesis program derives the formant frequencies of an incoming vowel sound by systematically generating internal signals that consist of combinations of possible F_1's, F_2's, and F_3's and comparing the incoming signal with the internally synthesized signal. The internal synthesized signal that best matches the incoming signal is selected as the model signal. The formant frequencies of the model signal are reasonable approximations of the incoming signal. The fundamental frequency of phonation can also be calculated, though with less certainty, by using a computer program that takes account of many of the possible variations in the fundamental frequency pattern (Gold, 1962).

Motor Theories of Speech Perception

These computer programs in a sense are derived from the traditional motor theories of speech perception (Zinkin, 1968), which claim that we perceive speech in terms of the way that we produce speech. Motor theories can be viewed as a particular model of a match between an animal's peripheral anatomy and its central perceptual system. Early versions of the motor theory, which dates back to the nineteenth century, claimed that it was necessary to move our lips, tongue, velum, and so on, at a "subliminal" level in order to perceive speech (Zinkin, 1968). Various data were presented in support of this view. Some people, for example, habitually move their lips as they read (many people, of course, do not). Some advocates of traditional motor theories thus claimed that there always are subliminal movements of our lips, tongue, and other organs of speech articulation when we listen to speech. Other motor theorists abandoned the claim that any movements of the articulatory apparatus were necessary to perceive speech; they instead proposed that we have an internal, neural representation of the possible acoustic consequences of articulatory maneuvers. According to these versions of the motor theory, we perceive speech by internally generating a model signal and "perceiving" the internally generated signal that best matches the acoustic characteristics of the incoming speech signal. Although motor theories were not in the mainstream of American academic psychology, they were and still are the dominant theory for the perception of speech in other schools of psychology, particularly in the Soviet Union. Zinkin (1968) for example, provides a detailed account of the development of motor theories in Soviet psychology. The chapters that follow discuss experiments and data that indicate that human speech has special properties that make it an efficient mode for vocal communication. These data also led to an explicit, quantitative version of the motor theory of speech perception and to experiments which demonstrated that human beings, like frogs, are equipped with neural devices that are matched to the salient acoustic characteristics of human speech. Some of these devices, like the cells in a frog's auditory nerve, appear to respond to structured signals in terms of the acoustic constraints imposed by our speech-producing apparatus.

SUMMARY

Comparative studies demonstrate the presence of neural systems matched to peripheral anatomy through the process of natural selection. Matched neural systems are involved in the control of respiration, swallowing, and walking as well as communication. The communicative matched systems respond to signals that a species can produce.

Human beings appear to have neural devices that are matched to their speech-producing anatomy. Human speech production can be described in terms of the source-filter theory. The airways of the supralaryngeal vocal tract — the pharynx, nose, and mouth — act as an acoustic filter. The source or sources of acoustic energy filtered by the supralaryngeal airway are phonations generated by the action of the larynx and turbulent "noise" generated by air movement through constrictions. The vowels of English normally are produced with laryngeal phonation. The rate at which the vocal cords of the larynx open and close determines the fundamental frequency of phonation, which we perceive as pitch. The frequencies at which the supralaryngeal airways permit local energy maxima to occur are the formant frequencies. The pattern of formant frequencies determines the phonetic class of the vowel. Different vowels have different formant frequency patterns — the perceptual response to a given pattern is the phonetic class of a vowel. Detailed electrophysiologic and acoustic data show that bullfrogs have neural devices that are tuned to the formant frequencies of their mating croaks. Similar matched systems may exist in other animals, including *Homo sapiens.*

CHAPTER 7

Speech Is Special

IF YOU HAVE EVER TURNED THE dial on a short-wave radio, you know it is difficult to find much in common among the sounds that different languages use. The biblical story of the Tower of Babel comes to mind. We cannot understand what people are trying to say when they are using a language unfamiliar to us. We often cannot even differentiate or imitate the sounds they are using. Phoneticians have to train for years in order to make transcriptions of unfamiliar languages or dialects. Indeed, the obvious rejoinder to any claim that people are like bullfrogs — that they have innate neural mechanisms that structure the sounds of speech — is that we all do not use the same sounds. All bullfrogs make the same sounds, but all people do not. It depends on where a person grows up and what language or dialect she or he hears — so how can we claim that there are innate neural mechanisms adapted to the perception of the sounds of human speech? Would not a more plausible theory be that we just string more or less arbitrary sounds together to form words and sentences? What is wrong with a theory of speech acquisition that claims that we, as infants and children, learn the sounds that happen to be used in our language by simply imitating them? After all, we learn the letters of the alphabet a few years later and again learn to string these letters together so they form words and sentences.

These are not merely rhetorical questions that I am inventing to change the pace of this exposition. They were at one time or another implicit or explicit hypotheses that led to attempts to engineer complex "talking machines." A rather common opinion concerning language is that its phonetic aspect is trivial and indeed finally irrelevant to the serious study of human language and its evolution. Simpson, for example, in reviewing attempts to trace the evolution of language, notes that "audible signals capable of expressing language do not require any particular phonetic apparatus, but only the ability to

138

produce sound, any sound at all" (1966, p. 473). If Simpson's claim were true, any sequence of sounds that people found tolerable would serve as a vehicle for communication in a linguistic mode. We could, for example, communicate with each other by using the sounds that spoons and forks make when tapped on a wall. The system would be limited in its scope, but people in fact have used this system. The codes that prisoners sometimes devise to "talk" to each other through walls are an example. Morse code is another similar system that makes use of sequences of dots and dashes transmitted by short and long beeps. These systems are slow, however; the fastest speed that a Morse code operator can achieve is about 50 words per minute, that is, about 200 to 250 letters per minute. Moreover, at this rate the Morse code operator has to devote full attention to transcribing a message. The operator usually does not even remember what was transcribed and has to rest after an hour or two to recover from the fatigue engendered by transcribing at this rate. In contrast, we can easily follow a lecture delivered at a rate of 150 words per minute. The fastest rate at which people can produce and perceive speech sounds is about 20 to 30 sounds or "letters" per second, or about 1200 to 1800 phonetic units per minute. The research reviewed here demonstrates that human speech has special properties that make possible the high rate at which we can communicate.

VOCODERS

This research started in the years before World War II. Bell Telephone Laboratories has for many years been one of the most active centers for the quantitative study of the acoustic properties of human speech. It is obvious why this should be. Telephones are used to transmit human speech, and progress in making telephones that are better, more reliable, or less expensive can be enhanced if we know more about the nature of speech. By the mid-1930s the Bell Telephone research group under the direction of Homer Dudley knew how to make what engineers call a real-time analysis-synthesis speech transmission system. What they did seemed at first to be rather cumbersome, pointless, and expensive. But the device they invented, the VOCODER, was to become one of the components of the top-secret speech transmission systems developed for cryptographic purposes during World War II. The VOCODER later made it possible to start a project directed at developing a reading machine for blind people. In the course of that engineering project, it was found that the sounds of human speech are not like the sounds of the alphabet.

The VOCODER, however, was developed by Bell Telephone Laboratories for none of the above reasons. It was developed to save money for the telephone company. I hope that the connection between "practical" engineering projects and advances in "theoretical" science will become evident as we follow this story. The arbitrary division between engineering and science becomes meaningless when engineers find that the theories they were supposed to be implementing do not work.

As I noted earlier, when we talk we are controlling two anatomical systems. We control the source of acoustic energy, for example, the larynx, for a "voiced" sound like the vowel [i]. We also control the positions of our tongue, lips, and velum (which closes our nose to our mouth) to set up the supralaryngeal "filter" that specifies this vowel. Similarly the VOCODER operates by first electronically tearing the speech signal apart into electrical signals that specify the characteristics of the source and electrical signals that specify the filter. These electrical signals are then transmitted by a wire or radio transmitter to a special synthesizer that puts these electrical signals together to reconstitute the speech signal. The VOCODER system thus consists of a separate analyzer and synthesizer. The analyzer represents the character of the source using three parameters, or signals, that must be extracted and transmitted. The filter function is represented by at least sixteen parameters that also must be derived from the incoming speech signal and transmitted. The system was quite complicated; the 1936 version filled a small room with a mass of vacuum tubes and electronic circuits.

The economic motivation for the development of the VOCODER was that this mass of electronic equipment could reduce the frequency range necessary to preserve speech intelligibility in telephone circuits from about 5000 to 500 Hz. The range of frequencies that can be transmitted on any particular electronic channel is inherently limited. A particular circuit, or channel — for example, the telephone cable between the United States and England — has a given capacity, say 50,000 Hz. By using electronic techniques, it is possible to squeeze about eight separate conversations that need a channel of 5000 Hz each into the 50,000 Hz available. (Some frequency "space" has to be left between the 5000 Hz channels necessary for each individual conversation.) The VOCODER made it theoretically possible to squeeze ten times as many conversations into the same Atlantic telephone cable. If a battery of VOCODERS first processed the telephone conversations, each telephone conversation's frequency range could be reduced to 500 Hz. Eighty conversations then could be squeezed into the trans-Atlantic cable. An Atlantic telephone cable is a very expensive item and has a limited lifespan. The cables deteriorate as sea water leaks into them, and the conductors and electronic amplifiers deteriorate. If you can squeeze ten times as many messages onto a cable and thereby avoid laying nine additional cables, you have saved a considerable amount of money even if the VOCODER equipment costs millions of dollars.

VOCODERS never were placed into regular service on the normal commercial Atlantic telephone cables. The voice quality of the VOCODER system was judged by Bell to be too poor for commercial applications. In time, other speech compression systems were designed that were able to squeeze extra conversations down the same cable while they preserved good voice quality.[1] The VOCODER analysis made many errors that resulted in a loss in speech intelligibility and a "Mickey Mouse" voice quality. The system, however, proved invaluable for military cryptographic systems in which the parameters derived by the VOCODER analyzer were digitized and scrambled. The scrambled signals could be put together at the receiving end in the VOCODER synthesizer by using suitable cryptographic devices. Winston Churchill, in his memoirs, notes that he used what appears to have been a VOCODER system to converse with Franklin Delano Roosevelt. It was not possible to keep the principles on which VOCODERS are designed secret during World War II, since they had been described in the open scientific literature in 1936. However, the actual equipment was classified. Nazi Germany never developed a useful secure speech transmission system despite a great deal of effort. Work on the VOCODER systems still goes on throughout the world. The Soviet Union was not supplied with VOCODER systems under the World War II lend-lease program. The imprisoned Zeks in Solzhenitsyn's *First Circle* are, for example, apparently working on building a VOCODER system and sound spectrograph. Israeli intelligence was able to glean information from clear radio transmissions between Arab heads of state during the 1967 Six-Day War because the Soviet Union had not supplied its client states with VOCODER crypto systems.

Speech Synthesis

Another application of the VOCODER was pointed out by Dudley at Bell Telephone Laboratories. The VOCODER synthesizer could be used to generate artificial speech sounds. Since the synthesizer started with a set of electrical signals that specified the acoustic signal, it was possible to generate either modified versions of actual speech signals or completely synthetic speech signals that had never been spoken by a human speaker. Modified versions of speech signals could be produced by changing one or more of the electrical signals from the analyzer that controlled the synthesizer. Completely synthetic sounds could be generated by specifying the entire set of electrical control signals. Synthesized, modified, and synthetic speech sounds provided a new tool for determining the salient acoustic correlates of the phonemic distinctions of human speech.

Phonemic distinctions are the meaningful sound contrasts of a language or dialect. For example, in English the difference between the vowels [i] and [I] is phonemic since this vowel distinction differentiates words like *heat* and *hit*. In contrast, the difference between [i] and [ĩ], where [ĩ] is a nasalized [i], is not phonemic in English since no English words are differentiated by means of nasal versus nonnasal vowel oppositions. (In Portuguese nasal versus nonnasal vowel distinctions are phonemic.) Speech synthesizers allowed experimenters to determine systematically what acoustic factors actually conveyed phonemic distinctions. An experimenter could, for example, determine whether the fundamental frequency of phonation played any part in determining whether a listener, whose native language was English, would hear a vowel as an [i] or an [e]. Vowel stimuli that had the formant frequencies of these vowels could be synthesized with different fundamental frequencies. The synthesized vowels then could be copied a number of times in random sequence on a tape recording. A psychoacoustic listening test could then be conducted in which listeners would be asked to write down on an answer sheet whether they perceived each particular synthesized vowel to be an [i] or an [e]. Psychoacoustic tests with synthesized speech signals, in fact, showed that fundamental frequency had only a slight effect on vowel perception (Fujisaki and Kawashima, 1968).

FORMANT FREQUENCY TRANSITIONS

Formant frequency patterns, and in particular dynamic, time-varying formant frequency patterns, however, turned out to be the most salient acoustic cues in the perception of human speech. The sound spectrograph, the instrument designed at Bell Telephone Laboratories in the 1930s for the analysis of speech, made it possible to see the dynamic pattern of formant frequencies as functions of time. Although it is possible to produce sustained vowels in which the formant frequency pattern does not change, the formant frequencies of the

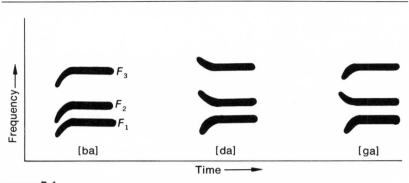

FIGURE 7-1.
Formant frequency patterns for the sounds [ba], [da], and [ga].

speech signal continually change in the course of normal speech production. In Figure 7-1 the formant frequency patterns of the sounds *ba*, *da*, and *ga* are shown as dark bars. Note that the formants of the sound *ba* all start at a lower value and then abruptly rise to a rather steady level. The symbols F_1, F_2, and F_3 in Figure 7-1 have been used to label the representations of the first, second, and third formant frequencies of the *ba*. The changing part of the formant frequency pattern at the start of the *ba* is called the *transition;* the steady part, the *steady-state*. (Engineering jargon is quite transparent compared with the jargon of other professions.)

The questions that the technique of speech synthesis allowed scientists to address at first seemed almost simple-minded: What part of the formant frequency pattern of the *ba* in Figure 7-1 is the acoustic correlate of the isolated sound [b]? What part of the acoustic pattern of the *da* is the acoustic correlate of the isolated sound [d]? What is the acoustic correlate of the soung [g]? The questions seemed almost simple-minded because everyone "knew" that the sounds [b], [d], and [g] were discrete consonants. The phonetic representation of speech since the invention of the alphabet over five thousand years ago had been in terms of discrete segments. Speech was supposed to consist of a sequence of phonetic segments. Indeed the usual image was that of beads on a string. It thus seemed to be an almost trivial problem to isolate the discrete acoustic correlates of consonants like [b], [d], and [g].

The program of research which demonstrated that human speech was an encoded signal in which the acoustic cues that specified a segmental consonant like a [b], [d], or [g] might be spread across an entire syllable had as its immediate goal a practical device. Haskins

Laboratories, a privately endowed laboratory, was established in New York City shortly after the end of World War II in an old factory loft in what was then a low-rent district, East 43rd Street off Third Avenue. The laboratory was distributed over three floors of the building and was served by a freight elevator.

One of the goals of the laboratory was to develop a machine that would read books aloud to blind people. Although the ultimate goal of the project was to develop a reading machine, the focus of the research from the outset was the basic problems that a reading machine would have to address, rather than the actual mechanics or circuits of the machine. A reading machine must solve three different problems. First, the machine, if it is to "read' printed texts, must have an electro-optical device that can recognize printed alphabetic characters and punctuation—a print reader. The second functional element in a reading machine is the orthographic-to-phonetic converter, a device that can, in effect, regularize the spelling of English. The third functional element is the device that converts the string of phonetic symbols to sound—an acoustic converter. A practical reading machine would have to include page-turning devices, indexing schemes, and so on, but these ancillary systems obviously were irrelevant if the basic parts of the system still had to be devised.

The key to the project was the acoustic converter. Although print readers were not available at the time, the reading machine could initially operate with the texts of new books. At some stage in the production of a book a typesetting process takes place. Thus there always would be a possibility of starting with a machine representation of the printed text by using a special typesetting machine that would provide a control tape for the reading machine. The process of converting the orthographic text to a phonetic text was not trivial, but at worst it would entail a large dictionary in which all the words of English would appear with their orthographic and phonetic spelling. At the time the acoustic converter did not seem to present any unusual problem. The individual phonetic symbols would have to be sequentially converted to acoustic signals.

As already noted, the prevailing view was that the sounds of speech were individual, segmentable beads on a string. That is what phonetic transcriptions implied. The word *cat*, for example, in a phonetic transcription is segmented into the initial stop consonant [k], plus the vowel [ae], plus the final stop consonant [t]. (A stop consonant is one that is made by abruptly closing, or "stopping," the supralaryngeal airway.) The stop consonant [k] in the word *cat*, furthermore, is in theory supposed to be identical to the initial consonant of the word *kite* or the final consonant of the word *back*. In a phonetic alphabet a given symbol has the same sound quality wherever it appears. This principle is implicit in all traditional phonetic theories. If the phonetic units did not have the same sound quality, you seemingly would not be able to have a phonetic transcription.

PHONETIC SEGMENTATION

The engineering solution to the problem of converting phonetic symbols to sound that was first attempted made use of the linear properties of magnetic tape recording. Suppose you had recorded a sequence of sounds on a tape recorder. If you had, for example, recorded a person clapping his hands, followed by a person sneezing, followed by a person singing, you would be able to unreel the tape and isolate each event by cutting out the piece of the tape on which it had been recorded. The tape recording would have allowed you to segment the sequence of acoustic events. You would be able to take the short sections of magnetic tape and splice them together in different sequences, so that the sneeze would come after the singing, or the singing before the clapping. This technique seemed to be an appropriate tool for isolating the phonetic segments of English. If you started by recording a speaker carefully reading a selected list of words, you could easily record the total phonetic inventory of English. The tape recording could then be copied and sliced up into sections of tape that each corresponded to a phonetic element (Harris, 1953; Peterson, Wang, and Sivertson, 1958). If, for example, you had a tape recording of the word *cat*, you should be able to slice off the section of tape that corresponded to the initial [k] and then slice off the final [t], leaving the third remaining [ae] section of the tape recording. If you went through the same process with a tape recording of the word *tea*, you would be able to segment out a [t] and an [i]. The segmentation of the word *ma* would yield [m] and [a]. If a phonetic transcription were simply a linear sequence of individual and invariant segments, you then would be able to combine the individual sounds recorded on the sections of tape into new words. Given even the small set of words that we used as examples of the tape-cutting process, you would, for instance, be able to form the English words *mat*, *me*, and *tack*.

The "solution," however, did not work. When new words were put together out of the phonetic segments that had been segmented, the speech signal was scarcely intelligible. It was in fact impossible to even segment out sounds like stop consonants without hearing the vowels that followed or preceded them in the words where they had occurred. It was, for example, impossible to cut out a pure [k] from the tape recording of the word *cat*. No matter how short a segment of tape was cut, one would always hear the vowel sound [k] plus the [ae] vowel that followed it.

ENCODING

The Haskins Laboratories research program established that it was inherently impossible to isolate a stop consonant without also hearing the adjacent vowel. The difficulty was not that the speech-segmenting technique lacked precision. The speech signal is inherently encoded at the acoustic level (Liberman et al., 1967). The formant transitions, which follow from the physiologic properties of the human supralaryngeal vocal tract, represent a melding of the consonants and vowels of the speech signal. The acoustic cues of the stop consonants and vowels in sounds like [ba], [da], and [ga] are "squashed together." A human speaker, when producing a sound like [ba], starts with the supralaryngeal vocal tract (lips, tongue, and so on) in the positions that are necessary to produce a [b]. The speaker initially closes the lips to produce the "stop," but then opens them while moving the tongue toward the shape necessary to produce the vowel [a]. The tongue cannot move instantly; there is an interval in which it is moving toward the "steady-state" position of the [a]. During this interval the formant transitions of the [b] are produced. The formant transitions represent the acoustic signal that results as the speaker goes from the articulatory configuration that would be necessary to produce a [b] to that necessary to produce an [a]. When a human listener hears these transitions, the [ba] is heard. No matter how fine a slice of the transition one cuts, if it is interpreted as speech at all, it will be heard as the consonant plus the vowel.

The speech-encoding process is not limited to consonant-vowel pairs. In producing a word like *bat* in fluent discourse, the speaker does not necessarily attain the articulatory configuration or the formant frequency pattern of the steady-state vowel after having produced the [b]. The speaker instead starts toward the articulatory configuration of the [t] before reaching the steady-state values that would be characteristic of an isolated and sustained vowel. The articulatory gestures are melded together into a composite characteristic of the syllable. The sound pattern that results from this encoding process is itself an indivisible composite. Just as there is no way of separating the [b] gestures from the vowel gestures (you cannot tell when the [b] ends and the vowel begins), there is no way of separating the acoustic cues that are generated by these articulatory maneuvers. The sound pattern that results is a composite. The acoustic cues that characterize the initial and final consonants are transmitted in the time slot that would have been necessary to transmit a single, isolated vowel.

The encoding of speech thus has an important functional property: it yields the high rate of signal transmission that I noted earlier. A simple experiment that you can perform without any complicated instruments will illustrate the difference between the transmission rate of encoded human speech and that of segmental nonspeech sounds. The experiment requires two persons, a pencil, and a watch with a sweep second hand. The object of the experiment is to determine the fastest rate at which you can count the number of pencil taps that occur in five seconds. One person taps the pencil while the other counts and looks at the watch. If you perform this experiment, you will discover that most people can, with a little practice, tap a pencil faster than the rate at which you can count the taps. The fastest counting rate is about 7 to 9 taps per second, that is, 35 to 45 taps in five seconds. The rate at which we identify the individual sounds of speech ranges from 20 sounds per second for normal rates of speech to about 30 sounds per second (100 to 150 "taps" in five seconds). It is impossible to attain this rate with sequences of segmented nonspeech sounds (Liberman et al., 1967). At rates that exceed 15 sounds per second, the individual sounds merge into a buzz. We cannot even resolve the individual sounds, much less identify them.

The process that allows human speech to attain this high rate of transmission appears to involve the encoding of phonetic events into a speech signal that consists of units whose minimum length is the syllable in the production of speech. The segmental phonetic elements appear to have a psychological status as programming instructions for the speech production apparatus (Harris, 1974, 1977). Human listeners appear to decode the speech signal by using neural devices that inherently take account of the constraints of speech production —that is, perceptual devices "matched" to speech production.

Motor theories of speech perception are not new; Zinkin (1968), for example, presents a comprehensive review of Russian research that dates back to the nineteenth century. However, the Haskins experiments of the 1950s and 1960s provided the first convincing evidence that speech perception was structured in terms of the constraints of speech production. The Haskins experiments relied on careful, controlled psychoacoustic experiments in which listeners

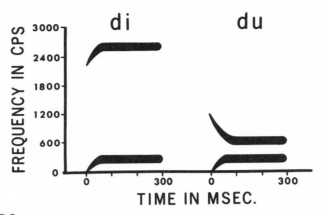

FIGURE 7-2.
Formant frequency patterns for F_1 and F_2 that will produce the
sounds [di] and [du].

were asked to respond to synthetic speech stimuli. Synthesized speech
allowed experiments to be run using stimuli that differed along known
acoustic parameters. In Figure 7-2, for example, stylized spectrograms of the formant frequency patterns that were used in a typical
Haskins experiment are presented. The spectrogram shows only the
first and second formant frequencies. These two formant patterns,
however, when transformed to speech signals by the synthesizer, will
be heard as the sounds [di] and [du] (the English words *dee* and *due* are
reasonable approximations). Note that the second formant transition
is different for the two synthesized syllables [di] and [du]. The transition is falling in the [du], rising in the [di]. However, listeners hear an
identical [d] at the start of these two synthesized sounds.

The theory developed by the Haskins Laboratories group proposes that these two different acoustic patterns are heard as the same
[d] because the listener is decoding the speech signal by using an
internal computer which knows that these different acoustic patterns
will occur when a speaker puts his or her tongue into the configuration that is used to produce a [d] before either [i] or [u]. In other
words, we hear the same [d] because a [d] articulation will produce
different formant frequency transitions in the encoded speech output
before either an [i] or a [u]. The Haskins theory did not claim that we
interpret speech by moving our lips, and so on, and generating silent
speech signals that we use to compare with the incoming speech signal.
Older, traditional versions of motor theories of speech perception

claimed that we, in effect, talk to ourselves quietly in order to perceive the sounds of speech. The data of the early Haskins experiments have been replicated many times with improved synthesizers. As we gain a better understanding of the process of speech perception, it seems more and more likely that many aspects of speech perception involve our using neural devices that respond selectively to the acoustic patterns that are typical of those of human speech. In other words, in some ways we are not so different from bullfrogs.

HUMAN SPEECH AND THE HUMAN INPUT-OUTPUT SYSTEM

The studies on the perception and production of bullfrog mating calls which I discussed earlier are consistent with the hypothesis that bullfrogs have perceptual mechanisms that are "tuned" to respond to the acoustic characteristics of their species-specific mating calls. These species-specific acoustic parameters are, in turn, constrained by the morphology of the bullfrogs' larynges and supralaryngeal vocal tracts (Capranica, 1965; Frishkopf and Goldstein, 1963). The matched system that is in place in bullfrogs appears to be relatively simple and involves "mechanisms" that are located in the peripheral auditory system. The Frishkopf and Goldstein (1963) study monitored the electrical output of the frogs' eighth cranial nerve, which in essence is the channel from the basilar membrane of the ear. The data of human speech perception suggest that a similar though more complex system exists in human beings. The human system is more complex insofar as our linguistic responses appear to involve the activity of a number of central nervous system mechanisms that decode the speech signal. Though we appear to use auditory mechanisms that follow from our mammalian heritage for the perception of some linguistically salient acoustic cues, other aspects of human speech perception appear to involve specialized mechanisms that are probably species-specific. These specialized mechanisms derive linguistically significant parameters like formant frequency patterns that are not directly present in the acoustic signal — parameters that can be calculated with certainty only if one takes into account the physiologic constraints of human speech production.

FORMANT FREQUENCY EXTRACTION

The calculation of formant frequency patterns is probably one of the basic steps in the perception of human speech. Although other acoustic parameters, such as the fundamental frequency of phonation and the presence or absence of noise excitation, provide linguistically salient cues, the pattern of formant frequency variation is probably the primary acoustic event. What is striking is that formant frequencies are *not* realized directly in the acoustic speech signal. Formant frequencies are instead the properties of the supralaryngeal airways that filter the acoustic source or sources involved in speech production (Hermann, 1894; Fant, 1960). The formant patterns plotted in Figures 7-1 and 7-2 were schematic diagrams of the *control* pattern of a speech synthesizer. The actual acoustic signals that were presented to human listeners had nothing that could be directly identified as a formant frequency.

Figure 7-3 illustrates the concept that formant frequencies are not *directly* present in the acoustic speech signal. The top graph shows the filter function of the supralaryngeal airways that would yield the vowel [i]. The three relative maxima — F_1, F_2, and F_3 — are the first three formant frequencies. Note that these three local peaks necessarily form part of a total, continuous filter function that extends across the audible frequency spectrum. The filter function will pass acoustic energy through it at all the frequencies that are plotted in accordance with the values shown. Relative energy maxima will occur at the formant frequencies, but energy will pass through the filter at other frequencies. Formant frequencies are frequencies at which maximum energy will pass through the supralaryngeal airways acting as an acoustic filter relative to nearby frequencies. The formant frequencies are thus local properties of the supralaryngeal filter.

The middle diagram shows the spectrum of the periodic energy that could be generated by the larynx. The fundamental frequency of phonation is 500 Hz, which is apparent in the position of the first bar of this graph. This vertical line or bar represents the amplitude of the fundamental component of the glottal excitation. The bars that occur at integral multiples of the fundamental frequency — 500 Hz, 1000 Hz, 1500 Hz, and so on — represent the amplitude of the harmonics of the fundamental. The empty spaces between the bars indicate that there is no acoustic energy between the harmonics. Together the ensemble of fundamental and harmonics represents the power spectrum of the glottal sound source in the frequency domain. A human listener normally would not have access to this acoustic signal because it is filtered by the supralaryngeal airways that are interposed between the larynx and the speaker's lips. If a speaker's supralaryngeal airway assumed the configuration that is appropriate to generate the vowel [i], a listener would hear an acoustic signal whose spectrum would be the product of the spectrum of the glottal excitation and the filter

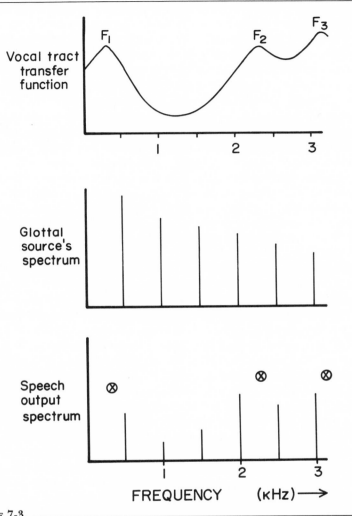

FIGURE 7-3.
Top: Filter function of the supralaryngeal airway for the vowel [i].
Middle: Spectrum of glottal source for a fundamental frequency of
500 Hz. Bottom: Spectrum of the speech signal that would result if
the filter function shown in the top graph were excited by the
glottal source noted in the middle graph. Note that there is no
acoustic energy present at the formant frequencies which are noted
by the circled Xs.

function. The result would be the spectrum sketched in the bottom graph of Figure 7-3.

Note that the listener does not have access to the filter function sketched in the top graph. The signal that the listener hears instead has energy only at the fundamental frequency and the harmonics, which in essence "sample" the supralaryngeal filter function. Note that no energy is present at the formant frequencies. The absence of any acoustic energy at the formant frequencies in the speech signal is a consequence of there being no energy in the periodic laryngeal source, except at the fundamental frequency and its harmonics. The fundamental frequency of phonation and its harmonics are controlled by the activity of the laryngeal muscles and the air pressure generated by the lungs. The control of the fundamental frequency of phonation and its harmonics is independent of the control of the supralaryngeal airways filter function. In general, the harmonics of the fundamental frequency do not fall on the formant frequencies.

The bottom graph sketched in Figure 7-3 does not represent some extreme, odd condition. The fundamental frequency of phonation of many women and some men can exceed 400 Hz during connected discourse. The fundamental frequency of children under the age of 6 years typically exceeds 500 Hz. The upper limits of fundamental frequency for 2-to-3-year-old children is at least 1.5 kHz (Keating and Buhr, 1978). The spectra of speech sounds that tend to be used as illustrations in introductory texts on speech usually show signals that have low fundamental frequencies. In Figure 7-4 the fundamental frequency is low, 100 Hz. It is easy to see where the formant frequencies are *if* the supralaryngeal filter function is sampled by the closely spaced harmonics of low fundamental frequency laryngeal sources. The formant frequencies thus seem to be present in the speech signal when we view spectra like that in Figure 7-4. The 100-Hz fundamental in the figure samples the filter function thirty-five times between 100 Hz and 23.5 kHz. A 500-Hz fundamental, in contrast, samples the filter function only seven times in this same frequency interval. The increased uncertainty of formant measurements from the bottom graph in Figure 7-3 follows from the fact that we have to reconstruct the shape of the continuous filter function from the points sampled by the discrete harmonics of the fundamental. Only if we can reconstruct the filter function with sufficient detail to determine the local maxima can we then determine the formant frequencies. In other words, formant frequency extraction is a two-stage process. We first have to connect the sampled points to reconstruct the supralaryngeal filter function. The second stage appears to

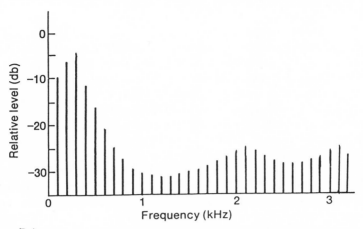

FIGURE 7-4. _____
Spectrum of the filter function noted in the top graph of Figure 7-3
excited by a glottal source having a fundamental frequency of 100 Hz.

involve reconstructing the filter function to derive the formant frequencies. The formants are the local peaks of the *reconstructed* filter
function.

It is notoriously difficult to calculate the formant frequencies of
sounds that have high fundamental frequencies by using sound spectrograms or other procedures that involve reconstructing the filter
function by means of simple interpolation between the sampled points
of the spectrum. There simply are not enough data available in the
points that are sampled by the few harmonics of high fundamental
frequencies. Recent psychoacoustic data (Ryalls and Lieberman, 1982)
show that human listeners also have more difficulty in determining the
formant frequencies of vowels as the fundamental frequency of phonation rises. In an experiment with computer-synthesized vowel stimuli that differed only in their formant patterns, the error rate for their
identification increased for higher fundamental frequencies. Human
listeners, however, are much better formant extractors than are
human viewers using sound spectrograms or other methods that are
limited to reconstructing the continuous supralaryngeal filter function from *only* the data derived from the sampling points provided by
the harmonics of the fundamental frequency. If we take into account
the way in which the supralaryngeal filter function is produced, we
can bring more information to bear on the process of reconstructing
the supralaryngeal filter function.

THE PSYCHOLOGICAL REALITY OF FORMANT FREQUENCY PATTERNS

Since formant frequency patterns are not directly present in the speech signal, one reasonable question is whether human listeners actually derive formant frequencies at any stage of the perceptual interpretation of speech. Do formant frequency patterns, in other words, have a psychological reality? This question was one of the underlying issues in the nineteenth-century controversy concerning the "harmonic" and "inharmonic" theories of vowels. Helmholtz (1863) had derived the harmonic structure of voiced vowels by means of acoustic analysis. Hermann (1894), in contrast, stressed the significance of the formant frequencies of the supralaryngeal vocal tract, which were inharmonic for the differentiation of vowels. Since the harmonic structure of a vowel is the simpler property of a vowel in that it is always physically present in the acoustic signal, it is reasonable to suppose that speech perception in human beings might not involve any stage of processing entailing a representation of the signal in terms of formant frequencies.

Some recent studies have proposed that this is the case — that linguistic distinctions are made from the spectrum of the acoustic signal without any direct reference to the underlying formant frequency pattern. Chistovich (1979), for example, claims that local spectral peaks are the salient cues for vowel perception. Bladon and Lindblom (1981) likewise propose that the perceptual "distance" between pairs of vowels depends on the difference between the spectral shapes between vowels. Blumstein and Stevens (1979) developed templates that characterize place of articulation in terms of the overall tilt or shape of the calculated onset spectrum for stop consonants followed by vowels. It is, however, not clear that the spectral data which these studies cite are, in fact, independent of the underlying formant frequency pattern. Fant (1956) demonstrates that the total shape of the spectrum is determined by the absolute frequency of formants for sounds whose supralaryngeal filter function can be specified by an all-pole network. This is the case for unnasalized vowels. Other studies, moreover, show that the formant frequency pattern as it is plotted in the $F_1 - F_2$ plane is a much better predictor of phonological distinctions than are gross spectral measures. The phonological vowel space relationships that have been traditional since the time of Hellwag (1781) are essentially isomorphic with F_1 versus F_2 vowel formant frequency plots (Joos, 1948; Nearey, 1978). As Bladon and Lindblom indeed note, their spectral measure accounts "for the experimental behavior of our listeners in only a rather gross fashion" (1981, p. 1414). The data of Blumstein, Isaacs, and Mertus (1982) again show that changing the overall tilt or shape of the onset spectrum has little or no effect on the perception of place of articulation for a stop consonant. The perception of place of articulation instead follows the absolute values of the formant and burst frequencies that can be derived from the onset signal.

The hypothesis that we perceive linguistic distinctions directly from the spectrum of the acoustic signal instead of extracting formant frequencies would be reasonable only if we were to limit speech perception to ideal acoustic environments, such as sound-treated rooms, anechoic chambers, or open fields on quiet days. In the real world this hypothesis runs into many difficulties because both the local and the overall characteristics of the spectrum of the acoustic signal that a listener hears are constantly subject to distortion from environmental sources. The spectrum of an acoustic signal that corresponds to the same sound, for example, can vary in different rooms. The acoustic spectrum that corresponds to a given sound can, in fact, vary as you turn your head (Beranek, 1949). A speech recognition scheme that had to derive linguistic contrast from measurements based on the "raw" acoustic spectrum would constantly have to take account of the effects of the external environment on the overall spectrum.

It is easy to demonstrate that changing the overall shape of the frequency spectrum that you hear has little effect on speech intelligibility.[2] Most high-fidelity music systems have tone controls that can effect great changes in the overall acoustic spectrum. The bass or low-frequency boost controls can tilt the acoustic spectrum up toward the low-frequency part of the spectrum, changing the overall energy balance of the spectrum. However, this does not change one's identification of speech sounds, even when isolated short-term onset spectra are presented to listeners in psychoacoustic tests (Blumstein, Isaacs, and Mertus, 1982).

A stage of formant frequency extraction appears to be necessary for speech recognition, whether it is effected by computer algorithms and electronic analysis (Hughes, 1961) or by human beings. Recent experimental data, moreover, show that human listeners can perceive sinusoidal replicas of formant frequency patterns as speech (Remez et al., 1981). In these experiments the formant frequency pattern for a sentence is first derived. The formant frequency pattern then is represented by a set of varying sinusoids, that is, "pure" tones, whose amplitudes are adjusted to follow the amplitudes of the formant frequencies derived from the speech signal. Some listeners are not able to hear these signals as speech; they hear them as "science fiction sounds," computer bleeps, bird sounds, animal cries, and the like. Other listeners, however, hear these sounds as speech and can identify the original sentences. The only property of these sinusoidal signals that bears any relation to the original speech signal is that "its time-varying pattern of frequency change corresponds abstractly to the potential products of vocalization" (Remez et al., 1981, p. 949). The only hypothesis that appears to explain the behavior of the listeners is that there is a psychologically "real" stage of formant frequency speech processing at which formant frequency patterns are represented and that the listeners were able, when primed, to relate the time-varying sinusoidal pattern to this stage of speech perception.

The data of Remez and his colleagues (1981) are consistent with earlier, more limited data (Bailey, Summerfield, and Dorman, 1977). They also explain how we may perceive the signals that "talking" birds produce as speech. Talking birds like mynahs generate signals that do not have the acoustic spectrum of human speech. Birds produce sounds by means of two syringes. One syrinx is located in each of the bifurcations of the trachea that lead to the bird's lungs. The larynx, which is positioned at the top of the trachea, takes no part in the production of sound in birds (Negus, 1949; Greenewalt, 1968). In phylogenetically advanced birds like mynahs, each syrinx can produce a different sinusoidal, pure tone. Mynah birds mimic human speech by producing acoustic signals in which a sinusoidal tone is present at the formant frequencies of the original human speech sound that the bird is mimicking. The sinusoids are, in addition, interrupted at the rate of the fundamental frequency of the mimicked human speech (Greenewalt, 1967; Klatt and Stephanski, 1974). We perceive these nonspeech signals as speech because they have energy at the formant frequencies.

FORMANT FREQUENCY EXTRACTION: A MATCHED SYSTEM

Given the fact that human beings respond to formant frequency patterns and can derive formant frequency patterns from speech signals, how are formant frequencies derived by human beings? One possibility is that formant frequency patterns are derived by the peripheral auditory system (Chistovich, 1979). Recent electrophysiologic experiments, however, show that this is probably not the case. The experiments of Sachs and Young (1979), for example, show that a spectrum containing formant peaks can be derived from the discharge patterns of cochlear nerve fibers of cats only when the fundamental frequency is low and the amplitude is low, about 40 db. These formant peaks disappear when the amplitude of the speech signal is increased to 80 db. The peripheral auditory system is probably not fundamentally different for human beings and cats. Since human listeners have no difficulties in perceiving speech at this level, higher-level processing in the human nervous system appears to be necessary to derive formant frequency information (Ainsworth and Pols, 1980, p. 9).

One promising avenue of research regarding formant extraction in human beings appears to involve "analysis by synthesis" in which knowledge concerning the physiologic constraints of speech production is brought to bear on the process. In analysis by synthesis (Bell et al., 1961), the formant extraction algorithm makes use of the fact that there is a fixed relationship between the frequency of a formant, its amplitude, and its effect on the total form of the overall filter function. Fant (1956) noted two crucial facts. First, the relative amplitudes of the formants of an unnasalized vowel sound are known once we know the values of the formant frequencies. Second, the shape of the total filter function is also known once we know the values of the formant frequencies. Each formant frequency, in effect, determines a partial specification of the total filter function. We can derive the total filter function by adding up the combined effects of the individual formant frequencies. Conversely, it turns out that a supralaryngeal filter function that is made up solely of formants (or "poles" — see Flanagan et al., 1970) can be resolved into the sum of a set of partial filter functions, each of which corresponds to an isolated formant frequency. We thus can determine the formant frequencies of a vowel even if there is no energy present at the exact formant frequencies in the acoustic signal, so long as we have enough acoustic information to establish the overall shape of the filter function. The analysis-by-synthesis procedure implemented as a computer algorithm by Bell and his colleagues (1961) calculated formant frequencies by matching the input signal against the combined patterns of three formant combinations. The algorithm also took account of what combinations of formant frequencies can occur in the production of human speech. The procedure of linear predictive coding (LPC) devised by Atal and Hanauer (1971) can be regarded as a modified version of this procedure in that the computer algorithm fits the input spectrum with a set of individual filter functions, each of which has the correct overall shape of a single formant.

Some of the perceptual effects that have been noted in psychoacoustic experiments with human listeners can be explained if we hypothesize that human beings extract formant frequencies by using the entire spectrum and by having some implicit knowledge of the physiology of speech production; that is, an analysis by synthesis in which we internally interpret the input speech signal in terms of how it could have been produced. The analysis-by-synthesis procedure, for example, takes into account the low-frequency part of the spectrum below the first formant frequency. This is consistent with Holmes's (1979) observation that high-quality speech synthesis requires a careful spectral match below the first formant frequency. Analysis-by-synthesis methods are also sensitive to the fundamental frequency of phonation. They become less accurate as F_0 increases, but that also is the case with human listeners (Ryalls and Lieberman, 1982). Finally, the presence of antiformants or zeroes in the filter function degrades their performance. This is also the case for human listeners.

Antiformants or zeroes represent points in the frequency spectrum where the supralaryngeal filter absorbs a local energy peak. The effect occurs when an airway other than the principal airway to the speaker's lips can divert some of the acoustic energy of the source. In the production of nasal sounds, the open nasal airway absorbs acoustic energy and introduces antiformants into the filter function (Fant, 1960). The presence of an antiformant in the filter function presents computational difficulties to an LPC algorithm and typically introduces errors (Atal and Hanauer, 1971). Similar computational difficulties would enter into an analysis-by-synthesis program of the type used by Bell and colleagues (1959). Human listeners again have more difficulty in identifying speech signals that differ by virtue of their formant frequency patterns when these sounds are nasalized. Bond (1976), in an experiment in which vowels were excerpted from nonnasal and nasal contexts, showed that the error rates of listeners who had to identify these stimuli increased 30 percent for the nasalized vowels. The Bond study made use of English-speaking listeners who normally are not exposed to phonemic variations among nasalized vowels. Similar results, however, occur when the responses of native speakers of Portuguese, a language that makes use of a full set of nasalized vowels at the phonemic level, are analyzed. Native speakers of Portuguese confuse Portuguese words that depend on minimal distinctions in nasalized vowels 30 percent more often than is the case for similar nonnasalized Portuguese words. The general phenomenon noted by Greenberg (1963), that the world's languages tend to avoid using nasalized vowels, probably follows from the relatively higher perceptual error rates that nasalization introduces. One of the interesting aspects of the restructuring of the hominid supralaryngeal vocal tract, which I will discuss later, is that it yields the ability to produce nonnasal sounds.

VOCAL TRACT NORMALIZATION

If formant frequency patterns are once removed from the physical attributes of the speech signal, their linguistic interpretation is at least one step more "abstract." Formant frequency patterns are generated by the supralaryngeal vocal tract; the absolute values of formant frequencies thus are a function of the length of the speaker's supralaryngeal airways (Chiba and Kajiyama, 1941; Fant, 1960). The formant frequencies of an [i] produced by a 2-year-old child thus are almost twice as high as those produced by the child's mother, since the length of the child's airway is about half that of the parents' (Goldstein, 1980). The absolute values of the formant frequencies of the "same" sounds produced by different adults also varies (Peterson and Barney, 1952). We come in all sizes, and the length of the supralaryngeal airway is different for different individuals. A stage of perceptual processing in which we normalize, or somehow take account of this fact, is an essential step in the linguistic categorization of speech.

A number of experiments and observations indicate that vocal tract normalization takes place in the perception of speech. The data of the Ladefoged and Broadbent (1957) psychoacoustic experiments, for example, demonstrate that an identical acoustic stimulus, a tape recording of a synthesized vowel of English, will be heard as an [I], an [ɛ], or an [ae] by normal listeners depending on their estimate of the length of the supralaryngeal vocal tract that produced the signal. In the Ladefoged and Broadbent (1957) experiment, a speech synthesizer was used to generate three "carrier" sentences that began with *The word you will hear is.* One carrier sentence had low formant frequencies, another higher formant frequencies, and a third still higher formant frequencies. A token of the vowel [ɛ] synthesized with formant frequencies appropriate for the mid-frequency carrier phrase was heard as an [ɛ] when it was presented to listeners immediately after that sentence. The same stimulus was heard as an [I] when it was heard after the low-frequency value carrier sentence and as an [ae] after the high-frequency value carrier sentence.

The basis for the listener's decisions is apparent if we consider the variations in formant frequency that characterize the same vowel for speakers who have different lengths of supralaryngeal vocal tract. In Figure 7-5 I have reproduced the Peterson and Barney (1952) plot of the first and second formant frequencies of the vowels produced by seventy-six adult male, adult female, and adolescent male and female speakers. The vowel symbols are plotted with respect to the absolute values of their first and second formant frequencies. The vowels were

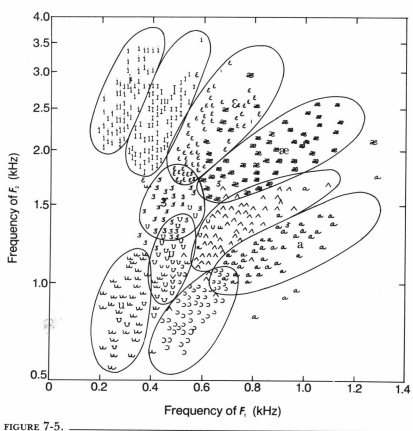

FIGURE 7-5.
Plot of first and second formant frequencies derived by Peterson
and Barney (1952) for the vowels produced by seventy-six different
speakers. The frequency of F_2 is plotted with respect to the ordi-
nate for each vowel token; the frequency of F_1, with respect to the
abcissa. The loops enclose 90 percent of the tokens produced for
each of the vowel categories of English by the speakers.

tokens derived from spectrograms of the speakers' reading of a list of
English words of the form *heed, hid, head,* and so on. The word initial
[h] resulted in noise excitation of the vowel that facilitates the mea-
surement of formant frequencies from spectrograms. The words were
all identified by listeners in a procedure wherein the words of ten
different speakers were presented in random order to the listeners. A
listener thus would not know whose voice or what word was coming

next. The loops on the plot enclose the vowel tokens that made up 90 percent of the tokens in each class. Note that there is overlap on the plot even though the 10 percent of the stimuli that overlapped most are *not* plotted. The data thus show that a sound intended by one speaker as an [ɛ] has the formant frequencies of another speaker's [I]. The plot in Figure 7-6, which is from Nearey (1978), perhaps makes the effect clearer. Nearey has plotted the averages of formant frequency for F_1 and F_2 that Peterson and Barney (1952) derived for their adult male, adult female, and adolescent speakers. Nearey has converted the plots of formant frequencies to a logarithmic scale. I have entered the stimulus marked "V" in Nearey's diagram. If a listener heard this stimulus and thought that it was being produced by a child, it would fall into the range of child [I]'s. If the listener instead thought that the stimulus V had been produced by an adult female, it would fall into the class of female [ɛ]'s.

The Supervowel [i]

The identification of vowels in relation to normalization is explored systematically in the work of Nearey (1978). Nearey notes several aspects of normalization. It is obvious that human listeners do not have to hear a complete sentence in order to arrive at an estimate of the hypothetical length of a speaker's vocal tract. The perceptual data of Peterson and Barney (1952), for example, involve the identification of isolated words by panels of listeners. Thus if vocal tract normalization were a psychologically "real" stage in the perception of speech, there must be some acoustic cues in the speech signal for normalization. The Peterson and Barney (1952) data yield an insight into the nature of some of these cues. The data of their speech perception experiment show that virtually all the [i] vowels produced by the speakers were identified as [i]'s by the listeners. There were only two errors out of over 10,000 trials. The [u]'s were subject to slight confusion; other vowels showed high error rates; for example, [ɛ] and [I] were confused 5 percent of the time. The vowels [i] and [u] thus might be perceptual anchor points for vocal tract normalization. If that were the case, it should be possible to build an automaton that would identify tokens of vowels, that is, assign acoustic signals to the phonetic categories intended by their speakers, in terms of acoustic cues derived from the vowels [i] and [u]. The algorithm developed by Gerstman (1968) in which normalization coefficients are derived from the F_1 and F_2 of a speaker's [i] and [u] is an example of a possible automaton. The Gerstman algorithm, however, in effect claims that a

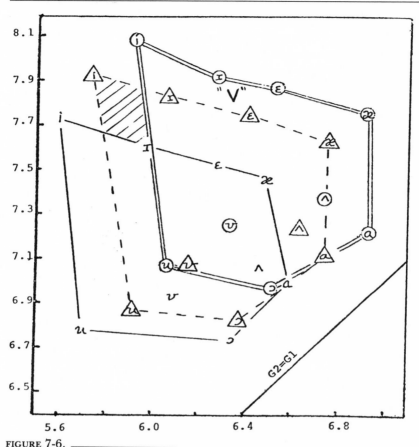

FIGURE 7-6.
Average values of formant frequencies derived by Peterson and
Barney for adult male speakers, adult female speakers (vowel points
enclosed by triangles), and adolescents (vowel symbols enclosed by
circles). The frequency values have been plotted on logarithmic
scales. The vowel points of each class of speakers are connected and
form relative vowel spaces. Note that the vowel spaces for the adult
females and the adolescents are transposed upward in frequency
from the vowel space of the adult males. (After Nearey, 1978.)

listener must defer her or his judgment of a vowel's identity until tokens that are known to be examples of [i] and [u] are heard for a given speaker. The CLIH algorithm developed by Nearey (1978) yields a solution that is more consistent with the perceptual responses of human listeners so long as it deals with a given language or dialect (Disner, 1980).

Nearey's (1978) CLIH normalization algorithm, in essence, claims that all the vowels produced by a given speaker can be assigned to their intended phonetic categories *if* the listener is provided with a token of at least one identified vowel. The CLIH algorithm is fairly simple, as it involves a linear rescaling of all formant frequencies; all the formant frequencies are divided by a constant that is equal to the ratio between a standard-length vocal tract's formant frequency pattern for a particular vowel and a token of that vowel for the speaker in question. Nearey further notes that the [i] vowels of all speakers are, in effect, always identifiable as [i]'s by virtue of their particular formant frequency patterns. The plot in Figure 7-6 illustrates this effect. Note that the formant frequency patterns of vowels in the interior of the vowel space overlap in the plot of the adult male, adult female, and adolescent averages. Vowels on the lower right boundary of the vowel space also can overlap; note that the adult males' and adolescents' [a] and [ɔ] overlap. The overlaps are consistent with the perceptual confusions that listeners made in the Peterson and Barney (1952) vowel study; for instance, [a] and [ɔ] confusions are quite common in their data. The only vowel that has a formant pattern that inherently cannot be confused with a token in some other vowel class is [i]. The [i] vowels of different speakers form the extreme upper left margin of the vowel space plotted for different-sized supralaryngeal vocal tracts. Nearey (1978) thus predicts that a token of a formant frequency pattern that specifies an [i] will always be heard as an [i] produced by a supralaryngeal vocal tract that has a particular effective length.

Nearey (1978, pp. 98–149) tests this hypothesis by means of a psychoacoustic experiment in which a listener hears a formant frequency pattern that corresponds either to an [i] produced by an adult male's relatively long supralaryngeal vocal tract or to an [i] produced by a child's shorter supralaryngeal vocal tract. Juxtaposed with the [i]'s are two formant patterns that range over almost the total possible range of vowels for adult speakers and children older than 7 years. The listeners were told to identify the vowel that they heard in comparison with their own dialect of American English. They were also asked to rate the naturalness of each [i-V] combination that they heard (where V = the vowel corresponding to the varying formant frequency patterns). There were four categories of "naturalness judgment," from "OK" to "very bad." The listeners' responses were consistent with the hypothesis that they derived "normalizing" information from the [i]'s.

Figure 7-7 shows the overall shift in the listeners' responses for the two conditions in terms of a "predominance boundary" plot. The phonetic symbols connected by lines represent the boundaries at which listeners identified formant frequency patterns as particular vowels. The boundaries for the tokens presented with the [i] of a longer vocal tract are connected with a solid line; those for the [i] from a shorter vocal tract, with a dashed line. Note that there is a general shift throughout the vowel space. The listeners clearly categorize the vowel formant frequency patterns that they hear in terms of the presumed length of the supralaryngeal vocal tract corresponding to the "carrier" [i]. The boundary for the vowel [ɛ], for example, shifts from F_2's of 2 kHz to F_2's of 2.5 kHz. The "naturalness" ratings that the listeners made also are consistent with the premise that they set up their expectations of the speech signal that they are listening to in terms of the range of formant frequency variation appropriate for a particular supralaryngeal vocal tract. Formant frequency patterns that are identified as "OK" tokens when presented with the shorter-length vocal tract [i] are identified as "very bad" when they are presented with the longer vocal tract [i] because they are outside of the formant frequency range of the presumed longer supralaryngeal vocal tract.

The effects of vocal tract normalization on speech perception have been noted in other psychoacoustic experiments. May (1976), for example, notes a shift in the boundary for the identification of the fricatives (s) and (š). The center frequency of the frictional (turbulent noise) portion of synthesized stimuli were shifted in ten steps from 2974 Hz to 4455 Hz. The boundary shifted to higher frequencies for the stimuli produced with an [ae] vowel corresponding to a shorter-length supralaryngeal vocal tract. Rand (1971) obtains similar results for the formant transition boundaries for the stop consonant pairs [b] versus [d] and [d] versus [g]. The results of experiments using adaptation paradigms again show the special status of the vowel [i], which appears to act as an optimum signal for keying vocal tract normalization (Morse, Kass, and Turkienicz, 1976; Sawusch and Nusbaum, 1979; Sawusch, Nusbaum, and Schwab, 1980). Studies of the effects of tongue movements on formant frequency patterns are consistent with the vowel [i]'s having a special status. The experiments of Fujimura and Kakita (in press) show the relative insensitivity of the formant pattern of [i] to changes in the magnitude of muscle contraction. The vowel [i]

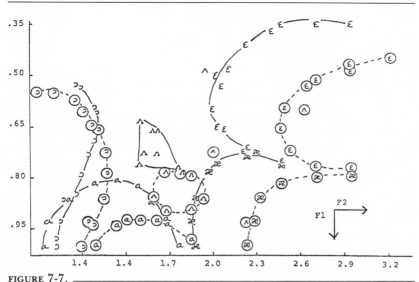

FIGURE 7-7.
Shift in listener's categorizations of synthesized vowel stimuli when
they heard the stimuli after the [i] vowel of either a long or a short
supralaryngeal vocal tract (circled symbols). Note that the identification boundaries shift upward in frequency for the short vocal tract
condition. (After Nearey, 1978.)

thus is less susceptible than other vowels to variation that follows from
differences in overall muscular effort. The consistently more reliable
identification of the vowel [i] in speech perception experiments that
occurs when isolated vowels are presented, or when tokens from
speakers who have different-sized vocal tracts are presented in random sequences, probably follows from this special status of [i]. The
vowel [u], as Nearey (1978) notes, also serves as a vocal tract size-cali-
brating signal, though to a lesser degree. The data of speech perception experiments again consistently show that [u]'s are identified more
reliably than other vowels, except [i] (Peterson and Barney, 1952; Bond,
1976; Fairbanks and Grubb, 1961; Ryalls and Lieberman, 1982; Fowler and
Shankweiler, 1978; Strange et al., 1976; Pisoni, Carrell, and Simnick, 1979).

CUES FOR NORMALIZATION

There has been some debate over the nature of the acoustic cues that
enable a listener to calculate the probable length of the supralaryngeal
vocal tract being heard. Several studies (Strange et al., 1976; Verbrugge,

Strange, and Shankweiler, 1976; Fowler and Shankweiler, 1978) have claimed that the primary cue for normalization is the acoustic patterning of consonantal formant transitions. These experiments contrasted the identification of isolated vowels with that of vowels presented in the environment of consonants, such as [pVp]. The vowels were identified more reliably when presented in consonantal environments. These effects, however, appear to follow from the relative facility with which phonetically untrained listeners can transcribe stimuli that correspond to English words, such as *pip, pup, poop*, versus isolated vowels (Kahn, 1978; Assmann, 1979; Pisoni, Carrell, and Simnick, 1979).

Human listeners probably make use of whatever cues are available to infer the probable length of a speaker's supralaryngeal vocal tract. For example, if the identity of a vowel is *known*, a listener can derive the length of the vocal tract that would have produced it. Thus vowels like [I] or [ae] and [ʊ], which are not as inherently specified for supralaryngeal vocal tract length (Lieberman et al., 1972; Gerstman, 1968; Nearey, 1978), can yield more reliable identification by serving as known normalization calibration signals (Verbrugge, Strange, and Shankweiler, 1976). The general occurrence of stereotyped opening phrases like *Hello, Hi, Hej* (in Swedish), which are "necessary" elements in telephone conversations, may follow from their role in providing normalization signals. A listener hearing these openers knows the intended phonetic targets; thus any stereotyped opener can serve as a calibrating signal for vocal tract normalization. However, there again seems to be a tendency to use the point vowels [i] and [u] in these openers.

THE NEURAL BASIS OF NORMALIZATION

One point should be stressed in regard to any claims that I appear to be making regarding the psychological reality of perceptual processes like vocal tract normalization. The implementation of these processes in the central nervous system clearly does not involve a computational process in which the listener derives any conscious knowledge of the size of the supralaryngeal vocal tract which is producing a speech signal. However, it is also clear that the sounds of speech cannot be identified, that is, placed into the phonetic categories that a speaker intended, unless the listener somehow takes account of the length of the speaker's supralaryngeal vocal tract. That the process takes place at an unconscious level need not surprise us; a similar process takes place when we identify images. We compensate for the size of the image that is projected on our retina when we identify someone's face. However, the principles that underlie the process whereby we compensate for distance as we identify visual data also are not part of our conscious experience. The discovery of the laws of perspective is comparatively recent. We have to be taught how to draw scenes with a "natural" perspective that takes into account the effects of distance on visual images. Infants, however, obviously have these principles built in; they learn to identify their mother's face, for example, without having to be taught to compensate for the effects of distance. Artists in the twelfth century likewise could "see" how far they were from a building; they had the appropriate internal algorithm that takes distance into account in making decisions concerning visual images. However, they did not consciously apply these principles when they painted. Similarly, the neural implementation of perceptual processes like vocal tract normalization or formant frequency extraction need not involve active computations like the analysis-by-synthesis procedure of Bell and colleagues (1961) or Nearey's (1978) CLIH computation, wherein the absolute values of an input formant frequency pattern are converted to a logarithmic scale and shifted to a "standard" template that defines the vowel space of a particular dialect. These computational processes conserve memory space in a computer at the expense of algebraic computations and sequential steps. They in effect trade memory space for sequential computations. The results that, for example, follow from the analysis-by-synthesis formant frequency "extractor" (Bell et al., 1978) could be derived from a process in which the input signal was simultaneously compared against the spectra that result from all possible combinations of F_1, F_2, and F_3 patterns using an ensemble of templates in a parallel operation that would save computational time. Each template of the ensemble would correspond to a possible vowel spectrum. The template that best matched the input spectrum would be selected by a decision-making process that simultaneously looked at the match in all the templates and selected the best fit. The parallel process would use much more memory than the analysis-by-synthesis process. The memory would equal the total number of possible combinations of F_1, F_2, and F_3. However, the system would not have to wait for an internal computer to systematically run through all possible combinations of F_1, F_2, and F_3 and calculate the difference between each computed combination and the input pattern signal. The relevant point about either the analysis-by-synthesis process or the parallel process, in the context of this discussion, is that both processes extract formant frequencies by using detailed information of the specific constraints of speech production. Both processes "know" that speech signals are generated by acoustic sources that are filtered by supralaryngel airways — specifically that vowels are generated by a periodic laryngeal source filtered by an all-pole network (Fant, 1960).

SUMMARY

The encoded nature of human speech yields special properties: a functional advantage in the high rate of speech compared with other acoustic signals and matched perceptual systems. Speech research with devices like the VOCODER, which was developed in the 1930s for telephone systems, enabled systematic experiments to proceed in which the acoustic cues that specify speech could be synthesized. Psychoacoustic experiments demonstrated that it is impossible to segment phonetic elements that correspond to the letters of the alphabet from the speech signal. Speech is instead "encoded" in a process that melds acoustic cues together in roughly syllable-sized segments. This allows human speech to transmit linguistic data at rates of 20 to 30 phonetic segments per second; we otherwise would be limited to rates of 7 elements per second.

The process of human speech perception appears to involve matched neural devices that extract formant frequency patterns from the acoustic signal. Formant frequency patterns appear to have a psychological reality, though they are not actually directly present in the speech signal that we hear. We act as though we calculate formant frequency patterns, using built-in knowledge about the possible acoustic characteristics of human speech. Traditional motor theories, as well as template theories, embody this claim. We also take into account the probable length of a human speaker's supralaryngeal vocal tract when we assign phonetic labels to formant frequency patterns. The process of vocal tract normalization is general; all speech signals necessarily must be normalized to take into account the differences in supralaryngeal vocal tract length that typify different human speakers. Psychoacoustic data show that certain speech sounds furnish acoustic cues that can direct the process of vocal tract normalization. The vowel [i] is an optimum cue for normalization.

CHAPTER 8
Linguistic Distinctions and Auditory Processes

THOUGH I BELIEVE THAT THE weight of evidence is consistent with the presence in human beings of neural mechanisms matched to the acoustic characteristics of human speech, it obviously must be the case that the initial stages of vocal communication in archaic hominids must have been based on neural mechanisms that are more general. The linguistic distinctions that occurred in our ancestors' speech probably were structured in terms of auditory mechanisms that are more general and that probably occur in many other animals. The model that I propose for the evolution of the species-specific neural mechanisms that make human speech special starts with vocal communication based on both the sound-producing capability that can be found in modern closely related animals like apes and the auditory mechanisms that can be found in these and other living animals. The anatomical and neural speech production and perception mechanisms that are species-specific to present-day human beings are the result of natural selection for enhanced vocal communication from this base. There would have been no selective advantage for the retention of fairly complex neural mechanisms matched to the species-specific aspects of human speech if some form of vocal communication had not already existed.

It is appropriate to note at this point that many of the linguistic distinctions conveyed by human speech are not so indirectly related to the acoustic signal as are the perception and categorization of formant frequency patterns. Clearly many of these linguistic distinctions may be structured in terms of the auditory mechanisms that are found in other animals. The continued presence of these linguistic distinctions reinforces the case for the gradual evolution of many aspects of human speech, starting from the auditory base that is present in all mammals. The perception of linguistic stress, for example, involves the integrating properties of the auditory system (Lifschitz, 1933). Both

169

the amplitude and the duration of a vowel are salient acoustic cues that determine where we hear "primary word lexical stress" in words like *rebel* (the noun) versus *rebel* (the verb). Analytic studies in which the duration and amplitude of the acoustic signal were measured (Jones, 1932; Lieberman, 1960) and perceptual studies using synthesized speech (Fry, 1958) show that these two parameters interact to yield the linguistic percept of lexical stress. Lifschitz (1933) showed that the perceived loudness of sinusoidal tones is a function of the integral of their amplitude with respect to time for durations under 500 msec. Since the duration of vowels in connected speech generally ranges from about 100 msec to 350 msec, our perception of lexical stress is structured by this auditory process.

In this regard some studies (Kuhl, 1981) differentiate between perceptual mechanisms that hypothetically are involved *only* in speech perception and perceptual mechanisms that structure all aspects of audition. I think that the distinction between *auditory* and *speech* mechanisms perhaps is more significant if we differentiate between speech mechanisms that have *evolved* for the specific end of facilitating vocal communication and auditory mechanisms subject to the general constraints of audition that do not reflect the selective pressure of communication. The distinction can be tricky since particular linguistically relevant sound contrasts may have evolved in human languages to take advantage of auditory mechanisms. It is also possible that some of the responses of human listeners to nonspeech sounds are, in turn, structured by neural mechanisms that initially evolved to facilitate the perception of speech. The emotive quality of sounds in a poetic framework, for example, may follow from the properties of the vowel space (Mandelker, 1982). However, some aspects of communication in human beings and other animals clearly reflect the presence of neural mechanisms that are specific to communication.

VOICE-ONSET-TIME AND AUDITORY PERCEPTUAL MECHANISMS

The perception of voice-onset-time distinctions (Lisker and Abramson, 1964) is an interesting example of a linguistically relevant distinction which appears to be structured in terms of an auditory mechanism that is present in many, if not all, mammals. However, though the linguistic distinctions conveyed by voice-onset-time distinctions often follow from acoustic signals that can be classified by means of an auditory mechanism, in other instances the linguistic distinction involves acoustic signals that appear to be perceptually interpreted by neural mechanisms matched to the particular acoustic characteristics of *speech*.

The voice-onset-time (VOT) cues that differentiate sounds like [p] from [b] in the English words *pin* and *bin* usually can be directly related to the presence or absence of periodic excitation in the speech waveform. Stop sounds like [p], [b], [t], and [d] are produced by a speaker's momentarily obstructing his or her supralaryngeal airway. For the labial sounds [p] and [b], the closure is effected by the speaker's lips. Alveolars like [t] and [d] are made by closing the airway with the tongue blade; velars like [k] and [g] involve obstructing the airway with the tongue body. On the release of the obstruction, air flows through the supralaryngeal airway. The acoustic consequence of the release is a burst of sound energy, which can usually be seen in the waveform of the acoustic speech signal. The voiced stops [b], [d], and [g] of English have periodic excitation present within 25 msec after the release of the stop. In their voiceless counterparts [p], [t], and [k], periodic excitation occurs after 25 msec. The linguistic distinction thus can usually be directly related to the presence or absence of a physical property of the acoustic signal.

Many independent studies of perceptual experiments with adult human listeners (Abramson and Lisker, 1970), human infants (Eimas et al., 1971), chinchillas (Kuhl and Miller, 1974, 1978; Kuhl, 1981), and monkeys (Waters and Wilson, 1976) show that listeners who are asked to partition sounds that differ *minimally* along the VOT dimension in terms of when periodic excitation occurs form two classes. Sounds that have VOTs of less than 25 msec form one class. This includes the English stop consonants [b], [d], and [g]. Sounds that have VOTs greater than 25 msec — for example, the English stop consonants [p], [t], and [k] — form the other class. The partitioning of sounds that differ with respect to the timing of periodic excitation into two classes at the 25-msec point also holds when human listeners are asked to form categories for nonspeech sounds (Pisoni, 1977). The effect probably follows from the properties of the mammalian auditory system (Hirsch and Sherrick, 1961; Lieberman, 1975; Kuhl, 1981). The VOT decision depends on a listener's being able to tell whether voicing occurred after the release burst of a stop consonant. The psycho-acoustic experiments of Hirsch and Sherrick (1961) show that 25 msec is the shortest interval that can separate two different acoustic signals for which human listeners can reliably make this decision. The strategy that a VOT-categorizing automaton could use for these acoustic signals would be fairly simple. The automaton would place signals in which voicing and the burst were coincident or had a short lag in one category. This category would include the English stops [b], [d], and [g]. Signals in which voicing occurred after the burst would form a second, long-lag category that would include the English stops [p], [t], and [k]. The automaton could potentially form a third category in which voicing occurred before the burst. This category is not the basis of a phonemic distinction in English, but it occurs in many other languages (Lisker and Abramson, 1964) and includes, for example, the Spanish "prevoiced" stops [b], [d], and [g]. The decisions of our hypothetical automaton would be structured by the 25-msec limit on the time resolution of the mammalian auditory system, which in effect sets up the "window" for the three VOT categories.

I have used the word *structure* to describe the probable consequence of this characteristic of the mammalian auditory system — its 25-msec time resolution — because the linguistic situation is not quite so simple. The acoustic signals that investigators like Kuhl (1981) uses in her experiments are simplified versions of human speech that have been generated by speech synthesizers. These simplified acoustic signals differ *only* with respect to the timing of periodic excitation. The speech signals that human beings generate and listen to are not that simple. Acoustic analyses show that human listeners can differentiate stop sounds that have identical VOTs by using the acoustic information that is carried in the bursts. Moslin (1979), for example, shows that speakers produce long-lag [t]'s that have short VOTs of less than 25 msec. The amplitude of the bursts of these [t]'s is, however, higher than that of a [d]. Listeners hear these stops as normal [t]'s; the amplitude of the burst is a sufficient acoustic cue. Moslin's data are derived from discourse — speech addressed to 70-week-old children by their mothers as well as their mothers' speech to other adults. In the speech directed to young children, some mothers seem to produce "hypercorrect" stop consonants that are clearly differentiated either by VOT or by means of the amplitude of their bursts (Moslin, 1979).

The cue value of burst amplitude may follow from a *speech*-perceiving mechanism adapted to the archetypal pattern for the production of stop consonants by human speakers. The burst of a long-lag VOT stop will, all other things being equal, have a higher amplitude than the burst of a short-lag stop. This follows from the fact that the vocal cords are open on the release of a long-lag stop. The larger glottal opening will allow a greater airflow through the supralaryngeal vocal tract on the stop's release; the greater airflow is more likely to produce a higher burst amplitude (Flanagan et al., 1970; Lieberman, 1977b). The Moslin (1979) data thus show a matched scheme for the production and perception of stops. Speakers produce either a long VOT or a higher burst amplitude, or both, for stops like [t]. A higher burst amplitude usually is concomitant with a long VOT, but a speaker can generate a higher burst amplitude with a short VOT. The higher burst amplitude serves as a *sufficient* cue that identifies the stop as a [t]. Human listeners thus respond either to VOT or to the burst amplitude by using a recognition routine that is *matched* to the manner in which human speakers produce these stop consonants, though it is *structured* by a generalized auditory mechanism.

The linguistic distinction that results in a stop consonant's being heard as a [p] versus a [b] or as a [t] versus a [d] can also be cued by either the amplitude of the aspiration noise that follows the burst (Repp et al., 1978) or the duration of the vowel that precedes the consonant. Human infants also can categorize stop consonants into [p] versus [b] and [t] versus [d] by using the relative duration of the vowel that precedes the consonant relative to the duration of the syllable (Miller, 1981). The infants take into account the rate of speech. Their ability to make this decision is probably the result of innate, genetically transmitted perceptual mechanisms rather than their experience with speech since they differentiate these stimuli before their fourth month of life. The perceptual automaton that we would have to build to classify stop consonants using these acoustic cues would again exemplify a motor theory for speech perception since these cues are concomitant with the archetypal production of stop consonants. Both higher aspiration noise and shorter vowel duration follow from the larger opening of the larynx at the release of stops like [p], [t], and [k] (Klatt, Stevens, and Mead, 1968; Klatt, 1976). The evolution of the neural device or devices that underlie the linguistic categorization of stop sounds with respect to VOT might have initially been based on the mammalian *auditory* system's time resolution. However, the process of natural selection appears to have produced a *speech*-perceiving system that is matched to the constraints of speech production. The speech-perceiving system for VOT operates in terms of the full set of acoustic cues that are generated when people produce these stop consonant distinctions.

CATEGORICAL PERCEPTION

One of the effects noted by the Haskins Laboratories group in their early experiments on the perception of speech was that many of the linguistically salient distinctions were perceived in a categorical mode. The voice-onset-time and place-of-articulation distinctions for stop consonants that we have been discussing were thus perceived. Human beings normally are much better at discriminating stimuli than they are at identifying them. A brief example will illustrate the effect. Suppose that we perform the following hypothetical experiment using a set of color samples that involve small as well as great differences in hue, saturation, and brightness. We obtain the inventory of lipstick colors of a department store and remove the labels. We assemble a panel of observers. The task of the observers is to identify and relabel the lipsticks under the following constraint: each lipstick is presented in isolation to the panel of observers. The observers will have to name all the different types of lipsticks and sort them. What will the result be? A mess. The observers will not be able to remember the categories that they set up as the "attempt to identify" the various shades of lipstick. Different samples of the same shade will be placed in different categories; different shades will be identified in a given category. Reliable identifications can be obtained only if the observers are content to establish a small set of general categories. In contrast, if we instead perform a discrimination test, the results will be quite different. A discrimination test with lipstick colors would involve taking two samples at a time from the set of lipsticks and asking the observers whether the two samples are the same or not. All the lipsticks probably will be reliably discriminated if our observers have normal color vision. Experiments in which observers had to discriminate and identify acoustic stimuli that differed in the dimensions of frequency, amplitude, and duration (Pollack, 1952) show that human observers generally cannot reliably identify more than five to nine categories along a single dimension. In contrast, they can discriminate between hundreds of stimuli along these acoustic dimensions. George Miller (1956), in a provocative paper, "The Magical Number Seven, Plus or Minus Two," showed that the effect is general and that it probably reflects some basic properties of our sensory and cognitive capacity.

The phenomenon that is termed "categorical perception" was first noted in connection with the identification and discrimination of stop consonants. The experiments are fairly simple. An experiment investigating the perception of place of articulation for stop consonants could have the following form (Liberman, 1970). A set of synthetic speech stimuli that vary with respect to the starting point of the transition of the second formant frequency are prepared. In Figure 8-1 the set of formant frequency transitions is sketched. The second formant frequency transition of stimulus 0 starts at 1.600 kHz; stimulus +1, at 1.685 kHz; stimulus +2 at 1.770 kHz. The stimuli are presented to listeners in two listening tests. In one test the listeners are asked to discriminate between the pairs of adjacent stimuli, such as stimuli 0 and +1 or stimuli +1 and +2. The task is a simple discrimination judgment; the stimuli are presented in triplets in an *ABX* format where the listener is asked to state whether token *X* is the same as stimulus *A* or *B*. In the identification test each stimulus is presented

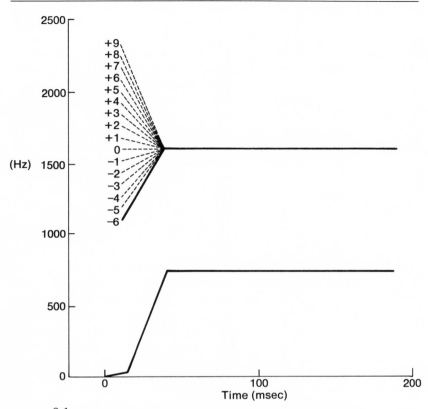

FIGURE 8-1.
Schematic representation of two formant frequency patterns that,
when used to control a speech synthesizer, will produce the sounds
[bæ], [dæ], and [gæ]. The numbers −6 through +9 show the
starting points of the different stimuli that result when starting at
these particular values of F_2. (Adapted from Liberman, 1970.)

in isolation in a random sequence; the listeners are asked to identify
the entire set of stimuli. Since these synthesized stimuli are modeled
on the formant frequency patterns of the English CV (consonant-
vowel) syllables [ba], [da], and [ga], they are asked to identify the
stimuli by using these phonetic labels.

The results were that in the identification experiment the listeners usually did not hear any sounds that were between a [ba] and a
[da] or between a [da] and a [ga]. The responses of a listener in a
typical identification experiment are plotted in Figure 8-2. The horizontal scale shows the starting points of the stimuli sketched in Figure

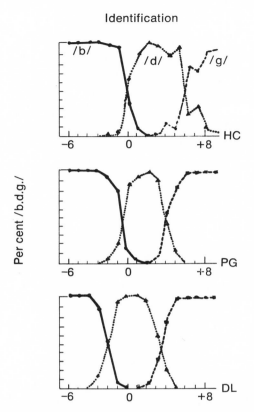

FIGURE 8-2.
Identification functions of three listeners, HC, PG, and DL, to the synthesized stimuli schematized in Figure 8-1. (Adapted from Liberman, 1970.)

8-1. The vertical scale shows the percentage of the time that each stimulus was identified as a [ba], a [da], or a [ga]. Note that the identification abruptly shifts from one category to another. In Figure 8-3 the responses of the same listener (Liberman, 1970) are presented for the discrimination test that was run with these same stimuli. The percentage of the time that the listener was able to discriminate between two adjacent stimuli is plotted on the vertical axis. If the results of the discrimination test for these speechlike stimuli were like the discrimination of acoustic stimuli other than the sounds of speech, the discrimination function would be a straight line at or near 100

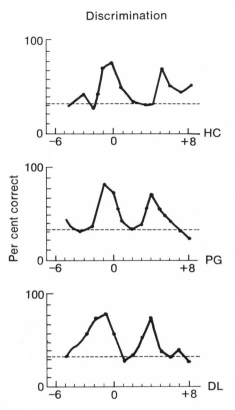

FIGURE 8-3. _____

Discrimination functions of three listeners to the synthesized stimuli
schematized in Figure 8-1. (Adapted from Liberman, 1970.)

percent. But it is not; the listener is guessing, that is, performing at the
chance level of 50 percent except at points along the horizontal scale
near the identification boundaries of Figure 8-2. The listener is not
able to discriminate any better than in the identification test that
requires placing the stimuli in different categories. In other words,
listeners are not able to tell the difference between different [ba]'s no
matter how hard they listen to them in the *ABX* discrimination experiment.

The phenomenon of categorical speech perception is very odd in
the context of our ability to make fine discriminations between other
stimuli. In our hypothetical lipstick discrimination experiment the

observers were able to discriminate between shades of red that they had put into the "same" category in the identification experiment. The same results obtain in actual experiments involving auditory stimuli. Listeners, for example, can reliably differentiate between pure tones that are 5 Hz apart from each other in an *ABX* discrimination test, though these tones are placed in the "same" category in an identification test. The two psychological tasks are quite different. In an auditory discrimination test the listener's task is simply to compare two signals that are presented in the same temporal frame. In an identification test the listener has to remember the salient characteristics of the auditory categories that he or she is setting up and place each new stimulus into the appropriate category. It is therefore surprising to find that listeners cannot differentiate between the four stimuli in the [ba] category in Figure 8-1. The start of the second formant transition that specifies these four [ba]'s is 100 Hz apart for each stimulus. These same listeners can differentiate between pure tones that differ by 5 Hz. Why cannot they differentiate between these [ba]'s?

The situation is all the more odd in that only some speech sounds are categorically perceived. Vowel sounds, for example, tend to behave like nonspeech auditory signals. Listeners are able to discriminate vowels within their identification categories. For example, though listeners may place a set of five different formant frequency patterns within their [I] category in an identification test, they can reliably differentiate between these different [I]'s in a discrimination test. In contrast, different [b]'s all sound the same. The different [I]'s, in other words, all sound slightly different though they are all appropriate [I]'s. Different theories were proposed that attempted to account for the categorical perception of the stop consonants. Fujisaki and Kawashima (1968), for example, suggested that the phenomenon followed from the short duration of the second formant frequency transition. Lane (1965) proposed a theory, framed in terms of Skinnerian reinforcement theory, that claimed that categorical perception was a "training effect." However, the best account for the phenomenon of categorical perception follows from the neural mechanisms that are involved in the perception of speech. Categorical perception occurs, for example, in the discrimination of speech stimuli that differ with respect to voice onset time. Although human listeners (Carney, Wilden, and Viemeister, 1977) and chinchillas (Kuhl, 1981) can discriminate between stimuli whose VOTs differ by 10 msec throughout the range of VOTs typical of speech, there is a peak in the discrimination function at the point of the phonetic boundary that differentiates sounds like [d] and [t] in identification experiments. This phonetic boundary, as I noted earlier, probably reflects an auditory mechanism. Chinchillas are members of the simplest class of mammals — rodents. The similar behavior of humans and chinchillas in response to stimuli that differ with respect to VOT leads Kuhl to propose that auditory mechanisms "provide a selective pressure on the phonetic oppositions used by the world's languages" (1981, p. 340).

Kuhl interprets the data of experiments that explore the perception of place-of-articulation cues by nonhuman animals to support the claim that *all* the phonetic oppositions of human language follow from auditory mechanisms. This clearly is not the case for the VOT distinctions that human listeners make on the basis of burst amplitude, aspiration amplitude, and vowel duration. The categorical perception of the formant frequency transitions that can cue place of articulation for stop consonants also does not appear to depend on an auditory mechanism. If the categorical perception of place of articulation followed from auditory mechanisms, we might expect to find similar discrimination functions for human and nonhuman listeners. However, the categorical discrimination functions for humans and for the only nonhuman animals yet tested, rhesus monkeys, differ. Whereas human infants do *not* discriminate between stimuli that differ with respect to formant transition patterns that are within a phonetic category (Eimas, 1974; Morse, 1976), rhesus monkeys are able to discriminate between these "within-category" stimuli (Sinnott, 1974; Morse and Snowden, 1975).

One of the intriguing possibilities raised by Kuhl's perceptual experiments with chinchillas is whether their natural vocal communications make use of VOT distinctions. Chinchillas have a vocal apparatus that can produce signals that differ with respect to the interval between the release of a stop and the start of phonation. Whether they produce vocal signals that convey meaningful information in their communications is an open question. Animals like apes likewise can produce stop consonants that differ with respect to VOT. Again, ethological studies have not addressed this question, which would shed some light on the possible form of the earliest stages of hominid vocal communication.

THE PERCEPTION OF CONSONANTAL PLACE OF ARTICULATION: A MATCHED SYSTEM

The explanation for the categorical perception of consonantal place of articulation in *Homo sapiens* which makes most sense to me is that it reflects the presence of neural mechanisms that represent a "match" with the constraints of the human supralaryngeal vocal tract. As I noted earlier, the motor theory of speech perception developed by the Haskins Laboratories research group (Liberman et al., 1967) accounted for the perception of an "identical" [d] in stimuli like those schematized in Figure 7-2. The Haskins theory noted that placing the tongue blade in the [d] position before either an [i] or a [u] vowel will yield two different formant frequency transition patterns. We hear these two patterns as the same [d] sound, the theory claims, because we have neural mechanisms that embody this knowledge of the constraints of human speech production. In other words, we have *speech*-perceiving neural mechanisms that, like a frog's, are matched to the physiologic constraints of our sound-producing system. The filter functions of the supralaryngeal vocal tract are similar when a speaker forms the initial [d]'s of the syllables [di] and [du] by moving the tongue against the palate (Perkell, 1969). The filter function is, however, quite different for the vowels [i] and [u]. The formant transitions thus are quite different for the syllables since they start from approximately the same starting point and go to different end points. According to the original Haskins motor theory of speech perception, human listeners hear identical [d]'s because they decode the speech signal in terms of this implicit knowledge of the manner in which speech is produced.

The Haskins theory (Liberman et al., 1967) implied that the decoding process involved active computations: the listener hypothetically matched the incoming speech signal against an internally generated signal. The process was not very different from the analysis-by-synthesis model of Halle and Stevens (1959), which was implemented in the formant frequency "extractor" computer program of Bell and colleagues (1961). However, the process could also be implemented by means of a "template" model in which the formant frequency patterns of all admissible syllable forms of a given language or dialect could be stored in a larger memory. The memory requirements of an active template model in which incoming speech signals were matched against an inventory of all possible syllable forms would be greater, but computational speed would be faster. I will return to the question of template versus active computational models for speech perception.

One of the deficiencies of the Haskins motor theory was that it did not explain why speech perception should be categorical. There were some vague claims that the articulatory gestures involved in speech are discrete. That is true to a very limited degree since labial stop consonants are, of course, effected by the lips, whereas other stop consonants — alveolars, dentals, velars — are generated by means of tongue maneuvers. The claim was made that different parts of the tongue are used for alveolars and velars. The tongue blade effects the constrictions that are necessary for the production of dentals and alveolars, whereas the tongue body is active in the production of velars. However, that does not really explain why velars are generated by means of an obstruction at the midpoint of the supralaryngeal vocal tract or why the tongue blade generates an obstruction at the points of articulation that are actually used in the production of dentals and alveolars. Cineradiographic studies of the motion of the tongue like those made at Haskins Laboratories in the 1960s, for example, show that the tongue can generate an obstruction at any point along the hard palate. Why then do the languages of the world make use of a limited number of places of consonantal articulation? Why do these places of articulation correspond to the discrete categories that are evident in the response patterns of 1-to-3-month-old human infants?

The answer I think rests in a match that has occurred through the process of natural selection between some of the neural mechanisms that we use in perceiving speech and some of the functional, physiologic properties of the human supralaryngeal vocal tract. These physiologic properties are discussed by Stevens (1972) in his "quantal" theory. Stevens demonstrates that the locations at which human languages most often generate the obstructions of stop consonants yield formant frequency patterns that have certain advantages as acoustic signals. In Figure 8-4 I have sketched a stylized model of the supralaryngeal vocal tract with an extreme constriction. The constriction represents the situation that results a few milliseconds after the release of a stop consonant. There is no anatomical reason why the position of the constriction cannot be shifted to any point along the supralaryngeal vocal tract. Stevens (1972) modeled the formant frequency patterns that would result from shifting a constriction along the supralaryngeal vocal tract. He noted that at certain points there was (1) a convergence of two formant frequencies that (2) furthermore did not change very much as the constriction's position was moved a centimeter forward or backward. Both of these effects yield functional advantages to the sounds that are generated at these locations. The convergence of two formants (1) yields a spectral peak in the filter function of the supralaryngeal vocal tract (Fant, 1956). Signals with distinct spectral peaks, such as the vowel [i], are more reliably perceived. The local insensitivity of the converging formant frequency patterns with respect to the exact position of the constriction (2) likewise yields a functional advantage. The speaker does not have to be precise in positioning the tongue to yield a signal with a

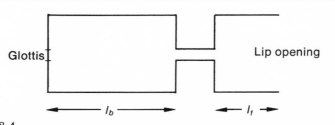

FIGURE 8-4. _____

Stylized model of the supralaryngeal vocal tract showing the
constriction that would occur immediately after the release of a stop
consonant; l_b is the length of the vocal tract behind the constriction, l_f the length before the constriction.

well-defined spectral peak. The plot in Figure 8-5 illustrates the
effect. The curved bars indicate the converging, stable formant frequency patterns that occur at the quantal points of articulation.

The spectral peaks that define these consonantal points of articulation occur quite abruptly, or "quantally," because of the physical
properties of the human supralaryngeal vocal tract and the principles
of acoustics. The result is that there are well-defined locations along
the supralaryngeal vocal tract at which a consonantal constriction (one
that occurs either on the release of a stop or during a fricative) will
yield peaks in the acoustic spectrum. These locations correspond
quite closely to both the points of articulation of traditional phonetic
theory (Bell, 1867) and the articulatory correlates of Prague School
"distinctive features" (Jakobson, Fant, and Halle, 1952). The effects of
categorical perception again reflect the acoustic patterns that correspond to these quantal locations. My claim is that we have acquired, by
the process of natural selection, neural devices that are tuned to
respond to the formant frequency patterns and spectral peaks that
correspond to these quantal places of articulation.

The selective value of quantal signals may perhaps be clarified by
the following example. Suppose that you have to set up a signaling
system and can use either a set of bells or a violin. The set of bells
consists of ten bells that are mounted in a row on a frame. Each bell is
about a foot from the next bell and is tuned so that its characteristic
resonance frequency is at least 200 Hz higher than the bell to its left.
The bell sounds are made by people who hit the bells with mallets.
The "meaningful" bell claps that make up the bell code will be
quantal. A person can either hit a bell or not. If a bell is hit, it will
always produce a characteristic sound. In contrast, violins produce a

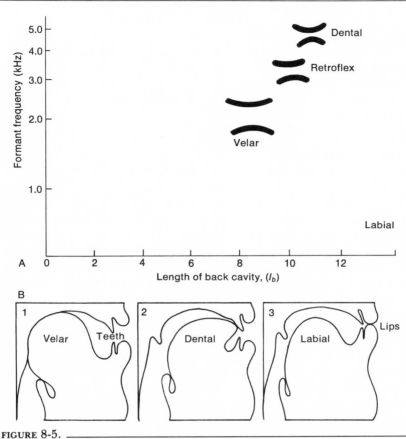

FIGURE 8-5.
"Quantal" spectral energy concentrations that occur as the constriction shifts to various points along the supralaryngeal vocal tract. Sketches for the velar, dental, and labial consonantal articulations that occur in English are also shown. (Adapted from Lieberman, 1977b.)

range of intermediate sounds as a player shortens the length of a string or changes the bowing. Violinists have to be quite careful when they play if they want to produce consistent sounds.

In the course of hominid evolution the development of the human supralaryngeal vocal tract yielded the ability to produce a range of quantal consonantal articulations. The sounds that could be generated at these quantal locations have distinct spectral peaks.

The quantal stop sounds thus would have an initial value for vocal communication in early hominids who had a general-purpose auditory, perceptual system similar to that present in nonhuman primates. There, however, would be a selective advantage for the retention of alletic variations that were present in the hominid population or mutations that would suppress within-category responses, yielding the "phonetic" perceptual mechanisms that are present in modern *Homo sapiens*.

ADAPTATION EXPERIMENTS

Further evidence that is consistent with the theory that human beings have a set of neural mechanisms adapted for speech perception comes from psychoacoustic experiments which make use of the "selective adaptation" paradigm. Since the introduction of this paradigm (Eimas and Corbit, 1973), a number of studies have indicated the presence of feature detector mechanisms that are analogous to those found in the auditory and visual systems of frogs, cats, and monkeys. Experiments that make use of this paradigm use the following procedure. Listeners are first asked to identify speech stimuli that differ with respect to an acoustic continuum, such as second formant frequency transitions that will cue the consonantal place of articulation. This initial session establishes the phonetic boundaries along this continuum. In a later listening session the same subjects first listen to several trials of an *adapting* stimulus, such as a stimulus that has been identified as a [ba], followed by five or so stimuli drawn from the test continuum. The outcome of selective adaptation is that a phonetic boundary shifts. If listeners adapt to a [ba], stimuli that were previously identified as [ba]'s that were near the [ba]-[da] boundary (see Figure 8-2) will now be identified as [da]'s. The theoretical interpretation of selective adaptation is as follows. A neural feature detector is, by definition, a hypothetical mechanism that responds to some particular attribute or attributes of an input signal. For speech, it essentially is a hypothetical neural embodiment of a Jakobsonian "distinctive feature" (Jakobson, Fant, and Halle, 1952). If speech signals are hypothetically identified by triggering feature detectors, then the location of a phonetic boundary represents a point along a continuum where two detectors are responding with equal strength. Fatiguing one of these detectors by presenting a number of trials would reduce the response of the feature detector that responds to the adapting stimulus. This would yield a change in the balance point along the continuum where both feature detectors respond with equal strength. A shift in the phonetic boundary toward the adapting stimulus thus is consistent with this theory and has been interpreted as evidence for feature detectors for speech perception.

A number of studies have used the selective adaptation paradigm and have demonstrated boundary shifts for VOT and place of articulation (Cooper, 1974; Diehl, 1975; Eimas, 1974; Miller and Eimas, 1976). There is some controversy as to whether adaptation involves the fatigue of feature detectors that respond directly to auditory — that is, acoustic — properties of speech signals or whether it involves the fatigue of feature detectors at a more abstract "phonetic" level (Cooper, 1974). Adaptation at an exclusively auditory level would involve a shift in the boundary if, and only if, the adapting stimulus had most of the acoustic properties of the stimuli that were shifted. What usually happens in adaptation experiments is that the greatest shift along a continuum will take place when the adapting stimulus most closely matches the acoustic parameters of the other signals that the subjects identify. If, for example, we presented synthesized speech signals to listeners along an acoustic continuum that elicits the voiced stops [b], [d], and [g], we would shift the phonetic boundary closer to [b] if the listeners heard an adapting [b] stimulus than if they heard an adapting [m] sound. The sounds [b] and [m], according to phonetic theory, both have a *labial* place of articulation, though [b] is an unnasalized stop and [m] a nasalized continuent. The shift in the phonetic boundary for a stop sound continuum is twice as great when we use a [b] adapting stimulus as when we use an [m]. However, though the greater shift associated with acoustically identical stimuli supports the view that adaptation occurs at an auditory level, the shifts that do occur when the phonetically similar [m] sound is used are consistent with the presence of effects at a *phonetic* level. The adaptation shifts with the [m] sound refute the theory that adaptation is taking place exclusively at an acoustic level.[1]

SYLLABLE TEMPLATES

One of the interesting aspects of the continuing controversy regarding the selective adaptation paradigm is that the discussion usually implicitly accepts the hypothesis that speech is perceived on a segmental basis. Most of the controversy centers, as I have noted, on the question of whether feature detectors are fatigued at an abstract phonetic level that roughly corresponds to the distinctive features in the linguistic model proposed by Jakobson, Fant, and Halle (1952) or whether the boundary shifts follow from the fatigue of neural devices that respond directly to the acoustic properties of the signals. Given the encoded nature of the speech signal that was demonstrated in the data that led to the development of the Haskins Laboratories motor theory, it is difficult to see how the perception of speech can occur without a level of neural processing at the syllabic level. The Haskins motor theory model of speech perception made use of an active comparator that, like the analysis-by-synthesis model (Halle and Stevens, 1959), incorporated the listener's knowledge of speech production in terms of algorithms that generated an internal signal that a listener hypothetically compared with an input signal. However, the constraints of speech production can also be captured in a model of speech perception if we hypothesize that a listener has an ensemble of fully specified syllable templates. Speech perception hypothetically could involve a listener's first segmenting the input signal into a sequence of CV and VC syllable patterns of burst frequencies, formant patterns, noise spectra, and the like and then comparing these patterns against an internal inventory of possible syllable patterns. The syllable pattern that was the best fit with the input signal, after normalization of the input parameters, would be perceived as the phonetic signal. The ensemble of internal templates would be constrained by language-universal physiologic properties of speech, such as the quantal properties of the supralaryngeal vocal tract, and language-specific constraints that the listener would have to learn, such as the admissible phonetic shape of syllables. This model is not parsimonious, in that it would use many more memory locations than would a model that computed the acoustic effects of admissible vocal tract maneuvers. However, the acoustic template model seems to be a better fit with psychological reality. Syllable templates as minimal units formally indicate the encoded nature of the acoustic cues for speech. What I propose at the neural level is that the neural mechanisms that we use to "detect" the sounds of speech are syllable sized (Lieberman, 1976c; Klatt, 1979).

CONSONANTAL ONSET SPECTRA

In this light the interpretation of the data of experiments that make use of the selective adaptation paradigm should be at the syllabic level. The results of the data of speech perception experiments involving encoded formant frequency transitions fit this model. The results of recent experiments that show the cue value of the onset spectra of stop consonants for place-of-articulation distinctions are also consistent with this theory, though these experiments originally were focused on deriving invariant cues for traditional phonetic segments. A number of recent studies (Stevens and Blumstein, 1978; Blumstein and Stevens, 1979; Chapin, Tseng, and Lieberman, 1982) show that consonantal place of articulation can be cued by the short-term onset spectrum of a stop consonant. In Figure 8-6 a schematized four-formant-plus-burst pattern that will yield the syllable [da] is shown. The burst is schematized by the vertical bar at approximately 3.5 kHz. This particular syllable was one of a number synthesized in a psychoacoustic study by Stevens and Blumstein (1978). When listeners are asked to identify the place of articulation for synthesized stimuli limited to 5, 10, 20, or 40 msec from the onset of the stop, they can still identify place of articulation. For example, they correctly identify place of articulation 90 percent of the time when they are presented with only the first 5 msec of the stimuli. Listeners can also hear the vowel of the syllable, though they have heard only the first 5 msec. Listeners thus can use the onset of the syllable to derive this phonetic distinction in the absence of explicit specification of the formant frequency transitions or the steady-state vowel. The effect occurs even when we present 15-msec onset signals computer-edited from the first words of 70-week-old children (Chapin, Tseng, and Lieberman, 1982). Short-term onset cues whose acoustic spectrum reflects the quantal properties of the supralaryngeal vocal tract (the converging formant frequency and burst energy concentration) thus can signal consonantal place of articulation as well as the syllable's vowel. If we hypothesize that the neural mechanisms that respond to these sounds as linguistic events in human beings are complete, fully specified syllabic "templates," we can explain both the categorical perception of speech and many of the effects of selective adaptation as well as the psychoacoustic data that support motor theories like the Haskins model. The process of adaptation thus would involve fatiguing a syllable detector that was specified in terms of the entire temporal pattern. If we adapted with a stimulus that had only *some* of the acoustic properties of the fully specified template for the [da] syllable detector, we would fatigue the syllable detector less than we would if we adapted with a *fully specified* match to the syllable template.

An interesting test of this hypothesis already exists. The selective adaptation experiment reported by Blumstein, Stevens, and Nigro (1977) used synthesized consonant-vowel stimuli like that schematized in Figure 8-6, which had bursts and formant frequency transitions as well as synthesized syllables that lacked bursts. The adaptation experi-

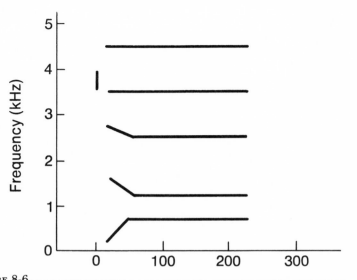

FIGURE 8-6.
Schematized representation of format frequency and burst pattern
that will produce the sound [da] when it is used to control an
appropriate speech synthesizer. The burst produced on the release
of the stop is represented by the vertical line. (After Blumstein,
Stevens, and Nigro, 1977.)

ments used either fatiguing stimuli that were fully specified and had
bursts or stimuli that lacked bursts. The most robust boundary shifts
for stimuli that *lacked* bursts occurred when the fully specified fatiguing stimulus *with* a burst was used. In other words, a smaller boundary
shift occurred when the condition of acoustic similarity between
adapting stimulus and the stimuli that formed the continuum was met!
The data thus again refute the hypothesis that adaptation takes place
solely at an acoustic level. The adaptation effect can be explained if we
hypothesize that humans have somewhere inside their brains a functionally equivalent representation of the complete, fully specified
acoustic pattern that specifies a possible syllable. This hypothesis
would predict that the greatest boundary shift would occur when the
fatiguing stimulus best matched the internal representation of the
syllable template.

    Fully specified syllable templates obviously would take up more
memory locations than feature templates or "rules" that internally
generate an acoustic pattern. The fully specified template theory can

be realized in terms of a motor theory computational algorithm that computes acoustic patterns that are constrained by the possible articulatory maneuvers and physiologic properties of the human supralaryngeal vocal tract. The template model again trades memory locations for parallel processing, redundancy, processing speed, and psychological reality. Both the motor theory model and the syllable template model predict that at some level of processing, encoded acoustic patterns constitute a more primitive level of speech perception than a phonetic-segment or distinctive-feature level of representation. Distinctive features and phonetic segments could be regarded as derived properties that perhaps reflect the structuring of the inventory of syllable templates in terms of the constraints of speech production and acoustic similarity (Lieberman, 1976c, 1979a; Klatt, 1979). A syllabic level for speech perception is consistent with other data, such as those on the diadic synthesis of speech (Fujimura and Lovins, 1978) as well as data on phonetic symbolism in reading (Rozin, Poritsky, and Sotsky, 1971; Gleitman and Rozin, 1973). Fully specified syllable templates for the perception of speech, in effect, constitute a strong version of the claim that we have perceptual mechanisms matched to the particular constraints of human speech production.

LATERALIZATION AND THE PERCEPTION OF SPEECH

As I noted in Chapter 1, the human brain is functionally lateralized; although the reasons for lateralization are not clear, it is apparent that the two hemispheres of the brain do not participate equally in the perception of speech and other structured tasks (Bradshaw and Nettleton, 1981). The role of the dominant hemisphere, which is usually the left one, in linguistic tasks was first noted by Broca in 1861. Broca observed that lesions in the anterior region of the left hemisphere resulted in linguistic deficits in his patients. The deficits of aphasia, however, represent extreme conditions that follow from permanent damage to the brain; they do not occur in normal subjects. The phenomena that have surfaced through the study of speech perception, in contrast, occur in normal subjects and reflect the normal processing activity of the human brain. The first hint that speech might be processed differentially by the two hemispheres of the human brain came through one of the accidental observations that trigger significant advances in science. The British Post Office operates the telephone system of the United Kingdom. Like its counterpart, the private Bell telephone system, it also maintains a laboratory for research and development connected with improving telephone communications. The telephone system of the United Kingdom in the 1950s was a splendid example of the state of the art of 1930. It was undoubtedly better than many of the continental telephone systems. The most advanced equipment then in use in France had been installed by the German occupation forces in World War II. Some of the telephone lines in use in the Soviet Union are said to have been erected during the reign of Czar Nicholas. However, the British were not content to profit from these comparisons and desired to catch up to, if not to surpass, their American cousins. They thus started on the development of a new telephone system and new standards for testing telephone equipment.

The test that the British Post Office's research laboratory, the Joint Speech Research Unit, devised was elegant and simple. Different telephone systems were used by pairs of people who used the telephones to transmit information necessary to play games of chess under different conditions of line noise. The telephones were also used to transmit long lists of words. One person would read the list of words while the other person wrote the transmitted words down. These tests also were conducted with different telephone systems under different conditions of line noise. The measures of telephone quality were derived from assessments of their effectiveness in playing games and from the number of errors made in the transmission of word lists. Telephone systems that had the fewest number of errors and allowed people to play chess when the line noise was at a higher level than the level that would be tolerable in other telephones were judged to be better.

A number of control procedures had to be followed in order to evaluate the different telephone designs. The word lists had to be balanced to include a representative sample of the sounds of the various dialects of English spoken in the United Kingdom; the listeners who used the telephones likewise had to be familiar with the sounds of these different dialects. One control procedure had to be introduced that was not part of the original experimental design. The listeners had to be instructed to consistently put the telephone receiver against their right ear. This was necessary because the experiments showed that there was a right-ear advantage of approximately 3 dB over the listeners' left ears (Swaffield, Shearme, and Holmes, 1961). A telephone system would work at the same level of performance at a line noise level that was 3 dB higher if the people using the telephones listened with their right ears instead of with their left ears. A difference of 3 dB roughly corresponds to a noise level that sounds twice as loud (Fant, 1960).

The basis of this right-ear advantage probably derives from the functional lateralization of the human brain that was discovered 100 years earlier by Broca. The right ear is connected to the left, dominant hemisphere of the brain by a major contralateral pathway. In contrast, it is connected to the right hemisphere by a smaller ipsilateral pathway. Speech presented to the right ear thus apparently has a better pathway to the left dominant hemisphere of the brain (Shankweiler and Studdert-Kennedy, 1967). The left ear conversely has a major pathway to the right and a minor pathway to the left hemisphere of the brain.

Lateralization also appears to play a role in the perception of conspecific calls by nonhuman primates (Peterson et al., 1978). In an experiment that monitored the responses of monkeys to vocal signals, monkeys of several Old World species (there is a general distinction between Old World and New World monkeys) were trained to push bars in response to particular monkey vocalizations. The sounds were presented to the monkeys monaurally over headphones so the effect of listening with the right versus the left ear could be explored. The data showed that Japanese macaque monkeys *(Macaca fuscata)* had a right-ear advantage when they responded to one of their species-specific vocalizations. The other monkeys did not show a right-ear advantage in response to these Japanese macaque sounds, nor did the Japanese macaque monkeys show a right-ear advantage in response to the calls of other monkeys. The Japanese macaque monkeys, moreover, responded to salient acoustic properties of their calls, a relative peak in the fundamental frequency contour, and ignored the absolute value of the fundamental frequency contour which varies from one monkey to another (Zoloth et al., 1979). This is also what human beings do when they respond to the intonation contour of a sentence (Lieberman, 1965, 1967; Atkinson, 1973). The Japanese macaque monkeys also required very little training to respond to their species-specific calls, whereas the monkeys of other species could not be taught to respond to the salient fundamental frequency peak of the Japanese macaque call.

The differential effects of right-ear versus left-ear perception of the sounds of human speech have been explored by hundreds of experiments that use the technique of "dichotic" presentation (Shank-Weiler and Studdert-Kennedy, 1967). Recent versions of the dichotic technique make use of computer-generated speech signals and a two-channel tape recorder and headphones. The technique presents two competing signals to a listener. In a typical example, the computer is used to generate two synthetic syllables, a [ba] and a [da]. The two signals are recorded on the channels of a two-track tape recorder so that pairs of syllables always appear simultaneously on the two channels of the tape recorder. A tape recording thus is prepared using the computer in which a [ba] will appear on the right channel while a [da] appears on the left channel in one instance, and a [da] will appear on the right channel while a [ba] appears on the left channel in another instance, and so on. The tape recording that results thus consists of many [ba] versus [da] pairs. When normal listeners are asked to listen to the tape through headphones, they will not hear a blend of the two sounds. They instead hear either a [ba] or a [da]. The dominant hemisphere of the human brain can be determined by using a test in which the two hemispheres of the brain are selectively anesthetized (Kimura, 1967). Listeners who have dominant left hemispheres consistently tend to hear the stop consonant, the [da] or the [ba], that was presented to their right ear. The reverse is usually true for listeners who have dominant right hemispheres.

The relevance of lateralization to the perception of speech is not clear. Although syllables that start with stop consonants show a right-ear advantage in dichotic listening tests, other sounds show no right-ear advantage. Sinusoidal pure tones show a left-ear advantage; steady-state vowels show neither a left- nor a right-ear advantage (Mattingly et al., 1971). Signals that have some of the characteristics of human speech generally show more of a right-ear advantage than do other signals (Cutting, 1974), but it is not clear why certain speech sounds show more of a right-ear advantage than do other sounds. As Bradshaw and Nettleton (1981) point out in their review article on the nature of neural lateralization, the dominant hemisphere of the brain appears to be in some way adapted to handling tasks that involve keeping track of serial order. Differential neural activity thus occurs in a variety of tasks that are not limited to the perception of speech. Lateralization perhaps may be a consequence of the preadapted functioning of the motor association areas of the brain for rule-governed activity.

Summary

The perceptual mechanisms that are involved in "decoding" human speech are structured, in part, by auditory constraints. The identification of stop consonants in terms of their voice onset time (VOT) thus appears to follow from a basic constraint of the mammalian auditory system. The VOT decision depends on a listener's being able to tell whether voicing occurs before or after the release burst of a stop consonant. The shortest interval for which human listeners and other mammals can make this distinction is 25 msec. This 25-msec interval structures the primary categories for phonetic VOT distinctions across many human languages. Human listeners, however, can make VOT distinctions by using acoustic parameters like burst amplitude, aspiration amplitude, and vowel duration, which have no clear auditory basis. The perception and identification of consonantal place of articulation likewise appear to involve neural devices adapted specifically for "phonetic," that is, speech, distinctions rather than general auditory mechanisms. The phenomenon of categorical perception of speech may follow from the presence of neural mechanisms adapted to speech perception and matched to the constraints of the human supralaryngeal vocal tract. Experimental paradigms like adaptation and dichotic presentation yield data that are consistent with the presence of such specialized neural devices in *Homo sapiens* that operate off encoded syllable-sized segments.

CHAPTER 9

The Man on the Flying Trapeze: The Acquisition of Speech

> He was talking of Malaysia, palm-trees, the little wives of rajahs in colored sarongs — or perhaps not sarongs? — crouched round him on the ground; he himself cross-legged on the ground teaching the little wives of rajahs to use sewing machines! Moored to a rotting quay — as it might have been Palembang, but of course it was not Palembang — was his schooner. His schooner had in its hold half a cargo of rifles under half a cargo of sewing machines. The rajahs, husbands of the little wives, did not like their Dutch suzerains and in that country War had lasted not five but three-hundred and fifty-five years . . . The Conrad of those days was Romance. He was dark, black-bearded, passionate in the extreme and at every minute; rather small but very broad-shouldered and long in the arm. Speaking English he had so strong a French accent that few who did not know him well could understand him at first.
>
> (Ford Madox Ford on Joseph Conrad; Ford, 1971, pp. 245, 155).

ONE OF THE LINGUISTIC mysteries is how children acquire their first language. If the process simply involved logically deducing the syntax and sound pattern, then we might expect adults to be able to acquire a foreign language with equal facility. Yet we know that acquiring the sound pattern of a foreign language with native proficiency is essentially impossible for most adults. The syntax and semantic structure of a foreign language usually can be acquired by adults, given sufficient study and motivation. However, it is almost impossible to attain the phonetic proficiency of any normal child. There appears to be a critical period, a time after which we cannot master the sound pattern of a foreign language.

The difficulties that most adults experience in learning to speak a foreign language without an accent do not appear to follow from deficiencies in general intelligence, motivation, or indeed facility with language. Adults who have acquired two or three different languages

194

as children often have as much trouble learning to speak a new foreign language as adult monolinguals do. We all know some adults who are good at learning foreign languages. These fortunate individuals, particularly when they become academics, often imply that other people who cannot master a foreign language are lazy, unmotivated, or perhaps simply stupid. Whenever I get into an argument with my learned colleagues who claim that anyone can learn to speak five languages without an accent, I fall back on Joseph Conrad, who is my staff, my support.

The chronology of Conrad's linguistic background is consistent with the presence of a critical period that limits the acquisition of phonetic ability. Conrad's native language was Polish, though he was born in the Ukraine. In his youth he learned to speak and write French as well as Polish. He drifted to Marseille at the age of 17, where he sailed for two years on French ships. During this period he acquired a native Marseillaise accent. At the age of 20, with hardly any knowledge of English, he qualified as a seaman on an English ship and two years later sailed as third mate on a voyage to Australia. Though Conrad became a ship's master in the British merchant service four years later and is one of the masters of English prose, he always spoke English with a strong Marseillaise accent. As Ford describes the situation, it was usually impossible for strangers to understand Conrad.

Conrad's case is by no means unusual. The speech of Henry Kissinger is another example. Kissinger's English syntax is flawless; his accent is Germanic. In contrast, Kissinger's brother, who was a few years younger when the brothers came to the United States from Germany, has no accent. Studies of the acquisition of Hebrew by the children of immigrant families living in Israeli kibbutzes show the same pattern. There is an early critical period that limits the acquisition of a language without a foreign accent. The syntax and semantic structure of a language, in contrast, can usually be mastered by adults.

THE CRITICAL PERIOD

The concept of a critical period derives from behavioral and electrophysiologic studies on various animals. A number of studies have, for example, shown that the structure and function of the mammalian visual system are affected by the early experience of an animal. The studies of Hubel and Wiesel (1970) show that kittens fail to develop their normal complement of binocular cortical neurons when they are deprived of vision in one eye between age 4 weeks and 12 weeks.

Deprivation of binocular vision after that period has little effect. The
kitten likewise will develop normally if its vision is restored during the
critical period before 12 weeks. If an animal is deprived of normal
visual stimuli throughout the critical period, the structure of the
visual cortex fails to develop normally.

The concept of the critical period embodies the claim that innate
neural devices exist in the visual cortex. These innately determined
neuronal structures are elements for important visual attributes.
However, they must be exposed to appropriate "normal" visual
inputs during the critical, or sensitive, period. The electrophysiologic
techniques that can be used with cats obviously cannot be used to
study human subjects, but humans who have been deprived of visual
inputs during their critical period show behavioral deficits that are
similar to those of cats with regard to binocular vision (Freeman,
Mitchell, and Millodot, 1972; Mitchell et al., 1973). The critical period for
human binocular vision, however, seems to be somewhat longer than
it is for cats, starting several months after birth and extending to age 3
years (Banks, Aslin, and Letson, 1975). Behavioral experiments with
human subjects show that deficiencies in visual acuity can be traced to
a deficiency of specific features in the early visual input. Visual
resolution for normal people is almost equal for vertically and hori-
zontally oriented patterns. People who suffer at an early age from
ocular astigmatism, which blurs visual details in a particular orientation, are later unable to resolve detail in this orientation even when
the ocular deficiency is corrected (Freeman and Thidos, 1973). The
deficiency again appears to follow from reorganization of the visual
system that is a consequence of early abnormal visual input.

The effects of early experience appear to be general and pervasive. Fairly simple avoidance training of kittens in a normal visual
environment produces massive neural traces in both the visual and the
somatic cortices. Spinelli and Jensen (1978) first trained kittens to
move their forelegs up or down in response to visual stimuli. Electrophysiologic data revealed modification of cells in both the visual
cortex and regions of the cortex that are associated with control of the
foreleg and visual "association." Learned visual tasks in chicks result
in an alteration of the overall blood flow pattern to the brain (Bondy
and Harrington, 1978). Changes in neural organization have been
found in primates that appear to be the consequence of the general
social and physical environment. Both the complexity of the physical
environment and exercise during early development thus affect the
cerebellum in monkeys (Floeter and Greenough, 1979) and mice (Pysh
and Weiss, 1979):

The neuronal organization of the cerebellum is similar from fish to humans, a consistency through vertebrate phylogeny that has contributed to doubt that the cerebellum might be modifiable by experience. This evidence for plasticity in cerebellar circuitry indicates that phylogenetically stable structures, as well as phylogenetically newer ones, are not "hardwired" and can be modified by environmental experience . . . the cerebellum, like the neocortex, is a structure that integrates a variety of incoming information into an appropriate output. In terms of both maturation and function, plasticity of the cerebellum is perhaps no more surprising than the earlier demonstrations of plasticity in the hippocampus or neocortex.

(FLOETER AND GREENOUGH, 1979, P. 229)

The effects of early experience on communication are particularly evident in birds (Marler, 1976). Birds that are raised in isolation without being exposed to the normal repertoire of bird song appropriate to the species later fail to develop their normal song repertoire. The process by which children acquire speech, however, differs in a crucial way from the acquisition of bird songs by birds. Birds will acquire their normal song repertoire if they are simply exposed to the bird songs. The birds do not have to participate in the full range of activities that constitute the normal activity of the species. They do not have to fly about in their normal environment, make nests, forage, and so on. Simple exposure to the songs apparently will trigger an innately determined "template" that results in the bird's producing the range of songs normally produced in the species (Marler, 1976).

Human children, in contrast, have to *use* speech productively in order to acquire the sound pattern of a language. Snow (1977) reports that Dutch-speaking children who are exposed to German television programming for many hours each day do not acquire German. Dutch-speaking children will, of course, acquire German if they are raised in a bilingual environment in which German is used in a productive manner for communication. It is not enough merely to expose them to the sounds of German. Similar effects occur when children are raised in bizarre, culturally deprived situations. Wolff (personal communication) reports on two 4-year-old children who were neglected and left for the most part in a playpen with a television set turned on. The children did not acquire speech even though they heard commercials, talk shows, soap operas, and the like. Their linguistic and social development was quite deficient. The clinical record shows extreme linguistic and cognitive deficits in children who have been raised in isolation (Singh and Zingg, 1942; Curtiss, 1977) or in deaf children who have been raised without instruction in sign language or other forms of communication (Lenneberg, 1967). The critical period in human beings, unlike birds, thus involves the range of social behavior that places speech and language in a productive, communicative framework. Though the neural mechanisms that regulate song in birds may be isolated from the neural devices that regulate other aspects of bird life, people are not birds. Children apparently have to map the uses of language onto the real world if they are to acquire linguistic competence. It is difficult in this light to see how linguistic ability can be isolated from the neural substrate that underlies the social and cognitive behavior of human beings.

A MODEL FOR THE ACQUISITION OF SPEECH

The general and pervasive difficulty that normal adults have in acquiring a second language thus can be viewed, in itself, as strong evidence for a critical period, if the abundant electrophysiologic and behavioral data on the neuronal bases of communicative behavior in other species, and vision in all species, are relevant in any sense to human communication. Note that the critical-period explanation of the difficulty that human adults have in acquiring the sound pattern of a foreign language makes sense *only* if we first have accepted the hypothesis that human phonetic ability involves neural structures, or "devices," that are necessary for the perception and/or production of the sounds of human speech.

If we accept this premise — neural devices that are affected by early experience and are limited by a critical period structure human phonetic ability — we still have several options open to us concerning the nature of these devices and the innateness question. The "strong-innate" position of linguists like Chomsky claims that the neural structures that determine the possible forms of human languages are *all* innate. Though Chomsky (1980a, 1980b) is concerned with the syntactic aspects of language, his position is compatible with and probably derives from the phonologic theories of Jakobson. Jakobson's position, which is developed in a number of works (Jakobson, Fant, and Halle, 1952; Jakobson, 1940; Chomsky and Halle, 1968), is that the meaningful phonemic sound contrasts of all human languages can be captured by a limited set of features. These features differentiate meaningful sound contrasts like the difference between the [p] and [b] of the English words *pat* and *bat* or the [b] and [d] of *bad* and *dad*. Jakobson (1940) claims that all children produce the sounds of all languages in their first months of life when they babble. According to

Jakobson, children lose the ability to produce the sound contrasts that they do not hear in their linguistic environment. If we were to construct a neural analog of this theory, we would have to equip it with a full set of innately determined neural devices that would account for the sound contrasts that occur in all human languages. Specific neural devices would atrophy if they were not used within the critical period. This aspect of Jakobson's phonologic theory is embodied in the "natural phonology" of Stampe (1973) and in recent theories concerned with the "learnability" of syntactic rules (Pinker, 1979; Williams, 1981).

Although a strong-innate theory is consistent with much of the data that we now have on speech perception in infancy, it does not account for all aspects of speech perception, nor does it account for the data of speech production. Infants do not, for example, initially produce the sounds of all human languages when they babble (Port and Preston, 1972; Lieberman, 1980). Two other options are open. We could propose a "plasticity" model in which infants and children gradually build up neural devices that are specialized to perceive various speech sounds while they also build up neural, automatized motor control "circuitry" to produce the sounds. The neural perceptual circuitry would be plastic until the critical period. However, a model for speech acquisition that involves only plasticity clearly cannot account for the data of speech perception and certain aspects of speech production.

A mixed system involving both specialized innate neural mechanisms and neural plasticity is the only model that seems to account for the data that I will discuss here. Much of the data of the acquisition of speech perception and some aspects of speech production are consistent with a strong-innate model. Innately determined, that is, genetically transmitted, neural devices are the most plausible explanation for these phenomena. The acquisition of speech production clearly involves the innately determined maturation of the supralaryngeal vocal tract, larynx, and respiratory system, as well as certain neural control mechanisms. However, the major factor in the development of speech production appears to be the gradual formation of automatized neural "circuits" that control the production of speech. A mixed system that involves both innate, genetically transmitted neural devices and neural devices acquired within the lifetime of the organism by the process of plasticity furthermore provides a conceptual framework for the evolution of specialized neural devices for speech perception that is consistent with both comparative and paleontological data.

The process of speech acquisition, contrary to the claims of adherents of a strong-innate theory for human language, takes years of practice. It does not resemble the rapid unfolding of innately determined motoric activity that is apparent in the establishment of flight in birds or swallowing in human infants (see Chapter 11). Though innately determined neural mechanisms appear to structure the perception of speech, the acquisition of the neural "programs" for speech production may be no different in kind from that necessary for other activities like performing on the flying trapeze, playing the violin, or classical ballet dancing. Like speech production, these activities all appear to involve a critical period. But there is nothing uniquely linguistic about the critical period. The situation for the acquisition of speech thus is similar to that of mastering the flying trapeze. The perceptual mechanisms that structure human vision are necessary elements in mastering the flying trapeze and are undoubtedly innately determined. But no one would claim that the motoric skills that are necessary for performing on the flying trapeze are innate. That also seems to be the case for the production of speech. The acquisition of speech by human children thus appears to entail a mixed system—a neural substrate that involves both specialized, innate neural mechanisms and neural plasticity shaped by the general cognitive process.

Babble, Play, and Speech Perception in Infancy

Most children begin to produce meaningful words between their first and second birthdays. The acquisition of language in children after they enter this stage of develoment, the "phonologic" stage, has been studied in detail in many works. In contrast, relatively little attention has been paid to the earliest, infantile stages of speech acquisition. This distinction, of course, reflects the common view that there is little, if any, linguistic aspect to infants' early crying and babbling. Crying is usually viewed outside the linguistic frame of reference as an aspect of the innate expression of emotion, a vestige of our link to other animals (Darwin, 1872). Again, the babbling of infants has been stated to be a sort of play in making the sounds of speech (Lewis, 1936; Jakobson, 1940; Lenneberg, 1967). Although we normally may think of play behavior as frivolous conduct that has no serious purpose, play behavior in young animals is important for their normal development. The notion of play as a sort of mechanism that simply allows an animal to dispose of surplus energy derives from Spencer (1878). Spencer's view of the source of play is consistent with Victorian theories concerning child rearing: children are little savages; play drains their surplus energy.

It is difficult to measure the long-term effects of play or its absence, but it is apparent that play is not simply a mechanism for draining surplus energy. When animals experience food shortages under adverse environmental conditions, they nonetheless maintain play activity. We thus can conclude that there is a selective advantage in maintaining play activity in that the growing animal is willing to pay in order to maintain play, especially in conditions of food shortage (Muller-Schwarze, Stagge, and Muller-Schwarze, 1982). Studies of play behavior have postulated that it is important in establishing about thirty different functions in a variety of animals — functions such as general neuromuscular development, learning about the environment, and developing social skills (Baldwin and Baldwin, 1977). In short, we could claim that kittens and puppies play to establish the skills that are important to cats and dogs and that the babbling play of human infants establishes the neuromotor skills necessary for human speech.

I would like to enlarge on the claim that babbling constitutes a necessary, innately determined type of play behavior that establishes the neuromotor control necessary for speech production. The hypothesis I would like to propose is that speech acquisition in infancy largely involves the infant's mastering of speech production. One of the surprising discoveries of the past decade is that infants appear to be equipped at or shortly after birth with the neural devices that we use to perceive speech. Though the precise nature of these devices has yet to be determined, it is clear that human infants respond to and differentiate between the different fundamental frequency patterns, formant frequency patterns, bursts, voice-onset-time differences, and the like that convey linguistic information in speech.

A detailed discussion of the perception of speech by infants would, in itself, involve a book. Experiments which explore the perception by infants of the full range of sound contrasts that can occur in all human languages have furthermore not been run. Indeed we do not really know the nature of all the sound contrasts that can occur in all languages. However, infants can discriminate between the acoustic cues that signal a variety of phonologic contrasts. Kuhl (1979), in her review of the data on speech perception in infancy, for example, lists the following sound contrasts that are reliably discriminated:

VOT — prevoiced/coincident/delayed
Place of articulation for stops — labial, alveolar, velar with and
    without burst cues

Fricatives — voiced versus voiceless, e.g., va/sa: strident versus
  nonstrident, e.g., fi/ei
Liquids and glides — ra/la and wa/ya
Vowels — a/i, i/I, a/o
Stress distinctions — ba 'ba/ 'baba
Pitch contours — rising versus falling, monotone versus rise-fall

SOME EXPERIMENTAL TECHNIQUES

Progress in experiments on the discrimination of speech by infants
largely follows from the introduction of techniques that allow the
experimenter to infer when an infant can discriminate between two
signals. It is obviously impossible to ask an infant to push a button
when a sound is perceived as being different. Various techniques have
been devised to gauge the responses of infants. One technique involves monitoring the infant's heart rate (Morse, 1976). However,
high-amplitude sucking and head-turn techniques have been used in
most recent experiments on the perception of speech by human
infants. The sucking technique was first used in 1969 in experiments
with visual stimuli (Siqueland and Delucia, 1969). The sucking technique
works best for infants under 4 months of age. It essentially depends on
the infant's becoming bored with a stimulus. The experiment starts
with an infant sucking on a nipple connected to a pressure transducer.
When the infant sucks on the nipple, the pressure transducer registers
the force of the infant's sucking. A speech sound is presented to the
infant contingent on the suck's force exceeding a threshold. The
infant typically continues to suck forcefully as the speech sound is
presented contingent on a forceful suck. This pattern continues for a
while, the same speech sound being presented in response to a forceful suck. After a minute or so the infant learns that a sound will be
presented if the suck is forceful. The rate at which the infant sucks
gradually increases as the infant reaches the criterion of contingent
sound presentation. After a few more minutes the infant, however,
becomes habituated, that is, bored with the sound, and the rate of
sucking falls. If a new sound is then presented — a sound that the
infant can perceive as being different — the infant "dishabit-
uates," or becomes interested in the new sound, and the rate of
sucking again increases. If the infant cannot perceive the difference
between the new and the old sound or if the same sound continues in a
control condition, the rate of sucking will not rise at the point where
the experimenter shifts to the new sound.

  The head-turn technique complements the sucking technique in that it works for infants between 5½ and 10 months. The infant is trained to turn his or her head when a particular speech sound is presented (Eilers, Wilson, and Moore, 1977). The infant is rewarded by associating a pleasing visual stimulus, such as a toy monkey beating a drum, with a sound. The infant, for example, would be trained to turn left on hearing the vowel [i] and right on hearing the vowel [a]. The head-turning technique makes it possible to determine whether infants will respond to the phonetic class of the vowels across different speakers' voices. The infant is initially trained to respond to the [a] versus [i] vowels of one speaker. After the infant's head-turning responses have been established, the [a] and [i] vowels of other speakers are introduced (Kuhl, 1979).

There are still many open questions concerning the speech perception of infants. Some speech contrasts are more robust than others. The contrast between stop sounds that differ with respect to voice onset time is greater between the short-lag and long-lag categories (English [b] and [p]) than it is between prevoiced and short-lag sounds (Spanish [b] and English [b]) (Eimas, 1975). This holds true even in children whose first language, Kikuyu, makes use of a phonemic, prevoiced versus short-lag VOT contrast (Streeter, 1976). The VOT contrast that is used in English was present in the Kikuyu-speaking children even though their native language does not use this contrast. Again, the English [f] versus [Ɵ] contrast is not reliably present in 6- and 8-month-old infants raised in an English-speaking environment. It was observed in 12- and 14-month-old children in the context of [fi] versus [Ɵi], but not of [fa] versus [Ɵa] (Eilers, Wilson, and Moore, 1977).

The results of Eilers, Wilson, and Moore's study (1977) are revealing in that more energy is present in the high-frequency part of the spectrum that is necessary for the [f]-versus-[Ɵ] distinction when these consonants occur before the vowel [i]. Children thus may have to learn to focus on the less robust acoustic difference to perceive this sound contrast. Whatever the reason is for some sound contrasts being present earlier than others—whether more exposure to the linguistic environment or maturation of the auditory system is involved—the available data show that some sound contrasts are present earlier than others and are more robust.

Studies of the acquisition of meaningful words by young children reinforce this view. Olmsted (1971) studied the phonetic structure of the words that 100 children between the ages of 15 and 54 months produced in one-hour recording sessions. The phone substitutions that the children produced in these words compared with the exemplars provided by their mothers were analyzed. The children's consonantal errors corresponded to the rank order of the perceptual errors noted by Miller and Nicely (1955) for adults. More substitutions occurred for the sound contrasts that are more susceptible to errors in perception. The children's vowel substitutions, moreover, were consistent with the quantal aspect of speech production (Stevens, 1972) discussed earlier. The vowels [i], [u], and [a] were subject to fewer substitution errors than other vowels except [ae], which is differentiated by duration in English from other nonquantal vowels. The data of Blasdell and Jensen (1970) in which twenty children between the ages of 28 and 39 months were asked to imitate four-syllable nonsense CVC syllables also show that sounds which are easier to perceive will be repeated with the fewest errors. Stressed syllables, which have longer durations and amplitudes (Fry, 1958; Lieberman, 1960), were repeated with the fewest errors. The vowel [i], Nearey's (1978) "supervowel," again was repeated with the fewest errors. The substitution error data derived from children's attempts at producing words are, in general, consistent with the perceptual mechanisms for some vowel contrasts like the quantal or "point" vowels [i], [u], and [a] being in place at a very early age, with other vowel contrasts being shaped up as the children are exposed to speech in a meaningful context. The vowel categories of different languages divide up the formant frequency space into an almost infinite set of possibilities (Lieberman, 1976c). Given the variety of vowel distinctions across different languages and dialects, it is difficult to see how we could be equipped at birth with a complete set of innately determined vowel feature detectors.

LOSING VERSUS BUILDING UP PHONETIC CONTRASTS

One of the claims of the strong-innate theory for speech perception is that we lose the ability to discriminate sound contrasts that are not present in our linguistic environment within the critical period. The data that we have so far are suggestive but not conclusive. Whereas infants can differentiate between the sounds [r] and [l] (Eimas, 1975), Japanese-speaking adults have great difficulty in keeping track of this distinction. Psychoacoustic data derived from Japanese-speaking adults, moreover, shows that their discrimination function does not peak at the [ra] versus [la] boundary as is the case for English-speaking listeners when they are presented with synthesized speech signals that present a continuum in third formant frequency transitions from [ra] to [la] (Miyawaki et al., 1975). These data thus support the theory that we *lose* the ability to perceive sounds that we do not use. However, the data on the perception of prevoiced versus short-lag stop sounds, such as [ba] versus [ba] (Eimas, 1975), show that English infants are not as sensitive to this contrast as are Spanish infants (Eilers, Wilson, and Moore, 1977). These data support the view that *some* phonetic contrasts are reinforced by exposure to the sound pattern of the infant's environment; that is, we *build up* neural devices in the period of neural plasticity. The data of infant speech perception so far are consistent with a mixed system that makes use of both neural plasticity and innately determined neural devices — whether these devices are "feature detectors" or "syllable templates."

GENETIC VARIATION

The common experience of adults who learn a second language is that they usually can understand the language far better than they can speak it. We do not as yet have quantitative data on the acquisition of a variety of phonetic contrasts by adults. What would happen if Japanese-speaking adults were schooled in identifying the English [r]-versus-[l] contrast using the techniques that have been devised to teach the sounds of sonar signals to adults (Swets et al., 1962)? It is possible that the plasticity of adult speech perception varies. Some adults might be much better than others in learning to perceive new sounds. The issue of genetic variation also has hardly been explored in connection with speech perception. If there are innate neural devices for speech perception that are genetically transmitted, it is almost certain that variation will exist across the human population. As I noted in Chapter 1, the degree of alletic variation in human beings is at least 7 percent (Ayala, 1978).

Human beings differ with respect to basic biological mechanisms like those that govern the efficiency with which we transfer oxygen into our bloodstream. The mammalian respiratory system is the result of tens of millions of years of evolution by means of natural selection toward solving the problem of supplying oxygen to the bloodstream. However, we still find great variations in the efficiency of different people's oxygen transfer ability. The amount of oxygen that must be transferred to the bloodstream increases during strenuous exercise. As the CO_2 level rises in the bloodstream, the chemoreceptors that regulate respiration increase the amount of air transferred through a person's lungs (see Chapter 5). The respiratory system thus delivers more oxygen to the bloodstream by transferring more air through the lungs. The efficiency of the total oxygen transfer process, however, varies from one person to another. Some people do not "extract" as much oxygen from the air that they breathe in and out of their lungs, and they may have to transfer four times as much air through their lungs at a given CO_2 level than another normal adult does (Bouhuys, 1974).

The plots in Figure 9-1 show the relation between CO_2 level and the volume of air that a person transfers through the lungs. Respiratory physiologists use four different functions to account for the behavior of this sample of 33 normal adults. The different plots show the presence of variant patterns of respiratory behavior. The fact that the subjects do not all differ from each other but instead fall into four different groups argues for the presence of different underlying genetically transmitted mechanisms for oxygen transfer. These data are not surprising. We know from other data that people differ from each other in this respect as they do in others. Some people have the respiratory ability to run marathons; others do not. The four different functions thus reflect the fact that alletic variations in the biological mechanisms that determine oxygen transfer still exist in the human population despite a hundred million years or so of evolution involving the respiratory system. By studying the pattern of variation, the physiologist can, however, predict the behavior of an individual once he knows what group the individual falls into.

Consider instead the treatment of these physiologic data that would occur if they were cast into the competence-performance model that derives from the linguistic theories of Saussure and Chomsky. The linguist-physiologist would attempt to find a single biological mechanism that reflects the underlying "respiratory competence" of all 33 subjects. The differences in behavior would, to the linguist-physiologist, reflect the presence of mysterious "performance" factors outside the domain of linguistic physiology. Faced with these data, the linguist-physiologist might derive an "average" function that accounts for the behavior of none of the subjects. Most likely the linguist-physiologist would have to conclude that since no single competence function could be derived that accounted for the behavior of all the subjects, the problem was outside the proper domain of linguistic physiology.

The data of speech perception in adult human listeners are replete with references to individual differences. Remez and colleagues (1981), for example, note that some of their subjects heard sine-wave equivalents to speech as speech signals, while other subjects heard the sounds as "science fiction" noises, buzzes, and so on. The data of Pisoni (1971) show different categorization functions for different listeners for the stop sounds [ba], [da], and [ga]. Pisoni used the

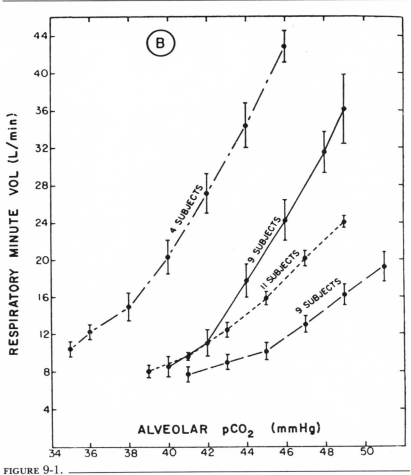

FIGURE 9-1.
Plots of airflow through lungs versus CO_2 gas in lungs. As the
percentage of CO_2 rises, people increase the amount of air that they
move through their lungs. Note the different behavior of the four
groups of individuals plotted. Some people have to move almost
four times more air through their lungs at the higher levels of CO_2
that usually occur during sustained muscular activity. (Adapted
from Kellogg, 1964.)

tape recordings made by the Haskins Laboratories group that constitute the stimuli for the original and many subsequent studies of
categorical perception in adult listeners as well as in children and
infants. The pattern of variation observed by Pisoni is probably typical
for all these studies. Similar variations exist in studies using other
synthetic and natural stimuli.

GENETIC VARIATION AND THE HIERARCHY OF ACOUSTIC CUES

The variations between different subjects can become quite extreme.
Tallal and Piercy (1975), for example, show that children who are
diagnosed as having developmental aphasia cannot perceive sound
contrasts that involve perceiving rapidly changing acoustic events,
such as stop sounds. Recent data (Schupack et al., 1983; Lieberman, in
press b) show variation in the identification of place of articulation for
stop consonants and for the vowels of American English in a population of adult dyslexic subjects. These subjects, who are otherwise
normal, were asked to identify a variety of computer-edited and
computer-synthesized speech stimuli in psychoacoustic tests. The test
procedure involved asking the dyslexic subjects to repeat the stimuli
that they heard; this procedure avoided transcription problems that
otherwise might occur with subjects who had reading, writing, and
spelling deficits. The subjects, for example, had no difficulty in correctly repeating full CVC syllables of the form *bat, pet, peat, gut, did*,
and the like that had been recorded by an adult, phonetically trained
speaker. They also had no difficulty in a second psychoacoustic test in
which they repeated words like *had, head, heed*. These tests demonstrated that the subjects could identify and correctly repeat the stop
consonants and vowels of American English. A pattern of errors,
however, emerged when the dyslexic subjects were asked to repeat
computer-synthesized 200-msec long-vowel stimuli and short computer-edited consonant-vowel syllables. The dyslexics' responses were
transcribed by phonetically trained observers who also made use of
visual cues in the case of the stop-consonant identifications.

The vowel stimuli were synthesized by using the average formant
frequencies of F_1 and F_2 found by Peterson and Barney (1952). These
stimuli had been used in a previous experiment with a group of
nondyslexic subjects (Ryalls and Lieberman, 1982). The average error
rate for vowel identification of the nondyslexic subjects for these
stimuli was 9 percent. Table 9-1 shows the error rate for each
dyslexic subject. These error rates exclude [a] versus [ɔ] confusions,
which are characteristic for many dialects of American English. Note

TABLE 9-1. Variations in Speech Perception, IQ, and Oral Reading of Dyslexic Subjects

Subject	Sex	Constant errors				Vowel errors		IQ			Oral reading grade
		Average	[b]	[d]	[g]	Total	w/o [a/o]	Average	Verbal	Performance	
1	M	18	22	17	22	27	30	105	97	116	2.0
2	M	11	.28	2	4	16	30	93	90	99	3.7
3	M	45	52	60	23	63	71	93	89	99	5.7
4	F	12	23	5	7	31	40	122	122	120	10.3
5	M	12	22	0	13	–	–	85	93	77	9.0
6	M	47	13	53	77	12	16	102	98	106	3.7
7	M	16	28	7	12	45	51	110	111	107	8.7
8	F	33	17	34	50	13	16	91	87	98	2.6
9	M	50	48	43	58	0	9	123	115	131	11.0
10	M	21	27	8	27	38	36	119	118	117	6.4
11	F	10	7	3	20	40	45	106	108	102	5.4
12	F	–	–	–	–	59	66	89	86	96	5.1
13	F	23	17	15	33	33	37	84	89	80	3.9
14	M	13	27	2	12	21	25	98	93	106	3.7
15	M	11	8	3	20	12	16	108	104	111	9.7
16	M	6	3	3	10	23	26	111	112	107	3.4
17	M	–	–	–	–	9	11	102	103	100	5.4
18	M	–	–	–	–	10	15	79	76	86	3.6
19	M	–	–	–	–	13	23	100	92	110	5.1

that there is extreme variation between dyslexic subjects: some have extremely high vowel error rates—for example, 38, 45, and 59 percent; others perform at or close to the level of the normal control group. The dyslexic subjects were retested on these vowel stimuli a second time, and their responses were tape recorded and transcribed using a double-blind procedure by an expert phonetician. The same pattern of error rates for vowel identification was observed with this procedure, in which the phonetician knew neither the correct responses nor the initial results.

The constant-vowel stimuli were used in psychoacoustic tests in which the dyslexic subjects were asked to repeat the stop consonant with which each syllable started. The syllables started with a [b], a [d], or a [g]. These stimuli were ones that had been used in a previous study (Chapin, Tseng, and Lieberman, 1982) with subjects who had no difficulty in reading. The stimuli were prepared by computer-editing samples of discourse from the utterances of a 1½-year-old child who was talking with her mother. The duration of each syllable was limited to the first 135 msec of each syllable starting from the release of the stop consonant. The average error rate of the nondyslexic subjects was 7 percent when they were asked to identify the initial stop consonant. The normal control group's error rates for [b], [d], and [g] identifications were 5, 5, and 10 percent, respectively. Table 9-1 notes the error rates for stop-consonant place of articulation for each dyslexic subject.

The data in Table 9-1 appear to reflect discrete speech perception deficits. These deficits are not present in the entire population of dyslexic subjects, nor is there a uniform pattern of errors in identification of vowels and stop-consonant place of articulation. Though some subjects, for example, subjects 7, 10, and 11, have higher error rates for both consonants and vowels, other subjects show different patterns. Subjects 6 and 8 thus have high error rates for stop consonants and low error rates for vowels. However, these generalizations fail to capture the variation in the pattern of errors for particular consonantal place-of-articulation contrasts. Note the variation in the error rates for the identification of [b], [d], and [g] in Table 9-1. The dyslexic subjects who were all voluntarily enrolled in the reading clinic of the Language Disorders Unit of the Massachusetts General Hospital had been tested using a full complement of intelligence and reading tests. The subjects, moreover, had no general auditory deficits. There was no correlation between error rates and IQ scores. High vowel error rates occur for subjects whose verbal IQ scores differ by 32 points. High consonantal error rates also occur for subjects whose verbal IQ scores differ by 32 points.

In Chapters 7 and 8, data and theories were discussed which propose that specific genetically transmitted neural mechanisms are involved in the perception of speech. The perceptual data of Table 9-1 are consistent with these theories. It is apparent that many forms of dyslexia are genetically transmitted. Recent studies of families with a three-generation history of dyslexia, for example, show a pattern of alletic variation on chromosome 15 (Smith et al., 1983). The data of Table 9-1 thus are consistent with the presence of alletic, or genetic, variation in these speech perception mechanisms. That variation exists is not surprising. Linguists often assume that a nativist position regarding the biological basis of language necessarily leads to the claim that linguistic ability is uniform throughout the population that makes use of a given language or dialect. As I have noted before, this position is simply wrong. Even the most basic and central biologically determined aspects of human life, such as the anatomical and neural mechanisms that effect and regulate respiration, vary in the present human population (Bouhuys, 1974). The biological bases of respiration, moreover, have been filtered by the selective forces that are relevant to respiration in terrestrial animals for hundreds of millions of years. Despite this long evolutionary history we find genetic variation in the biological mechanisms that structure respiration. The specific acoustic parameters that specify vowel distinctions and consonantal place of articulation — formant frequency patterns and onset spectra — derive from the properties of the human supralaryngeal vocal tract. The data that will be discussed in Chapters 11 and 12 are consistent with the evolution of the human supralaryngeal vocal tract and matching neural speech perception mechanisms in the recent past (500,000 to 250,000 years ago). Thus, in the ability of human listeners to identify these sounds, it is not surprising to find patterns of variation that appear to have a genetic basis.

It is likely that some aspects of speech perception as well as other aspects of human linguistic ability (for example, specific components of syntactic ability) are more basic in that their biological determinants are more uniformly distributed in the present human population. It is possible that the cues that are most uniform throughout the human population may be those that have the longest evolutionary history. If this is true, we would expect distinctions that involve voice onset time to be more robust than place of articulation. Voice-onset-time perception, as noted earlier, may derive from properties of the mammalian auditory system, which is about 200 million years old (Pilbeam, 1972).

Adaptations that had a selective advantage in the more recent past obviously will be more unevenly distributed throughout the population that defines a species than adaptations that had a selective advantage in an earlier period — all other things being equal. Thus the ability to digest cow's milk is unevenly distributed throughout the present human population. Cows were domesticated only about ten to fifteen thousand years ago. Before that time there would have been no selective advantage in being able to digest cow's milk. We find that people who are descendants of populations that traditionally kept cows are more likely to be able to digest cow's milk than people whose ancestors did not keep cows. The probability of the occurrence of the genetically transmitted mechanisms that allow people to digest cow's milk thus varies with the time-depth of the selective advantage.

We can perhaps gain new insights into the hierarchy of the

acoustic cue structure of human speech by studying the actual pattern
of variation. I would predict that the cues that are most often perceived by infants and children with little or no exposure to their
linguistic environment are also the cues that are most often perceived
by different adults. These cues also probably will be the most highly
valued sounds of human speech and will be the most resistant to
confusion in the presence of noise. The processes of sound change
may in many instances reflect a shift from less perceptually salient
sounds to more highly valued ones. The vowel shifts that have occurred in many languages toward the vowel [i] may reflect this process
(Lieberman, 1976c).

THE ACQUISITION OF INTONATION BY INFANTS

The acquisition of intonation by infants appears to represent an
interesting interplay between maturation and interaction with the
infants' adult caretakers. As previously noted, adult speakers typically
lengthen the duration of the expiratory phase of respiration during
speech. The length of an expiration is equal to the length of a
sentencelike unit of speech. Adult speakers maintain a steady subglottal air pressure during the nonterminal phase of the expiration. They
effect this level air pressure by holding back on the elastic recoil force
of the lungs with the intercostal muscles that can expand the rib cage.

There is one crucial difference between the intonation signals
that newborn infants produce and those typical of older human
speakers. Newborn infants cannot regulate subglottal air pressure by a
"hold-back" intercostal muscle gesture. The hold-back, that is, inspiratory, function of the intercostal muscles is a mechanical consequence
of the fact that the ribs are angled downward and outward from the
spine in human beings after the age of about 3 months. At birth, the
ribs in newborn infants are almost perpendicular to the spine. Newborn infants thus inherently cannot effect a steady subglottal air
pressure by working against the air pressure generated by the elastic
recoil of the lungs. The control of subglottal air pressure during long
expirations requires a hold-back function since the elastic recoil pressure at the start of the expiration will exceed the level of 8 to 10 cm
H_2O that is normally used during speech. Newborn infants can generate the air pressure functions that occur in short breath-groups because the air pressure that results from the elastic recoil is quite low, in
the order of 2 cm H_2O. Newborn infants can supplement this pressure with their abdominal muscles to generate the subglottal air
pressures necessary for phonation. They, however, cannot regulate

air pressure during long breath-groups because the increased lung volume generates a subglottal air pressure function that is initially too high. Although adult speakers tend to produce short breath-groups that again involve the simpler pressure regulation scheme of the newborn infant (Froscher, 1978), they can also produce very long breath-groups. Human infants begin to produce long episodes of phonation after their third month of life when their rib cage has restructured toward the adult configuration (Langlois, Baken and Wilder, 1980).

The regulatory patterns that are involved in generating the air pressure functions typical of speech are quite complex even for the relatively simple situation that occurs when we produce short breath-groups and do not have to program an intercostal hold-back function. The elastic recoil function still must be supplemented by the precisely coordinated activity of the "expiratory" intercostal and abdominal muscles. It is striking that newborn infants do as well as they do, and it is reasonable to hypothesize an innately determined mechanism that has evolved to regulate subglottal air pressure during phonation. The presence of such an innate mechanism would not be surprising since the larynx clearly has evolved over a period of 300 million years to facilitate the production of sound at the expense of respiratory efficiency (Negus, 1949).

The data of Truby, Bosma, and Lind (1965), Stark, Rose, and McLagen (1975), and Langlois, Baken, and Wilder (1980) all show a pattern of respiratory activity for newborn infants in which the expiratory phase is about five times longer than the inspiratory phase. Newborn infants appear to generate an initial positive alveolar air pressure by means of abdominal contraction about 100 msec before the onset of phonation. There also is an abrupt decrease in alveolar air pressure at the end of phonation as the infant goes into the inspiratory phase of respiration (Truby, Bosma, and Lind, 1965, p. 73).

Three aspects of the intonation pattern of the normal human newborn cry are similar to the patterns that adult speakers usually use:

1. The duration of the expiratory phase is usually longer than that of the inspiratory phase and can vary. The cry patterns noted in the work of Truby, Bosma, and Lind (1965) have expiratory phases whose durations varied over a two-to-one range.

2. The alveolar air pressure function rapidly rises prior to the onset of phonation and then falls rapidly at the end of phonation as the infant enters the inspiratory phase of respiration. Phonation occurs until the end of expiration. The abrupt shift in the alveolar air

pressure function at the end of phonation reflects a basic vegetative constraint since a negative air pressure is necessary for inspiration. The infant must maintain a positive air pressure during expiration, and so an abrupt transition must take place at the end of the expiratory cycle coincident with phonation. Numerous studies (Ohala, 1970; Atkinson, 1973; Shipp, Doherty, and Morrissey, 1979) have found that the effect of changes in subglottal air pressure on the fundamental frequency of phonation is approximately 10 Hz/cm H_2O. Thus, all things being equal, F_0 will fall at the end of an expiration. If the larynx does not maintain its phonatory configuration until the end of phonation but instead begins to open toward its inspiratory position, the terminal fall in F_0 will be enhanced as the laryngeal muscles relax (Van Den Berg, 1962; Atkinson, 1973).

Most traditional perceptually based phonetic theories (Armstrong and Ward, 1926; Pike, 1945; Trager and Smith, 1951) and many instrumental studies (Lieberman, 1967; Hadding-Koch, 1961; Vanderslice and Ladefoged, 1972; Atkinson, 1973; Tseng, 1981; Landahl, 1981) agree insofar as a falling F_0 and amplitude contour form the *terminal* of a breath-group. The terminal intonation contour whose acoustic correlates are a falling F_0 and amplitude thus is the cue that signals the end of a declarative sentence or phrase in most human languages (Lieberman, 1967). This signal follows from the vegetative constraints of respiration. It reflects the biological necessity of a transition in alveolar air pressure from the positive air pressure of expiration to the negative air pressure of inspiration.

3. The third aspect wherein the intonation pattern of the newborn cry is similar to the adult pattern is that the F_0 contour tends to be almost level in the nonterminal portion of the breath-group. About 70 percent of the F_0 contours noted in the spectrograms of Truby, Bosma, and Lind (1965) and the corpus that formed the data base sampled in the work of Lieberman and colleagues (1972) had a relatively steady nonterminal F_0 contour. The other cry patterns involved either gross perturbations of the F_0 pattern where the infant blew his or her vocal cords apart because of excessive subglottal air pressure relative to medial compression (Van Den Berg, 1962) or exhibited other patterns of F_0 variation. What was not noted was the steady declination that some recent studies claim in the base form for intonation (Maeda, 1976; Sorenson and Cooper, 1980; Liberman, 1978; Pierrehumbert, 1981). The declination theory claims that a general fall in F_0 throughout the breath-group characterizes the intonation contours of most languages. According to Pierrehumbert (1981), this hypothetical gradual fall in F_0 follows from some as yet unknown basic property of

speech production that is manifested in the initial utterances of infants and children. The intonation pattern of the newborn cry does not show a consistent F_0 declination that fits any version of the declination theory. (Different versions of the declination theory characterize the hypothetical F_0 fall in different ways.)

EARLY IMITATION OF INTONATION

Traditional perceptually based accounts of the acquisition of speech state that infants start to imitate the sounds that they hear toward 8 to 10 months (Lewis, 1936). Recent studies that make use of the techniques of instrumental analysis, however, show that the process of imitation can start much earlier. Acoustic analysis of a "conversation" between a Japanese-speaking mother and her 6-week-old son, for example, shows the infant imitating the absolute F_0 and shape of the mother's intonation (Lieberman, Ryalls, and Rabson, 1982). Figure 9-2 shows the mother's F_0 contour for an utterance directed to an adult (one of the members of the recording crew) immediately before she turned to talk to her infant son. Figure 9-3(a) shows the F_0 contour of the sustained m-like sound that she directed to her son. Note that the average F_0 of the speech directed to the infant is over 300 Hz in contrast to the mother's average F_0 of 200 Hz in her speech directed to adults. The mother appears to be using a "motherese" register in which her average F_0 is within the infant's F_0 range (Keating and Buhr, 1978), facilitating imitation.

Figure 9-3(b) shows the F_0 contour of the infant imitating the sound whose F_0 is plotted in Figure 9-3(a). The infant has matched both the absolute F_0 and the shape of the sound that his mother directed to him. Note, however, that the infant's imitation is only 680 msec long, whereas the duration of the mother's utterance was 1100 msec. The infant at age 6 weeks lacks the rib cage anatomy necessary to produce a long expiration at a controlled subglottal air pressure. He thus responds with a shorter intonation contour that, however, preserves the absolute F_0 and shape of his mother's intonation contour. The infant's imitations of his mother's speech in this "conversation" involved three interchanges in which the infant's responses were limited to durations of approximately 700 msec. The mother appeared to initiate this conversation when she moved quite close to her son's face and directed the infant's first m-like sound, which she in turn imitated, followed by the infant imitating that sound, and so on. Infants by these procedures may learn that it is appropriate to imitate speech sounds. There, of course, may be a genetically transmitted

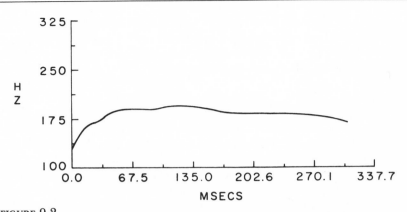

FIGURE 9-2. _____
Fundamental frequency of phonation plotted as a function of time
for a mother's utterance directed to an adult.

tendency for children to imitate sounds and for mothers to accultur-
ate their children to the imitation of speech. However, whether or not
there are any innate mechanisms that are specifically designed to
facilitate the imitation of speech sounds, it is evident that infants begin
to imitate the intonation contours that occur in their native language
at a very early age. These instrumental data thus are consistent with
the traditional, oft-repeated claim that children acquire the characteristic intonation patterns of their native language in the first year of
life (Lewis, 1936).

By age 3 months infants can match the duration of their mother's
intonation contours as well as the absolute F_o. The data of Sandner
(1981) show a 3-month-old infant imitating the fundamental frequency contours of his German-speaking mother during a five-minute
"conversation." The infant is imitating the detailed, nonterminal
modulations of fundamental frequency that his mother produces.
Sandner presents no physiologic data on the infant's subglottal air
pressure; however, an adult human speaker would normally maintain
an even subglottal air pressure and imitate the details of the nonterminal fundamental frequency contour by adjustments of the laryngeal
muscles (Ohala, 1970; Atkinson, 1973). It otherwise would be extremely
difficult, if not impossible, to imitate long, detailed fundamental
frequency contours. The speaker would have to compensate for the
constantly changing subglottal air pressure that would be generated
by the decreasing elastic recoil function. As already noted, phonation
during newborn cry, where subglottal air pressure is not regulated,

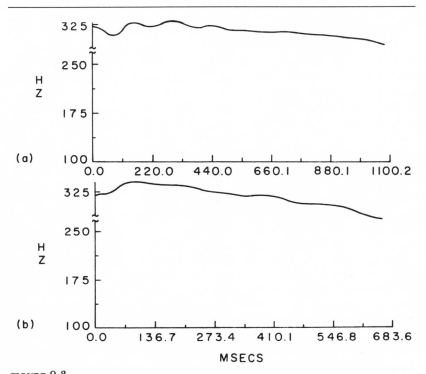

FIGURE 9-3.
Fundamental frequency contour of a mother's *m*-like sound
directed to her infant son (*a*). Fundamental frequency contour of
the utterance that the infant produced immediately afterward (*b*).

tends to be interrupted with intervals of aspiration when the vocal
cords are blown apart by an excessively high subglottal air pressure.
The infant in Sandner's study thus in all likelihood was regulating
subglottal air pressure by using his intercostal muscles. It is difficult to
see how a 3-month-old infant could have "learned" to regulate his
subglottal air pressure since the development of his rib cage would not
have allowed him to use his intercostal muscles to regulate air pressure
until the third month of life (Langlois, Baken, and Wilder, 1980). In other
words, the infant in Sandner's study appears to regulate subglottal air
pressure and imitate intonation contours as *soon* as his anatomy develops to the point where he can regulate subglottal air pressure. The
pattern of anatomy and muscular control suddenly appears. It thus is
quite likely that the neural muscular control pattern for the regulation
of subglottal air pressure is innately determined.

VOWEL PRODUCTION

The anatomy of the supralaryngeal vocal tract of human infants at birth is similar to that of nonhuman primates. Human infants initially do not produce vowels like [i], [u], and [a] (Lieberman et al., 1972; Stark, Rose, and McLagen, 1975; George, 1978; Buhr, 1980). Though the neural control for speech production may not be well developed at birth, the anatomy of the supralaryngeal vocal tract in itself is a limiting factor until it restructures at about the age of 3 months. Studies in which the supralaryngeal vocal tract typical for newborn infants is modeled by using a computer-implemented simulation show that it is inherently impossible to produce these vowels[1] (Lieberman and Crelin, 1971; Lieberman, Crelin, and Klatt, 1972; Lieberman, 1975a). The tongue in the human newborn is long and thin and is positioned entirely within the oral cavity. The newborn's tongue contour does not have the almost-circular shape of the posterior margin of the adult human tongue (Nearey, 1978). This difference in tongue shape, which follows from the high position of the newborn's larynx, makes it impossible for newborns to produce the supralaryngeal vocal tract area functions that are necessary to produce these sounds (Fant, 1960; Stevens and House, 1955).

The phonetic categorization of the vowels that infants produce in their noncry utterances is not easy. The range of fundamental frequencies that infants use when they babble, which may range from low-frequency "fry" phonation to F_o's of 1.5 kHz (Keating and Buhr, 1978), confounds the transcription problem. Although perceptions of vowel quality and pitch normally are almost independent, extremes of F_o can influence vowel perception (Fujisaki and Kawashima, 1968). Furthermore, we usually do not know what words or sounds infants are trying to produce or whether they are attempting to produce words at all. This in itself makes the transcription problem difficult. Studies of speech perception show that we usually make use of the pragmatic context of a conversation to aid our perception of phonetic detail. We tend to "hear" sounds that are consistent with an interpretation of a read passage or a conversation that "makes sense" (Lieberman, 1963). It is necessary to listen to about 0.8 second of a conversation in order to identify individual words correctly (Pollack and Pickett, 1963). Anyone who has ever attempted to make a transcription of the proceedings of a conference knows that it is often impossible to understand what a speaker is saying unless one is familiar with the topic under discussion. Much of the phonetic detail that we hear depends on our knowledge of what the speaker most likely said.

Despite these difficulties, perceptually based phonetic transcriptions of the sounds that infants make in their first three months of life are in substantial accord (Irwin, 1948; Stark, Rose, and McLagen, 1975; George, 1978). The transcriptions of phonetically trained listeners responding to the sounds that infants produce in their noncry utterances are restricted to the "front" vowels of English, except [i], for infants raised in an English-speaking environment. At age 3 months the vowel [i] and the "back" vowels of English, including [u] and [a], appear (George, 1978; Buhr, 1980; Lieberman, 1980). What is interesting in regard to the development of speech-producing anatomy and the motor control of speech is that infants appear to exploit their speech-producing anatomy to its fullest capacity. The vocal output of human infants thus stands in marked contrast to the behavior of both juvenile and adult chimpanzees in this regard (see Chapter 10).

EARLY IMITATION OF VOWELS

Recent data show that some infants and mothers establish a pattern of interactive vowel imitation when the infant is as young as 3 months (Lieberman, Ryalls, and Rabson, 1982). These data are consistent with the hypothesis that two different aspects of human behavior are involved in the early stages of speech acquisition. The general cognitive process of imitation characterizes the behavior of both the infant and the mother as the infant and mother interact, taking turns. However, the vowels that the mother and infant produce as they imitate each other are not simple imitations of the formant frequency patterns that define vowels. The infant's imitations of the mother's vowels have formant frequency patterns that are much higher, being scaled to the infant's shorter supralaryngeal vocal tract. The infant at age 3 months acts as though he were equipped with an innately determined neural device that enables him to effect the process of vocal tract normalization.

Figure 9-4 shows the frequencies of F_1 and F_2, the first two formants of the sustained vowels, and the end points of the diphthongs that were produced by a Japanese-speaking mother and her 3-month-old son while they were imitating each other. These data were derived from the same Japanese-speaking mother-infant pair discussed earlier in regard to the early imitation of intonation. The speech sample was recorded in the infant's home in the course of a study investigating the early development of speech. A recording crew visited the infant's home at two-week intervals and recorded an

mented analysis (Buhr, 1980; Lieberman, 1980; Lieberman, Ryalls, and Rabson, 1982).

The vowel imitations whose formant frequencies are plotted in Figure 9-4 were produced after an interlude in which the infant was spontaneously producing sustained [ae]- and [u]-like vowels[2] as well as [ae]-to-[u] diphthongs. The duration of these utterances ranged from 950 to 1120 msec. The mother initiated the conversation when she placed her head close to her infant son and imitated one of his vowels that had a phonetic quality intermediate between [ae] and [a]. After a short pause, she produced a sustained 870-msec-long diphthong in which she started with [a] and ended with [u]. The infant responded even as she was phonating, starting with an [a]-like vowel and ending with an [u]-like vowel. The duration of the infant's imitation was 700 msec. The mother then responded by producing a second diphthong starting with a slightly centralized [a] and ending with [u] in a 966-msec-long diphthong, which the infant again imitated. The infant's imitation was 790 msec long. The mother then produced a third [a]-to-[u] diphthong, which the infant again imitated. The tempo of the conversation then changed as it came to an end. The mother produced a series of shorter, 300-msec [ae]'s and [a]'s, which the infant at first imitated. The conversation ended with the infant's producing an [u]-like vowel in response to his mother's [a].

The tape recording shows a pattern of conversational turn-taking developing in which the infant and mother respond to each other's utterance. The acoustic formant frequencies plotted in Figure 9-4 also clearly show that the child does not attempt to mimic the absolute values of the formant frequencies of his mother's vowels. Note that the infant's formant frequencies are always higher than his mother's. He imitates the *phonetic* class into which her vowels fall in terms of her acoustic vowel space; that is, he imitates her [a]-class vowels[3] with [a]'s that have higher formant frequencies which are appropriate to his acoustic vowel space, and her [u]'s with vowels that again have higher absolute formant frequencies which are appropriate to his acoustic vowel space.

Figure 9-4 shows that the infant could produce a fair approximation to the absolute values of the formant frequencies of his mother's [a]'s. Point X lies within the infant's vowel space. He could imitate his mother's [a]'s with a sound having these formant frequencies, which would better approximate the absolute values of her formant frequencies for this vowel, but he does not do so. The infant instead acts as though he were equipped, at age 3 months, with an innately determined neural vocal tract normalization device.

THE INNATE BASIS OF VOCAL TRACT NORMALIZATION

As noted earlier, we do not respond to the absolute values of the formant frequency pattern of speech when we are in the phonetic "mode." When we imitate the words that another person produces, we do not attempt to replicate the absolute formant frequency pattern. We instead produce sounds that have appropriate relationships but are frequency-scaled to the length of our own supralaryngeal vocal tract. We are not consciously aware of this. When we, for example, imitate the vowel [a] that is produced by a 2-year-old, we are not conscious of producing a formant frequency pattern whose absolute values may be half those of the child's. What we have to do is to set up an equivalence class between the vowels that we produce and the child's vowels. We have to know that our [a] is the same as the child's even though the formant frequencies differ by a factor of two. The process is not conceptually very different from the way in which we correct for the size of the image projected on the retina of the eye. We recognize Uncle Joe's face whether he is 5 feet or 10 feet from us. The image that is projected on our retina is twice as large when Uncle Joe is 5 feet away, but we automatically compensate for the absolute differences in size and instead pay attention to the relational form of the image. We also recognize speech sounds as being the same in terms of relational attributes. Like the recognition of faces, which is apparent in early infancy, the recognition of the sounds of speech appears to be based on innate normalization devices. It is most unlikely that a 3-month-old infant could learn, through a process of trial and error, to establish equivalence classes based on formant frequency normalization when he imitates the vowel sounds that his mother makes. The infant at age 3 months has barely acquired the supralaryngeal vocal tract anatomy necessary to produce the full range of vowel sounds when he imitates his mother.

Data on the development of vowel production in other infants as they mature are again consistent with the presence of an innately determined vocal tract normalization device. In Figures 9-5 and 9-6, formant frequency data derived from a child who was in the word-producing stage of language acquisition are presented. Note that the formant frequencies are lower as the child grows. The child's vowel space adjusts to his longer supralaryngeal vocal tract. The acoustic vowel space also better approximates the form of the adult vowel system (Nearey, 1978; Lieberman, 1979a, 1980). There is a gradual and consistent improvement in children's production of the vowels of English from the earliest stages of babbling well into the stage (at age 3 years) where the children are producing multiword sentences and are conversing with adults (Landahl, 1982).

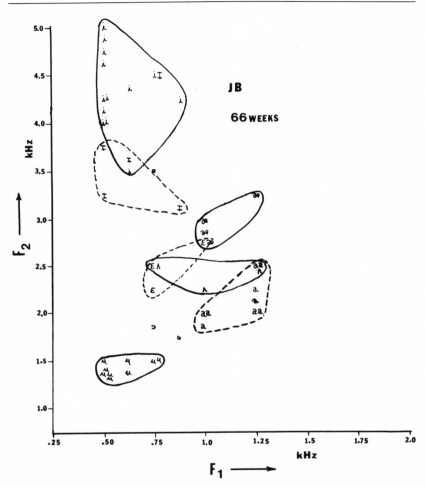

FIGURE 9-5.

Formant frequencies of vowels produced by child JB at age 66 weeks. The phonetic class of each vowel is indicated. (After Lieberman, 1980.)

ACQUIRING MOTOR CONTROL PATTERNS

Children's acquisition of consonantal sound contrasts has also been studied in recent years with the use of instrumental techniques. Studies of the acquisition of voice-onset-time distinctions, for example, show that children start by producing stops that are either prevoiced or have short lags. The short-versus-long-lag contrast is not

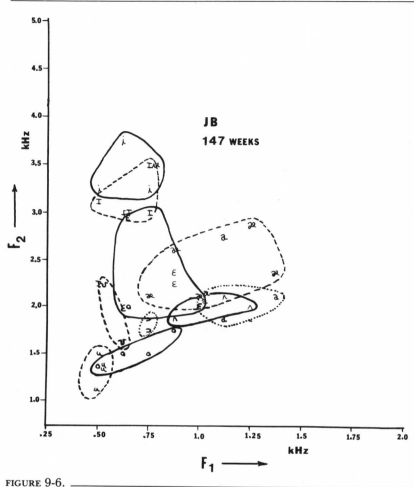

FIGURE 9-6. _____

Formant frequencies of vowels produced by child JB at age 147
weeks. (After Lieberman, 1980.)

apparent until children are about 18 months old (Oller and Ross, 1976;
Port and Preston, 1972). The situation is thus similar to that of vowel
perception. Infants can perceive phonetic distinctions long before
they can produce them. Whereas the human speech perception system seems to respond to acoustic cues that have an innate basis and are
in a sense invariant,[4] there is not much evidence for the presence of
any innate invariant articulatory maneuvers for speech production.

Cineradiographic data on the speech production of adult speakers thus show that there is no invariant set of supralaryngeal vocal tract shapes that all speakers of a language use to generate the vowels of that language (Russell, 1928; Ladefoged et al., 1972; Nearey, 1978). Different speakers, for example, use different supralaryngeal vocal tract maneuvers to generate the vowels [I] and [ɛ]. Electromyographic data again show that even simple articulatory distinctions like nasalization involve different patterns of motor control for different speakers (Bell-Berti, 1973). These data show that human children cannot be innately equipped with a set of uniform, invariant instructions for the control of their vocal tracts for the production of speech. Speech production, like other activities involving complex and precise motor coordination, appears to involve gradually setting up patterns of automatized motoric activity. The data that have been obtained through the study of children acquiring their first language show that it takes years for children to acquire these automatized motor control patterns.

SUMMARY

The acquisition of speech by human children appears to involve both innate neural mechanisms that are specific to speech, such as vocal tract normalization and air pressure regulation, and general cognitive processes, such as imitation. Critical periods appear to be involved in the acquisition of speech by human beings. However, critical periods — that is, periods in which an organism must be exposed to some stimulus in order to achieve "normal" behavior — are not limited to speech acquisition or to human beings. Electrophysiologic and behavioral data show that critical periods structure the acquisition of binocular vision in cats, visual acuity in cats and human beings, bird calls, and so on.

Recent instrumental data show that infants begin to imitate the intonation patterns of their mothers from age 6 weeks, and vowels by age 3 months. Genetic variation may account for some of the variations in the pattern of speech acquisition as well as ultimate adult linguistic ability. Whereas some aspects of speech perception appear to involve genetically transmitted innate neural mechanisms, the motor routines involved in speech production probably are, for the most part, learned automatized patterns that are no different in kind from those necessary for other skilled activities.

CHAPTER 10
Apes and Children

IT IS CURIOUS TO SEE HOW LONG IT takes to resolve a scientific issue. The common view of science is that scientists are objective beings who quickly devise "crucial" experiments that test conflicting theories and establish "laws." The lead in the March 21, 1980, "Research News" section of *Science* is "Ape-Language Controversy Flares Up," an issue that has been hotly debated since the seventeenth century. The issue of ape-language became a theological as well as a scientific question in the seventeenth century when it was linked to the question of our special status — the creation of human beings in the image of God. Then as now, the study of anatomy, physiology, and animal behavior was reducing the sharp distinction between human beings and the lower animals. Tyson's (1699) comparative anatomy, for example, showed the similarities between the structures of the human body and those of the apes, including the nervous system. Live apes were also observed in contact with human beings. The entry in Samuel Pepys's *Diary* for August 1661 thus notes, "it is a great baboon, but so much like man in most things . . . I do believe it already understands much English; and I am of the mind it might be taught to speak or make signs." Little progress in teaching apes either to talk or to sign followed Pepys's *Diary* entry until the recent studies of ape-language that I will discuss here. Apes raised in a humanlike environment can be taught to communicate by means of American Sign Language. The apes' linguistic progress does not appear to be equivalent to that of normal children raised in normal environments. Indeed, extra care may have to be taken to establish the concept of communication by means of sign in nonhuman hominoids. However, the ape-language data that are presently available indicate that chimpanzees have the biological capability for communicating in a linguistic mode. That result in itself addresses one of the central issues concerning hominid evolution in general and the evolution of human language in particular. The fact that chimpanzees *can* acquire language, albeit at a level found in young children, is consistent with the hypothesis that the initial steps toward the evolution of human language could have started with the hominoids ancestral to both human beings and apes. Further specializations in the direction of enhancing cognitive and linguistic ability have widened the gap.

LANGUAGE VERSUS COMMUNICATION

The issue in studies that teach a language like American Sign Language to a chimpanzee is not, of course, whether the chimpanzee will then become human. Rather, the comparative psychologist or linguist in studies of the acquisition of communication by young chimpanzees must somehow determine whether the communication is similar to that of human children, in that some aspects of the communication are in a "linguistic" mode. The difficulty that people have in deciding whether some aspects of ape-human communication are linguistic reflects the more general problem that linguists have in deciding what aspects of human communication are linguistic. Some cases are as obvious as determining if a bird is flying or not. Your reading this sentence is clearly an example of communication in a linguistic mode.

The usual definitions of languge — that (1) it allows us to transmit "new" information; (2) it allows us to generate infinitely long sentences; (3) it allows us to generate an infinite number of sentences — offer little guidance when we, for example, attempt to differentiate the "linguistic" from the "nonlinguistic" communications of young children. There are clear cases. A child clutching its side when he howls with pain from a stomach ache is not communicating in a linguistic mode. But is a child asking for a cookie, while he utters the sound [gUk] and looks up at his mother, communicating in a "linguistic" or in a "nonlinguistic" mode? Studies of the acquisition of language will classify such utterances as linguistic if the sound [gUk] is a member of a class of phonetically related sounds that the mother reacts to appropriately and that the child produces when he wants a cookie. We know that, in time, the child's utterances will take on the characteristics of adult speech — which we surely want to classify as linguistic. Thus we see continuity between the fully specified, stable adult form of the language and the child's first, imperfect attempts at communication in a linguistic mode.

More elaborate definitions of human language that are supposed to differentiate it from the communications of other animals also do not work when we examine the actual communications of young children. The "design" features of Hockett (1960), for example, do not fit the communications of young children. Hockett's list of design features includes features 4, interchangeability; 10, displacement; and 11, productivity, which clearly do not characterize the one- and two-word stages of language acquisition.

Design feature 4, interchangeability, for example, claims that the phonetic form of a particular word that a person utters is similar to, or interchangeable with, the phonetic form of the "same" word that he hears. The phonetic shapes of the words that children produce typically differ from the adult forms. At age 4 my son's phonetic forms of the word *raisin*, for example, were quite different. He would produce the phonetic sequence [wIno], though he responded to normal adult versions of *raisin* and would stop and interrupt adults who would direct the phonetic form [wIno] to him. The "correct" adult word for him was *raisin*. The effect is general and pervasive: children typically produce different phonetic forms of adult words. These phonetic equivalents, moreover, change as the child matures (Olmsted, 1971; Landahl, 1982). Children's early utterances also do not involve design feature 10, displacement; that is, they do not typically discuss situations displaced in time and place. Moreover, the actual utterances of young children do not manifest design feature 11, productivity. Children do not produce an infinite set of sentences; they do not produce utterances like "She has green hair" in the absence of green-haired individuals.

TRANSFORMATIONAL GRAMMAR

The formal methods of transformational, generative grammar at face value would appear to offer a theoretical framework by which we could decide whether the utterances of a child or a chimpanzee constituted communication in a linguistic mode. Chomsky indeed claims that "modern linguistics has provided a great deal of new information concerning a wide range and variety of languages. It has sought, with much success, to achieve significantly higher standards of clarity and reliability than those reached in earlier studies of language" (1966, p. ix). Chomsky, in 1966, also hoped that the methods of formal transformational linguistics would yield an understanding of the specific characteristics of the mental abilities that underlie language:

> It does not seem unrealistic, therefore, to hope that research of the sort that can be undertaken at present may lead to a plausible and informative account of the mental abilities that underlie the

achievement of normal linguistic competence, abilities that may be as individual and species-specific as that of a bird to learn a particular set of songs, of a beaver to build dams, or of a bee to integrate its own actions into the intricate social activity of the hive.

(1966, p. ix)

Chomsky's more recent statements indicate that he believes that the studies in transformational grammar which have since occurred have solved the problem. We now supposedly have isolated the salient species-specific aspects of the syntax of human language. Chomsky thus speaks with certainty when he comments on Premack's (1980) discussion of communication between human beings and chimpanzees:

> What they [experimenters working with chimpanzees] are not going to discover is the possibility of imposing on that species, however hard they try, a system that has *any* of the properties of language in the domain that I'm talking about . . . I don't expect that they are going to be able to impose on that species a system that has, for example, recursive rules meeting the condition of structure dependence (to take the most simple property of human language).
>
> (Chomsky, 1980, p. 181)

Chomsky is also quite certain as to the locus of the biological deficiency that prevents chimpanzees from being able to handle structure-dependent transformational rules. "One thing is missing: that little part of the left hemisphere that is responsible for the specific structures of human language" (Chomsky, 1980, p. 182).

Despite these heady claims, there is some doubt as to whether the theory of transformational grammar has any validity. One of the basic tests of any scientific theory is that it must be able to describe the range of data that is within the scope of the theory. Hundreds of papers and books have explored various issues using the techniques of transformational grammar. However, as Gross notes, "no linguist has been able to construct a transformational grammar with the type of coverage that traditional grammars used to provide" (1979, p. 859). Gross and his co-workers attempted to build a formal transformational grammar that would describe a significant portion of French. Their corpus contained more than twelve thousand lexical items and constituted a classification of the simple predicates of French. The attempt failed. In contrast, a nontransformational grammar of six hundred rules and conditions for the application of those rules described the data. Similar difficulties occurred when Gross attempted to construct and study the generality of a single transformational rule for a large corpus of French sentences. The transformational mechanisms involved in Equi-NP deletion (a phenomenon in which particular noun phrases are deleted) were studied by Gross (1968, 1975, 1979) over a ten-year period. What happened was that "each time we introduced a new example, the rule had to be applied in a way different from that used in all previously studied cases" (Gross, 1979, p. 861). Gross's assessment of the state of modern transformational linguistics is that

> today there is no longer any distinction between generative syntax and a substantial part of generative phonology; the sole object of both is symbolic manipulation of a few well-known facts, intended to show that the human mind can be reduced to a formal class of abstract automata. The universities which have built linguistics departments with the aim of increasing knowledge about language now find themselves equipped with philosophy departments of a strange specialization, perhaps not altogether desirable. Linguistics has vanished . . . any attempt or even proposal to collect systematic data is instantly qualified as anti-theoretical, and eliminated from what has been institutionalized as linguistics. Normally a specialist who invents some abstract mechanism should propose some way to verify its adequacy, or verify it himself; this can and should be done by applying the mechanism to all relevant parts of well-studied languages. This elementary rule is almost never followed.
>
> (1979, p. 879)

Gross concludes that both the theory and the practice of linguistic studies in the transformational school have become mired in "pseudo-Cartesianism." Despite over twenty years of research no transformational theory has, for example, been used to explore any language, even English, as completely as possible. If you want a description of the syntax of English, you will find it in the works of Jesperson's (1909) traditional grammar. You will not find any transformational grammar that can describe more than a fraction of the corpus, imperfectly and in a cumbersome and opaque manner. There is no transformational metric, a generative philosopher's stone that will tell us whether a chimpanzee or a child is communicating in a linguistic mode.

APE CULTURE

Before comparing the acquisition of communication in apes and human children, I would like to note some of the data which suggest that we probably do not know what or how chimpanzees communicate in the state of nature. It is common to state that chimpanzees do not exhibit any linguistic behavior in their native habitat. However, recent close observations of changes in chimpanzee culture are puzzling in that regard. In contrast to bees and other insects, the social relations of chimpanzees, like those of human beings, are not immutable. Rapid changes in chimpanzee *culture* have been observed. Goodall (1979), for example, records two rapid changes in the pattern of social interactions in the Gombe Stream site.

The first change involves behavior that in a human community would be characterized as warfare. The life cycle of a chimpanzee is not very different from that of a human being. As Goodall notes, infancy lasts about five years; adolescence lasts from about age 9 to age 14; old age sets in at about 35. Affectionate bonds exist between mothers and their children and between siblings, and these bonds may persist throughout life. Aggressive behavior within a group of chimpanzees usually consists of threatening gestures and calls. Fights between members of the same community may occur. These fights may involve individuals competing for food or males competing for a female, but they seldom last more than a minute and rarely result in serious wounds. Fights between chimpanzees belonging to different communities, however, are more serious and can be to the death.

Each chimpanzee community has a home range within which the chimpanzees roam foraging for food. The home range of the chimpanzees in the main study group followed by Goodall at Gombe has fluctuated between 5 and 8 square miles. The home range is patrolled by groups of adult males in a military manner:

> The adult males, usually in groups of two or three, quite regularly patrol the boundaries, keeping close together, silent, and alert. Sometimes they climb a tall tree and stare out over the "hostile" territory of an adjacent community. As they travel, they may sniff the ground or pick up and smell leaves and twigs. They seem to be searching for clues to locate strangers.
>
> If the patrol meets up with a group from another community, both sides, after exchanging threats, are likely to withdraw discreetly back into home ground. But if a single individual is encountered, or a mother and child, then the patrolling males usually chase and, if they can, attack the stranger. Ten very severe attacks on mothers or old females of neighboring communities have been recorded since 1970; twice the infants of the victims were killed.
>
> (Goodall, 1979, p. 594)

What is relevant to the present discussion is that in 1970 the main chimpanzee community at Gombe divided; seven males and three females established themselves in the southern part of the home range. Starting in 1974 the chimpanzees who had split off to form the new community were killed by their former compatriots in savage, sustained attacks in which they were hit, kicked, and bitten. The attacks persisted until all of the chimpanzees who had split off were exterminated. How did the chimpanzees of the two groups reorder their allegiance? Clearly membership in the community was not determined by genetically transmitted factors since the chimpanzees that formed the two warring groups all were members of the same community until 1970. Again, how did the chimpanzees communicate to each other the new community relationships? The social change was sudden and profound. The chimpanzee conceptual system and communications system would have to indicate and transmit the changes in group membership.

The second cultural change that Goodall observes is the establishment of cannibalism in one family of chimpanzees. Passion, an adult mother, attacked another chimpanzee mother and seized and killed her baby. Passion shared the cannibal feast with her children, who went on to kill and eat other infant chimpanzees. The pattern of cannibalism apparently was established in a period of two or three years. Cannibalism was probably quite common in many human communities. It has apparently persisted for hundreds of thousands of years. One of the problems that makes it difficult to reconstruct the supralaryngeal airways of many fossil hominids (see Chapter 12) is that the skull base has been destroyed in the region of the foramen magnum. The skulls probably were opened at the foramen magnum so that the brains could be removed and eaten.

The pattern of cultural change in the chimpanzee community with regard to the establishment of cannibalism again demonstrates that chimpanzee behavior is not *determined* by genetic factors and is quite fluid. Insofar as the cannibalistic behavior of Passion and her family involves a measure of deception and stealth—it never occurs in the presence of adult males who might interfere and protect the infants—there must be both the concept of wrongdoing, that is, deviation from the established community norm that might be punished, and the communication of that concept in Passion's family.

The behavior of chimpanzees in the Gombe Stream colony also shows tool making and the transmission of a tool-making tradition. Goodall (1968) observes a chimpanzee mother stripping leaves from a branch to make a "termite stick" while she is closely observed by a juvenile chimpanzee. The termite stick is used by the chimpanzee to fish termites out of their holes. The termites then are licked off the stick by the chimpanzee (Goodall, 1968). Neither tool use nor tool making is exclusively a human or primate attribute. The California sea otter, for example, also uses stone "tools" to open shellfish. The sea otter holds a stone under a flipper until it acquires a supply of shellfish. It then floats on its back and cracks the shellfish open on the stone (Kenyon, 1969). The sea otter anticipates its need for the stone tool, as does the chimpanzee making its termite stick. The oft-repeated claim that animals do not have a sense of the future or past (Hockett's design feature of displacement) does not appear to be true. The degree to which chimpanzees may reflect on the past or speculate on the future undoubtedly differs from that of some human beings. However, there is a great deal of variation with respect to human preoccupation with the past or the future — Proust's reflections are, after all, unusual — and so it seems inappropriate to claim, as Hediger (1981, p. 16) does, that the "crucial" element of human thought and language that "makes" us human is the ability to "talk about a past or future event."

One of the aspects of speculation on the origins of human language that tends to trivialize its study is the continual attempt to find *the* factor that led to its evolution. It is obvious that communication in a linguistic mode affects all aspects of human life. Any element of human culture that could result in a selective advantage that could be further developed through the presence of human language could enhance the value of the biological substrate that structures human language. It is becoming apparent that almost all the elements that can occur in human culture can also be observed in a reduced degree in other animals. Chimpanzees in their natural environment, for example, use a range of greetings similar to those of human beings, such as handshaking, back patting, embracing (Goodall, 1968, 1979). Nonhuman primates engage in paternal as well as maternal care to infants. Male baboons often carry their offspring to protect them from attacks from other males (Busse and Hamilton, 1981). It thus is unlikely that the evolution of human language involved some sudden all-or-nothing process that yielded a behavioral attribute which cannot be found in closely related species. For example, human language, as Hegel observed in the nineteenth century, probably does enhance cooperative endeavors, but baboons in captivity learn to cooperate to use tools in novel situations (Beck, 1973). Chimpanzees are capable of cooperative problem solving in captivity (Nissen and Crawford, 1936). Both chimpanzees and baboons act cooperatively to hunt in their native environment (Goodall, 1968). Thus, though linguistic communication undoubtedly enhances cooperative activity, it does not *in itself* make

cooperative activity possible and exclusively hominid. The same statement may be made with respect to the reduction of aggressive conduct
that human language can *sometimes* enhance within a social community. As Goodall (1979) notes, chimpanzees within the social group
often use threatening expressions and calls to establish their position
in the hierarchy of the group before they resort to physical attacks.

Chimpanzees are, of course, not people. There are many important differences in their behavior. They are comparatively silent
animals. Though they do produce loud sounds when they are aroused
(Marler and Tenaza, 1978), they in general are silent (Goodall, 1968).
Their vocal activity thus stands in marked contrast to that of human
beings, who continually vocalize from birth onward. Human beings
act as though they were innately predisposed for communication in a
vocal mode; chimpanzees show much less vocal activity. The patterns
of chimpanzee and human social organization also differ fundamentally with respect to group cohesiveness and altruism. As Goodall's
(1979) observations demonstrate, wounded chimpanzees are not
cared for by their associates. The wounded chimpanzees dragged
themselves off into the bush, where they died of their wounds. The
fossil evidence of hominid evolution, in contrast, shows that the
injured and infirm were nursed back to health in periods as distant as
60,000 to 100,000 years before the present. Altruism is, of course, a
selective advantage for the preservation of a population. The adaptive
value of altruism with respect to the value of older individuals is
enhanced to the degree that they can communicate their life's experi-
ences to the younger members of the community. Enhanced linguistic
communication thus enhances the adaptive value of altruism. Altruis-
tic behavior is also a selective advantage in the preservation of the
community when the infants and children of slow-breeding animals
like chimpanzees and human beings are cared for after the death of
their natural parents. Chimpanzee communities again differ in this
respect from human societies. The infant and juvenile dependents of
a chimpanzee typically die shortly after their mother dies. The other
adult members of the chimpanzee community will not "adopt," or
take care of, the orphaned chimpanzees.

TEACHING APES HUMAN LANGUAGE

Attempts to teach apes human languages probably date back to at least
the time of LaMettrie (1747), who claimed that we could teach an ape
to talk by using the methods that had been developed to teach deaf
children language. The ape, LaMettrie claimed, would then be "a

perfect little gentleman." Success in this endeavor dates back to the project initiated by Alan and Beatrix Gardner in 1965. The Gardners considered the failure of attempts to teach chimpanzees to communicate vocally. Both the disappointing results of the attempt by Hayes and Hayes (1951) and observations of chimpanzees in their natural habitat indicated that chimpanzees might be better adapted for communication using gestures or other visual cues. The supralaryngeal vocal tracts of chimpanzees and other apes are inherently incapable of producing the full range of sounds necessary to speak a language like English (Lieberman, 1968a). Chimpanzees, however, do not even produce the full range of sounds that they could produce (Lieberman, 1976a). Chimpanzees simply do not appear to be adapted biologically for vocal communication with the complexity of human speech.

The procedure that the Gardners adapted was brilliant in its simplicity. Human children acquire speech and language when they are exposed to a normal linguistic and social environment. The biological differences between chimpanzees and human beings could be assessed if a chimpanzee were raised in conditions similar to those of a human child. The Hayes and Hayes (1951) project had, in fact, attempted to raise an infant chimpanzee in a normal human environment with spoken English the mode of communication. The Gardners instead used American Sign Language (ASL), the gestural language that is usually used by deaf people in North America. The Gardners thus raised Washoe, a female chimpanzee who was about 10 months old at the start of the project, in an environment in which people communicated with her by using ASL. The initial Washoe project, which was reported in a number of papers (Gardner and Gardner, 1969, 1971, 1974, 1975a, 1975b) and motion pictures (Gardner and Gardner, 1973), suffered from the deficiency that some of Washoe's human companions were not proficient signers of ASL. Washoe's exposure to ASL also did not start until she was 10 months old. Another project, in which four chimpanzees were raised in an ASL environment from birth onward, was subsequently started by the Gardners (Gardner and Gardner, 1978, 1980).

The Gardners have documented the procedures they employed to assess the vocabularies of the chimpanzees, the training procedures, and the comparative analyses of the linguistic skills of ASL-using chimpanzees as compared with normal human children acquiring speech and deaf children acquiring ASL. The analyses presented in the work of Gardner and Gardner (1974) show that Washoe's progress during the first three years of ASL exposure qualitatively was similar to the children studied by Brown (1973) and Bloom (1970). The chimpanzee's utterances were similar to those of children in the one- and two-word stages of language acquisition. Locatives like *in, out,* and *there* occurred frequently, as did appropriate responses to Wh-questions, that is, sentences like *Where is John?* The analyses presented in the studies of Gardner and Gardner (1978, 1980) reported comparisons of the number of different utterances, the number of utterances per hour, and the grammatical categorization of the early vocabulary of chimpanzees versus that of children as well as the relations between Wh-questions and the chimpanzees' replies.

Table 10-1 reproduces one of these comparisons from the work of Gardner and Gardner (1978). The utterances that Washoe made in a number of sessions that were approximately twenty minutes long each were transcribed in a procedure modeled on the techniques developed by Brown (1973) and Bloom (1970). A team of two persons was necessary. One person whispered a spoken transcription of the signing, together with notes on the context, into a cassette recorder, while the other person performed "the usual roles of teacher, caretaker, playmate and interlocutor" (Gardner and Gardner, 1978, p. 57). The output of the chimpanzee is within the range reported both for the English-speaking children studied by Brown (1973) and Bloom (1970) with whom the chimpanzee is compared and for children using ASL in a study that made use of videotapes (Hoffmeister, Moores, and Ellenberger, 1975). A complete corpus of Washoe's expressive vocabulary after fifty-one months of training is presented in Gardner and Gardner's study (1975b). The 132 signs listed and described met a criterion of reliable usage that was rather conservative. The sign first had to be reported on three independent occasions by three different observers. It then had to occur spontaneously and appropriately at least once on fifteen consecutive days. The list thus probably underestimates Washoe's vocabulary. The list notes the usage of each sign and the configuration of the sign, that is, the place where the sign is made, the shape of the active hand, and the movement involved.

The four young chimpanzees who were exposed to ASL almost from birth began to use signs in combination before they were 1 year old. The rate of acquisition of signs and sign combinations for the chimpanzees was similar to that reported for children acquiring ASL. The age at which the chimpanzees had produced ten different sign combinations was 6 to 7 months. The children started to produce sign combinations, or phrases, at 9 to 10 months (McIntire, 1977). Both the chimpanzees and the signing children were somewhat more advanced than children acquiring English; the age at which English-speaking children produced ten different phrases ranged from 16 to 24 months

TABLE 10-1. Parallel Grammatical Categorizations for the Early Vocabulary of Children and Chimpanzees

Categories Used by Nelson	Nelson's Data for Children (N = 18)		The Data for Chimpanzees (N = 3)	
	Examples	Mean percentage of 50-item vocabulary	Examples	Mean percentage of 50-item vocabulary
I. Nominals				
specific	Mommy, Daddy, Dizzy	14	Betty, Pili, Susan	7
general (includes pronouns)	doggie, light, milk	51	dog, light, milk	49
II. Action words	go, out, up	13	go, out, up	24
III. Modifiers	big, hot, mine	9	good, hot, mine	8
IV. Personal-Social	no, please, want	8	no, please, refusal	11
V. Function words	for, That? Where?	4	—	0[a]

[a] Before reaching a 50-item vocabulary, our fourth subject, Tatu, was using That? which is identical to the name-asking questions categorized as function words for children.

SOURCE: Gardner and Gardner, 1978, p. 51, table 2.

237

in Nelson's (1973) study. Data derived in our studies at Brown University indicate that some children are even slower and have produced ten two-word utterances at age 30 months. It is evidently easier for chimpanzees and children to master signs than speech.

THE "CHILD" CHIMPANZEE

The chimpanzees in their first twelve months of life produce utterances that refer to their immediate environment, such as *There drink, There eat, There diaper, Susan brush, Gimme drink, Potty can't.* The output is essentially similar to that of young children.

One of the most interesting results of the primate research of Goodall and her co-workers is that chimpanzees have an extended childhood and adolescence that is quite similar to that of human beings. Chimpanzees under natural conditions are weaned at about age 5 years and live with their mothers until they are 8 to 10 years old. Throughout this period there is close interaction between the chimpanzee and its mother.[1] The environment that the Gardners set up for their chimpanzees took advantage of the possibility for close interaction between the infant chimpanzee and its human caretakers. As Gardner and Gardner note,

> chimpanzee subjects can be maintained in an environment that is very similar to that of a human child . . . their waking hours follow a schedule of meals, naps, baths, play and schooling, much like that of a young child. Living quarters are well stocked with furniture, tools, and toys of all kinds, and frequent excursions are made to other interesting places—a pond or a meadow, the home of a human or chimpanzee friend. Whenever a subject is awake, one or more human companions are present. The companions use ASL to communicate with the subjects, and with each other so that linguistic training is an integral part of daily life, and not an activity restricted to special training sessions. These human companions are to see that the environment is as stimulating as possible and as much associated with Ameslan [ASL] as can be. They demonstrate the uses and extol the virtues of the many interesting objects around them. They anticipate the routine activities of the day and describe these with appropriate signs. They invent games, introduce novel objects, show pictures in books and magazines, and make scrapbooks of favorite pictures, all to demonstrate the use of ASL.
>
> The model for this laboratory is the normal linguistic interaction of human parents with their children. We sign to the chimpanzees about ongoing events, or about objects that have come to

their attention as mothers do in the case of the child. We ask questions, back and forth, to probe the effectiveness of communication. We modify our signing to become an especially simple and repetitious register of Ameslan, which makes the form of signs and the structure of phrases particularly clear. And we use devices to capture attention, such as signing on the chimpanzee's body, which are also used by parents of deaf children (Schlesinger and Meadow, 1972).

(1980, p. 335)

It is significant to note that chimpanzees raised under these conditions will "initiate most of the interchanges by themselves, with their own questions, requests and comments" (Gardner and Gardner, 1980). The chimpanzees, like human children, "talked" to themselves. Washoe, for example,

often signed to herself in play, particularly in places that afforded her privacy, i.e., when she was high in the tree or alone in her bedroom before going to sleep. While we sat quietly in the next room waiting for Washoe to fall asleep, we frequently saw her practicing signs . . . Washoe also signed to herself when leafing through magazines and picture books, and she resented our attempts to join in this activity. If we did try to join her or if we watched her too closely, she often abandoned the magazine . . . Washoe not only named pictures to herself in this situation, but she also corrected herself.

Washoe also signed to herself about her own ongoing or impending actions. We have often seen Washoe moving stealthily to a forbidden part of the yard, signing *quiet* to herself.

(Gardner and Gardner, 1974, p. 20)

As I noted earlier, one of the functional features of human language is that it makes use of *words* rather than *signals*. Words are not simply labels for particular things or actions. They are rather flexible concepts that can take on a number of related references. The word *table* does not have one particular reference, nor are its references restricted to a particular type of table. It thus can refer to a chair when we use a chair as a table. The referents of the ASL signs that chimpanzees acquire when they are raised in a humanlike environment, like the referents of children's words, are not restricted to single items. The ASL signs function as words. The referent of the sign for *car* thus is the class of vehicles that are cars; the sign for *tree* will be used when chimpanzees are asked to identify a wide variety of trees, and so on. The chimpanzees attached new referents to words themselves. The sign for *meat*, for example, was used to identify raw meat wrapped in supermarket packaging, though meat was never presented and identified to the chimpanzees in that form. The chimpanzees on visits to the Gardner household formed the association themselves.

The signing chimpanzees also, like children, often used signs in combination to describe objects that were not represented by a sign in their vocabulary. Washoe, for example, referred to a swan as a *water bird*. Terrace and his colleagues (1979) have discussed this example in detail. They claim that there is no evidence that chimpanzees ever extend the semantic referents of an Ameslan sign or that chimpanzees create "new" words. The *water bird* sequence to Terrace is *not* an example of the chimpanzees creating a new word through the novel combination of signs. "Washoe may have simply been identifying a body of water and a bird, in that order" (Terrace et al., 1979, p. 895). The *water bird* sign sequence is, however, not an isolated occurrence, and Terrace would have to "explain" away other instances in which chimpanzees use sign sequences to describe new stimuli. Gardner and Gardner (1980), for instance, report the following examples:

> *Listen drink* for chimpanzee Moja referring to Alka Seltzer in a glass
> *Metal hot* for a cigarette lighter
> *Metal cup drink coffee* for a thermos bottle
> *Dirty good* for Washoe referring to a potty chair

The chimpanzees, like children, describe new objects in terms of either descriptive properties or functional attributes of the items (Clark and Clark, 1977).

TERRACE'S OBJECTIONS

These points are important since Terrace, in a widely publicized book and several papers (Terrace et al., 1979; Terrace, 1979a, 1979b) claims that "apes can learn many isolated symbols (as can dogs, horses, and other nonhuman species), but they show no unequivocal evidence of mastering the conversational, semantic, or syntactic organization of language" (1979, p. 901).

Although rigorous criticism is a necessary element in scientific discourse, the attacks that Terrace and his colleagues have launched on ape-language studies are excessive and are not consistent with published data. In the discussion of the *water bird* example, Terrace and his colleagues state that "there is no basis for concluding that Washoe was characterizing the swan as a 'bird that inhabits water.'

Washoe had a long history of being asked *what that?* in the presence of objects such as birds and bodies of water. In this instance, Washoe may have simply been answering the question, *what that?*, by identifying correctly a body of water and a bird, in that order" (1979, p. 895). The *water bird* example that Terrace discusses is drawn from the data of Fouts (1975), which Terrace cites. Fouts's description of Washoe's use of the sign sequence *water bird* departs from the scenario that is essential to Terrace's "explanation": "I often take Washoe for boat rides in a pond surrounding a chimpanzee island at the Institute. The pond is inhabited by two very territorial and nasty swans. Since I do not have a sign for swan I refer to them with the *duck* sign. Washoe does not have the *duck* sign in her vocabulary so she refers to the swans as *water birds*" (Fouts, 1975, p. 385). Washoe consistently refers to swans as *water birds* whether they are in or out of the water. Terrace's explanation implies that Washoe's use of the sequence *water bird* was limited to a single instance in which she replied to the question *What there?* by describing the constituents of the scene before her — the water and the bird. Washoe instead coined a new word by using the same perceptual criteria that human beings used when they coined the new word *steamboat.* You could argue that someone producing the sequence *steam boat* for the first time was merely describing what he saw; but the new word's semantic reference is to the boat that is mechanically powered. Washoe's word *water bird* refers to the animal that she saw, just as *steamboat* refers to the mechanically powered boat, *flatiron* to the device that people use to press clothes, and *toothbrush* to the object that Professor Terrace uses each day.

Terrace's bias is also evident in the way that he limits his discussion of the chimpanzee sign combinations reported in the work of Fouts (1975) to the single example, *water bird,* that might plausibly fit his facile explanation. This selectivity on the part of Terrace perhaps follows from the fact that the data would refute his claim that the sign communications of chimpanzees are "unstructured combinations of signs, in which each sign is separately appropriate to the situation at hand" (Terrace et al., 1979, p. 893). Fouts (1975), for example, reports that chimpanzee Lucy identified citrus fruits as *smell fruits,* a radish as a *cry fruit* or a *hurt fruit* after she tasted it, a watermelon as a *drink fruit* or a *candy fruit.* These examples are reported in the paragraph that precedes the *water bird* example. It is difficult to see how Terrace could have been unaware of these data.

Fouts (1975) also reports examples of chimpanzees inventing their own Ameslan signs for new objects. Washoe invented a sign for *bib.* Lucy invented a sign for the leash on which she was walked along a busy highway. Washoe also extended the referents of the sign *dirty* from its initial association with feces and soiled items. As Fouts notes,

> I was about to teach Washoe the sign *monkey* and while I was preparing the data sheet she turned around and began to interact with a particularly obnoxious macaque in a holding cage behind us. They threatened each other in the typical chimpanzee and macaque manner. After I had prepared the data sheet I stopped the aggressive interaction and turned her around so that she was facing two siamangs. I asked her what they were in ASL. She did not respond. After I molded her hands into the correct position for the *monkey* sign three times she began to refer to the siamangs with the *monkey* sign. I interspersed questions referring to various objects that she had signs for in her vocabulary. Next, I turned her toward the adjacent cage holding some squirrel monkeys and she transferred the *monkey* sign immediately to them. After she called the squirrel monkeys *monkey* several times I turned her around and asked her what her previous adversary was, the macaque, and she consistently referred to him as a *dirty monkey*. Up until this time she had used the *dirty* sign to refer to feces and soiled items; in other words as a noun. She had changed the usage from a noun to an adjective. In essence, it could be said that she had generated an insult. Since that time she has similarly used the dirty sign to refer to me as *dirty Roger* once when I signed to her that I couldn't grant her request to be taken off the chimpanzee island *(out me)* and another time she asked for some fruit *(fruit me)* and I signed *sorry but I not have any fruit*. Lucy has also used the *dirty* sign in similar manner. Once she referred to a strange cat she had been interacting with aggressively as a *dirty cat*, and she has also referred to a leash (which she dislikes) as a *dirty leash*.
>
> (1975, p. 387)

Terrace, in a public lecture at Brown University in December 1979, dismissed the *dirty* example out of hand. He claimed that Washoe undoubtedly was signing *dirty* in order to distract Fouts by indicating that she wanted to defecate.

Do Chimpanzees Sign Spontaneously?

One of Terrace's conclusions, which has been cited widely, is that whereas children's utterances are spontaneous, apes either imitate utterances made by their human interlocutors or are prompted. If this were true, it would mean that apes do not really communicate by using sign language. The data that I have already discussed—the observations of Washoe, for example—refute this claim. Terrace, however, supports his claim with a statistical procedure that he has applied to the utterances of Nim, the chimpanzee who was tutored in the project that he directed, as well as to some of the data reported for Washoe and the chimpanzees studied by Miles (1976). An examination of the procedure used by Terrace is illuminating. It shows that different criteria have been used to classify the utterances produced by children and by chimpanzees.

Over the years a fairly standard set of criteria has been developed to classify the utterances of children with respect to whether they are spontaneous and "novel." These criteria are rather straightforward. Thus Brown (1968), in his pioneering studies, considered children's responses to Wh-questions to be novel utterances. A response to a Wh-question has to be linguistically novel. If someone were to ask you, *What's that?*, you could not appropriately reply with the imitation *What's that?* Wh-questions thus serve as probes of a child's linguistic knowledge. The child also cannot appropriately respond to the question *What's that?* with the imitation *What's that?* The child's linguistic ability thus can be assessed by the interlocutor's careful use of Wh-questions.

Further refinements in the classification of children's utterances as to whether they are novel utterances, expansions, reductions, or simple imitations have since Brown's work (1968) been based on the overlap between the children's utterances and the immediate prior utterance of the parent or adult interlocutor (Bloom, Rocissano, and Hood, 1976). Terrace implicitly accepts these criteria, which structure the data base for the studies of children's speech with which he compares the sign communication of apes. Terrace, however, departs from these well-established procedures when he analyzes conversations with apes.

The Gardners, for example, followed Brown's (1968) criteria and reported an utterance as spontaneous "only if there had been no prompting other than a question such as *What that?* or *What you want?*" (Gardner and Gardner, 1978, p. 48). Terrace, in contrast, considers responses to Wh-questions as prompts — unspontaneous utterances that are not novel. Terrace indeed considers *any* signing activity that occurs before a chimpanzee produces an utterance to be a prompt when he analyzes the conversations filmed in the motion pictures of Washoe signing, as in the film of Gardner and Gardner (1973). By using this idiosyncratic procedure, he concludes that the chimpanzee conversations in the studies of the Gardners, Fouts, and Miles are not spontaneous — while keeping in the background the fact that different procedures have been applied to children and chimpanzees. If we were to apply Terrace's procedures to the corpus of Landahl (1982), in which detailed transcripts of conversations with three normal human children between the ages of 52 and 105 weeks are presented, we would have to conclude that human children almost never produce spontaneous utterances!

Terrace appears to have directed his attention toward devising peculiar metrics that will demonstrate that chimpanzees have no linguistic "competence." For example, he presents a statistical analysis in which he lumps together all of the utterances that a chimpanzee produces, without regard to verbal and pragmatic context, to look for the presence of fixed word-order relations like those that occur in the syntax of English. The statistical analysis is "objective" and "scientific," but it is irrelevant. Although some children do make use of word order at an early age, others do not. Different children make use of different strategies as they acquire language. The three children in Landahl's (1982) study differ in this respect. Only one of the children studied by Landahl, the child who adopted a "gestalt" approach in which she attempted to produce an entire sentencelike unit in one breath, used consistent word order in the early stages of language acquisition. In producing these utterances, however, this child tended to produce unintelligible sounds. The child who produced the largest number of intelligible words did not consistently use the word order of English.

Landahl's data do not represent an isolated occurrence. Many studies of the utterances of children have demonstrated that English-speaking children do *not* consistently make use of word order as a syntactic device in the early stages of language acquisition. This finding is generally accepted by psychologists and linguists; a discussion of the relevant studies can be found in the work of Clark and Clark (1977, pp. 311–312). Terrace's statistical analysis would show that human children also have no linguistic competence in the early stages of multiword utterances. It is possible that chimpanzees never will progress beyond that stage. That result would not be surprising, and it would provide us with some insight on the differences between hominids and closely related animals; but the interesting differences are unlikely to show up in a statistical analysis that removes all the context of an utterance.

Nim, the Wolf-Ape

One of the primary determinants of normal adult linguistic ability is the presence of "normal" social interaction in childhood. A normal environment in which normal discourse and interchange between parents and child occur is, for example, necessary to establish normal patterns of turn-taking in discourse (Kendon, 1975). A normal social environment is a necessary element in establishing human cognitive and linguistic ability (Singh and Zingg, 1942). Children raised in aberrant environments like Genie, the child who was locked into a room and tied to a toilet-training chair, generally fail to develop normal linguistic ability (Curtiss, 1977). "Wolf-children," children who were thought to have been raised by animals, form the extreme limiting state for the effects of social deprivation. Seen in this light, what is most peculiar about the studies of Terrace and his colleagues is their primary claim that "a team at Columbia University (Terrace, Petitto, Sanders, and Bever) attempted to replicate the experiments of the Gardners, Fouts, and Patterson" (Seidenberg and Petitto, 1981, p. 117). In contrast to the human environment in which the Gardners raised their chimpanzees, Terrace raised Nim in a very different manner. Nim's teachers were told that they should *not* treat him as though he were a child. Terrace, moreover, subjected Nim to long training sessions in a prisonlike environment. From the age of 9 months Nim was taken to a small 8-by-8-foot room. The room was empty except for a one-way mirror and was painted a uniform white. Terrace believed that a rich environment would distract the chimpanzee from the drill sessions that took place each day in three two-hour sessions. Instead of constant human companions who were proficient in ASL, an ever-changing staff of teachers, who were themselves novices in sign language, "cycled through Project Nim in a revolving door manner" (Terrace, 1979, p. 108). Terrace and the Columbia University team thus did *not* replicate the experiments of the Gardners, Fouts, and Patterson. Terrace applied strict Skinnerian theory and treated Nim as though he were a super-rat.

As Van Cantfort and Rimpau (1982) note, the difference in teaching and rearing conditions could easily account for the differences between Nim and the chimpanzees raised under conditions that more closely approximated those typical for normal human children. Van Cantfort and Rimpau also point out a number of other deficiencies in the procedures and analyses of Terrace and his associates. Frame-by-frame analysis of motion pictures, for example, is not appropriate for the analysis of sign language communications. Terrace and his colleagues (1979) made use of this procedure when they attempted to analyze the films of Washoe signing. It is *more* difficult to see dynamic events like signs when using frame-by-frame analysis than it is when viewing films in real time. Independent analysis of the Gardner films by experts in American Sign Language have replicated their observations (Stokoe, 1978). The major fault of the studies of Terrace, Seidenberg, and Petitto, however, is the systematic misrepresentation of other investigators' work, particularly that of the Gardners. Van Cantfort and Rimpau (1982) document these unfortunate lapses from objectivity.

CLEVER HANS: A CAUTIONARY TALE

Clever Hans was a horse who was supposed to be able to count. His trainer, Wilhelm von Osten, would ask Hans to add numbers together. Hans would count out the correct solution by moving one of his hooves and was the toast of Berlin until 1907. After much excitement it was discovered that Hans indeed was a very clever horse, though his skills in arithmetic had been overrated. Hans had discovered, on his own, that his trainer's eyebrows twitched as Hans pawed out the "correct" answer. The trainer, Wilhelm von Osten, apparently changed his facial expression when Hans had come to the correct solution. Hans noticed this (horses have very acute vision) and learned to stop pawing on this cue (Pfungst, 1970).

Ever since, psychologists cite the cautionary tale of Clever Hans in connection with experiments that demonstrate intelligent behavior in animals other than human beings. Thomas Sebeok (1981), who with Robert Rosenthal organized a conference on Clever Hans, believes that the Clever Hans effect invalidates all present studies of chimpanzee communication except that of Terrace. Although papers that discussed other topics were presented at this conference, the central theme of the organizers appeared to be that the methods of science cannot be trusted because of the Clever Hans effect. Sebeok thus notes that "the omnipresence of the Clever Hans phenomenon in all dyads — whether only one partner is human or both are — seems to me no longer at issue" (1981, p. 201).

The Clever Hans effect, however, can be eliminated by means of double-blind procedures, where the person administering or scoring a test given to an animal does not know the "correct" answer. For example, the vocabulary tests for chimpanzee Washoe and the other chimpanzees trained in the Gardners' ASL experiments used an elaborate system in which the apes were shown color slides of various objects presented in random order. The apes' signing responses were independently scored by two observers who could not see the slides (Gardner and Gardner, 1974, 1978, 1980).

The data of these naming experiments demonstrate beyond reasonable doubt that Washoe had the concept of a *word* and could name *classes* of objects. A typical vocabulary test with Washoe would involve her naming thirty-two different items, with four different exemplars of each. The item *car* thus would be represented by color slides of four different cars that Washoe had not previously seen. A typical test response (Gardner and Gardner, 1978) was 91 exemplars out of 128 correctly identified, that is, 71 percent correct identification. If Washoe had been performing at chance level and guessing, her score would have been 4 out of 32 exemplars correct, or 3 percent. The procedure and apparatus eliminate completely the possibility that the Clever Hans effect could have aided Washoe. She could not see the human beings who knew what the items presented were. The human observers scoring Washoe's sign responses likewise could not see the exemplars.

LANGUAGE AND COGNITION

Studies of chimpanzee communication can become mired in controversy as to whether they are using human language or not. The argument as to *what* would constitute human language can go on forever. Even Chomsky notes that there are different levels of linguistic ability in human beings. In discussing the acquisition of "moderately complex linguistic structures," for example, he states:

> I would be inclined to think . . . that there would be a correlation between linguistic performance and intelligence; people who are intelligent use language much better than other people most of the time. They may even know more about language . . . It may very well be (and in fact there is some evidence) that the steady state attained is rather different among people of different educational level, even if there is no reason to believe that there is a difference in intelligence.
>
> (Chomsky, 1980, p. 175)

Measures of vocabulary and complexity of utterances show that chimpanzees raised in a rich, humanlike environment are generally similar to those of many children through the age of 2 years (Gardner and Gardner, 1978) and in some respects to the age of 3. There is a fair amount of variation in the rate at which different children acquire language. Landahl's (1982) study shows, for example, three different patterns of language acquisition and achievement for three children through the age of 2 years. However, chimpanzees are not children; they are not as intelligent, and their utterances are qualitatively different in this respect. After listening to hundreds of hours of

recordings of children in the Brown University project on the early
stages of speech acquisition,[2] it is apparent to me that the utterances of
chimpanzees lack the variety and spontaneity of the utterances of a
clever, verbal child. Conversations between chimpanzees and
humans, nevertheless, show cognitive skills that are startling in a
nonhuman animal and that clearly demonstrate the factors of temporal and spatial displacement noted earlier in connection with Hockett's (1960) design features and that clearly are creative and "linguistic." Fouts and associates (1982), for example, note the following
conversation between Washoe and one of her human companions:

GEORGE: What you want?

WASHOE: Orange, orange.

GEORGE: No more orange, what you want?

WASHOE: Orange.

GEORGE: (Getting angry) No more orange, what you want?

WASHOE: You go car gimme orange. Hurry.

Washoe had not been in a car for more than two years when this
conversation took place. She clearly is discussing an activity, going off
in a car to buy oranges at the supermarket, that is displaced in time
and place from the immediate surroundings of the conversation. She
also knows that people drive off to the supermarket to get oranges and
that she might receive one of these oranges. Washoe clearly knows a
lot about the world that she can express in a linguistic mode.

If we contrast this conversation with Washoe to the converation
in Figure 10-1 with Duff, a boy, at age 78 weeks, the chimpanzee
appears to be more precocious. The line notations are Landahl's, as
are the detailed phonetic transcriptions of Duff's utterances.

Note Duff's constant repetitions as well as the degree to which his
phonetic output departs from the well-formed adult speech that he is
trying to approximate. Duff's conversational ability, however, im-
proves rapidly. In the transcript shown in Figure 10-2, Duff still
produces many repetitions, but he also produces multiword utterances. The topic that he is talking about, a story that he has invented in
which a king is placed in the dungeon of a castle, is more abstract than
that of typical published chimpanzee conversations.

Duff progresses rapidly. In the transcript shown in Figure 10-3
Duff, at age 105 weeks, is telling a story about a dog. Note the
repetitions, ill-formed phonetic output, and errors in syntax. However, the length and complexity of the story are hard to match in the
published transcripts of the sign conversations of any chimpanzee that

170. Mother: Can you tell the girls about what you saw on TV, Duff? Who was on TV?

171. Duff: *[tʰeɪ̯pʰ]
    * tape

172. Mother: Who was there?

173. Duff: *[ˈgɔˌgi | ˈkʰɔˌdi]
    * trolley trolley

174. Mother: That's the trolley.

175. Karen: Oh!

176. Mother: Sounds like "cruddy", but it's definitely, there's no question, it's "trolley".

177. Duff: *[ˈpɑˌdi]
    * trolley

178. Mother: Who?

179. Duff: *[ˈpɑˌdi]
    * trolley

180. Mother: Trolley!

181. Duff: *[ˈpɑˌdi]
    * trolley

182. Mother: Trolley?

183. Duff: *[ˈpɑˌdi]
    * trolley

184. Mother: Good!

185. Duff: *[ˌpɑˈdi]
    * trolley

186. Mother: Trolley?

187. Duff: *[ˈpɑˌdi]
    * trolley

188. Mother: Can you say "train"?

189. Duff: *[ˈheɪ̯ˌnə | ˈdæˌdi]
    * train Daddy

FIGURE 10-1. ————————————————————————

Transcript of part of a conversation with a 78-week-old boy, Duff. Duff's utterances are transcribed by using "close" phonetic notation and are also glossed as to their interpretation by the child's caretakers. (From Landahl, 1982, pp. 504–505.)

48. Duff: * [ɔ̃h]

    *

49. Karen: It has a dungeon? Your castle has a dungeon? Where is the
             dungeon, Duff?

50. Duff: * [ˋɪn'd>]

    * in there͞the

51. Karen: Huh? Where is it? Can you show it to me?

52. Duff: *[thaˆʌ]

    *

53. Karen: Oh, oh, oh, oh! The trapdoor!

54. Duff: *[dɪzˢ | dɪzˢ | dʊ̆zˢ̌ | ᶻɣɪs | dɪzˢ]

    * this   this   this   this   this

55. Karen: What about that grating there?

56. Duff: * [ɔ̃h]

    * V̇G

57. Karen: Huh? Where does that go?
58. Carol: Where's the king?
59. Mother: Where is King Friday, Duff?

60. Duff: *[ɪnˋdən'dənž̌ʌən]

    * in the dungeon

61. Mother: In the dungeon! Yes, he is!

FIGURE 10-2.
Transcript of part of a conversation with Duff at age 87 weeks.
(From Landahl, 1982, pp. 531–532.)

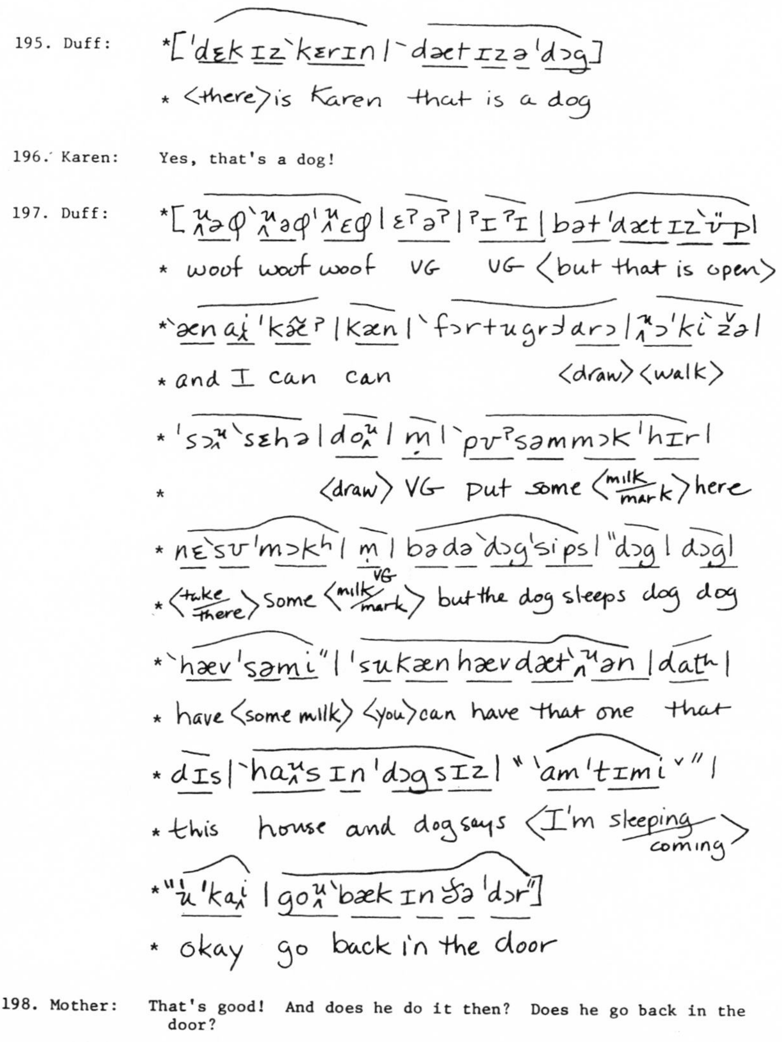

195. Duff: *[ˈdɛk ɪz ˈkɛrɪn | ˈdæt ɪz ə ˈdɔg]

  * ⟨there⟩ is Karen that is a dog

196. Karen: Yes, that's a dog!

197. Duff: *[ᵘəɸˋᵘəɸˈᴧɛɸ | ɛˀəˀ | ˀɪˀɪ | bət ˈdæt ɪz ˈᵛᵛp |

  * woof woof woof VG VG ⟨but that is open⟩

  *ˋæn aᵢ ˈkæˀ | kæn | ˈfɔrt u gr↓ɑrɔ | ˋᴧ ɔ ˈki ᵛ z̧ə |

  * and I can can ⟨draw⟩ ⟨walk⟩

  * ˈsɔᵘˋsɛh ə | doᵘ | m̩ | ˋpʊˀsɑmmɔk ˈhɪr |

  * ⟨draw⟩ VG put some ⟨milk/mark⟩ here

  * nɛ ˋsʊ ˈmɔkʰ | m̩ | bə də ˋdɔg ˈsips | ˈdɔg | dɔg |

  * ⟨take/there⟩ some ⟨milk/mark (VG)⟩ but the dog sleeps dog dog

  * ˋhæv ˈsəm i" | ˈsu kæn hæv dæt ˋᴧᵘən | datʰ |

  * have ⟨some milk⟩ ⟨you⟩ can have that one that

  * dɪs | ˋhaᵘs ɪn ˈdɔg sɪz | "ˈam ˈtɪmi ᵛ" |

  * this house and dog says ⟨I'm sleeping/coming⟩

  *"ᴧ ˈkaᵢ | goᵘ ˋbæk ɪn ʃə ˈdɔr"]

  * okay go back in the door

198. Mother: That's good! And does he do it then? Does he go back in the door?

FIGURE 10-3.
Transcript of part of a conversation with Duff at age 105 weeks.
(From Landahl, 1982, p. 605.)

have yet been published. A transcript of Duff telling us about a dog that woke him up while he was visiting his grandparents in Florida is presented in Figure 10-4. Duff related this account during the same recording session as the one in Figure 10-3, when he was 105 weeks old. The account is full of repetitions, but it again is qualitatively different from chimpanzee conversations.

We at present lack data that explore the limits of linguistic and cognitive ability in apes. Clever young children like Duff are often raised in a stimulating environment in which their parents read fanciful nursery tales to them. Would chimpanzees raised in a rich, humanlike environment invent fanciful stories if their human surrogate parents read such stories to them? Such attempts might yield interesting data since experiments like those of Premack and Woodruff (1978), which will be discussed below, show that chimpanzees can keep track of fairly complex story lines and conceptual problems.

LANGUAGE ABILITY ENHANCES COGNITIVE ABILITY

Studies with children (see Chapter 4) show that enhanced linguistic ability in the form of bilingual skill results in enhanced performance in nonlinguistic cognitive tasks (Ben-Zeev, 1977; Bain and Yu, 1980; Peal and Lambert, 1962). Premack's recent studies with chimpanzees that have been taught to communicate with human beings by using plastic symbols demonstrate that they also show improvements in cognitive skills (Premack, 1976; Premack and Woodruff, 1978). Premack's (1972) experiments were among the first to demonstrate communication between human beings and chimpanzees. In these experiments Premack used plastic symbols to communicate with chimpanzee Sarah, who was less than 1 year old when training commenced. Sarah mastered syntactic processes like negation and conjunction in lessons in which she had to place the plastic symbols in a prescribed order, similar to that which occurs in the syntax of English.

Premack's position with respect to the neural substrate involved in language is that the neural mechanisms also form part of the biological foundations of intelligence. In commenting on Chomsky's claim for a special neural "language organ," he notes that "there seem to be at least two varieties of innatism, one in which the factors that participate in language owe a great deal to genes but are nonetheless general—a part of intelligence at large—and a second in which the debt to the genes is equally large, but the factor is special to language. My impression is that Chomsky dismisses the first alternative too quickly" (Premack, 1980, p. 177). Premack's recent work has focused on chimpanzee intelligence. It has long been known that chimpanzees

225. Duff: *[`ʌ̃ʊf 'ʌ̃ʊf n̩ | `dɔg 'ʌeɪks ɔʌ̃pɛn |

* woof woof and dog wakes up and

*dɔg sɛz ʌ̃ʊf 'ʌ̃ʊf | `ɛn'hi | `ɛn'hi | `ɛn'i |

* dog says woof woof and he and he and he

*'ɔʌ̃pɛn [ɛ] 'tsʊ̀ ɪχə̥ | `hɔʌdz hɪm 'χʌ̃aɪ̯ ɪn |

* up and UG somebody hears him ⟨crying / calling⟩

* əp dæt 'ʌ̃ɪn dɔ̃ʌ |æn |æn | `ɪt ʌ̃əz 'maːmi·]

* ⟨up/out⟩ that window and and it was mommy

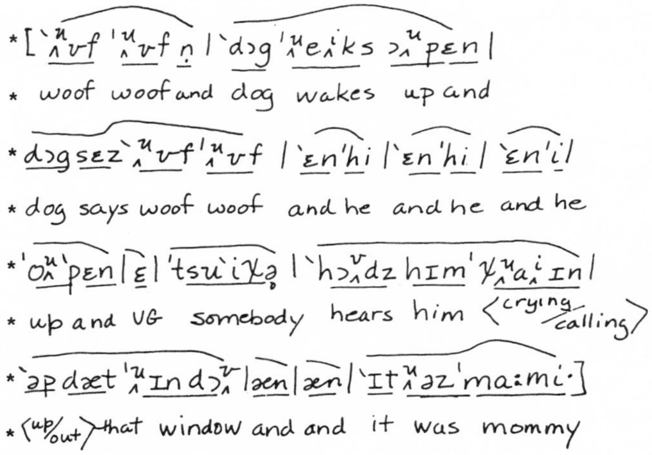

226. Karen: It was Mommy?

227. Mother: It was really Mommy all the time? This is because he frequently is awakened at night by dogs barking, see, and I go and get him, especially remember in Florida, Duff?

228. Duff: *[íə]

* yeah

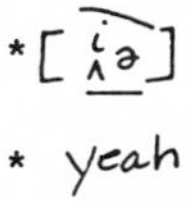

229. Mother: You used to hear those dogs barking? They were across, they lived right across the street.

230. Karen: And they'd wake you up at night?

231. Duff: *[nɔʌ̃]

* no

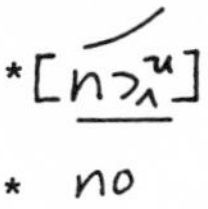

232. Karen: No?

FIGURE 10-4. _____

Transcript of part of same conversation as in Figure 10-3 with Duff at age 105 weeks. (From Landahl, 1982, p. 609.)

can solve fairly complex problems that involve tools. Köhler (1927), in his pioneering experiments, demonstrated that chimpanzees would fit poles together, stack objects to make ladders, remove obstructions, and pull objects with strings in order to get food that otherwise was inaccessible. However, much of the chimpanzees' behavior in these tests can be ascribed to innate mechanisms that are expressed in the normal play of the chimpanzee or to the process of trial and error. The problems that chimpanzee Sarah had to solve in the experiments reported by Premack and Woodruff have no counterpart in the natural environment of chimpanzees, nor can they be solved by trial and error. Their solution depends on the chimpanzee's first inferring the relationship between the elements that constitute the problem and then "solving" the problem.

Sarah was about 14 years old when these experiments took place. She was shown 30-second videotaped scenes in which a trainer struggled with a problem. In the last 5 seconds of each scene the videotape was put on hold, leaving an image of the problem at its peak on the TV monitor. Two different types of problems were videotaped in these 30-second dramas. One type replicated Köhler's work and showed an actor struggling to reach bananas that were placed out of reach, behind objects, and so on. The second set of 30-second dramas involved problems drawn from the laboratory routine that would have no direct counterpart in the "natural" environment of a chimpanzee; for example, a human was locked into a cage in one drama, a gas heater went out and had to be relit in one scene, and a phonograph had to be plugged into an electrical outlet. Sarah had to solve the problem presented in each drama by selecting one of two photographs from a box. One photograph showed a successful solution, such as the actor standing on a box to reach the bananas, or a key in a lock. The other photograph showed a failure—the actor falling off the box, or an item inappropriate to the solution of the problem. Sarah chose correctly in 21 of 24 trials. She did better on the problems that were solved in more concrete fashion—for example, with the actor standing on the box or moving objects—than on the more abstract problems in which the object that was crucial to the solution was shown. The analysis of Premack and Woodruff (1978) shows that Sarah's performance cannot be ascribed to rote memory, learning sets, and the like. In a variety of cognitive experiments (Premack, 1976), Sarah performed better than apes who had less exposure to communication. Chimpanzees who lacked "language" skills performed comparatively poorly compared with chimpanzees who had training in symbolic communication (Premack, 1981).

SUMMARY

Comparative studies of ASL communication in chimpanzees and other apes show that they communicate in a linguistic mode, albeit at a level equivalent to human children between the ages of 2 and 3.

Comparative studies of the culture of the chimpanzees also show patterns of behavior that in human societies would involve communication by means of language. These studies also show that nonhuman hominoids do not appear to make use of extensive vocal communication nor are they able to learn to imitate human speech. The evolutionary significance of these data is that some past biological substrate for aspects of human language other than speech apparently exists in living apes. The initial steps toward the evolution of human language could thus have started with the hominoids ancestral to both human beings and apes.

CHAPTER 11

The Evolution of Human Speech: Comparative Studies

HUMAN SPEECH HAS traditionally been identified as a unique defining characteristic of *Homo sapiens.* A discussion of the evolution of human speech thus necessarily involves the question of human uniqueness. The particular path that I shall take in following the possible evolution of human speech, however, touches on some broader questions regarding human uniqueness and the nature of the mechanisms of evolution. I have argued throughout this book that human linguistic ability is based on rather general neural mechanisms that structure the cognitive behavior of humans as well as other animals, plus a set of species-specific mechanisms that structure the particular form of human speech. Whereas the enhanced cognitive ability of modern *Homo sapiens* involves the gradual elaboration of neural mechanisms that can be found in other living animals, the species-specific aspects of human speech are unique and follow from anatomical specializations and matching neural mechanisms that are not present in other living animals. I will focus on the evolution of the human supralaryngeal vocal tract, using data derived by the methods of comparative anatomy.

These data are consistent with what I shall term a "functional branch-point" theory for natural selection. This theory differentiates between evolutionary change at the structural, anatomical level and the possibility for abrupt, qualitatively different *functional* selective advantages. A functional branch-point theory for evolution by means of natural selection claims that a process of *gradual anatomical* change can at certain points yield *"sudden" functional* advantages that will lead to qualitatively different patterns of behavior in a species. A functional branch-point theory accounts for the tempo of evolution, which, as Gould and Eldridge (1977) note, is not always even. Long periods of stasis marked by little change can occur, "punctuated" by intervals of rapid evolutionary change. The anatomical and fossil data relevant to the evolution of the human vocal tract, however, refute

Gould's (1977) claim that a special, "unique" evolutionary mechanism—neoteny—was operant in hominid evolution. Human uniqueness thus does not involve any unique evolutionary mechanism or the higher directing force implicit in Gould's model.

I will not here discuss in detail the evolution of other aspects of human language. I have already discussed such aspects as automatization, critical periods, the status of words as markers for fuzzy concepts, the role of pragmatic context, and the possible evolution of the neural bases for rule-governed morphophonemic and syntactic processes. Comparative data on the linguistic and cognitive ability of apes using modified versions of American Sign Language and other symbolic systems are relevant to the discussion of the evolution of these aspects of language since they reveal the cognitive base from which hominid evolution probably departed. Studies of the acquisition of language by human children likewise are relevant. I will note some of the features of hominid culture that are consistent with the presence of language. We know something about the tool kit of early hominids because they worked stone to make tools, and stones can survive thousands or millions of years. We also know a little about their burial rituals, habitation sites, and diet. Some aspects of the pattern of archaic hominid culture are apparent in the record of the fossil bones themselves, which show that the infirm were cared for. However, we have no record whatsoever of their actual utterances, which makes discussions of syntax, morphophonemics, word forms, and the like rather speculative, to say the least. Many discussions of the possible syntactic ability of early hominids have attempted to make use of the indirect evidence of hominid culture. Certainly the presence of burial rituals and of a fairly complex tool technology is consistent with the presence of language. However, at present I would not agree with even my own previous inferences (1975a, pp. 163–170) that posit a definite connection between a Lavaloisian tool culture and a transformational grammar. There are simply too many other cognitive strategies that could account for the steps that are necessary to make a stone tool for any conclusion on the precise nature of the syntax of the language of some archaic, extinct hominids to be anything but speculative.

CULTURE AND THE EVOLUTION OF LANGUAGE

Many discussions of the evolution of language have likewise attempted to key the "invention" or "appearance" of words or some putative "unique" quality of the syntax, morphology, semantic structure, and so on, of human language to some aspect of human culture.

Various aspects of human culture have been noted that hypothetically demonstrate a particular level of syntactic or morphophonemic complexity — for example, the division of labor in human societies, hunting, the nuclear family, cave painting, thin-bladed stone tools, burial rituals, manufactured objects that have hinges. I do not see how these proposals are particularly relevant in light of the cultural diversity of human society throughout even the historical period. Human linguistic ability did not change with the introduction of the wheel into different cultures, nor have changes in the structure of the American family had any significance with respect to our linguistic ability.

I also doubt that there is any *single* aspect of human culture that in itself provided *the* key to language or even yielded *the* factor that gave a selective advantage to variations that would enhance human linguistic ability. Cultural patterns like the division of labor that hypothetically provides a selective advantage for the evolution of human language also occur in nonhuman primates like baboons. Though a phenomenon like mother-to-infant communication may be a factor that will enhance the selective value of communication, it likewise can be observed in the behavior of modern chimpanzees (Goodall, 1974). Markers like the presence of a stone-tool technology appear to be exclusively hominid patterns of behavior, though we can see similar but simpler parallels in animals like the California sea otter (Kenyon, 1969). However, how can we possibly test the inferences that we may draw regarding the syntactic or morphologic ability of hominids who made stone axes? Would any linguist dare to predict the syntactic system or morphology of a present-day human culture if he or she had only a sample of bowls, pots, pans, and knives to work with? We could arrange a test of such speculations using the comparative method. Linguists who thought that they could deduce the form of syntax or inventory of words from indirect cultural evidence could be presented with the artifacts of contemporary human isolates. If they were able to predict the different linguistic forms from the evidence of pots, pans, arrows, baskets, agriculture, and the like, their theories would have some merit.

The data that we need to study the evolution of language are those of language. We do not have any record of the sentences or words that archaic, extinct hominids or our more immediate ancestors uttered 1 million, 100,000, or 30,000 years ago. We therefore cannot say much about how they put words together (their syntax) or how they modified words (their morphology). If we knew more about the neural bases of syntax and morphology, we might be able to make some inferences through reconstructions of the brains of fossil hominids — though that would be difficult since the soft tissue of the brain is never preserved long after death. However, I believe that we can derive some insights regarding the evolution of human language by studying the evolution of human speech.

As I have noted throughout this book, human speech is an integral element of human language. The species-specific aspects of *human* language indeed may be at the level of speech production and speech perception, which appear to reflect the presence of specialized neural devices that interface with a cognitive, general-purpose neural "computer." The properties of human speech, if this view is correct, then must reflect the neural devices that govern the production and perception of speech. By studying speech, we can derive some insight into the function and organization of the brain. Although we again have no direct evidence of the speech of various fossil hominids, the physiology of speech production is known, and so we can deduce some aspects of the nature of the sounds that various fossil hominids could have produced if we can determine their speech-producing anatomy. This last problem is not trivial, but we can make use of the methods of comparative anatomy to derive the general form of the supralaryngeal airways of fossil hominids.

RECONSTRUCTING THE SUPRALARYNGEAL VOCAL TRACTS OF EXTINCT HOMINIDS

The supralaryngeal airways of animals are defined by soft tissue muscles, ligaments, and so on, as well as by some bones. Soft tissue sometimes is preserved long after death, as when an animal's body rests in a peat bog or in ice. Soft tissue can also be indirectly preserved when an animal's body leaves an impression in mud that subsequently hardens. However, we at present lack any material that directly indicates the morphology of the soft tissue of the supralaryngeal airway of extinct hominids.

Despite the lack of direct evidence, it is possible to reconstruct these supralaryngeal airways. The process of reconstruction and the problems are similar to those involved in the reconstruction of other soft tissue. The muscles of dinosaurs, for example, can be reconstructed even though we have no samples of dinosaur muscle tissue. The methods of comparative anatomy and the overall continuity of evolution make these reconstructions possible. First of all muscles, as Campbell (1966) notes, "leave marks on bones." You can easily feel, for example, the facets or points of attachment where your digastric muscles are attached to, or inserted into, the lower border of the inside of your mandible (lower jaw). The facets are shallow nubbled pits. Since muscles are essentially "glued" to the bones or cartilages, a greater surface area yields a stronger glue joint. A shallow pit yields a greater surface area than would be the case if it did not exist. The larger the surface area of the facet, the bigger the muscle that is glued to the facet. When electrically stimulated, muscles pull on the bones or cartilages that they are attached to. A big muscle will exert a greater force on the bones than a smaller muscle; hence the facets of bigger muscles have greater surface areas. Thus we can deduce the size of a muscle that once was attached to a bone by looking at the surface area of its facet. Small bumps, nubbling, also increase the area of the "glue joint." The principle is again quite similar to that relevant to carpentry, where the surface of a joint frequently is roughened to yield a stronger glue joint.

Note that the digastric muscle in Figure 11-1 runs down and back from the mandible to the hyoid bone. The hyoid bone is a small semicircular bone that supports the larynx. Note, for the moment, that the "tilt" of the facets by which the digastrics are attached to the mandible lines up with the direction in which the digastrics run between the mandible and the hyoid. This arrangement represents good engineering since the force that the digastrics apply to the mandible is exerted in the direction in which they run. The glue joint at the facet thus is oriented perpendicular to the direction in which the muscle exerts a force. Figure 11-1 sketches this relationship. The strength of the glued muscle-to-mandible joint therefore is its *tensile* strength. The tensile strength of most materials is substantially greater than their shear strength. If you, for example, attempt to pull apart a stick of chalkboard chalk *along* its length, you will not succeed because its tensile strength is too high. But you can easily snap it in two *across* its long dimension because its shear strength is much lower. The situation is similar for muscles and their glue joints. Muscles and their facets tend to be lined up so that shear forces are minimized in the normal action pattern of the muscles. Muscles and ligaments are often "pulled" when they are stressed in some odd direction — a direction in which large shear forces pull the bone-to-muscle joint asunder. We thus can infer the probable direction in which a muscle was inserted into a bone by examining the geometry of the facets and bones.

These general observations about the arrangements of bones and muscles are, however, only one aspect of the comparative method. Animals are functional complexes of bones and soft tissue. All living animals are related; they are, moreover, related in various degrees to all extinct animals, of which extinct hominids form a subclass. We can

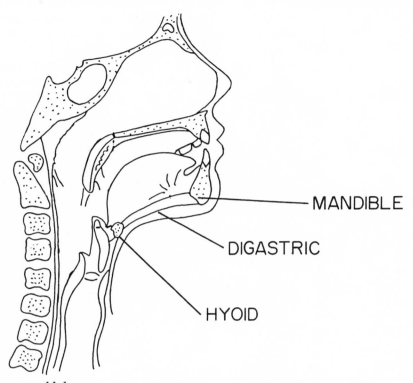

FIGURE 11-1.
The anterior belly of the digastric muscle in relation to its insertion
in the mandible and the hyoid bone. The digastric runs down and
back from the mandible to the hyoid. The lower inside surface of
the mandible where it is attached is angled to minimize shear forces.

derive reasonably certain reconstructions of the soft tissue structures
of extinct hominids by comparing the bones of extinct forms with the
bones and soft tissue of related, living animals. The problem of
reconstructing the supralaryngeal airway of an extinct hominid, say
Australopithecus africanus, is similar to the problem of reconstructing
the neck or the legs of a dinosaur. We can look at the bones and facets
for the muscles of the fossilized extinct animals. If we are reconstructing dinosaurs, we can also look at the bones and muscles of living
lizards that have bones which resemble those of extinct dinosaurs and
that are closely related to these extinct animals. The bones and
muscles of lizards "go together" in a consistent pattern; there are

variations in the pattern, to be sure, but there is an overall "normal" pattern that has been optimized through the process of natural selection. We thus can make a reasonable reconstruction of an extinct dinosaur.

ONTOGENY AND PHYLOGENY

The living animals that give us an insight into the relation of the soft tissue of the supralaryngeal vocal tract to the fossil remains of australopithecines and other extinct hominids are the living nonhuman primates and newborn human beings. Human neonates are qualitatively different from human adults. The ontogenetic development of all animals necessarily proceeds from the simple stage that exists after conception to the complexity of the adult stage. The process of development is not complete at birth. The situation is similar for all primates. Newborn chimpanzees, gorillas, and the like, all differ from adult members of their species. Human neonates likewise differ from adult human beings.

The adult forms of virtually all animals differ from the newborn and late embryonic stages. Darwin (1859, pp. 439–450) discusses the similarities between related species in their embryonic stages in detail. Haeckel's (1866) "Biogenetic Law: Ontogeny Recapitulates Phylogeny" was actually formulated by Darwin, who attributes the observation to Louis Agassiz:

> In two groups of animals, however much they may at present differ from each other in structure and habits, if they pass through the same or similar embryonic stages, we may feel assured that they have both descended from the same or nearly similar parents, and are therefore in that degree closely related. Thus community in embryonic structure reveals community of descent.
>
> As the embryonic state of each species and group of species partially shows us the structure of their less modified ancient progenitors, we can clearly see why ancient and extinct forms of life should resemble the embryos of their descendants, — our existing species. Agassiz believes this to be a law of nature; but I am bound to confess that I only hope to see the law hereafter proved true.
>
> (1859, p. 449)

Darwin characteristically tested this "law" by experiments using the data of artificial selection. We know that the different breeds of domestic dogs have similar ancestors, that different breeds of pigeons have similar ancestors, and so on. Darwin compared greyhounds and bulldogs, which, though they appear so different in their adult state, "are most closely allied, and have probably descended from the same wild stock" (1859, p. 445). He measured old dogs and their 6-day-old puppies and "found that the puppies had not nearly attained their full amount of proportional difference." Similar measurements involving horses and their foals and the nestling birds of different varieties of domestic pigeons replicated these data. Human adults and human newborn infants differ in their own special way as much as newborn chimpanzees or nonhuman primates differ from their parents.

It is apparently difficult for people to notice that familiar animals that they *know* are similar are really different. Thus when Darwin measured dogs and puppies as well as full-grown cart horses and racehorses and their foals, he was told by breeders that the puppies and foals of different breeds differed from each other as much as their parents did. The claim that human adults resemble newborn infants more than is the case for other primates probably rests on this same lack of objectivity regarding familiar animals that we know are the "same." Who could be more human than our infant sons and daughters? It is furthermore easy to overlook the anatomical and physiologic data that demonstrate that we differ from newborn human infants. The first comprehensive anatomical atlas of the human newborn, Crelin's, for example, was published in 1969.

The theory of neoteny that has been revived by Gould (1977) and Gould and Eldridge (1977) claims that human evolution involves a unique process: neoteny. We supposedly retain the morphology and physiology associated with the newborn. In contrast, all other primates grow up. Gould and Eldridge claim that the rapid pace of human evolution follows from modification of the regulatory genes that govern human development. They thus explain the rapid changes that have occurred in the last ten million years of hominid evolution by the process of "neotenization." We, however, do not resemble newborn infants; adult human beings diverge from newborn infants as much as, if not more than, other adult primates diverge from their newborns. Human newborn infants conform to the general principle noted by Darwin: they are closer to the newborn forms of nonhuman primates; they reveal our common ancestry. Human newborn infants, in particular, retain the supralaryngeal airways and associated skeletal morphology that occur in living nonhuman primates. We can use the skeletal similarities between newborn human infants, adult and juvenile nonhuman primates, and extinct fossil hominids too as a guide to the reconstruction of the fossil supralaryngeal airways.

Living human newborn infants and nonhuman primates thus serve the same function in the reconstruction of a hominid fossil's supralaryngeal airway as a lizard does for the leg muscles or neck of a dinosaur. The lizard is not a dinosaur, but it is closely related to extinct dinosaurs and has a similar skeleton. Newborn human infants likewise are not australopithecines or Neanderthal men or women, but they are closely related to these hominids and have similar skeletal structures. The process of reconstruction involves four steps.

1. We must note the correspondences between soft tissue and skeletal structure that occur in human neonates and nonhuman primates.
2. We then must evaluate the generality of these relationships by looking at the total range of nonhuman primates and other animals.
3. We must determine the functional significance of supralaryngeal morphology with respect to that of human neonates, nonhuman primates, and adult humans.
4. We can then extend our inferences concerning soft tissue, skeletal structure, and physiologic function to the reconstruction of the fossil supralaryngeal vocal tract, using the total skeletal complex as an anchor point for our reconstruction.

COMPARATIVE ANATOMY AND PHYSIOLOGY

Comparisons between the skeletal structure, brains, hands, and so on of humans and other primates date back to the first anatomical studies of apes at the end of the seventeenth century. Victor Negus's comprehensive study of the comparative anatomy and physiology of the larynx is, however, the primary model for the comparative study of the upper respiratory system. Negus's data and conclusions are presented in two works, *The Mechanism of the Larynx* (1928) and *The Comparative Anatomy and Physiology of the Larynx* (1949). Negus traces the evolution of the larynx from its appearance in ancient fish, who, like similar living fish such as the African lung fish and the mud fish of the Amazon, could breathe air (1949, pp. 2–8). Negus points out the selective advantage of the larynx in these air-breathing fish vis-à-vis still more "primitive" air-breathing fish like the climbing perch, which lack a larynx. The function of the larynx in air-breathing fish is to prevent water from entering the lung. The larynx in these animals is essentially a valve that is positioned in the floor of the pharynx. When the fish is in the water, the laryngeal valve closes; when the fish is out of the water, the larynx opens and allows air to be swallowed and forced into the fish's lung. The laryngeal valve in these fishes consists of a simple sphincter. It is interesting to note in this regard that the human embryo, when it is about 5 mm long, shows a slit in the pharyngeal floor "much like that of the Lung Fish" (Negus, 1949, p. 6).

The origin of the larynx was to facilitate air breathing in fish that *already* could breathe air. The initial developments that allowed primitive fish which resembled living forms like the climbing perch to breathe air follow from the process of "preadaptation"—"the highly important fact that an organ originally constructed for one purpose, namely flotation, may be converted into one for a wholly different purpose, namely respiration" (Darwin, 1859, p. 190). The swim bladders of fish, which are homologous with the lungs of vertebrates, evolved for flotation. Fish can extract dissolved air from water by means of their gills. The swim bladders of fish are elastic sacs that can be filled with air extracted from water by a fish's gills. Air-breathing fish instead filled their swim-bladder/lung by swallowing air, which then was transferred to their bloodstream from the swim bladder serving as a lung. The change in *function* of the swim bladder constitutes a *functional branch-point.* The new behavior is disjoint with the previous behavior of fish. Life out of water is quite different and novel compared with a watery existence.

Given these new conditions of life — life out of water — there are selective advantages for the further development of the larynx. *The presence of the larynx itself yields the possibility for further changes.* As Negus points out, the next stage in the evolution of the larynx was the development of fibers to pull the larynx open to allow more air into the lungs during breathing. Further stages of evolution yielded cartilages that facilitate the opening movements of the larynx. The elaboration of the larynx yields a second functional branch-point when it can act as a sound-generating device. The process of phonation, in which the vocal cords move rapidly inward and outward to convert the steady flow of air from the lungs into a series of "puffs" of air, can occur in the larynges of animals like frogs. Negus's (1949, pp. 40–42) comparative studies again demonstrate that many of the larynges of many animals are specialized for phonation at the expense of respiration.

FUNCTIONAL BRANCH-POINTS

Figure 11-2 illustrates these functional branch-points in the evolution of the upper respiratory system. A branch-point marks the point at which the course of evolution can potentially be changed by virtue of selection for a new mode of behavior that is of value to a group of

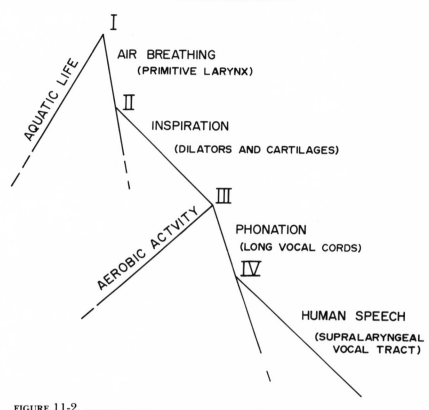

FIGURE 11-2. _____

A functional branch-point diagram for the evolution of the upper
respiratory system.

animals. The new function may conflict with the old function, and
rapid divergence can occur that ultimately will result in speciation as
different populations retain different genetically transferred anatomical structures that have a selective advantage for either the new or the
old function. The divergence can become quite extreme, as specializations for a given behavioral function can themselves lead to new
functional branch-points. The concept of functional branch-points is
not new (Mayr, 1978). However, this aspect of evolution by means of
natural selection is often overlooked. A theory of natural selection
that incorporates functional branch-points accounts for both the uneven tempo of evolution (Gould and Eldridge, 1977) and the value of
small changes.

The selective value of small steps is apparent in the gradual changes that occur within a functional continuum, such as the differences in the dilators of the larynx (Negus, 1949, p. 7). Darwin's eloquent comment on the value of small changes holds true within a functional continuum:

> For as all the inhabitants of each country are struggling together with nicely balanced forces, extremely slight modifications in structure or habits of one inhabitant would often give it an advantage over others; and still further modifications of the same kind would often still further increase the advantage. No country can be named in which all the native inhabitants are now so perfectly adapted to each other and to the physical conditions under which they live, that none of them could anyhow be improved.
>
> (1859, p. 82)

Although I do not advocate a neo-Darwinian model for economic development, it is obvious that the branch-point model holds true for the marketplace. For example, in the "struggle for existence" that occurs in the development and sale of automobiles, small differences yield a selective advantage. The differences between competing cars is often so small that slight differences in cost, performance, or reliability have profound effects. The changes that occurred in the American marketplace in the 1970s derive from small advantages in the price and fuel efficiency of imported Japanese cars. The trend toward higher sales of Japanese cars can probably be arrested by similar small changes in the design and price of American-made cars. The competition between car makers represents a state in which they are "struggling together with nicely balanced forces." In contrast, earlier in the century there was an abrupt change when automobiles began to compete with horse-drawn carriages. The nature of the contest was inherently different. Finely designed carriages could not compete, no matter how well made or how durable they were. Automobiles were qualitatively different; a functional branch-point occurred, and new selective forces entered into the competition.

An observer charting the evolution of conveyances would see a long period extending over centuries in which gradual changes improved horse-drawn carriages. The period of horse-drawn carriage improvement would appear to be a "static" period compared with the "sudden" introduction and improvement of the automobile. However, the evolution of the automobile also was long and had its roots in the gradual improvements in engines that had been going on for several centuries. Improvements in metallurgy, manufacturing, and the like that also had occurred gradually were all necessary factors for the invention of the automobile. A branch-point theory for natural selection accounts for the tempo of evolution. It differentiates between the slow, gradual process of change within a functional modality and the abrupt shifts in function that occur at a branch-point with the consequent opportunity for rapid change. Within a functional modality slight structural changes yield small selective advantages. At a branch-point small *structural* changes, such as alterations of the cartilages of the larynx that yield phonation, can produce an abrupt, great *functional* advantage by virtue of the selective advantage of the new mode of behavior.

LARYNGEAL MODIFICATIONS FOR RESPIRATION

A branch-point diagram captures phylogenetic divergence. The data of Negus (1949) are consistent with the four functional branch-points sketched in Figure 11-2. Negus discusses the anatomical bases of the first three stages in detail. The anatomical modifications that yield more efficient and controlled phonation at branch-point III, for example, impede efficient respiration. Different species went their own way with regard to the modifications of the larynx that would yield either more efficient respiration or phonation. Negus, for example, demonstrates that animals like horses have a larynx that is "designed" to maximize the flow of air to and from the lungs. In contrast, the human larynx is designed to enhance phonation for the process of vocal communication. Canids, which are social animals that also communicate by using vocalizations but that run down their game, represent an intermediate solution to the competing selective forces deriving from respiratory efficiency and phonation.

Figure 11-3 shows the relative area of the trachea, or windpipe, compared with the maximum opening of the larynx for a horse, a dog, and a human being (Negus, 1949, p. 31). The larynx acts as a valve with respect to the flow of air through the trachea, which leads to the lungs. Obviously a valve that can be opened wider will offer less resistance to the flow of air through the airway that leads to the lungs. All other things being equal, a wider opening will result in a greater airflow. You can demonstrate this to your own satisfaction by using a hydraulic analogy — opening the faucet of your kitchen sink. Animals that run long distances at a fast speed have to maintain aerobic conditions; that is, they have to transfer enough oxygen to their lungs to maintain the higher metabolic rate of sustained running. Horses thus have to

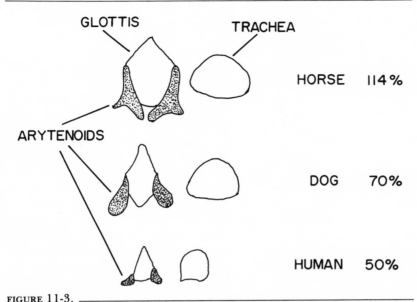

GLOTTIS   TRACHEA

HORSE   114%

ARYTENOIDS

DOG   70%

HUMAN   50%

FIGURE 11-3. ——————————————————————————
Relative opening of the larynx and trachea in horse, dog, and
human being. The arytenoid cartilages are stippled in these
transverse views looking down on the larynx. Note that the maximum opening of the larynx is smaller than that of the trachea in
human beings, where it is 50 percent of the tracheal area. The
human and canid larynges thus obstruct the airflow to the lungs
even when they are wide open.

maintain a high flow rate of air to their lungs. The larynx of the horse
and of other ungulates that use the strategy of running for long
distances to escape from predators thus has evolved to open wide to
yield the minimum resistance to airflow.

Figure 11-3 also shows the mechanics of the larynx that affect its
maximum opening. Horses have a larynx that has long arytenoid
cartilages. These cartilages swing apart to open the larynx for respiration. The sketch shows the two arytenoid cartilages abducted to the
maximum open position. The cross section of the trachea immediately
below the larynx is sketched to the right of the diagram of the
transverse section of the open larynx. Note that the opening of the
horse larynx is larger than the cross-sectional area of the trachea.
The horse's larynx thus does not impede the airflow to the horse's
lungs during respiration. Horses, in a sense, are optimally designed

for sustained long-distance running. Their hooves, legs, and larynges have evolved with the selective value of running as the crucial parameter in natural selection.

The sketch of the larynx of a dog (a staghound), in contrast, shows that the dog's larynx presents an obstacle to airflow even when it is at its maximum opening. The airway to the dog's lungs is restricted to 70 percent of the tracheal cross section. The sketches of the human larynx in its open respiratory state in Figure 11-3 shows that our airway also is restricted, to 50 percent of the tracheal cross section. The relative deficiencies of the dog and human larynges with respect to respiration follow from the short length of the arytenoid cartilages. The larynx opens for respiration by swinging the arytenoid cartilages outward from their posterior pivot point. Negus (1949, pp. 40–42) demonstrates that the optimum length of the arytenoid cartilages for maximizing the opening of the larynx relative to the trachea is about 0.7 times the diameter of the laryngeal opening. The nearest approach to this optimum length occurs in the Persian gazelle. The Persian gazelle can sustain speeds of 60 miles per hour. Human beings, in contrast, have almost the shortest arytenoid cartilages of any mammals relative to their tracheal cross section. Short arytenoid cartilages, however, have a functional advantage for phonation. High-speed motion pictures of the larynx show that phonation usually involves the anterior vocal cords, which run from the ends of the arytenoid cartilages to the thyroid cartilage (Timcke, von Leden, and Moore, 1958; Lieberman, 1967).

LARYNGEAL MODIFICATIONS FOR PHONATION

The soft parts of the larynx — the vocal cords, which consist of the vocal ligaments, and the thyroarytenoid and cricoarytenoid muscles — move during phonation. The heavy arytenoid cartilages normally do not move during steady-state phonation. In human beings phonation involving a heavy arytenoid cartilage usually yields a low-frequency "fry" or "creaky" laryngeal source. The average glottal (laryngeal) opening is large in fry phonation; airflow thus is high compared with the acoustic energy of fry phonation. Given the high mass of the arytenoid cartilages, fundamental frequency also is not so easy to control as it is in the normal registers for human phonation (Van den Berg, 1958). The functional trade-off therefore is between respiration and phonation. Animals who take the right branch-point at level III in Figure 11-2 thus retain changes that yield smaller arytenoid cartilages and more efficient phonation. These animals, as Negus notes, are social animals that rely on vocal communication. The leftward branch at level II takes the direction of selection for more efficient respiration as part of a total behavior complex that stresses sustained, high-speed running.

THE STANDARD-PLAN SUPRALARYNGEAL VOCAL TRACT

The functional branch-point at level IV denotes the modifications of the supralaryngeal vocal tract that typify anatomically modern *Homo sapiens.* Negus, in his comprehensive *Comparative Anatomy,* noted the differences between the supralaryngeal vocal tract that is typical of modern human beings and the vocal tract characteristic of all other terrestrial mammals. Negus also noted some of the selective disadvantages of the adultlike human supralaryngeal tract, and in collaboration with Sir Arthur Keith he reconstructed the supralaryngeal vocal tract of a Neanderthal fossil (1949, p. 195). However, he was not able to evaluate the functional significance of the differences between the human and nonhuman supralaryngeal vocal tracts. This deficiency was not Negus's; the physiologic and perceptual studies of human speech production and perception that are germane to assessing this difference were carried out long after Negus's active days. In brief, the functional divergence at branch-point IV involves the competing demands of selection for vegetative functions like breathing, swallowing, and chewing versus phonetic efficiency for high data-rate communication. I will attempt to demonstrate that the "unique" supralaryngeal airways of anatomically modern *Homo sapiens* evolved to enhance vocal communication at the expense of these vegetative functions. I will also argue that until comparatively recent times, 50,000 years before the present, there were different groups of hominids, some of whom retained the primitive standard-plan supralaryngeal airway.

The peculiar deficiencies of the adult human supralaryngeal airways with respect to swallowing have long been noted. We simply are not very well designed with respect to swallowing, and thousands of deaths occur every year when people asphyxiate because a piece of food lodges in the larynx. Charles Darwin, for example, noted "the strange fact that every particle of food and drink which we swallow has to pass over the orifice of the trachea, with some risk of falling into the lungs" (1859, p. 191). These deficiencies do not occur to the same degree with the standard-plan supralaryngeal airway, which is also better adapted for breathing and chewing. Negus's primary contribu-

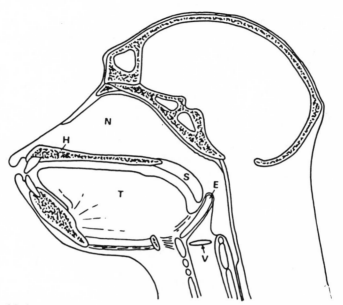

FIGURE 11-4. ⸻
Midsagittal view of the head of an adult chimpanzee: *N*, nasal
cavity; *H*, hard palate; *S*, soft palate, *E*, epiglottis; *T*, tongue; *V*,
vocal cords of larynx. (Adapted from Laitman and Heimbuch, 1982.)

tion with respect to our view of the physiology and evolution of the
human supralaryngeal airway was his demonstration that there is a
standard-plan airway from which we diverge in both an ontogenetic
and a phylogenetic sense.

Figure 11-4 shows a schematic midsagittal section of the head of
an adult chimpanzee and is a reasonable introduction to the anatomy
of the nonhuman standard-plan supralaryngeal airway. If we were to
slice a head in two on a plane midway and perpendicular to a line
between the eyes, we would be able to see a midsagittal view. You can
see the nasal and oral cavities of the supralaryngeal airway in the
sketch. The animal's tongue is long and thin compared with that of an
adultlike human being, and it is positioned entirely within the oral
cavity, the animal's mouth. The larynx is positioned *behind* the tongue
and is close to the roof of the nasopharynx, which leads into the nasal
cavity. The roof of the nasopharynx consists of the bones that form
part of the base of the skull. This fact is crucial to the reconstruction of

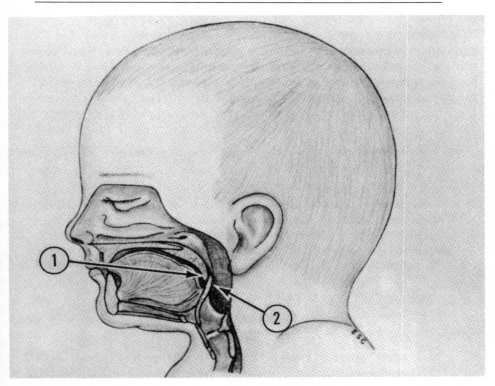

FIGURE 11-5. ────────────────────────────────
Diagram of human newborn showing the larynx locked into the
nasopharynx during quiet respiration. The soft palate "1" and
epiglottis "2" overlap. (After Laitman, Crelin, and Conlogue, 1977.)

the supralaryngeal airways of fossils. The hard palate, which is also a
bony structure that is often present in hominid fossils, forms the
anterior (front) part of the roof of the animal's mouth. The posterior
(back) part of the roof of the mouth is the soft palate, or velum. The
velum can be pulled upward and backward by levator and tensor
muscles (Bell-Berti, 1973).

The functional logic behind the morphology of the standard-plan
supralaryngeal airway is apparent when we look at the position of the
larynx during respiration. Figure 11-5 is a diagram of a human
newborn showing the larynx locked into the nasopharynx during
quiet respiration. The newborn infant moves the larynx upward into
the nasopharynx. The high position of the larynx relative to the

nasopharynx of the standard-plan supralaryngeal airway allows the newborn to do this. Note that the epiglottis and soft palate overlap and form a double seal. The diameter of the larynx of the newborn is small in relation to the distance between the end of the bony hard palate and the base of the spinal column. There is also room for food or water to pass on either side of the elevated larynx. The larynx, in effect, functions as a tube that extends upward from the trachea into the nasopharynx. The soft palate, epiglottis, and pharyngeal constrictors seal the airway that is formed through the nose into the larynx and trachea and to the lungs. Newborn infants can simultaneously swallow fluids while they breathe. The fluids enter their mouths, pass to either side of the elevated larynx, and enter the pharynx and esophagus positioned *behind* the larynx. Since their airway for breathing runs from the nose through the larynx-to-nasopharynx seal, liquids cannot fall into the larynx and trachea to choke the newborn infant. The neural mechanisms that control respiration are also matched to the standard-plan supralaryngeal morphology of the human newborn. Human newborns are obligate nose breathers. As Crelin notes, "Obstructions of the nasal airway by any means produces an extremely stressful reaction and the infant will submit to breathing through the mouth only when the point of suffocation is reached" (1973, p. 28).

The standard-plan morphology of the human newborn is typical of *all* other mammals, adult and young, which can elevate their larynx to form an airway through the nose to the lungs that is sealed from the mouth. Ibexes, horses, dogs, monkeys, apes—all can simultaneously breathe and drink (Negus, 1949; Laitman, Crelin, and Conlogue, 1977). Figure 11-6 shows the supralaryngeal airways of an ibex and a dog. Note that both have long, flat tongues that are positioned entirely within the mouth. The larynx is positioned high close to the base of the skull. The epiglottis of the larynx thus is positioned so that it can easily make contact with the soft palate. These animals are obligate nose breathers. The ingestion of fluids and small, solid objects can take place while these animals breathe; the fluid is routed around either side of the larynx.

Two other vegetative functional differences that distinguish adultlike human beings from other mammals can be correlated with the morphology of the standard-plan airway. The first difference is in respiration—the larynx exits directly into the nose. Compared with the adultlike human supralaryngeal airway, there is less of a bend in the airway. As Negus (1949, p. 33) notes, this results in a lower airflow resistance. The second vegetative functional difference is in chewing.

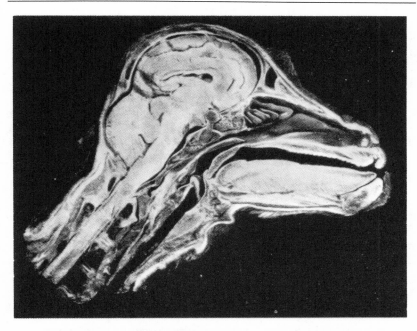

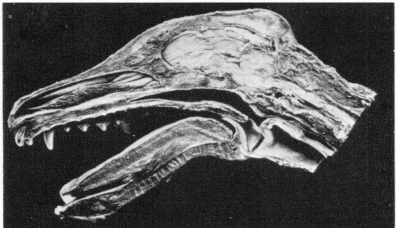

FIGURE 11-6.
Sections of the heads of an ibex (above) and a dog (below) showing the nonhuman standard-plan supralaryngeal airway. The high position of the larynx and the tongue's location in the oral cavity are apparent. (After Negus, 1949.)

The body of the mandible is relatively long compared with its ramus, consistent with the long, thin tongue. There is more room for teeth in the standard-plan morphology. Efficiency of chewing, all other things being equal, is a function of the tooth area that comes into contact during chewing. Studies of the efficiency of chewing that were directed at perfecting dentures show that a "swept tooth area" is the most important determinant of chewing efficiency (Manley and Braley, 1950; Manley and Shiere, 1950; Manley and Vinton, 1951). I will return to this topic in connection with the anatomical specializations of classic Neanderthal hominids (Trinkaus and Howells, 1979), which I think represent a hominid line that specialized for chewing at the expense of phonetic efficiency at branch-point IV.

THE HUMAN SUPRALARYNGEAL VOCAL TRACT

Figure 11-7 shows a midsagittal view of an adult human supralaryngeal vocal tract. The restructuring of the supralaryngeal vocal tract in human beings is quite pronounced by age 3 months (George, 1978). Negus again noted that the human supralaryngeal vocal tract gradually takes form in the course of ontogenetic development:

> There is a gradual descent [of the larynx] through the embryo and foetus and child. The reason for this descent depends partly on the assumption of erect posture, with the head flexed on the spine, so as to bring the eyes into a line of vision parallel to the ground . . . But this alone would not account for the position, since similar changes have occurred in the higher Apes without a corresponding descent of the larynx. The determining factor in Man is recession of the jaws; there is no prognathous snout . . . The tongue however retains the size it had in Apes and more primitive types of Man, and in consequence it is curved, occupying a position partly in the mouth and partly in the pharynx. As the larynx is closely approximated to its hinder end, there is of necessity descent in the neck; briefly stated the tongue has pushed the larynx to a low position, opposite the fourth, fifth and sixth cervical vertebrae.
>
> (1949, pp. 25–26)

Negus, in other words, does not treat the descent of the larynx as an isolated event. It is necessarily related to the total skeletal support system and the tongue. Still x rays and cineradiographic data derived from many normal speakers (a total sample size in excess of 200 subjects) show that the tongue body moves as an almost undistorted

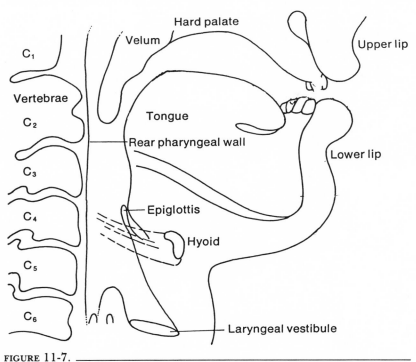

FIGURE 11-7.
Midsagittal view of the adult human supralaryngeal vocal tract.

body during the production of speech. The contour of the tongue body that forms the floor of the mouth and anterior wall of the pharynx, moreover, is, as Negus noted, curved. Its shape can be closely approximated by an arc of a circle (Nearey, 1978).

Human speakers, when they produce the vowels of a language like English (where tongue blade maneuvers are not used), move their tongue about in the space defined by the roof of the mouth and the spinal column. Figure 11-8 shows the position of the tongue for the production of the vowels [i] and [a] of American English. Nearey derived these data from cineradiographic x-ray movies of normal adult speakers. The tongue contours and center points for all the vowels of American English were derived by Nearey. The "horizontal" top part of the tongue body effectively determines the cross-sectional area of the mouth; the vertical back part of the tongue determines the cross-sectional area of the pharynx. The intersection

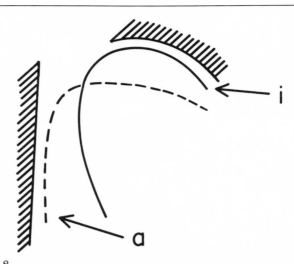

FIGURE 11-8.

Midsagittal view showing the contour of the tongue with respect to the hard palate and rear pharyngeal wall during the production of the vowels [i] and [a]. The contours were traced by Nearey from a cineradiographic film of an adult speaker of American-English. (After Nearey, 1978.)

of the planes defined by the vertebral column and the palate of the mouth yields an approximate right angle. The angle at which the pharynx and oral cavity intersect does not change when you bend your neck. X rays of people bending their necks forward and backward to the extreme limits of flexion (Shelton and Bosma, 1962) show that the bend takes place below the pharynx to the oral cavity bend, between the third and the fifth cervical vertebrae.

The speaker moves the tongue within this space. If the tongue is moved upward and toward the lips to produce the vowel [i], the tongue will yield the two-tube airway sketched in Figure 11-9. The cross-sectional area of the oral cavity will be constricted. In contrast, the cross-sectional area of the pharyngeal cavity will be quite large. The discontinuity at the approximate midpoint of the supralaryngeal airway will generate a vowel sound that has the quantal properties identified by Stevens (1972). The vowel [a] likewise is produced by a two-tube airway in which the pharyngeal tube is constricted and the oral tube expanded. The speaker in this case moves the tongue downward and back toward the vertebral column.

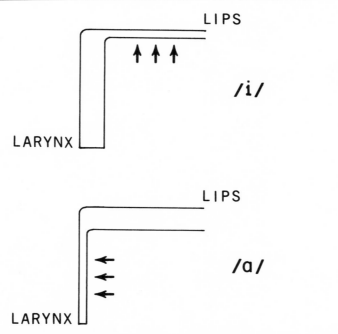

FIGURE 11-9.
Schematized adult human two-tube supralaryngeal airway.

THE PHONETIC DEFICIENCY OF THE STANDARD-PLAN AIRWAY

Computer-modeling studies in which the supralaryngeal airways of rhesus monkeys (Lieberman, Klatt, and Wilson, 1970), chimpanzee, and newborn human beings (Lieberman, Crelin, and Klatt, 1972) were systematically perturbed through the possible range of area-function variation show that the standard-plan supralaryngeal airway cannot produce vowels like [i], [u], and [a]. This deficiency follows from the fact that ten to one area-function variations are necessary to produce these vowels (Stevens and House, 1955). As I noted above, these area-function variations can be generated at the midpoint of the human supralaryngeal vocal tract by simply shifting the curved "fat" human tongue around in the right-angle space defined by the spinal column and palate. It is not possible to generate these abrupt area-function discontinuities in the nonhuman standard-plan supralaryngeal vocal tract. The standard-plan vocal tract is essentially a single-tube system in which the long, thin tongue defines the floor of the mouth. There is

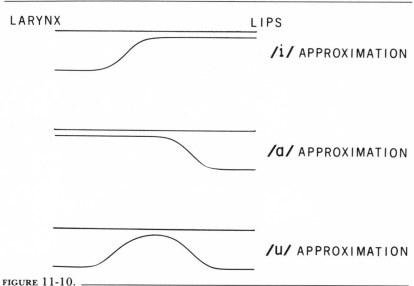

FIGURE 11-10.
Schematized nonhuman one-tube supralaryngeal airway in approximations to human vowels [i], [a], and [u].

no natural discontinuity in the system at which an abrupt area-function change can be generated along the tube. Figure 11-10 perhaps makes this point clear. A constriction necessarily must gradually give way to an unconstricted area of the single tube since the tongue muscle cannot itself form an abrupt discontinuity. Cineradiographic studies of newborn cry show this to be the case (Truby, Bosma, and Lind, 1965).

BREATHING, SWALLOWING, AND CHEWING

Human adults, unlike other adult mammals, are not obligate nose breathers. Negus connects this change in our breathing pattern with the descent of the larynx. Using the method of comparative anatomy, he compares the human airway with the airways of fast-running animals. In these animals the airways are relatively straight. In deer, for example, the nasal passage has only a slight curve "so designed as to cause no interference with the rapid passage of air" (Negus, 1949, p. 33). In contrast, the human airway is "a tortuous channel, the nasopharynx failing to reach the larynx and the air current turning through two right-angles; any disability due to angulation can, however, be partly overcome by opening the mouth" (Negus, 1949, p. 33). Negus is, of course, correct when he notes that mouth breathing is useful when we want to optimize airflow through the human supralaryngeal airways. Anyone who has run more than a mile knows that mouth breathing is necessary for strenuous aerobic exercise. It is interesting to note that human infants usually begin to breathe through their mouths at age 3 months (Laitman, Crelin, and Conlogue, 1977), after the first major restructuring of the supralaryngeal vocal tract toward its adult configuration (George, 1976, 1978; Goldstein, 1980). Whether mouth breathing is a consequence of adaptations for human speech or is a precursor of changes in the supralaryngeal airway that ultimately yielded human speech is an interesting question that I shall return to.

The pattern for swallowing that occurs in adultlike human beings is also quite different from that of other primates. We pull the larynx up and forward by tensing muscles like the anterior digastrics. If you refer back to Figure 11-1, you will see that in an adult human the hyoid bone, from which the larynx is suspended, is positioned below the mandible. In order to avoid having food fall into our larynx, we pull the larynx forward and upward, tucking the opening of the larynx behind the pharyngeal section of the tongue as we simultaneously push the bolus of food toward the opening of the esophagus. The food is rapidly pushed past the critical point at which it could lodge in the pharynx, which is a common food-and-air pathway (Negus, 1949, pp. 176–177; Bosma 1975; Laitman and Crelin, 1976). Figure 11-11 shows the food and air pathway of an adult human being.

The powerful pharyngeal constrictor muscles aid in propelling the bolus of food down the pharynx into the esophagus. Unfortunately the adult human pharynx is also part of the respiratory airway, owing to the ontogenetic descent of the larynx into the pharynx. An error in timing can propel the bolus of food into the larynx with results that are often fatal. It is not uncommon to find cadavers in a medical school dissection with a preserved piece of steak blocking the larynx. In the standard-plan airway, the pharynx lies behind the larynx (see Figures 11-4 and 11-5). Food that is being propelled down the pharynx thus cannot block the respiratory airway. Claims like those of Falk (1975, 1980) to the effect that fossil hominids could not have had nonhuman supralaryngeal airways because they supposedly would *not* be able to swallow in an upright position are thus wrong. The nonhuman supralaryngeal airways are *better* adapted for swallowing in any position; chimpanzees and monkeys habitually swallow food while they sit upright (Lieberman, 1982a, 1982b).

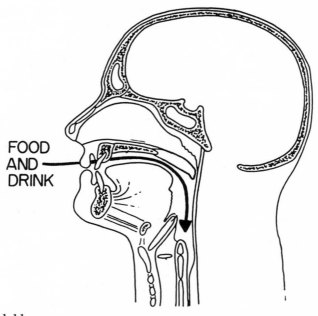

FOOD
AND
DRINK

FIGURE 11-11.
Diagram of adult human being showing pathway for the ingestion
of food. The food must pass over the opening of the larynx.

The manner in which adult human beings open and close their
jaws is also somewhat different from that of other primates. DuBrul
(1976, 1977) points out that adult human beings open their jaws by
pulling the mandible down and back with the anterior digastric
muscles. If you refer back to Figure 11-1 again, you will note that the
anterior digastric muscles, which run between the hyoid bone and the
mandible, can pull the mandible downward if the hyoid bone is
simultaneously stabilized by the sternohyoid muscle, which runs between the hyoid and the sternum (collarbone).[1] The opening motion
of the human mandible is different from that of standard-plan airways
where the digastric muscles exert a backward force on the mandible
because the hyoid bone is positioned close to the base of the skull. The
hyoid bone supports the cartilages of the larynx, and so its position
depends on that of the larynx relative to the base of the skull.

The pattern of forces that open the mandible is quite different in
animals who have standard-plan vocal tracts. Their mandibles open by
a "camming" action in which the force generated by the pull of the
anterior digastric muscles is opposed by an equal and opposite force

from the bone structure of their tempromandibular joint, the joint into which the mandible fits on the skull. Apes consequently have a massive tempromandibular joint that is quite different from that of an adult human being. The apes' tempromandibular joint has to be more massive to cope with the force generated in the camming action. The presence of an apelike tempromandibular joint in a fossil hominid thus is consistent with the fossil's having a nonhuman standard-plan supralaryngeal airway. DuBrul (1976, 1977) argues that fossil hominids like the La Chapelle-aux-Saints classic Neanderthal could not have had a standard-plan vocal tract because they would not be able to open their jaws like modern adult human beings. DuBrul, however, overlooks the pongid character of the La Chapelle-aux-Saints fossil's tempromandibular joint, which Boule (1911–1913) noted in the original descriptions of this fossil. DuBrul thus is "hoist with his own petard"; the pongid characteristics of the classic Neanderthal tempromandibular joint are consistent with its opening and closing like a gorilla's or a chimpanzee's. The massive brow ridges of classic Neanderthal fossils are also consistent with the pongidlike tempromandibular joint. Gorillas are not very pretty by human standards, but they have powerful jaw muscles and massive jaws that can exert a powerful bite. Neanderthal fossil hominids also have massive jaws and doubtless had powerful masseter muscles, whose presence we can infer from the facets on their skulls and mandibles. Though they too probably would not win any beauty contests today, their bites were undoubtedly more powerful than ours.

The long body of the mandible that is a characteristic of the standard-plan supralaryngeal airway is necessary to keep the tongue within the oral cavity. As Negus noted in his comparative studies, all animals except adult human beings have long mandibles with long bodies. There is plenty of space along the nonhuman mandible and upper jaw for teeth. This increases the efficiency of chewing. As I noted earlier, studies of the efficiency of chewing demonstrate that, all other things being equal, a greater tooth area will yield more effective chewing (Manley and Braley, 1950; Manley and Shiere, 1950; Manley and Vinton, 1951). The reduction in the length of the mandible that Negus first noted in connection with the movement of the tongue down into the pharynx is thus counterproductive for chewing.

The picture that emerges with regard to the vegetative functions of breathing, swallowing, and chewing is that the adult human supralaryngeal airway, and its associated skeletal structure, is less effective in these functions than the nonhuman standard-plan arrangement. This conclusion is not very surprising, given the ubiquitous occurrence of the standard-plan morphology.

NEOTENY

The superiority of the standard-plan supralaryngeal airway in these vegetative functions also explains the retention of this airway in newborn human infants. There is a selective advantage in being able to breathe and suckle simultaneously. Vocal communication is not as important in the first months of life as weight gain, efficient respiration, and avoidance of asphyxiation. Newborn human infants thus retain the "base form" mammalian supralaryngeal airway. As they develop, they deviate from the mammalian standard-plan airway. The nonhuman primates, in this regard, retain their functional "neoteny," so they are examples of "neotenous" development, not we. Adult nonhuman primates differ from their infants in other ways (Schultz, 1968; Laitman, Heimbuch, and Crelin, 1978; Laitman, 1983). In general, as Louis Agassiz and Charles Darwin observed over a hundred years ago, the adult forms of animals deviate from their infantile states. The theory of neoteny as propounded by Gould (1973, 1977) is refuted by the data of human and primate ontogenetic development, as well as by those of phylogenetic evolution.

THE SKELETAL CORRELATES OF THE SUPRALARYNGEAL AIRWAY

I have already noted some of the skeletal correlates of the standard-plan and adult human supralaryngeal airways. The base of the skull and the jaw, the basicranium and the mandible, are the skeletal features that support the soft tissue of the supralaryngeal vocal tract. The basicranium, moreover, itself defines the upper (superior) border of the supralaryngeal airways. Negus obviously saw the connection between the morphology of the skull base, mandible, and soft tissue of the supralaryngeal airway. The reconstruction of the airways of a Neanderthal fossil that he attributes to Sir Arthur Keith (Negus, 1949, pp. 195–200) is quite similar to recent reconstructions (Lieberman and Crelin, 1971; Laitman, Heimbuch, and Crelin, 1978; Grosmangin, 1979). Negus unfortunately does not discuss in detail the anatomical features that are the bases of the reconstruction. His discussion of the anatomical principles for reconstructing the fossil supralaryngeal airway is limited to the comment that I noted earlier, that the low position of the larynx in modern human beings derives from "the recession of the jaws" (Negus, 1949, p. 25) and to the comment that the larynx descends in human infants after birth "as a result of alteration in the vertebro-occipital and pituitary angles, together with downward movement of the tongue in the pharynx" (1949, p. 175).

Recent studies indicate that the basicranium is appreciably different from the other bones of the skull and is an extremely reliable guide both for the reconstruction of the supralaryngeal airways of fossils and for the assessment of phylogenetic relationships. The basicranium is first a very conservative region of the skull in an evolutionary sense. As Laitman (1983) notes, the numerous openings in the basicranium (the basicranial foramina) through which the cranial nerves and blood supply of the brain enter and exit the skull preclude drastic, uncoordinated changes in its form. Whereas deformations of the other bones of skull are usually not life threatening, abnormalities of the skull base frequently either are not viable (Bosma, 1975) or have profound behavioral consequences (Pruzansky, 1973). The special status of the basicranium is reflected in its composition. It is largely derived from cartilage. In contrast, the greater part of the rest of the skull is derived embryologically from membranous bone. Recent studies have shown that cartilage cells are more sensitive to growth-regulating hormones. This increased sensitivity to regulatory hormones is consistent with the restructuring of the skull base that occurs in the ontogenetic development of infants and children. It allows the precise changes that must occur if life is to be sustained as the basicranium changes its shape. As Laitman concludes,

> The basicranium is thus appreciably different from other components of the skull both in its largely endochondral development and its involvement with inviolable nervous and vascular structures. Due to these factors the basicranium is an evolutionary conservative area. Unlike the more plastic bones of the face or vault the configuration of the mature mammalian basicranium shows comparatively little variation within, or even among species. This evolutionary conservatism and stability has implications both for interpretation and reconstruction of fossil remains and for the assessment of phylogenetic relationships. The constant and predictable relationships among foramina and landmarks permit basicranial reconstruction with a degree of accuracy not possible for the more variable facial or neural bones. Similarly, phylogenetic change can often be monitored through the use of the basicranium as a guide. Since the basicranium is such a conservative feature, any alteration may indicate change of a more substantial nature than the more frequent, and easily achieved, changes in the more plastic parts of the skull.
>
> (1983, p. 9)

As we shall see, whereas there is little difference between the basicraniums of human newborns and other infantile or adult primates, who all have standard-plan supralaryngeal airways, there are profound differences between these skulls and the basicraniums of normal adult human beings. The selective forces that led to the restructuring of the human basicranium thus must have had extremely high selective value. In short, two facts emerge at this juncture.

1. The evolution of anatomically modern *Homo sapiens* does *not*, as Gould (1973, 1977) claims, involve the putative process of neoteny. Whereas adult apes differ from the juvenile "base" form with respect to differences involving the more plastic bones of the skull, we differ with respect to the basicranium.

2. The selective value of the functional consequences of the restructuring of the human basicranium must have been extremely high. The selective value of encoded, high-speed vocal communication is the factor that I think was involved. High-speed vocal communication coming together with the enhanced cognitive power of the hominid brain in the late *Homo erectus* stage of human evolution probably yielded human language. In more advanced cultural settings the communicative language of modern *Homo sapiens* may have yielded the selective advantage that outweighed the vegetative advantages of the nonhuman supralaryngeal airway.

CHAPTER 12

The Evolution of Human Speech: The Fossil Record

THE COMPARATIVE STUDIES THAT I have just discussed allow us to trace the evolution of the human supralaryngeal airway through the fossil record. The correlation between the soft tissue of the supralaryngeal airways and the basicranium was established, and the conservative nature of the basicranium and the selective value of human speech were noted. I shall start the analysis of the fossil record with a qualitative discussion of the recent classical Neanderthal fossils that will hopefully point out the relevant issues. I shall then discuss quantitative, statistically based methods and the evolution of the supralaryngeal vocal tract in other archaic hominids.

The classic Neanderthal hominids are of particular interest because they were quite advanced in many ways but nonetheless appear to have retained certain primitive features. They lived until comparatively recent times, had large brains, developed an advanced culture, and coexisted with populations of anatomically modern *Homo sapiens.* They, however, preserved the archaic features of the general mammalian basicranium noted in Chapter 11. Figure 12-1 shows inferior views (looking up) of the basicraniums of a newborn human infant, the La Chapelle-aux-Saints Neanderthal fossil, and a modern adult man. Figure 12-2 shows lateral views of these skulls and the mandibles. The skulls and mandibles have been drawn to the same size. There are many similarities between the newborn and Neanderthal skulls and mandibles. Note the length of dimension S, the distance between the posterior border of the palate and the anterior border of the foramen magnum, relative to dimension P, the length of the palate. Whereas dimension S is equal to or longer than dimension P in the human newborn and the adult Neanderthal fossil, it is usually shorter in adult human beings. In only two out of a sample of fifty modern adult human skulls were these dimensions equal (Lieberman and Crelin, 1971).

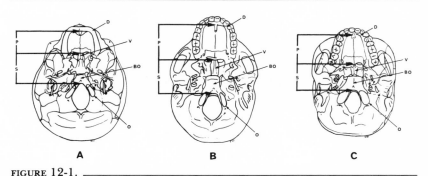

FIGURE 12-1.

Views of the bottoms of the skulls of modern newborn (*A*) and adult
(*C*) *Homo sapiens* and the La Chapelle-aux-Saints Neanderthal fossil
(*B*). *D* indicates the dental arch; *V*, the vomer bone; *BO*, the basilar
part of the occipital bone; and *O*, the occipital condyle. The skulls,
which are quite different in size, have been drawn to the same scale.
(After Lieberman and Crelin, 1971.)

Distance *S* is quite long, 6.2 cm, in the Neanderthal fossil. It is
also quite long relative to the short length of the newborn skull:
2.6 cm average with a range of 2.5 cm to 2.7 cm. The anterior-poste-
rior length of the newborn larynx is about 2 cm (Crelin, 1973). The
newborn skull thus has sufficient room for its larynx to be positioned
high relative to the basicranium, almost in line with the tongue, so that
it can lock into the nasopharynx during respiration. The length of the
largest adult male larynx illustrated in the work of Negus (1949) is
4.5 cm. The range, as estimated from Negus's data (1949, p. 177) and
Goldstein's compilation (1980, p. 65), is about 3.5 cm to 4.5 cm for
adult males. Consequently there is more than enough room for the
larynx to be positioned in a *similar* place in the Neanderthal fossil. In
contrast, in the fifty skulls of modern adult males measured in Lieberman and Crelin (1971), dimension *S* averaged 4.1 cm with a range of
3.6 cm to 4.9 cm. There just is not enough space in a modern adult
human skull between the hard palate and the spinal column for a
larynx that is positioned close to the basicranium with the pharynx
located behind the opening of the larynx.

The high laryngeal position and respiratory "locking" function
of the larynx in the standard-plan airway is also apparent in the lateral
views of Figure 12-2. The basicraniums of the newborn human and
the Neanderthal fossil are flattened out in the region between the end
of the palate and the basion (the anterior edge of the foramen

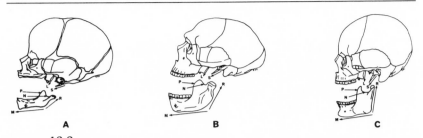

A   **B**   **C**

FIGURE 12.2. ───

Lateral views of skulls of modern newborn (*A*) and adult (*C*) *Homo
sapiens* and the La Chapelle-aux-Saints Neanderthal fossil (*C*). *L*
indicates angle of pterygoid lamina; *S*, angle of styloid process; *R*,
ramus of mandible; *M*, body of mandible. (After Lieberman and
Crelin, 1971.)

magnum). The roof of the nasopharynx in the newborn and Neanderthal skulls is a relatively shallow and elongated arch, whereas in adult
human beings it forms a deep, short arch. In the skulls that support a
standard-plan supralaryngeal airway, the occipital bone between the
foramen magnum and the sphenoid bone of the skull is only slightly
inclined away from the horizontal plane (Bergland, 1963; Lieberman
and Crelin, 1971; Laitman, Heimbuch, and Crelin, 1978).

The relationship between the bones that form this part of the
basicranium is again different in newborns compared with adult
human beings (Lieberman and Crelin, 1971; Laitman and Crelin, 1976).
The distance between the vomer bone and the synchondrosis of the
sphenoid and occipital bones is relatively long in newborns (Crelin,
1973). As children mature, this distance decreases. The vomar often
overlaps the synchondrosis in adults (Takagi, 1964). The skeletal features that support the muscles and ligaments of the supralaryngeal
vocal tract and mandible are similar in newborn *Homo sapiens* and the
Neanderthal fossil. For example, the pterygoid process of the sphenoid bone is relatively short, and its vertical lamina is more inclined
away from the vertical plane than is the case in adult human skulls.
The medial pterygoid plate, which is one of the points where the
superior pharyngeal constrictor muscle is attached, is also similar in
the modern newborn and fossil Neanderthal skulls. This muscle plays
a part in swallowing (Bosma, 1975) and in speech production (Bell-Berti,
1973). It is active in the production of nonnasal sounds, where it helps
seal the nasal cavity, and in the production of sounds like the vowel [a],
where it pulls the tongue body back.

The body of the newborn mandible, dimension *M* in Figure 12-2, is longer than the ramus, dimension R. The length of the body of the mandible in the newborn skull is consistent with the fact that the newborn tongue is long and is positioned entirely within the month. The length of the mandible has to be long to hold the tongue. The body of the newborn mandible is thus about 3.5 cm compared with the 2.0-cm length of the ramus. The proportions of the Neanderthal fossil's mandible are similar to those of the newborn's mandible. In contrast, the lengths of the mandibular body and ramus are usually almost equal in adult human beings (Crelin, 1973). Other details of the newborn and Neanderthal mandibles also differ from those of adult modern *Homo sapiens.* The posterior border of the mandibular ramus is more inclined away from the vertical plane. There is a similar inclination of the mandibular foramen leading to the mandibular canal through which the inferior alveolar artery and nerve pass. The mandibular coronoid process is broad, and the mandibular notch is relatively shallow (Lieberman and Crelin, 1971).

The skeletal features of the human newborn and the classic Neanderthal La Chapelle-aux-Saints fossil that make up what Le Gros Clark called "the total morphological pattern" supporting the soft tissue of the supralaryngeal airways are so similar that by following the methods of comparative anatomy, the Neanderthal fossil would most likely have had a supralaryngeal airway quite similar in form to that of a human newborn. These similarities probably led Negus and Sir Arthur Keith to conclude that the airways of the classic Neanderthal were similar to that of a newborn. They led Edmund S. Crelin to the similar reconstruction reported in Lieberman and Crelin (1971) and the similar independent reconstruction by Grosmangin (1979). A diagram of Crelin's reconstruction is presented in Figure 12-3. Note the position of the tongue with respect to the palate. The tongue, like that of a human newborn, is positioned almost entirely within the mouth. The larynx is positioned close to the base of the skull; the pharynx is positioned behind the larynx. The supralaryngeal airway differs markedly from that of a modern adult human being. It essentially is a nonhuman single-tube system.

COULD A NEANDERTHAL SKULL SUPPORT A MODERN VOCAL TRACT?

Although one can argue about using correlations between skeletal morphology and soft tissue, it is reasonably clear that the skeletal morphology of the Neanderthal skull could *not* support an adult human supralaryngeal vocal tract. The relevance of the length of the

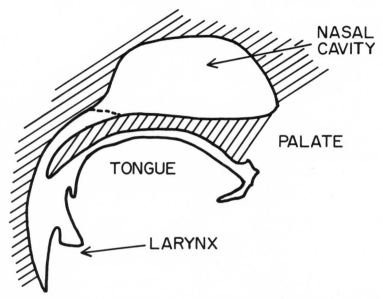

FIGURE 12-3. ——————————————————————————————
Reconstruction of the supralaryngeal vocal tract of the La Chapelle-
aux-Saints Neanderthal hominid. Note the high position of the
larynx relative to the palate and the tongue, which is positioned
almost entirely within the oral cavity. The pharynx lies behind the
larynx. (After Lieberman and Crelin, 1971.)

palate to the reconstruction of the supralaryngeal airway has been
discussed before (Lieberman, 1975a, p. 137; Lieberman, 1979, 1982).
The length of the palate in a fossil like the La Chapelle-aux-Saints
Neanderthal, for example, precludes that hominid's having a modern
human supralaryngeal vocal tract. It is straightforward to demonstrate, even if I were to limit this discussion to the length of the classic
Neanderthal palate, that a modern human supralaryngeal vocal tract
most likely could not occur with a classic Neanderthal skull. In the
debate concerning the reconstruction of Lieberman and Crelin (1971)
a number of authors, including LeMay (1975), Carlisle and Siegel
(1974), DuBrul (1977), and Falk (1975), have claimed that classic
Neanderthal hominids had normal human adult vocal tracts. I shall go
through the steps of a reconstruction, keeping in mind the length of
the palate, and see whether this is possible.

The first step entails placing the La Chapelle skull on a "normal"

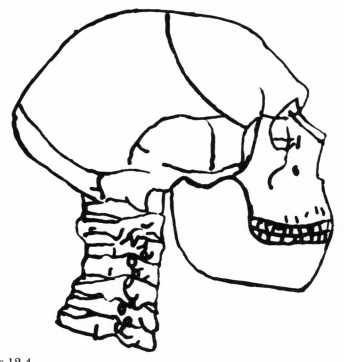

FIGURE 12-4.

Can one give a Neanderthal hominid a modern human vocal tract?
Step 1. The La Chapelle-aux-Saints skull and mandible are placed
on a modern vertebral column.

vertebral column, as shown in Figure 12-4. This follows the observation of Strauss and Cave (1957) and yields normal upright posture. Strauss and Cave found that the La Chapelle-aux-Saints fossil suffered from arthritis during his life. Boule (1911–1913) did not take account of the arthritic condition of the fossil and incorrectly reconstructed the normal posture of classic Neanderthal fossils as a stoop. Though the Neanderthal vertebral column is not quite similar to that of a normal human adult, having some infantile features (Crelin, 1973), it would not have resulted in a habitual stoop. The reconstruction reported in Lieberman and Crelin (1971) also starts with a normal human vertebral column. Comments like those of Carlisle and Siegel (1974) and DuBrul (1977), which imply or claim that an "error" was thereby introduced into the reconstruction noted in Lieberman and

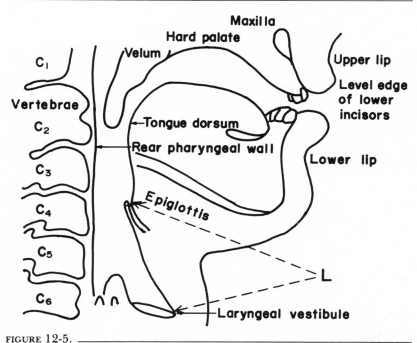

FIGURE 12-5. —————————————————————————————
Step 2. Cross-sectional view of a normal adult human male supralaryngeal vocal tract. Note that the tongue obviously fills the oral cavity. The various pellets and the coin were markers used in a cineradiographic study of speech, from which this view was taken. (After Perkell, 1969.)

Crelin (1971) by not taking note of the arthritic condition of the La Chapelle fossil, are thus irrelevant. Note the distance between the front of the palate and the vertebral column.

Step two involves considering the morphology of the normal human adult supralaryngeal vocal tract. Figure 12-5 shows a cross-sectional view of a normal adult male vocal tract derived from a cineradiographic study of speech production (Perkell, 1969). As I have noted before (see Figures 11-7 and 11-8), the curved tongue body forms both the floor of the oral cavity and the anterior wall of the pharynx. The posterior contour of the tongue body is almost circular (Nearey, 1978). The laryngeal opening is quite low, but it is positioned *within* the neck between the fifth and sixth cervical vertebrae. The distance between the front of the hard palate and the vertebral column in this figure has been made identical to that of Figure 12-4. The length of the vocal tract between the epiglottis and the laryngeal vestibule has been marked with the letter L.

The next step in this reconstruction involves considering the range of variation in the proportions of the tongue body. That there is a range of variation is evident in radiographic studies like that of King (1952). During the production of human speech the larynx, moreover, moves up and down. It is usually at its lowest level in the production of a vowel like [u]. It is high during the production of a vowel like [i] (Fant, 1960; Perkell, 1969; Ladefoged et al., 1972; Nearey, 1978). As will be seen in step four, the *lowest* position of the larynx is a crucial factor regarding the validity of a vocal tract reconstruction. Hence, granting the Neanderthal fossil the benefit of the doubt, I will give him a tongue contour that is derived from x rays of human speakers producing acute, or front, vowels like [i], [I], and [e], in which the larynx is not lowered. The tongue contours in Figure 12-6 are thus derived from the data of Ladefoged and associates (1972) for normal adult speakers producing these vowels. Note that the tongue contour is approximately circular, except that the vertical pharyngeal sections tend to be longer than the oral section. I will, however, again "tilt" the reconstruction to give the La Chapelle fossil the benefit of the doubt by using tongue contour T, in which the pharyngeal and oral sections have equal lengths. This tongue contour will keep the larynx positioned as high as possible, and I will give the Neanderthal skull a normal human vocal tract.

In step four the vocal tract is put together. Figure 12-7 shows the Neanderthal skull in relation to the putative vocal tract. I have placed tongue contour T plus laryngeal section L (from epiglottis to laryngeal vestibule) on the Neanderthal skull and vertebral column. Note that the larynx is positioned *below* the seventh cervical vertebra at the level of the sternum. This position is most unlikely, if not impossible, since no primate has a larynx in its chest. The difficulty stems from the long span between the front of the Neanderthal palate and the vertebral column. This span is consistent with the probable nonhuman Neanderthal supralaryngeal anatomy. If I were to insist on spanning this distance with an adult human tongue, I would end up with an anatomical monster. If I had used one of the other five tongue contours from Figure 12-6, the larynx would be even lower! It thus is most unlikely that classic Neanderthal hominids had normal human supralaryngeal vocal tracts. Similar considerations apply to the skeletal morphology and supralaryngeal vocal tracts of the australopithecine and *erectus*-grade fossils that I will discuss. The length of the palate is simply too

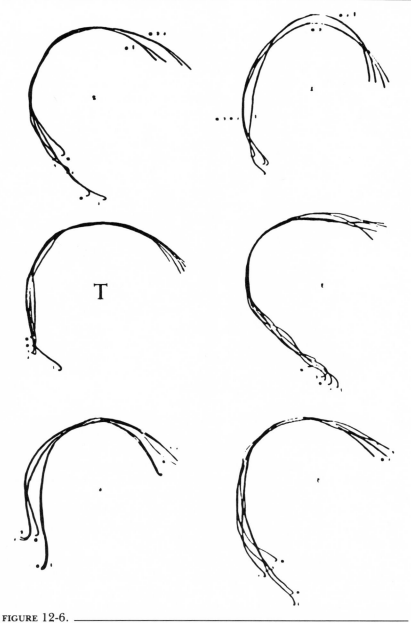

T

FIGURE 12-6.
Step 3. Tongue contours for normal adult human speakers. These
tongue contours were derived from a cineradiographic study of
vowel production (Ladefoged et al., 1972). They are shown in this
figure in the scale that would be necessary for them to fit the skull in
Figure 12-4. The tongue must fill the oral cavity of the Neanderthal
fossil, just as it fits the modern oral cavity in Figure 12-5.

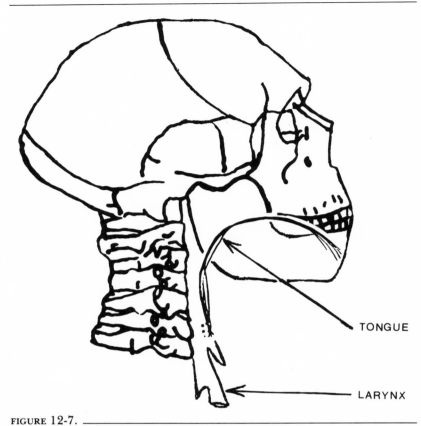

FIGURE 12-7.
Step 4. Tongue contour *T* from Figure 12-6 has been placed under
the Neanderthal skull, as has the modern human laryngeal section *L*
from Figure 12-5. Note that this places the larynx below the
cervical vertebrae in the Neanderthal chest! It is essentially impossible to give a Neanderthal hominid a modern human vocal tract.
The modern human tongue has the wrong shape.

long. If one insists on giving these hominids human tongues that are
thick and have equally long oral and pharyngeal sections, then their
larynges must be placed in their chests! Since no primate at any
phylogenetic level — lemur, monkey, ape, human being — has its larynx in its chest, this "solution" is essentially impossible. The long
palates of australopithecine, *Homo erectus,* and classic Neanderthal
fossils instead must support nonhuman standard-plan supralaryngeal
vocal tracts in which the tongue is long and thin and is positioned
almost entirely within the oral cavity.

QUANTITATIVE STATISTICAL COMPARISONS

The comparisons of skeletal morphology that I have already discussed can be applied on an individual case-by-case basis to all existing fossil hominid skulls. However, there are variations between each of these skulls, just as there are variations between the skulls of modern adult human beings. Human observers are very good in recognizing similar shapes and forms when confronted with a set of skulls, each of which varies slightly. As Le Gros Clark noted, there is a "total morphological pattern" that is the skeletal correlate of a function like upright bipedal posture that trained human observers can recognize in the pattern of individual variation. The total morphological pattern that is the skeletal correlate of the standard-plan versus the modern adult human supralaryngeal vocal tract is also evident when trained observers look at skulls that are at the end points, that is, skulls that have either standard-plan or adultlike human vocal tracts. Quantitative statistical methods that group skulls in terms of their shape, however, force us to generate explicit hypotheses concerning the specific anatomical features that we think are significant and allow us to test these hypotheses against large sample sizes. Quantitative statistical procedures, moreover, are especially well suited to analyzing the tempo of evolution — whether evolutionary changes in the bones of the skull are gradual or instead occur in spurts — and to determining whether these changes are correlated with other factors like upright posture.

Recent studies that make use of quantitative measures of the flexure of the basicranium make it possible to compare large numbers of skulls within the population that defines a species and to compare the skulls of different species. Figure 12-8 shows three views of the skull of an adult female chimpanzee with craniometric points that are appropriate for comparing the flexure and form of the basicranium. The basion, point E in Figure 12-8, is, as I noted earlier, the anterior margin of the foramen magnum. Point D is the sphenobasion — the point where the sphenoid and occipital bones meet. The occipital bone spans the distance ED. The hormion, point C, is the posterior margin of the vomer bone. Point B, the staphylion, is the posterior limit of the bony palate. The distance AB thus is an accurate measure of the length of the palate.

Figure 12-9 shows these points for a newborn and an adult human skull. The study of Laitman, Heimbuch, and Crelin (1978) derived these measures from a sample of 228 primate skulls. Table 12-1 shows the number of skulls used for each species and the age of each individual at time of death as defined by the dental stage. Stage 1 included skulls of individuals who died prior to the eruption of

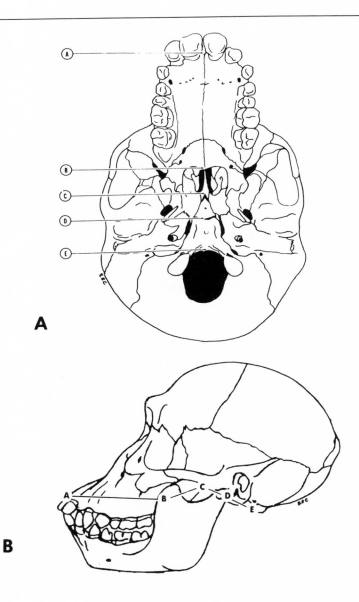

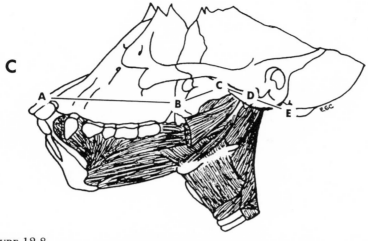

FIGURE 12-8. _____

A: Craniometric points on the midline of the basicranium of an
adult female chimpanzee (*pan troglodytes*) — *A*, prosthion; *B*,
staphylion; *C*, hormion; *D*, sphenobasion; *E*, endobasion. Note the
exposed sphenoid bone between points *C* and *D*. *B:* Topographic
projection of the basicranial line on the skull of an adult female
chimpanzee. *C:* Topographic projection of the basicranial line on
the skull of an adult chimpanzee, lateral view, with the left half of
the mandible removed to show the muscles of the tongue, the
pharyngeal constrictors, and some of the extrinsic muscles of the
larynx. (After Laitman, Heimbuch, and Crelin, 1978.)

deciduous dentition. Stage 2 included skulls of individuals between
the eruption of the first central incisor to the completion of deciduous
dentition; stage 3, the eruption of the first permanent molar; stage 4,
the eruption of the second permanent molar; and stage 5, the eruption of the third permanent molar. Previous studies (Bergland, 1963)
demonstrated that the angular relationships and distances in the
region of the skull defined by points *B–E* in Figure 12-9 were quite
stable in a sample of 223 Norwegian and Lapp skulls. Bergland also
demonstrated that these craniometric measures differed from ones
derived from nonhuman primates. As Bergland points out, the difference between humans and other primates with regard to the flexure
of the basicranium in the nasopharynx, the region defined by points
B–E, has been noted since the end of the nineteenth century.

The statistical procedures used by Laitman, Heimbuch, and
Crelin (1978) replicate these earlier studies as well as the qualitative

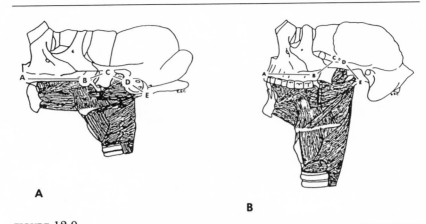

A

B

FIGURE 12-9. _____

Topographic projections of the basicranial line on the skulls of
newborn (A) and adult (B) human skulls, lateral views with the left
half of the mandible removed to show muscles of pharynx, tongue,
and some extrinsic laryngeal muscles. Note the relative orientation
of line *DE* in the newborn and adult. The superior pharyngeal
constrictor muscle runs forward and down almost perpendicular to
line *DE*, which defines the plane of the basioccipital. (Adapted from
Laitman, Heimbuch, and Crelin, 1978.)

observations of recent comparative studies (Negus, 1949; Lieberman,
1968, 1975a, 1979; Lieberman and Crelin, 1971, 1972; Laitman and Crelin,
1976). Nonhuman primates and stage-1 human beings have a basicranium that is essentially nonflexed from the posterior border of the
palate to the basion. Gibbons (Hylobates) and macaque monkeys
(Macaca) show little change as they develop. The basicranium becomes flatter as these nonhuman primates develop. In contrast,
human beings show a unique developmental pattern. They start with
the same basicranium as other primates. The statistical metrics that
involve multivariate analysis of variance and discriminant analysis
consistently placed stage-1 humans and other primates in the same
class. They then flex. After stage 2, modern human specimens were
misidentified only with other human specimens; stage-5 individuals
were sometimes misassigned to stage 4. The pattern of change in
basicranial flexure can be seen in Figure 12-10, in which the basicranial lines derived from gorilla, chimpanzee, and human skulls by
Laitman, Heimbuch, and Crelin (1978) are shown. The diagrams
show the basicranial lines drawn to the same scale since the statistical
metrics operate in terms of shape, ignoring absolute size. Note that

TABLE 12-1. Number of Primate Skulls Studied for 7 Species

Dental stage	1	2	3	4	5	Total
Macaca arctoides	0	3	1	4	6	14
Hylobates species	1	5	5	5	11	26
Symphalangus syndactylus	0	1	2	5	10	18
Pongo pygmaeus	2	4	7	7	9	29
Pan troglodytes	0	5	7	6	11	29
Gorilla gorilla	1	5	3	6	9	24
Homo sapiens	24	12	11	13	28	88
Total	28	35	35	46	84	228

SOURCE: Laitman, Heimbuch, and Crelin, p. 969.

the human newborn basicranial line is similar to that of the chimpanzee *(Pa)* and stage-1 gorilla *(Go)*. The chimpanzee basicranial line becomes somewhat flatter while the gorilla's becomes very flat, as Gould (1977) correctly notes. However, the human basicranium also changes, becoming *more* flexed, with the greatest change occurring between stages 1 and 2. The difference in the orientation of the basioccipital reflects the direction and size of the pharyngeal constrictor muscles in the standard-plan versus the adultlike human supralaryngeal airway. The descent of the tongue and larynx in human beings, which yields the human pharynx, results in a change in the direction in which the pharyngeal constrictors run (see Figures 12-5 and 12-9). The angulation of the adultlike human basioccipital segment *ED* in these figures corresponds to the uniquely human pharyngeal musculature.

The independent craniometric data of George (1978) and Grosmangin (1979) are consistent with these results. The major restructuring of the human basicranium takes place quite early in life. George (1976, 1978) derived her data from x rays of a sample of sixteen boys and sixteen girls. The x rays form part of a cephalometric series and were taken at ages 1 month, 3 months, 9 months, and thereafter once a year until 5 years 9 months. George's data complement the measurements derived from skulls by Laitman and Crelin (1978). George measured the cranial base deflection by five sets of angles. Statistical analysis shows a major decrease in the angle size by 9 months, with significant changes between 1 and 3 months for some individuals. The mean cranial base angle changed from 137 degrees at 1 month to 125 degrees at 9 months. This angle is 134 degrees in the La Chapelle-aux-Saints Neanderthal fossil (Howell, 1951). A cranial base angle of 125 degrees is within the human adult range. George (1978) concludes that the change of the human cranial angle is almost complete by age 1

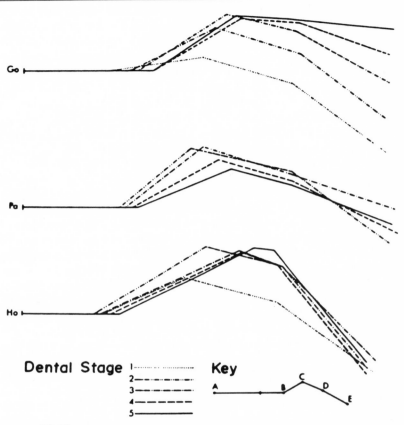

FIGURE 12-10.
Ontogenetic development of the basicranial line in modern human
beings; *Ho*; chimpanzees, *Pa*; and gorillas, *Go*. The measurements
were derived from the sample noted in Table 12-1. (Adapted from
Laitman, Heimbuch, and Crelin, 1978.)

year 9 months. George's study is significant since its data are derived
from x rays of living subjects and replicate observations derived from
either cadavers or dried skulls.

The independent study of Grosmangin (1979) is based on a
detailed series of craniometric measures of the basicranium that
includes, among other points, the series measured by Laitman, Heimbuch, and Crelin (1978, 1979). Grosmangin's sample includes a series
of twenty-five infants and children from newborns to 19-year-olds,

thirty European adults, a series of six non-European adults selected to establish the limits of variability, a series of nonhuman primate skulls including adults and juveniles, and five fossil hominid skulls. The fossil skulls include the classic La Chapelle-aux-Saints Neanderthal, La Ferrassie I, Pech de l'Aze, and La Quina skulls, plus the archaic but anatomically modern Cro-Magnon skull (Oakley, Campbell, and Molleson, 1971). Grosmangin documents her measurements and analysis in detail. Her conclusions (pp. 134–154) regarding the development of the basicranium in human beings compared with nonhuman primates is consistent with those of Laitman and Crelin (1976). She, however, concludes that the classic Neanderthal skulls are closer to those of juvenile chimpanzees (that is, they are less flexed) than to those of human newborns[1] (Grosmangin, 1979, pp. 186–191).

The analyses of Laitman, Heimbuch, and Crelin (1979), Laitman (1983), and Laitman and Heimbuch (1982) involve consideration of the flexure of the basicranium in the skulls of a large population of modern human beings and living primates. These studies and the independent studies of Bergland (1963), George (1978), and Grosmangin (1979) show that a flexed basicranium supports a humanlike supralaryngeal airway. Laitman, Heimbuch, and Crelin apply these metrics to fourteen fossil hominid skulls. Their analysis shows that there "appear to be at least two pathways taken in the evolution of man's upper respiratory system after a common pongid-like stage exhibited by the australopithecines. One line appears to have terminated with the Classic Neanderthals. The other line, encompassing those hominids with basicrania and upper respiratory structures of more modern appearance, may have given rise to modern man" (1979, p. 15). These conclusions, which are based on the statistical analysis of the flexure of the basicranium, are similar to the hypothetical scheme for the late stages of hominid evolution noted in Chapter 11 (Lieberman, 1968a, 1973, 1975a). The discussion that follows refers to the supralaryngeal airways of human beings as the "vocal tract." The claim implicit in this terminology is that the supralaryngeal airways of humans have a distinct function in the production of speech and that they evolved, in part, to serve this function. In other words, at functional branch-point IV (see Figure 11-2), the course of human evolution diverged from that of other hominids to select for variations that enhanced our phonetic ability.

Figure 12-11 shows a number of cranial base lines that are derived from Laitman, Heimbuch, and Crelin (1978, 1979) and Grosmangin (1979). I have restored the sections of the hard palate that were removed in the illustrations of Laitman and his co-workers.

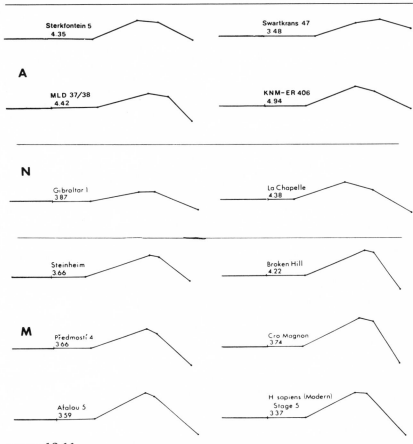

FIGURE 12-11. _____

A: Basicranial lines showing entire length of palate for the gracile
australopithecine Sterkfontein-5 and MLD-37/38 fossils and the robust australopithecine Swartkrans-47 and KNM-ER-406 fossils. N:
Basicranial lines for the Neanderthal Gibraltar-1 and La Chapelle-
aux-Saints fossils. M: Basicranial lines for the Steinheim and Broken
Hill fossils, fossil skulls that are archaic but have anatomically
modern basicranial lines, and modern adult *Homo sapiens*.

Palatal length, however, was preserved in their statistical analyses.
The length of the palate is an important element in determining the
functional aspects of the supralaryngeal vocal tract if one is concerned
with the properties of *human* speech. If you recall the discussion of the
quantal properties of human speech production in Chapter 8, the
special acoustic properties of the vowel [i] follow from the fact that

abrupt changes in the cross section of the vocal tract occur at its approximate midpoint. We thus have to keep track of two factors in the evolution of the human supralaryngeal vocal tract. The formation of a pharynx that is at a right angle to the oral cavity is one factor. The osteological features that are relevant in this regard are the flexure of the basioccipital bone and the shape and length of the basicranium between the basion and posterior border of the palate. These features are analyzed in detail by Laitman, Heimbuch, and Crelin (1978, 1979). The proportion of the pharynx relative to the oral cavity is the second factor. As noted earlier, the length of the palate in relation to the length of the neck is the osteological feature that is relevant to this factor.

A MODEL FOR THE EVOLUTION OF SPEECH AND LANGUAGE

The diagram presented in Figure 12-12 is an attempt to pattern one important aspect of the "recent" stages of hominid evolution — the evolution of human speech and language. The claim implicit in this model is that the recent stages of hominid evolution involved anatomical adaptations that yielded the special characteristics of human speech at the expense of vegetative functions like chewing, swallowing, and breathing in the archaic hominids who are among our more direct ancestors. The model further proposes that these anatomical adaptations have been matched by corresponding neural changes that in their totality yield encoded, high-speed human speech. The characteristic high rate of human speech, again coupled with the general cognitive power of the large hominid brain, yields human language — both our "thinking" language and our special "communicating" language. The biological cost of these changes is the relatively inefficient, distinctively human pattern of swallowing, breathing, jaw opening, and chewing as well as the crowding of the mandible with an excessively large complement of teeth.

The starting point in Figure 12-12 is the column at the top of the chart that includes the various gracile and robust australopithecine fossils. This column will be used to designate fossils that fall into the categories *Australopithecus africanus, Australopithecus robustus,* and *Australopithecus bosei* (Pilbeam, 1972). Although the fossils that have been so classified can be grouped in other ways, the data that I will review are consistent with this general classificatory scheme. The line to the left of the australopithecine column notes the *afarensis* fossils that have been described by Johanson and White (1981). These fossil hominids may be ancestral to the australopithecines grouped in the main column. The line to the right of the australopithecine column designates

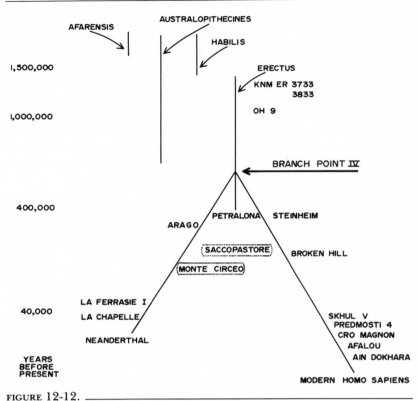

FIGURE 12-12.
The evolution of the modern human supralaryngeal vocal tract:
branch-point IV.

the *Homo habilis* fossils described by Leakey (1973), which may be
intermediate between the fossils to the left and *Homo erectus* – grade
fossils; further data will, it is hoped, resolve this issue.

A number of fossils that lived during this period have been
studied with respect to their probable supralaryngeal vocal tracts.
Studies of the STS-5 gracile australopithecine female from the Sterkfontein caves of South Africa are reported in Lieberman (1973,
1975a), Laitman, Heimbuch, and Crelin (1979), Laitman (1983), and
Laitman and Heimbuch (1982). The basicranium of this fossil shows
that it supported a nonhuman standard-plan upper airway in which
the larynx locked into the nasopharynx during respiration. The
palatal length and the angulation of the basicranium are both consist-

ent with this interpretation (see Figure 12-11). Analyses of other gracile and robust australopithecine material from South and East Africa show similar characteristics (Laitman and Heimbuch, 1982; Laitman, in press). These include the STS-19, Sterkfontein, and MLD-37/38 Makapansgat Lime Deposit craniums. All three of these fossils have been grouped in the taxon *Australopitheus africanus,* the "gracile" australopithecines (Howell, 1978). The "robust" australopithecine fossils KNM-ER 406 and 407 from East Africa and SK 47 from South Africa show differences compared with the gracile forms (Laitman, in press). However, these differences are similar to those that occur in the living species of apes — variations in the degree to which the basicranium is not flexed.

Laitman and Heimbuch (1982) apply these statistical procedures to a range of Plio-Pleistocene fossil hominids that lived prior to one million years before the present. With the exception of the OH-24 fossil, these hominids (STS 5, KNM-ER 406, MLD 37/38, Olduvai 5, Taung, Swartkrans 47, 48, and 83)

> all exhibit traits characteristic of the Pongidae and markedly differ from those of adult or subadult *Homo.* Overall these fossil hominids show relatively little exocranial flexion between the posterior border of the hard palate . . . and the most anterior point of the foramen magnum . . . The distance between the base of the vomer . . . and the spheno-occipital synchondrosis . . . is relatively large, as is characteristic of nonhuman primates and Stage 1 (infant) *Homo.*
>
> (Laitman and Heimbuch, 1982, p. 333)

The OH-24 fossil is the only specimen in the Laitman and Heimbuch (1982) study that has been classified as an example of the genus *Homo* (Howell, 1978). Its cranial capacity is in the order of 600 cc, about 50 percent greater than that of the other australopithecine-grade fossils studied. The reconstruction of the OH-24 *Homo habilis* basicranium appears to be distorted; the statistical analysis of the measurements derived from the present reconstruction also differs from that of the other australopithecine specimens studied by Laitman and Heimbuch (1982). Given the possible significance of this fossil, additional examination of the entire cranium with the view of refining the reconstruction of the basicranium is warranted. Thus, with the possible exception of specimens of *Homo habilis* up to one million years before the present, these hominids retained the standard-plan mammalian supralaryngeal airway. The configuration of the airway during breathing, swallowing, and vocalization is shown in the reconstructions of

FIGURE 12-13a. ──
Reconstruction of the head and neck of a Plio-Pleistocene hominid
during normal respiration. The reconstruction was based partly on
the cranium of the australopithecine Sterkfontein-5 cranium, whose
basicranial line is plotted in Figure 12-11. The mouth is closed since
the individual probably was an obligate nose breather.

Laitman and Heimbuch based on the STS-5 gracile australopithecine
shown in Figure 12-13.

The changes in the upper airway that occurred during the stage
of human evolution generally identified with the taxon *Homo erectus*
may have yielded the adaptive basis for functional branch-point IV.
The designation *Homo erectus* incorporates a variety of fossil hominid
specimens that generally are dated between 1 million and 500,000
years before the present, although some specimens dated at 1.5
million years before the present have been found in East Africa
(Howells, 1980). Cranial capacity ranges up to 1000 cc. The internal
volume of the skulls of *Homo sapiens*–grade fossils, in contrast, is at
least 1300 cc. Unfortunately the features of the basicranium of *Homo*

FIGURE 12-13b.
Reconstruction of the upper respiratory system during normal
respiration. Note the high position of the larynx and the concomitant positioning of the tongue within the oral cavity. The epiglottis is
in contact with the soft palate, providing a direct, sealed airway
from the nose to the lungs.

erectus skulls have not been studied in great detail owing to the absence
of this region in most specimens and to a general lack of interest
regarding the basicranium by most physical anthropologists. Howells
(1980), for example, in his survey article "The state of information on
Homo erectus," scarcely refers to any of the skeletal features of the
basicranium. Laitman (1983), however, has derived some preliminary
observations from recent finds in East Africa and the recently cleaned
skull from Petralona in Greece (Stringer, Howell, and Melentis, 1979).
The Petralona skull is probably at least 400,000 years old and is
generally considered to be an "advanced" *Homo erectus* (Howells,
1980). The African material consists of two craniums from East Turkana, KNM-ER 3733 and KNM-ER 3883 (Leakey et al., in prep.) and

FIGURE 12-13c. ———————————————————————————————
Reconstruction of the upper airways during the ingestion of liquid
material. The larynx is elevated maximally. The airway from the
nose to the lungs will remain sealed as liquid moves from the oral
cavity, around both sides of the larynx via the piriform sinuses, and
on to the esophagus (arrow). The hominidlike modern nonhuman
mammals can simultaneously ingest liquids and breathe.

the Olduvai Gorge fossil OH 9 (Rightmire, 1979). The KNM-ER-3733
fossil is conservatively dated at 1.5 million years before the present
and thus is contemporaneous in East Africa with the robust australopithecines as well as with the *Homo habilis* remains that also occur in
this region. The ER-3733 fossil's cranial capacity is about 830 cc. The
OH-9 fossil is dated at about 1.2 million years before the present and
has a cranial capacity of about 1070 cc. The ER-3733 and OH-9 fossils
are similar in many features (Rightmire, 1979) and suggest the persistence, with little change, of an *erectus*-grade hominid population
from about 1.5 million years to 400,000 years ago (Howells, 1980).

   The basicranium in these specimens of *Homo erectus*, though it
does not show the flexion of anatomically modern *Homo sapiens*, is
different from that of the australopithecines. Preliminary study of the

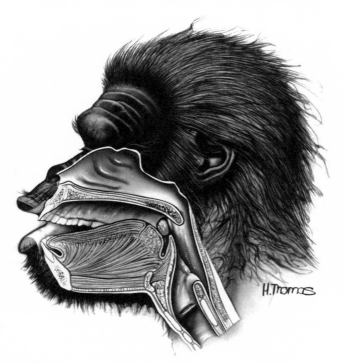

FIGURE 12-13d.
Reconstruction of the upper respiratory system during vocalization.
The larynx is slightly depressed, and the epiglottis and soft palate
are not in contact. Note that the nasal cavity is open, which yields a
nasalized acoustic signal. The tongue is positioned entirely within
the oral cavity, yielding a one-tube vocal tract that inherently
cannot produce formant frequency patterns of sounds like the vowel
[u] or [i]. (Figures 13a–d are after Laitman and Heimbuch, 1982.)

casts of the OH-9 and Petralona fossils shows that the distance between the vomer bone and the spheno-occipital synchondrosis, which
is a prime indicator of the degree of basicranial flexion, is much
smaller than is the case in living apes or in australopithecine-grade
hominids (Laitman, 1983).

    This change may have been retained for its role in facilitating
mouth breathing. As Laitman notes,

> The gradual attainment of flexion may well have corresponded
> to the partial descent of the posterior third of the tongue, hyoid
> musculature and larynx. Laryngeal descent, while probably not

comparable to the extreme descent found in modern *sapiens*, would surely have caused a separation between the epiglottis and soft palate to occur. As a result the larynx could no longer lock into the nasopharynx, providing a direct airway from the nasal cavity to the lungs. This change in respiratory structure would have altered the breathing and swallowing abilities of these hominids from the basic mammalian pattern . . . the tendency for oral tidal respiration would have been greatly increased. Due to the permanent separation of the larynx and nasopharynx, a patent airway during the ingestion of liquids could no longer have been possible. The mammalian ability to breathe and swallow liquids simultaneously could no longer exist.

(1983, p. 6)

As I noted earlier, the neural control of respiration in human infants is coordinated with the restructuring of their supralaryngeal airways. Human newborns are obligate nose breathers; their neural mechanisms that control respiration are matched to their standard-plan airways to minimize the possibility of choking. Although newborn infants could breathe through their mouths, they do not do so because they would have to lower the larynx and food could fall into it. It is safe to breathe through the nose, given the standard-plan mammalian airway in which the larynx is locked into the nasopharynx. At about age 3 months, when the larynx has begun its descent (George, 1976, 1978), the neural mechanisms that regulate breathing in human infants change, and voluntary mouth breathing usually can occur (Laitman, Crelin, and Conlogue, 1977). Since the larynx no longer locks into the nasopharynx, there is no selective advantage to obligate nose breathing — liquids can fall into the lowered larynx whether the air comes from the nose or from the mouth. There is instead a selective advantage for voluntary mouth breathing since respiration can continue even when the nose is blocked. The neural mechanisms that control respiration thus restructure in synchrony with the changes in the supralaryngeal airway, from obligate nose breathing to voluntary mouth breathing.

A similar synchrony involving the neural mechanisms that regulate respiration and the supralaryngeal airway probably occurred somewhere in the evolution of *Homo erectus*. The process may have started in the earlier *Homo habilis* lineage that perhaps is ancestral to *erectus*-grade *Homo*. Whenever the process started, however, voluntary mouth breathing would have had a selective value insofar as it would permit respiration when the nose was blocked. It would also have had the more important function of decreasing the resistance of the primate airway to the flow of air, particularly at high flow rates when turbulence is generated at the "bends" in the nasal pathway (Negus, 1949).

Mouth breathing thus would have had a selective value during strenuous physical activities. The heavily constructed *Homo erectus* skull was heavily muscled compared with that of the modern human being (Howells, 1980); life in the primitive conditions that occurred one million years ago undoubtedly depended more on the expenditure of muscular power. Hence there would have been a strong selective value for mouth breathing and for the anatomical and neural adaptations that make mouth breathing possible. Other factors, as Laitman (1983) notes, may have been involved in the restructuring of the *erectus* supralaryngeal airway, such as the effects of cerebral enlargement and the anterior movement of the foramen magnum to improve head balance. Probably no single factor was involved. Whatever the causes, once the respiratory system was restructured, the possibility would be present for further changes directed at increasing phonetic ability through the further descent of the tongue and larynx. The *erectus*-grade of hominid evolution thus yields a functional branch-point. Two main pathways can follow from the *erectus* solution to coping with the problems of life. One pathway is the one that our ancestors followed — toward increased communication and linguistic-cognitive ability. The other pathway, while it undoubtedly involved the enhancement of cognitive ability, relied to a greater extent on retaining and enhancing muscular ability.

MOSAIC EVOLUTION AND THE HUMAN VOCAL TRACT'S EVOLUTION

The divergence that follows functional branch-point IV, which is implicit in the *erectus*-grade airway, cannot really be viewed as a simple, binary bifurcation. A number of anatomical components are involved in the restructuring of the human supralaryngeal airway from the probable *erectus* configuration. These anatomical features are under separate genetic regulation in the present human population. Orthodontists thus are constantly correcting undershot and overshot bite patterns since an individual's mandible does not always match his or her maxilla. More extreme mismatches also occur which demonstrate that we are put together in bits and pieces that are under separate genetic regulation. The skeletal features that are related to the restructuring of the supralaryngeal vocal tract from the standard-plan mammalian to the modern human configuration involve the reduction of the distance between the front of the palate and the vertebral column and the flexure of the basicranial line, particularly in the basioccipital region (region *DE* in Figure 12-8). Variations, or "experiments of nature," involving the way in which these components go together can be seen in the present human population; extreme variations are considered to be "craniofacial anomalies" (Pruzansky, 1973) and can result in speech deficiencies (Landahl, Peterson-Falzone, and Lieberman, 1978). The fossil record also shows the presence of many experiments involving the way in which these features go together. The successful experiment—the anatomically modern human vocal tract and its supporting skeletal structure—appears to be the result of evolutionary experiments that go back at least to the *erectus*-grade hominid.

The line radiating to the right of the vertical *erectus* plot in Figure 12-12 indicates a hypothetical line of development toward the basicranium and supralaryngeal vocal tract of anatomically modern *Homo sapiens*. Some of the fossil hominids whose skeletal features conform to relevant skeletal features of the human basicranium are entered on this line with their approximate dating, which is derived from the recent survey paper of Howells (1980). The skeletal features of the Skhul-V hominid are within the range of modern human variation, as are those of the fossil hominids that follow. Fossils like Cro-Magnon from France, which is probably about 33,000 years old, have traditionally been considered archaic forms of anatomically modern *Homo sapiens* on the basis of both nonmetrical (Boule and Vallois, 1957) and metrical analyses (Howells, 1974, 1976) of skeletal features other than the basicranium. They also fall into the modern human range with respect to the morphology of their basicraniums. Both the length of the palate (line *AB* in Figure 12-8) and the flexure of the basicranial line (between points *B* and *E* in Figure 12-8) are human. Their vocal tracts would have had a human form. There simply is not sufficient room between the anterior margin of the palate and the basion for a larynx positioned high, close to the base of the skull, with the pharynx positioned behind it. The length of the palate and the mandible have been reduced, crowding the teeth together.

The Steinheim fossil, which is 200,000 to 400,000 years old (Butzer and Isaac, 1975), represents an experiment in which the length of the palate is clearly within the human range, though the basicranial line is somewhat less flexed than in modern human beings. The Steinheim skull, nevertheless, is closer to modern *Homo sapiens* with regard to its supralaryngeal vocal tract than it is to classic Neanderthal fossils like La Chapelle. Statistical multivariate analysis of its basicranium places it closer to modern *Homo sapiens* than to classic Neanderthal hominids (Laitman, Heimbuch, and Crelin, 1979). In contrast, multi-variate analysis of the more plastic bones of the skull place it close to classic Neanderthal forms (Trinkaus and Howells, 1979). The difference in classification follows from the skeletal features that one chooses to take into account. Trinkaus and Howells's comparison proceeds in terms of various facial features that, for the most part, have no known functional value. The basicranium, besides being a more conservative feature (Laitman, 1983), is related to the functional aspects of the supralaryngeal airways.

The Broken Hill fossil is more recent than the Steinheim fossil, probably somewhat older than 100,000 years B.P. (Klein, 1973). It represents an evolutionary experiment in which the basicranial flex-ure is great and falls into the human range (Laitman, Heimbuch, and Crelin, 1979). However, the palate is quite long by human standards. The Skhul-V fossil probably is not older than 40,000 years (Trinkaus and Howells, 1979). Its basicranium is completely human (Lieberman, 1973, 1975a), as are the more recent Predmosti-4 fossil from Czecho-slovakia and the Afalou, Taforlat-12, and Ain Dokhara fossils from North Africa.

The course of evolution along the line leading to modern *Homo sapiens* thus is not even, as would be the case if simply a regulatory gene changed the rate of development of the basicranium. There seem to have been various experiments that involved either selection of alletic variations in the existing hominid population or mutations that resulted in changes in the basicranial line's flexure and/or the length of the palate. Two of these experiments are entered in Figure 12-12 in the dotted boxes to the left of the human vocal tract line.

These experiments represent fossils that are usually identified as Neanderthal hominids. The Saccopastore fossil, which was found in Italy, lived in the last interglacial age, 130,000 years ago and has been identified as a precursor of classic Neanderthal man (Trinkaus and Howells, 1979). Its basicranial line is more flexed than the classic Neanderthal forms that I will discuss, but it has an extremely long palate and could not have had a modern human supralaryngeal airway in which the pharynx and oral cavities had the same approximate length. However, it represents a variation in the direction of modern *Homo sapiens* compared with later classic Neanderthal hominids. The Monte Circeo – 1 fossil, which was found in Italy, is undated. Its palate is shorter than that of Saccopastore 2, but it falls outside the human range with respect to the flexure of the basicranial line (Laitman, Heimbuch, and Crelin, 1979). However, it is more flexed than those of the other Neanderthal fossils. It is possible that the restructuring of the hominid basicranium occurred not only at the time of the hypothetical "initial" Neanderthal (branch-point IV) sketched in Figure 12-12 but also independently from early Neanderthal hominids. The fossil record, in short, is not consistent with the hypothesis of the sudden, coordinated restructuring of the basicranium and mandible. The various experiments of nature, such as long palates with flexed skull bases or short palates with unflexed skull bases, are instead consistent with the hypothesis of gradual mosaic evolution over the course of the past 250,000 years. Almost nothing appears to have happened with regard to the restructuring of the basicranium and mandible during the millions of years that intervened between the divergence of hominids from other primates until this recent period. However, we do not have to invoke any special mechanism of punctuated equilibria to explain this initial period of stasis. The standard-plan mammalian supralaryngeal vocal tract is well adapted for most of the vegetative aspects of life. The selective advantages of the standard-plan mammalian supralaryngeal airway for chewing, swallowing, and breathing have resulted in its retention in all other living animals.

NEANDERTHAL HOMINIDS

The line radiating to the left of the vertical *erectus* plot in Figure 12-12 represents the pattern of evolution that culminated in classic Neanderthal man. The name derives from the Neander valley in Germany, where fossil bones were discovered in 1856. Since that time Neanderthal remains have been found throughout Europe and Asia, from Portugal to Uzbekistan in Soviet Central Asia. They developed over a long period and diverged from the *erectus* base line and fossils like Petralona at least 400,000 years ago, through intermediate forms like the Arago fossils that were found in France, to the classic Neanderthal fossils like La Chapelle-aux-Saints and La Ferrassie, who lived about forty thousand to thirty-five thousand years ago (Trinkaus and Howells, 1979). Though the cranial capacity of classic Neanderthal skulls falls within the modern human range, these skulls are quite different from those of modern human beings or archaic forms of *Homo sapiens* like Skhul V and Predmosti, which were noted in the right branching line in Figure 12-12.

The data of detailed craniometric studies using recent populations from all major regions of the world show that classic Neanderthal skulls fall outside the pattern of variation that typifies either modern or archaic populations of *Homo sapiens* (Howell, 1951; Howells, 1970, 1974, 1976; Bergland, 1963; Laitman, Heimbuch, and Crelin, 1979; Trinkaus and Howells, 1979). The Neanderthal skull is massive and supports an array of teeth that are "positioned so far forward with respect to the face that in a profile view there is a gap between the last molar (the wisdom tooth) and the edge of the ascending mandible" (Trinkaus and Howells, 1979). The muscle that moves the mandible upward, the masseter, is massive and would generate a powerful bite. The swept tooth area involved in chewing would have yielded more efficient chewing. Neanderthal hominids would not have suffered from impacted wisdom teeth, which are our legacy as the human mandible has decreased in length, squeezing in the same number of teeth, albeit reduced in size. The Neanderthal ankle bones, finger bones, arches of the feet, shoulder blade, and so on likewise supported massive muscles that would have yielded superhuman strength, coupled with the full range of human dexterity. The full classic Neanderthal physique lasted for a period of about sixty thousand years down to the recent present, about forty thousand to thirty-five thousand years ago. The retention over this long period of the standard-plan mammalian supralaryngeal vocal tract in hominids who were completely bipedal (Straus and Cave, 1957) also argues against correlating the development of the human supralaryngeal vocal tract with upright posture.[2] Indeed the australopithecine and *erectus*-grade hominids also had bipedal upright locomotion (Campbell, 1966), though they had standard-plan nonhuman vocal tracts.

The data discussed so far, relating the basicranium to the supralaryngeal vocal tract, indicate that classic Neanderthal hominids like the La Chapelle fossil had vocal tracts that were close to the nonhuman, standard-plan system. As I noted earlier in connection with Figure 12-3, the reconstructed airway of the La Chapelle-aux-Saints fossil is functionally similar to that of a newborn human infant (Lieberman and Crelin, 1971). The tongue is positioned entirely within the oral cavity; the pharynx is positioned behind the larynx; and the larynx is positioned close to the base of the skull. The range of formant frequency patterns, which define the phonetic inventory of the Neanderthal vocal tract, does not include vowels like [i], the optimal vocal tract "calibrating" signal.

The basis for this assertion, that the Neanderthal vocal tract cannot produce vowels like [i], rests in computer-implemented modeling studies which have determined the range of formant frequency patterns that the reconstructed Neanderthal vocal tract can produce (Lieberman and Crelin, 1971; Lieberman et al., 1972). As I noted in Chapters 6 through 8, formant frequency patterns define vowel distinctions like [i], [u], [I]. Although the vowels of a language like English also differ in their intrinsic duration, the formant frequency patterns are necessary parameters for vowel quality in all known human languages (Chiba and Kajiyama, 1941; Fant, 1960; Greenberg, 1963). Formant frequency patterns also follow uniquely from the supralaryngeal area function. We could determine the formant frequency pattern that corresponds to a particular area function by constructing a physical model and "exciting" it with a source. The nineteenth-century experiments of Willis (1828) used this technique. However, computer-implemented models of the supralaryngeal vocal tract have been developed that allow us systematically to explore the effects of moving the tongue, lips, jaw, and larynx about in a reconstructed supralaryngeal vocal tract.

The Neanderthal modeling study reported in Lieberman and Crelin (1971) and Lieberman, Crelin, and Klatt (1972) used the computer model developed by Henke (1966). The area functions that we thought the reconstructed Neanderthal vocal tract could have assumed were derived with reference to cineradiographic motion pictures of the newborn vocal tract (Truby, Bosma, and Lind, 1965), the adult human vocal tract (Perkell, 1969), and the constraints imposed by the essentially nonhuman airway that does not allow abrupt changes in the cross-sectional area function. We actually skewed the modeling toward maneuvers that would be more typical of an adult human but that would be somewhat acrobatic in the reconstructed Neanderthal vocal tract or in the vocal tract of a living nonhuman primate (Lieberman and Crelin, 1971). Despite these acrobatic maneuvers, the reconstructed Neanderthal supralaryngeal vocal tract could not generate the formant frequency patterns of vowels like [a], [u], and [i] or the formant transitions that define the stop consonants [k] and [g].

The results of acoustic analyses of the cries of newborn human infants and the calls of nonhuman primates are consistent with this modeling study (George, 1978; Buhr, 1980; Stark, Rose, and McLagen, 1975; Richman, 1976; Lieberman, 1980).[3] It is important to derive acoustic data when discussing the possible sounds that an infant or a nonhuman primate produces. Our ears can play tricks on us. As George notes, "There was the general inclination to perceive the limits of the infant's vowel space as larger than actually was the case. Thus [ɛ] would be heard as [I] before [I] was produced and [I] would often be heard as [i] before an [i] . . . was produced" (1976, p. 82). The special properties of vowels like [i] with respect to vocal tract calibration follow from its particular formant frequency pattern (Nearey, 1978; Sawusch and Nusbaum, 1979). Though an [I] may sound like an [i], it will not serve this function.

Computer modeling of the range of formant frequency patterns that the newborn human and chimpanzee supralaryngeal vocal tracts can produce yield similar results (Lieberman et al., 1972). The newborn human infant computer modeling is consistent with the data derived by acoustic analysis of actual vocalizations (Lieberman et al., 1972; Stark, Rose, and McLagen, 1975; George, 1976; Buhr, 1980; Lieberman, 1980). Goldstein (1980) attempted to model the vocal tract of a newborn,[4] but she instead used measurements derived from the vocal tracts of 3-month-old infants. Her modeling is consistent with the phonetic repertoire of normal 3-month-old human infants (George, 1976; Buhr, 1980; Lieberman, 1980). Infants and chimpanzees inherently cannot produce the formant frequency patterns of vowels like [u], [a], or [i]. The reconstructed australopithecine supralaryngeal vocal tracts noted in Lieberman (1975a), Laitman and Crelin (1976), and Laitman and Heimbuch (1982) would be subject to the same restrictions. The vocal tracts of *erectus*-grade hominids (Laitman, 1983) probably would have a somewhat greater range of formant frequency variation but would not be able to produce an [i] vowel that had the properties noted by Nearey (see Chapter 8) that make it a "supervowel."

NEANDERTHAL SPEECH, LANGUAGE, AND CULTURE

The discussion of Neanderthal speech has become quite intense. This is not too surprising since the Neanderthal question has always been a problem. Virchow (1872), for example, claimed that the original fossil skull found in the Neander valley was that of an idiot who had died in the recent past rather than that of an archaic, extinct hominid. Virchow's claim is understandable since Down's syndrome, which results in the retention of neonatal morphology (Benda, 1969), had not been identified at that time. Virchow may have been comparing the Neanderthal skull with adult victims of Down's syndrome who were classified as idiots. Many other archaic hominid fossils have been found in Europe and elsewhere since that time. Some of these, such as Cro-Magnon, Chancelade, and Grimaldi, are unquestionably archaic specimens of anatomically modern *Homo sapiens*. Others, such as the La Quina–5, Le Moustier, La Chapelle-aux-Saints, and La Ferrassie fossils, are similar to the fossil that was found in the Neander valley. The genetic relationship of these fossils has posed a problem because fossil hominids like Cro-Magnon and Chancelade, whose morphology is within the range of modern *Homo sapiens*, were found in habitation sites that were close to the sites in which the Neanderthal fossils lived.

The replacement of Neanderthal fossils with ones that resemble modern *Homo sapiens* is startling in terms of its suddenness and extent and the subsequent changes in the cultural remains associated with the human populations who replaced the classic Neanderthal hominids. The dating in Europe, for example, indicates that the final Neanderthal occupation of sites in France occurred as late as 35,250 years ago. Carbon-14 datings across Europe indicate that modern human populations existed in these regions between 34,000 and 33,000 years ago (Trinkaus and Howells, 1979). The evidence of human culture again shows a series of rapid changes that occurred between 40,000 and 35,000 years ago. Although there is some continuity, the techniques of tool making and the inventory of tool types changed dramatically (Bordes, 1968). Again, though Neanderthal hominids had burial rituals, the development of art followed the replacement of Neanderthal hominids with modern human beings.

Two solutions to the Neanderthal problem have been proposed. One theory (Brace, 1964; Brose and Wolpoff, 1971) claims that the recent phases of hominid evolution, from the *erectus* grade to anatomically modern *Homo sapiens*, involve only one path. According to this theory, modern *Homo sapiens* evolved directly from Neanderthal hominids. This theory is plausible if, and only if, one includes in the Neanderthal classification fossils like Skhul V that indeed resemble modern *Homo sapiens*. Brace (1964) and Brose and Wolpoff (1971) in fact classify fossils like Skhul V and Broken Hill as Neanderthal, together with fossils like La Chapelle and La Ferrassie I. If the term *Neanderthal* is generalized to include *all* of these fossils, then it is true that the range of morphological variation of this redefined Neanderthal hominid level overlaps with many features of anatomically modern *Homo sapiens*. Natural selection then might have filtered out the variations that do not occur in anatomically modern *Homo sapiens* from this expanded, redefined Neanderthal class. However, the range of variation within this expanded class produces, as Howells notes, "a monster of which the morphological character is merely large cranial size and large brows, and of which the range of variation is simply illegitimate" (1976, p. 122). What Brace, Brose, and Wolpoff have done is to classify fossil hominids that have anatomical features that do not occur within the present population of *Homo sapiens* with fossils who in many ways are like us. Their motivation, as Howells (1976) notes, may involve the projection of the laudable "antiracist" sentiment of the 1960s into the fossil record. However, there is nothing racist in claiming that different groups of hominids lived between 250,000 and 35,000 years ago. The unique skeletal characteristics of classic Neanderthal hominids simply do not exist in the present population of *Homo sapiens*. For the theory proposed by Brace, Brose, and Wolpoff to work without any "special" evolutionary process, the hominids who traditionally have been classified as Neanderthals would have had to die without leaving any progeny. If, on the other hand, the classic Neanderthal hominids are supposed to be among our immediate ancestors, some rapid, special evolutionary process would have had to occur between 40,000 and 35,000 years ago that suddenly transformed Neanderthal hominids into modern human beings. If that were the case, we must wonder why this special evolutionary process applied only to hominids and why it suddenly stopped 35,000 years ago, leaving us with various maladapted structures. The curvature of the human spine is, for example, not particularly well engineered for upright posture, and we have too many large teeth crowded into our jaws. Despite these difficulties, advocates of the single-species hypothesis state that any claim that the Neanderthal hominids are not among our direct ancestors is an example of "hominid catastrophism." They instead propose that special evolutionary processes like neoteny rapidly transformed the progeny of the Neanderthal hominids into modern human beings (Gould, 1977).

The other, more conservative solution to the Neanderthal problem, which does not require any special, rapid evolutionary process restricted to human evolution, is that different forms of hominids lived until comparatively recent times. According to this theory, modern human beings are not directly related to the last of the Neanderthal hominids that were the contemporaries of our direct ancestors. According to this theory, hominid evolution did not involve a single path. Different hominid forms lived during the same epochs, and there are extinct hominid species just as there are extinct species of horses, rats, cats, and so on. Human evolution, in this view, does not involve any special mechanisms that would not be operant in the evolution of other animals. We thus do not "need" the putative mechanism of neoteny. We may be directly related to some of the Neanderthal hominids who lived some 200,000 years ago; some of their progeny may have retained changes in skeletal morphology that are species-specific characteristics of modern human beings. However, we are not directly related to their progeny, who instead retained the characteristic Neanderthal skeletal morphology and lived 35,000 years ago. Neanderthal fossils like La Chapelle-aux-Saints, according to this theory, are examples of a conservative hominid form that persisted into comparatively recent times.

As I noted earlier, the reconstruction of the supralaryngeal vocal tract of Neanderthal hominids and other fossils like Skhul V and Broken Hill is consistent with this second theory. The Skhul-V fossil can be readily differentiated from Neanderthal fossils like La Chapelle and La Ferrassie by using metics that do not directly bear on speech production (Howell, 1951; Howells, 1970, 1974, 1976; Trinkaus and Howells, 1979). Howells (1970), for example, derived discriminant functions by using a multiple discriminant analysis on seventy cranial measurements taken on seventeen recent human populations from all major regions of the world. Fifty individuals of each sex were in each population sample. The different groups were selected to represent the extremes of human skeletal morphology that approach those of classic Neanderthal fossils. Whereas measurements from Skhul V, which in all likelihood had a human vocal tract, fall within the range of normal human variation, the La Chapelle, La Ferrassie – I, and Shanidar-I Neanderthal fossils are extreme or fall completely out of modern limits. Measurements from the La Ferrassie – I skull, which is the most extreme of the Neanderthal types, fall between four and five standard deviations from the modern human mean. Similar results occur in univariate statistical studies (Howells, 1976; Howell, 1951).

The supralaryngeal vocal tract reconstructions and model for the evolution of speech and language discussed here are obviously consistent with the second theory, that there were parallel lines of hominid evolution that persisted until recent times. Some of the intense debate and claims that Neanderthal hominids could have produced the full range of human speech may be linked to this general debate on the nature of hominid evolution. Distinctions between Neanderthal fossils and other fossils based on speech, at the minimum, add to the distinctions noted by the independent studies of Howells, Howell, Trinkhaus, and others noted above. If one infers that the absence of human speech means the total absence of the other elements of human language and culture, then the distinction that I am making seems extreme and places Neanderthal hominids outside the *sapiens* range.[5] It is perhaps redundant to stress that I am not claiming that Neanderthal hominids lacked language and culture or could not reason because their phonetic ability differed from ours. The general theory for the biological bases of human language and their evolution that I have been discussing throughout this book argues against that. Neanderthal hominids would have had linguistic and cognitive abilities that are similar to ours if human language is built on neural mechanisms that structure the cognitive behavior of other species, plus a comparatively small number of species-specific mechanisms adapted to human speech. The genetic principle of mosaic evolution, in any case, argues against linguistic ability evolving as a complete system. Neanderthal hominids thus probably represent an interesting case of closely related hominids that had general cognitive and linguistic abilities similar to our more immediate ancestors but who lacked the special characteristics of human speech.

The evidence of Neanderthal culture indicates a highly developed tool-making and using culture, the use of fire, burial rituals, and a social order that cared for the elderly and infirm (Bordes, 1968; Pilbeam, 1972; Lieberman, 1975a; Trinkhaus and Howells, 1979). The fact that the La Chapelle fossil had severe arthritis (Strauss and Cave, 1957) and had lost most of his teeth years before he died argues, for example, for a culture in which the infirm were cared for. Other Neanderthal fossils likewise show signs of severe bone fractures that healed during their lifetimes (Trinkhaus and Howells, 1979). One of the adaptive values of human culture in which the aged, infirm, and injured are cared for is that these older people can impart their knowledge to the young. The group's collective knowledge thus is greater than the knowledge that a young, active member could possibly acquire through the process of trial and error. Obviously language enhances and indeed may be ultimately responsible for the adaptive value of this cultural pattern. I therefore find it hard to believe that Neanderthal hominids did not also have a well-developed language, particularly given the linguistic and cognitive ability of modern chimpanzees when they are taught sign language. Though it is, in the final analysis, impossible to state with certainty all the factors that might have differentiated the linguistic and cognitive ability of classic Neanderthal hominids from their anatomically modern human contemporaries, their speech ability was inferior.

SIGN LANGUAGE AND ISOLATING MECHANISMS

The evidence that Negus presents indicates that the primate larynx is adapted for vocalization at the expense of respiratory efficiency and argues against hominid language ever being exclusively a sign language, as Hewes (1973) claims. There indeed would be no selective advantage for *improved* vocal communication vis-à-vis either the *erectus* or Neanderthal levels if some form of vocal communication were not already in place.

A different form of vocal communication — the sounds that anatomically modern humans could have made compared to either *Homo erectus* or Neanderthal hominids — would undoubtedly have served as an isolating mechanism. Animals as different as wolf spiders (Stratton and Uetz, 1981) and cowbirds (King and West, 1979) will maintain breeding isolates on the basis of different "songs." Humans likewise will tend to form permanent bonds with members of the opposite sex who speak the same language or dialect (Neel and Ward, 1970). Different hominid populations thus would have lived and reproduced as isolates, given fundamentally different sound-producing ability. Similar isolates occur today as, for example, in the communities of Alpine Switzerland where until recent years dialect differences were a factor that maintained population isolates.[6] The differences that typify Neanderthal and anatomically modern populations of *Homo sapiens* are more profound than those that differentiate any human dialects. Vowels like [i], [u], and [a] are among the "universals" of human language and occur in all languages. Neanderthal hominids could not have produced these sounds. The speech of Neanderthal hominids would have lacked consonants like the velar stops, [k] and [g]; Neanderthal speech furthermore would have tended to be nasalized (Lieberman and Crelin, 1971). Neanderthal hominids would have lacked the innate, genetically transmitted neural mechanisms that human listeners use to decode place of articulation or velar stops. They would, at minimum, lack the innate neural mechanisms that human beings use to derive a "vocal tract length calibrating signal" from vowels like [i] and [u]. They probably lacked a fully encoded speech system.

THE SELECTIVE ADVANTAGES OF HUMAN SPEECH

The persistence of the standard-plan supralaryngeal vocal tract from its mammalian base through the australopithecines and its slight modification in *Homo erectus* and classic Neanderthal hominids argues for its selective advantages with respect to respiration, swallowing, and chewing. Only a relatively strong selective advantage with respect to some other aspect of human behavior could have provided a basis for the restructuring of the basicranium and vocal tract. Human speech is the probable basis for this last, most recent phase of hominid evolution. It provided one of the key elements of human society: rapid communication.

Human speech clearly is built on the biological base that is present in other primates. As I noted in earlier chapters, nonhuman primates use vocal call systems; electrophysiologic and psychoacoustic data show that some of these calls are perceived by means of innate neural mechanisms that are matched to the sound-producing mechanisms of the animals. The larynges of all primates are furthermore adapted for phonation at the expense of respiratory efficiency. Anatomically modern *Homo sapiens* continues this trend toward more efficient vocal communication. The fossil record indicates that the changes came over a period of time, in bits and pieces. The change could not have occurred instantly — the mechanisms of natural selection involve alletic variations that are present in a population and gradually diffuse through that population as more and more progeny survive because they have these variations. The presence of fossils like Saccopastore 2, which has some attributes of classic Neanderthal man but also has some aspects of the human basicranium, thus is not surprising. In a primitive period when muscular strength, efficient chewing, and less accident-prone respiration outweighed or were in balance with the advantages of a faster rate of information transfer, different hominid lines could coexist together with intermediate "experiments." As the central cognitive mechanism, the brain, gradually increased its power, the selective advantage of peripheral input-output mechanisms like human speech also would have increased. Moreover, any increase in the complexity of hominid culture would increase the selective advantage of human speech. Human speech, added to the technical and cognitive base already present, yielded our human ancestors a superior solution in their "infinitely complex relations to other organic beings and to external nature" (Charles Darwin, 1859, p. 61).

The presence of a fully encoded speech system in recent hominids may also have more directly contributed to the development of complex syntactic organization in human languages. The rapid data rate of human speech allows us to transmit a long sequence of words within a short interval. We can take the words that constitute a complex sentence into short-term memory and can effect a syntactic and semantic analysis. We have to keep track of the group of words that constitute a sentence in order to comprehend its meaning. Deficits like dyslexia, which interfere with a reader's ability to take in strings of words in a short time, thus often result in syntactic deficits. Dyslexic readers have difficulty in decoding the complex syntactic structures that occur in written material because they read words so slowly that they forget the words that started the sentence before they can analyze the sentence. The effects of a characteristically low rate of speech communication throughout an entire hominid population thus would probably limit syntactic complexity. Given the same constraints on short-term memory that are evident in modern *Homo sapiens,* a speech rate that was one-tenth that of modern human speech would limit vocal communication to very simple syntactic structures. You can easily perform the experiment of reading sentences to someone at a rate that is one-tenth of the normal rate. Your listener, and you, will forget the words that occurred at the start of anything other than a short, syntactically simple sentence. Rapid speech thus would, in itself, be an element that would provide a selective advantage for complex syntactic ability. It perhaps is again significant that pongids, which apparently lack the neural substrate that would allow them to produce human speech, do not seem able to progress beyond the two- or three-word stages of human language.

The vocal deficiencies of pongids and their comparative success in using sign language have led Hewes (1973) to propose that the initial modality for human language was sign and gesture. Human beings clearly can communicate rapidly by using manual gestures in a linguistic mode, as in American Sign Language. Present-day sign languages also can have a fairly complex syntax (Stokoe, 1978). However, it is probable that these systems work at a level comparable to vocal language only because we already have the neural substrate that evolved to structure vocal language. It is likely that our earliest hominid ancestors started from a syntactic and cognitive base that was only somewhat more advanced than that displayed by modern pongids. It is also likely that their communications were from the start vocal or that they at least made use of a wide range of vocal signals.

Sign languages inherently have a deficiency that is related to one of the crucial distinctions between human beings and other animals—habitual upright bipedal locomotion. The selective value of upright bipedal locomotion with respect to tool use and other manual tasks has long been recognized. One of the selective advantages of fully vocal language is that it enhances our ability to use tools, carry things, and indeed perform any of the tasks that involve using our hands. Vocal language thus continues the trend set by upright bipedal locomotion.

Vocal language has yet another inherent quality that structures human language. A spoken word is transitory and can have only an abstract relationship to a real object, event, or person. Words continually take on new references, perhaps in part because they are by their nature abstract. Manual signs, pictographs, and the like inherently can be iconic and thus may tend to have restricted references.

COLLECTIVE INSIGHT

Various "benefits" or contributions of language to human civilization have been noted. Language is supposed to reduce the degree of aggressive behavior, facilitate hunting and tool making, determine the person one will most likely marry, and so on. The fact is that language and speech enter into practically everything that we do or think about. Though some activities do not involve the overt use of language, such as brushing one's teeth, we first must learn what the function of a toothbrush is and why it is useful to brush one's teeth. The acquisition of these habits or modes of behavior almost always involves the use of human language. Imagine, if you will, a condition in which it takes ten times longer to communicate each thought. That undoubtedly was the situation in the course of hominid evolution before the encoded character of human speech communication evolved.

One of the mysteries of hominid evolution is the rapid rate at which cultural change has occurred in the last forty thousand years. Although there were changes in hominid culture in earlier periods, the pace of change seems to have quickened abruptly in the period of hominid evolution that is associated with anatomically modern *Homo sapiens* (Marshack, 1972; Pilbeam, 1972; Bordes, 1968; Boule and Vallois, 1957). Various proposals have been made to account for this fact. One possibility is that the data transmission rate of linguistic communication gradually increased throughout the course of hominid evolution through the process of speech encoding until it reached a level at which "collective" insight could function.

The process of problem solving usually is not "logical"; insight follows when a person suddenly sees the logical connections between various aspects of a problem that were previously opaque. Logic is not really a very useful process when we are confronted with a new problem. The logical connections are apparent only when we have solved the problem. Insight is the process wherein we consider the various parameters of a problem and then abruptly see the logical connections that we previously were not aware of. In a sense insight is akin to the process of artistic creation. It does not involve the principles of formal logic, though we usually can provide a formal logical analysis of a problem *after* we have had the flash of insight that allows us to solve the problem.

One of the steps necessary for the process of insight to operate is the preliminary step of data collection. If the mode of linguistic communication is rich enough to communicate the set of parameters that describe a problem, then more than one person can apply insight to the solution of that problem. This process of collective insight may be one of the factors responsible for the rapid advance in human culture that has occurred in the last forty thousand years. In a similar manner we can see the process of collective insight at work with regard to the advancement of science since the seventeenth century, when the crucial step of scientific publication took place. Publishing the results of experiments and scientific theories in journals that were accessible to comparatively large numbers of people perhaps was *the* crucial step in the development of the scientific age. It allowed collective scientific insight to be applied to problems. Many people could rapidly acquire the data that would let them apply their insight to the solution of a problem. It is possible that a similar though more general step occurred some forty thousand or so years ago when the rapid rate of speech communication that is typical of the linguistic system of anatomically modern *Homo sapiens became general throughout the hominid population.*

Precisely when the full system of human speech evolved is not clear. The evidence of the evolution of the human supralaryngeal vocal tract indicates that it probably occurred sometime in the last 250,000 years or so. However, it is impossible to know just when the neural mechanisms involved in "decoding" human speech were fully evolved. Even if we had a preserved fossil brain, it would not be possible to resolve this question, given our present knowledge of the brain. Attempts to identify gross features of the human brain that are not present in other primates and that presumably would indicate the presence or absence of language have been made, but they have not been successful (Falk, 1980). Saban's (1980, 1983) recent studies of the distribution of blood to various parts of the brain may lead to more definitive results. Saban traces the patterns of blood supply to those regions of the dominant hemisphere that are usually involved in the perception of speech by means of radioisotope techniques in living human beings and by charting the circulatory systems of fossil hominids from the impressions left on the inside surface of the skull. Saban notes that Neanderthal fossils like La Chapelle appear to have significantly fewer vascular connections to this area of the brain than do modern human beings. Saban's methods, however, have to be applied to a larger sample of both modern human and fossil hominid skulls before any definite conclusions can be drawn.

THE DEMISE OF THE NEANDERTHALS

Classic Neanderthal hominids thus appear to represent the terminal state of a conservative trend in hominid evolution. The muscular development of the *erectus* level is elaborated in classic Neanderthal hominids, together with increased neural development as evidenced by the large cranial capacity (though some of the cranial capacity may reflect their large muscles). The human beings who replaced these Neanderthal hominids had already developed elsewhere. The anatomically modern Mideastern Skhul-V and Jebel Qafzel fossils are contemporary with or slightly older than the last European Neanderthals. The most probable explanation for the replacement of the

European Neanderthals is that they were pushed out by an influx of modern human beings who may have come from Africa and the Mideast. The solution that I propose is neither novel nor peculiar. The historical evidence of human habitation in Europe is replete with documented instances of the migration of peoples forcing the previous inhabitants of a region out of their homeland. It is consistent with the mechanisms of evolution and change that follow from the synthetic theory of evolution (Mayr, 1942). Changes in a population isolate become distributed throughout the entire range of a species as the better-adapted isolate diffuses throughout the entire range.

The model or "picture" of hominid evolution that is consistent with its earlier stages, as Gould (1973) notes, resembles a bush more than it does a ladder. The various australopithecine species became extinct, though they lived in proximity to various forms of *Homo erectus* for 500,000 years. Various species of australopithecines probably became extinct at different times, while others survived somewhat longer (Pilbeam, 1972). Ultimately they all became extinct. The extinction of a species is not an unusual circumstance limited to hominid evolution. Most of the different species that ever lived on earth are now extinct. Extinction is a necessary correlate to the process of evolution by means of natural selection. As Darwin noted,

> It inevitably follows that as new species in the course of time are formed through natural selection, others will become rarer and rarer, and finally become extinct. The forms which stand in closest competition with those undergoing modification and improvement will naturally suffer most . . . Consequently, each new variety or species, during the process of its formation will generally press hardest on its nearest kindred, and will tend to exterminate them.
>
> (1859, p. 110)

Thus I propose that the extinction of Neanderthal hominids was due to the competition of modern human beings who were better adapted for speech and language. The synergetic effect of rapid data transmission through the medium of encoded speech and the cognitive power of the large hominid brain probably yielded the full human linguistic system. The rapid changes in human culture that occurred shortly after the replacement of the Neanderthals could be the result of a difference in the way in which humans thought. Though it is impossible to prove that human language and thought were the causative agents, the replacement of the Neanderthal population — adapted for strength and agility — by a population that was inferior save for enhanced speech abilities is consistent with this hypothesis.

Conclusion: On the Nature and Evolution of the Biological Bases of Language

FROM THIS BOOK, IT IS EASY TO conclude that I am claiming that human speech and the modern supralaryngeal vocal tract are the crucial factors that, in themselves, account for human evolution and human culture and indeed constitute the essence of "humanness." I have necessarily used many pages to discuss the special characteristics of human speech, speech perception, the anatomy of speech production, and the fossil record, viewed in terms of this particular theory for the evolution of the human supralaryngeal vocal tract. However, these elements alone would not have yielded human language, human cognition, or human culture. Many other factors were involved, essentially the total matrix that defines human culture. The process of human evolution, particularly its rapid pace over the past 10 million years and its ultrarapid pace in the past 250,000 years, can perhaps be seen as an evolutionary process involving positive feedback in which cultural behavior is inseparable from physical evolution.

The process of positive feedback can be illustrated by the following example. In the early years of the twentieth century automobiles were first introduced. The early automobiles were primitive and required better roads. Roads were built that enhanced the value of automobiles; more and better cars were built. As the "selective" value of cars increased, there was more pressure for building better highways. More and better highways enhanced the selective value of cars. As more cars were built and sold, they enhanced the selective value of better highways. In the course of this process of positive feedback, every phase of life in the United States became oriented to the highway-car couple, which in turn enhanced the value of cars and highways. Our behavior as we use cars to shop, play, and commute is as much a part of the pattern for the evolution of our car-based civilization as the physical stock of cars, the roads, the drive-ins, suburban sprawl, and the demise of alternate forms of transportation. Our cultural pattern too has evolved, as have the cars, the roads, and so on.

A similar process involving positive feedback may account for the rapid pace of human evolution through the intersection of language, communication, and cognition. Neural adaptations that would yield enhanced cognitive ability would be enhanced by communication in a linguistic mode. Linguistic communication essentially involves our exchanging conceptual information rather than signals that stand in a one-to-one relation with things or specific actions. The evolution of anatomical mechanisms that enhanced communication would have greater selective value in animals that had enhanced cognitive ability. Enhanced cognitive ability, in turn, would yield a greater selective value for adaptations that enhanced rapid communication. Various fortuitous circumstances may have entered into the evolution of human linguistic and cognitive ability. Rule-governed syntax and logic may have followed from the evolution of neural mechanisms adapted for motor control and automatized action. Automatized motor activity, in turn, is essential in allowing human beings to execute the rapid, precise articulatory maneuvers that underlie speech. But the ability to produce speech would be useless without the neural mechanisms that we use to "decode" speech sounds. Some of these neural mechanisms may derive from basic constraints of the mammalian auditory system. However, other aspects of speech perception, such as the "vocal tract normalization" that enters into the perception of speech, appear to be matched to the particular constraints of the human speech-producing system. The evolution of matched neural mechanisms for speech perception and specialized speech-producing anatomy again would be enhanced by the positive-feedback process. There would be an enhanced selective advantage for anatomical mechanisms which yielded the ability to produce stop consonants that had more distinct onsets and bursts in hominids that already had the neural mechanisms which structure the perception of voice onset time. There again would be an enhanced selective value for a neural mechanism which yielded vocal tract normalization in hominids that could produce sounds like the vowel [i], which yield unambiguous vocal tract reference information. The process of "matching" between neural mechanisms and peripheral anatomy is not unique to human beings. It occurs in many other species; only the particular result, the human speech production-perception system, is unique.

The acquisition of speech and language by children involves general cognitive processes like imitation and interaction with adult caretakers in a normal social environment. Recent experimental data indicate that the acquisition of speech by children also involves genetically transmitted, innate neural mechanisms that structure the perception of speech. Linguistic ability, particularly phonetic ability, appears to involve a "critical period" in which a child must be exposed to a language in a productive manner. Critical periods, however, cannot be regarded as an exclusively linguistic phenomenon. Critical periods are operant in the acquisition of normal visual processing in humans and other animals as well as in the acquisition of normal communicative behavior in other species.

Cognitive ability also appears to be present in phylogenetically "simpler" animals in simpler forms. Though it is still unclear how the brain works, distributed neural models based on the mechanism of synaptic modification are consistent with recent electrophysiologic data and provide plausible "learning" models for language. A distributed cognitive "computer" also is consistent with much of the data of aphasia. Though cortical activity undoubtedly plays a major part in human cognitive behavior, cognitive behavior can occur in animals that lack a cortex. Closely related animals like chimpanzees, when they are taught sign language and are raised in a "rich" humanlike setting, exhibit languagelike behavior. They acquire words, which they use to convey concepts; they can communicate in a manner similar to that of 2-year-old human children, though their utterances do not appear to approach the complexity and texture of the discourse of bright human children. Neither the early utterances of human children nor the utterances of chimpanzees consistently follow the syntactic "rules" of careful adult speech. The semantic interpretation of children's utterances depends to a greater extent on extralinguistic context than do the utterances of adult human beings, but sentences are almost never unambiguous in strictly linguistic terms. Pragmatic context always plays a part in guiding the semantic interpretation of an utterance. The linguistic and cognitive abilities of hominoids like chimpanzees are of signal interest, since they show that human language could have evolved by means of gradual Darwinian natural selection, starting with hominoids who resembled modern apes.

Some general perspectives have, I hope, emerged on the nature of human language, human cognition, and their evolution. The biological bases of human language are subject to the same principles that govern other biological systems. There is no linguistic "gene," nor is there a language "organ" that can be localized in the human brain. The biological bases of human linguistic ability involve the characteristics of the central distributed cognitive neural computer as well as the species-specific neural mechanisms that are involved in the perception and production of speech and some aspects of syntax. The distributed central computer of human beings, though it is bigger than that of any other species, probably is similar in form to the brains of closely related animals. It may function in a qualitatively different manner, but qualitative, functional differences can follow from quantitative, structural differences. The model of the brain that we have discussed posits a central distributed computer that performs cognitive and memory functions. Localized, peripheral neural devices feed information into and out of the central computer. Vision, for example, involves localized "neural transducers." Human speech, like the vocal, gestural, electric, and other communication systems of other species, appears to involve specialized, localized neural transducers.

The theory I have proposed for the evolution of the specific system for encoded speech that human beings use proposes that we can chart the evolution of some of the species-specific neural mechanisms involved in human speech through the fossil record. The picture that emerges is one that involves different evolutionary paths. After a long static period lasting until the *erectus* stage of hominid evolution, the specialized supralaryngeal anatomy for human speech developed in one lineage. The fossil record is consistent with the hypothesis of gradual, mosaic evolution of the species-specific skeletal structure of the skull and of the supralaryngeal vocal tract of modern *Homo sapiens* in the course of the last 250,000 years.

The late stages of human evolution may have involved the evolution of rapid, encoded human speech that follows, in part, from the species-specific human supralaryngeal vocal tract. Rapid human speech may not have been present in some recent hominid lines like the classic Neanderthals. Rapid information transfer that allows people to exchange information within the limits of memory span may have yielded a qualitatively different form of information transfer that resulted in "collective insight." Rapid information transfer through encoded speech thus may account for the replacement of the classic Neanderthals with anatomically modern human beings. Neanderthal hominids are interesting in this light since they may represent a hominid line that specialized for chewing and muscular strength at the expense of speech communication.

The principles of Darwinian natural selection and the mosaic principle that follows from classic genetic theory yield the synthetic theory of evolution. The synthetic theory can account for the uneven pace of evolution. There is no need to invoke special evolutionary processes like "neoteny" to account for either the facts of evolution in general or those of human evolution in particular. A Darwinian "branch-point" theory that differentiates between abrupt functional changes that can follow from gradual structural change probably can account for both the pace of evolution and the data of hominid evolution. The recent phases of hominid evolution, in particular, are not consistent with the theory of neoteny. The theory of punctuated equilibria invokes human neoteny as a putative fact and hence implicitly claims that human evolution involves a special species-specific evolutionary mechanism, neoteny. However, we do not resemble human newborns.

As for the linguistic study of human language, the traditional linguistic model that differentiates between "competence" and "performance" or "langue" and "parole" is not consistent with the data of biology. Genetic variability is typical of all populations and is apparent in some aspects of speech perception. To the degree that human linguistic ability involves genetically transmitted neural and anatomical mechanisms, we must expect variation. The only way that we can determine what aspects of human language are basic and universal is to study the actual pattern of variation. Logic is of little value; Cartesian introspection can be misleading. The nature and evolution of the biological bases of language can ultimately be ascertained only by studying the actual cognitive, linguistic, and communicative behavior of human beings and the other animals to whom we are all related.

References

Notes

Index

REFERENCES

Abramson, A., and L. Lisker. 1970. Discrimination along the voicing continuum: cross-language tests. In *Proceedings of the 6th International Congress of
Phonetic Sciences, Prague, 1967*, 569–573. Prague: Academic.

Ainsworth, W., and L. Pols. 1980. Summary of the session on "vowel percep-
tion" at the Gotland Workshop, August 15, 1979. In *Speech Transmission
Laboratory, Quarterly Progress and Status Report* 1/1980. Stockholm: Royal
Institute of Technology.

Anderson, J. A. 1972. A simple neural network generating an interactive
memory. *Mathematical Biosciences* 14:197–220.

Anderson, J. A., J. W. Silverstein, S. A. Ritz, and R. S. Jones. 1977. Distinctive features, categorical perception, and probability learning: some
applications of a neural model. *Psychological Review* 84:413–451.

Armstrong, L. E., and I. C. Ward. 1926. *Handbook of English intonation.*
Leipzig and Berlin: Teubner.

Asanuma, H. 1975. Recent developments in the study of the columnar
arrangement of neurons within the motor cortex. *Physiological Review*
55:143–151.

Assmann, P. F. 1979. The role of context in vowel perception. Master's
thesis, University of Alberta, Canada.

Atal, B. S., and S. C. Hanauer. 1971. Speech and synthesis by linear prediction of the speech wave. *Journal of the Acoustical Society of America* 50:637–
655.

Atkinson, J. R. 1973. Aspects of intonation in speech: implications from an
experimental study of fundamental frequency. Ph.D. diss., University of
Connecticut.

Ayala, F. J. 1978. The mechanisms of evolution. *Scientific American* 239:56–
69.

Bailey, P. J., Q. Summerfield, and M. Dorman. 1977. On the identification of
line-wave analogues of certain speech sounds. *Haskins Laboratories Status
Report on Speech Research* 51/52:1–15.

Bain, B., and A. Yu. 1980. Cognitive consequences of raising children bilin-
gually: one parent, one language. *Canadian Journal of Psychology* 34:304–
313.

Baldwin, J. D., and J. I. Baldwin. 1977. The role of learning phenomena in the ontogeny of exploration and play. In *Primate bio-social development: biological, social and ecological determinants*, ed. S. Chevalier-Skolnikoff and F. E. Poirier, 343–406. New York: Garland.

Banks, M. S., R. N. Aslin, and R. D. Letson. 1975. Sensitive period for the development of human binocular vision. *Science* 190:675–677.

Baru, A. V. 1975. Discrimination of synthesized vowels [a] and [i] with varying parameters (fundamental frequency, intensity, duration and number of formants) in dog. In *Auditory analysis and perception of speech*, ed. G. Fant and M. A. A. Tatham, 91–101. New York: Academic Press.

Bates, E. 1976. *Language and context: the acquisition of pragmatics*. New York: Academic Press.

Beck, B. B. 1973. Cooperative tool use by captive Hamadryas baboons. *Science* 182:594–597.

Beer, C. G. 1969. Laughing gull chicks: recognition of their parents' voices. *Science* 166:1030–1032.

Bekoff, M. 1977. Social communication in Canids: evidence for the evolution of a stereotyped mammalian display. *Science* 197:1097–1099.

Bell, A. M. 1867. *Visible speech or self-interpreting physiological letters for the writing of all languages in one alphabet*. London: Simpkin and Marshall.

Bell, C. G., H. Fujisaki, J. M. Heinz, K. N. Stevens, and A. S. House. 1961. Reduction of speech spectra by analysis-by-synthesis techniques. *Journal of the Acoustical Society of America* 33:1725–1736.

Bell-Berti, F. 1973. *The velopharyngeal mechanism: an electromyographic study*. Supplement to *Haskins Laboratories Status Report on Speech Research*.

Ben-Zeev, S. 1977a. The influence of bilingualism on cognitive strategy and cognitive development. *Child Development* 48:1009–1018.

———— 1977b. Mechanisms by which childhood bilingualism affects understanding of language and cognitive structures. In *Bilingualism: psychological, social, and educational implications*, ed. P. Hornby, 29–55. New York: Academic Press.

Benda, C. E. 1969. *Down's syndrome: mongolism and its management*. New York: Grune and Stratton.

Beranek, L. L. 1949. *Acoustics*. New York: McGraw-Hill.

Bergland, O. 1963. *The bony nasopharynx: a roentgen-craniometric study*. Acta *Odontologica Scandinavica* (Oslo) 21, suppl. 35.

Birdwhistell, R. L. 1970. *Kinesics and context: essays on body motion communication*. Philadelphia: University of Pennsylvania Press.

Bladen, R., and B. Lindblom. 1981. Modeling the judgment of vowel quality differences. *Journal of the Acoustical Society of America* 69:1414–1422.

Bloom, L. 1970. *Language development: form and function in emerging grammar*. Cambridge, Mass.: MIT Press.

Bloom, L. M., L. Rocissano, and L. Hood. 1976. Adult-child discourse. *Cognitive Psychology* 8:521–552.

Blount, B. G., and E. J. Padgug. 1976. Prosodic, paralinguistic, and interactional features in parent-child speech: English and Spanish. *Journal of Child Language* 4:67–86.

Blumstein, S. E. 1981. Neurolinguistics: language-brain relationships. In *Handbook of clinical neuropsychology*, ed. S. B. Filskov and T. J. Boll. New York: Wiley.

Blumstein, S. E., E. Isaacs, and J. Mertus. 1982. The role of the gross spectral shape as a perceptual cue to place of articulation in initial stop consonants. *Journal of the Acoustical Society of America* 72:43–50.

Blumstein, S. E., and K. N. Stevens. 1979. Acoustic invariance in speech production: evidence from measurements of the spectral characteristics of stop consonants. *Journal of the Acoustical Society of America* 66:1001–1017.

Blumstein, S. E., K. N. Stevens, and G. N. Nigro. 1977. Property detectors for bursts and transitions in speech perception. *Journal of the Acoustical Society of America* 61:1301–1313.

Bogert, C. M. 1960. The influence of sound on the behavior of amphibians and reptiles. In *Animal sounds and communication,* ed. W. E. Lanyon and W. N. Tavolga. Washington, D. C.: American Institute of Biological Sciences.

Bond, Z. S. 1976. Identification of vowels excerpted from neutral nasal contexts. *Journal of the Acoustical Society of America* 59:1229–1232.

Bondy, S. C., and M. E. Harrington. 1978. Brain blood flow: alteration by prior exposure to a learned task. *Science* 199:318–319.

Bordes, F. 1968. *The Old Stone Age.* New York: McGraw-Hill World University Library.

Bosma, J. F. 1975. Anatomic and physiologic development of the speech apparatus. In *Human communication and its disorders*, ed. D. B. Towers, 469–481. New York: Raven.

Bouhuys, A. 1974. *Breathing.* New York: Grune and Stratton.

Boule, M. 1911–1913. L'homme fossile de la Chapelle-aux-Saints. *Annales Paléontologie* 6:109; 7:21, 85; 8:1.

Boule, M., and H. V. Vallois. 1957. *Fossil men.* New York: Dryden Press.

Bowerman, M. 1973. *Early syntactic development: a cross-linguistic study with special reference to Finnish.* Cambridge: Cambridge University Press.

Brace, C. L. 1964. The fate of the "classic" neanderthals: A consideration of hominid catastrophism. *Current Anthropology* 5:3–46.

Bradshaw, J. L., and N. C. Nettleton. 1981. The nature of hemispheric specialization in man. *Behavioral and Brain Sciences* 4:51–92.

Bresnan, J. 1978. A realistic transformational grammar. In *Linguistic theory and psychological reality*, ed. M. Halle, J. Bresnan, and G. A. Miller, 1–58. Cambridge, Mass.: MIT Press.

Broca, P. 1861. Nouvelle observation d'aphémie produite par une lésion de la moitié postérieure des deuxième et troisième circonvolutions frontales. *Bulletin Société Anatomie* 6 (sér. 2): 398–407.

Bronowski, J. 1971. *The identity of man.* Garden City, N.Y.: Natural History Press.

——— 1978. *The origins of knowledge and imagination.* New Haven: Yale University Press.

Brose, D. S., and M. H. Wolpoff. 1971. Early upper paleolithic man and late middle paleolithic tools. *American Anthropologist* 73:1156–1194.

Brown, J. W. 1975. On the neural organization of language: thalamic and cortical relationships. *Brain and Language* 2:18–30.

———— 1976. The neural organization of language: aphasia and lateralization. *Brain and Language* 3:482–494.

Brown, R. 1968. The development of Wh-questions in child speech. *Journal of Verbal Learning and Verbal Behavior* 7:279–290.

———— 1973. *A first language.* Cambridge, Mass.: Harvard University Press.

Bruner, J. S. 1975. The ontogenesis of speech acts. *Journal of Child Language* 2:1–19.

Buhr, R. D. 1980. The emergence of vowels in an infant. *Journal of Speech and Hearing Research* 23:75–94.

Burdick, C. K., and J. D. Miller. 1975. Speech perception by the chinchilla: discrimination of sustained /a/ and /i/. *Journal of the Acoustical Society of America* 58:415–427.

Busse, C., and Hamilton, W. J., III. 1981. Infant carrying by male Chacma baboons. *Science* 212:1281–1283.

Butzer, K. W., and G. L. Isaac, eds. 1975. *After the australopithecines: stratigraphy, ecology and culture change in the Middle Pleistocene,* Appendix I: Correlational charts compiled at the symposium, 983. The Hague: Mouton.

Campbell, B. G. 1966. *Human evolution.* Chicago: Aldine.

Capranica, R. R. 1965. *The evoked vocal response of the bullfrog.* Cambridge, Mass.: MIT Press.

Carew, T. J., E. T. Walters, and E. R. Kandel. 1981. Associative learning in *Aplysia:* cellular correlates supporting a conditioned fear hypothesis. *Science* 211:501–503.

Carlisle, R. C., and M. I. Siegel. 1974. Some problems in reply to Neanderthal speech capabilities: a reply to Lieberman. *American Anthropologist* 76:319–322.

Carney, A. E., G. P. Wilden, and N. F. Viemeister. 1977. Noncategorical perception of stop consonants differing in VOT. *Journal of the Acoustical Society of America* 62:961–970.

Carter, A. 1974. The development of communication in the sensorimotor period: a case study. Ph.D. diss., University of California, Berkeley.

Cassirer, E. 1944. *An essay on man.* New Haven: Yale University Press.

Changeux, J.-P. 1980. Properties of the neuronal network. *Language and learning: the debate between Jean Piaget and Noam Chomsky,* ed. M. Piattelli-Palmarini, 184–202. Cambridge, Mass.: Harvard University Press.

Chapin, C., C. Y. Tseng, and P. Lieberman. 1982. Short-term release cues for stop consonant place of articulation in child speech. *Journal of the Acoustical Society of America* 71:179–186.

Chiba, T., and M. Kajiyama. 1941. *The vowel: its nature and structure.* Tokyo: Tokyo-Kaiseikan.

Chistovich, L. A. 1979. Auditory processing of speech. In *Proceedings of the 9th International Congress of Phonetic Science,* vol. 1, 83. The Hague: Mouton.

Chomsky, N. 1957. *Syntactic structures.* The Hague: Mouton.

———— 1965. *Aspects of the theory of syntax.* Cambridge, Mass.: MIT Press.

———— 1966. *Cartesian linguistics.* New York: Harper and Row.

———— 1980a. Initial states and steady states. In *Language and learning: the debate between Jean Piaget and Noam Chomsky,* ed. M. Piattelli-Palmarini, 107–130. Cambridge, Mass.: Harvard University Press.

———— 1980b. Rules and representations. *Behavioral and Brain Sciences* 3:1–61.

Chomsky, N., and M. Halle. 1968. *The sound pattern of English.* New York: Harper and Row.

Chomsky, N., M. Halle, and F. Lukoff. 1956. On accent and juncture in English. In *For Roman Jakobson,* ed. M. Halle, H. Lunt, and H. MacLean. The Hague: Mouton.

Clark, H. H., and E. V. Clark. 1977. *Psychology and language.* New York: Harcourt Brace Jovanovich.

Cooper, W. E. 1974. Adaption of phonetic feature analyzers for place of articulation. *Journal of the Acoustical Society of America* 56:617–627.

Crelin, E. S. 1969. *Anatomy of the newborn: an atlas.* Philadelphia: Lea and Febiger.

———— 1973. The Steinheim skull: a linguistic link. *Yale Scientific* 48:10–14.

Curtiss, S. 1977. *Genie: a psycholinguistic study of a modern-day "wild child."* New York: Academic Press.

Cutting, J. E. 1974. Two left hemisphere mechanisms in speech perception. *Perception and Psychophysics* 16:601–612.

Darwin, C. [1859] 1964. *On the origin of species:* Facsimile ed. Cambridge, Mass.: Harvard University Press.

———— 1872. *The expression of the emotions in man and animals.* London: John Murray.

Dawkins, R. 1976. Hierarchical organisation. In *Growing points in ethology,* ed. P. P. G. Bateson and R. A. Hinde, 7–54. Cambridge: Cambridge University Press.

Dejours, P. 1963. Control of respiration by arterial chemoreceptors. *Annals of the New York Academy of Sciences* 109:682–695.

Denenberg, V. H. 1981. Hemispheric laterality in animals and the effects of early experience. *Behavioral and Brain Sciences* 4:1–50.

deVilliers, J. 1974. Quantitative aspects of agrammatism in aphasia. *Cortex* 10:36–54.

Dewson, J. H., III. 1978. Some behavioral effects of removal of superior temporal cortex in the monkey. In *Recent advances in primatology,* vol. 1, *Behavior,* ed. D. Chivers and J. Herbert, 763–768. London: Academic Press.

Diehl, R. 1975. The effect of selective adaptation on the identification of speech sounds. *Perception and Psychophysics* 17:48–52.

Dingwall, W. O. 1979. The evolution of human communications systems. In *Studies in neurolinguistics,* ed. H. Whitaker and H. A. Whitaker, vol. 4. New York: Academic Press.

Disner, S. F. 1980. Evaluation of vowel normalization procedures. *Journal of the Acoustical Society of America* 67:253–261.

Dodart. 1700. Mémoires de l'Académie des Sciences de Paris. Noted in Müller (1848, 1002).

Dorman, M. F., and L. J. Raphael. 1980. Distribution of acoustic cues for stop consonant place of articulation in VCV syllables. *Journal of the Acoustical Society of America* 67:1333–1335.

Draper, M. H., P. Ladefoged, and D. Whitteridge. 1960. Expiratory pressures and air flow during speech. *British Medical Journal* 1:1837–1843.

Dresher, B. E., and N. Hornstein. 1976. On some supposed contributions of artificial intelligence to the scientific study of language. *Cognition* 4:321–398.

DuBrul, E. L. 1976. Biomechanics of speech sounds. *Annals of the New York Academy of Sciences* 280:631–642.

——— 1977. Origin of the speech apparatus and its reconstruction in fossils. *Brain and Language* 4:365–381.

Eilers, R. E., W. R. Wilson, and J. M. Moore. 1977. Developmental changes in speech discrimination in infants. *Journal of Speech and Hearing Research* 20:766–780.

Eimas, P. D. 1974. Auditory and linguistic processing of cues for place of articulation by infants. *Perception and Psychophysics* 16:513–521.

——— 1975. Speech perception in early infancy. In *Infant perception: from sensation to cognition,* ed. L. B. Cohen and P. Salapatek, vol. 2, 193–231. New York: Academic Press.

Eimas, P. D., and J. Corbit. 1973. Selective adaptation of linguistic feature detectors. *Cognitive Psychology* 4 (1):99–109.

Eimas, P. D., E. R. Siqueland, P. Jusczyk, and J. Vigorito. 1971. Speech perception in infants. *Science* 171:303–306.

Eldredge, N., and S. J. Gould. 1972. Punctuated equilibria: an alternative to phyletic gradualism. In *Models in paleobiology,* ed. T. J. M. Schopf. San Francisco: Freeman Cooper.

Escalona, S. 1973. Basic modes of social interaction: their emergence and patterning during the first two years of life. *Merrill-Palmer Quarterly* 19:205–232.

Evarts, E. V. 1973. Motor cortex reflexes associated with learned movement. *Science* 179:501–503.

Fairbanks, G., and P. Grubb. 1961. A psychological investigation of vowel formants. *Journal of Speech and Hearing Research* 4:203–219.

Falk, D. 1975. Comparative anatomy of the larynx in man and the chimpanzee: implications for language in Neanderthal. *American Journal of Physical Anthropology* 43:123–132.

———— 1980. Language, handedness and primate brains: did the Australopithecines sign? *American Anthropologist* 82:72–78.

Fant, G. 1956. On the predictability of formant levels and spectrum envelopes from formant frequencies. In *For Roman Jakobson,* ed. M. Halle, H. Lunt, and H. MacLean. The Hague: Mouton.

———— 1960. *Acoustic theory of speech production.* The Hague: Mouton.

Ferguson, C. A. 1964. Baby talk in six languages. *American Anthropologist* 66:103–114.

Fernald, A. 1982. Acoustic determinants of infant preference for "motherese." Ph.D. diss., University of Oregon.

Ferrein, C. J. 1741. Mémoires de l'Académie des Sciences de Paris, 409–432 (Nov. 15). Noted in Müller (1848, 1002).

Flanagan, J. L., C. H. Coker, L. R. Rabiner, R. W. Schafer, and N. Umeda. 1970. Synthetic voices for computers. *IEEE Spectrum* 7:22–45.

Floeter, M. K., and W. T. Greenough. 1979. Cerebellar plasticity: modification of purkinje cell structure by differential rearing in monkeys. *Science* 206:227–229.

Fodor, J. A., T. Bever, and M. Garrett. 1974. *The psychology of language.* New York: McGraw-Hill.

Folkins, J. W., and G. N. Zimmerman. 1981. Jaw-muscle activity during speech with the mandible fixed. *Journal of the Acoustical Society of America* 69:1441–1444.

Ford, F. M. 1971. *Memories and impressions.* Harmondsworth: Penguin.

Fouts, R. 1975. Capacities for language in great apes. In *Society and psychology of primates,* ed. R. H. Tuttle, 371–390. The Hague: Mouton.

Fouts, R., M. Hannum, C. O'Sullivan, and K. Schneider. In press. Chimpanzee conversations. In *Language development,* ed. J. Kuzo. Hillsdale, N.J.: Erlbaum.

Fowler, C. A., and D. P. Shankweiler. 1978. Identification of vowels in speech and non-speech contexts. *Journal of the Acoustical Society of America* 63, suppl. 1, S4 (A).

Freedle, R., and M. Lewis. 1977. Prelinguistic conversations. In *Interaction, conversation and the development of language,* ed. M. Lewis and L. A. Rosenblum. New York: Wiley.

Freeman, R. D., B. Mitchell, and M. Millodot. 1972. A neural effect of visual deprivation in humans. *Science* 175:1384–1386.

Freeman, R. D., and L. N. Thidos. 1973. Electrophysiological evidence that abnormal early visual experience can modify the human brain. *Science* 180:876–878.

Frishkopf, L. S., and M. H. Goldstein, Jr. 1963. Responses to acoustic stimuli from single units in the eighth nerve of the bullfrog. *Journal of the Acoustical Society of America* 35:1219–1228.

Froscher, M. M. 1978. The effects on respiratory function of sense-group duration. Ph.D. diss., Columbia University.

Fry, D. B. 1958. Experiments in the perception of stress. *Language and Speech* 1:125–152.

Fujimura, O., and Y. Kakita. In press. Remarks on quantitative description of the lingual articulation. In *Frontiers of speech communication research*, ed. B. Lindblom and S. Ohman. New York: Academic Press.

Fujimura, O., and J. B. Lovins. 1978. Syllables as concatenative phonetic units. In *Syllables and segments*, ed. A. Bell and J. B. Hooper, 107–120. Amsterdam: North-Holland.

Fujisaki, H., and T. Kawashima. 1968. The roles of pitch and higher formants in the perception of vowels. *IEEE Transactions on Audio and Electroacoustics*, AV-16:73–77.

Gall, F. J. 1809. *Recherches sur le système nerveux.* Paris: J. B. Baillière.

Gardner, R. A., and B. T. Gardner. 1969. Teaching sign language to a chimpanzee. *Science* 165:664–672.

——— 1971. Two-way communication with an infant chimpanzee. In *Behavior of nonhuman primates*, ed. A. Schrier and F. Stollnitz, vol. 4. New York: Academic Press.

——— 1973. *Teaching sign language to the chimpanzee Washoe.* 16mm sound film and transcript. State College, Pa.: Psychological Film Register.

——— 1974. Comparing the early utterances of child and chimpanzee. In *Minnesota Symposium on Child Psychology*, ed. A. Pick, vol. 8. Minneapolis: University of Minnesota Press.

——— 1975a. Early signs of language in child and chimpanzee. *Science* 187:752–753.

——— 1975b. Evidence for sentence constituents in the early utterances of child and chimpanzee. *Journal of Experimental Psychology* 104:244–267.

——— 1978. Comparative psychology and language acquisition. *Annals of the New York Academy of Sciences* 309:37–76.

——— 1980. Two comparative psychologists look at language acquisition. In *Children's language*, ed. K. E. Nelson, vol. 2. New York: Halsted Press.

Gazdar, G. 1981. Phrase structure grammar. In *The nature of syntactic representation*, ed. P. Jakobson and G. K. Pullum. Dordrecht, Netherlands: Reidel.

George, S. L. 1976. The relationship between cranial base angle morphology and infant vocalizations. Sc.D. diss., University of Connecticut.

——— 1978. A longitudinal and cross-sectional analysis of the growth of the postnatal cranial base angle. *American Journal of Physical Anthropology* 49:171–178.

Gerstman, L. 1968. Classification of self-normalized vowels. *IEEE Transactions on Audio and Electroacoustics* AV-16:78–80.

Geschwind, N. 1965. Disconnection syndromes in animals and man. *Brain* 88:237–294, 585–644.

——— 1981. The significance of lateralization in nonhuman species. *Behavioral and Brain Sciences* 4:26.

Geschwind, N., F. A. Quadfasel, and J. M. Segarro. 1968. Isolation of the speech area. *Neuropsychologia* 6:327–340.

Gleitman, L. R., and P. Rozin. 1973. Teaching reading by use of a syllabary. *Reading and Research Quarterly* 8:447–483.

Gold, B. 1962. Computer program for pitch extraction. *Journal of the Acoustical Society of America* 34:916–921.

Goldin-Meadow, S., and H. Feldman. 1977. The development of language-like communication without a language model. *Science* 197:401–403.

Goldman-Eisler, F. 1958. The predictability of words in context and the length of pauses in speech. *Language and Speech* 1:226–231.

Goldstein, U. G. 1980. An articulatory model for the vocal tracts of growing children. Sc.D. diss., Massachusetts Institute of Technology.

Goodall, J. 1968. The behavior of free-living chimpanzees in the Gombe Stream Reserve. *Animal Behavior Monographs* 1:161–312.

———— 1979. Life and death at Gombe. *National Geographic* (May):593–620.

Goodglass, H. 1968. Studies in the grammar of aphasics. In *Developments in applied psycholinguistics*, ed. S. Rosenberg and J. Koplin. New York: Macmillan.

———— 1976. Agrammatism. In *Studies in neurolinguistics*, ed. H. Whitaker and H. A. Whitaker, vol. 1. New York: Academic Press.

Goodglass, H., S. E. Blumstein, J. B. Gleason, M. R. Hyde, E. Green, and S. Statlender. 1979. The effect of syntactic encoding on sentence comprehension in aphasia. *Brain and Language* 7:201–209.

Goodman, D., and J. A. S. Kelso. 1980. Are movements prepared in parts? Not under compatible (natural) conditions. *Journal of Experimental Psychology: General* 109:475–495.

Gould, S. J. 1973. *Ever since Darwin.* New York: Norton.

———— 1977. *Ontogeny and phylogeny.* Cambridge, Mass.: Harvard University Press, Belknap Press.

Gould, S. J., and N. Eldredge. 1977. Punctuated equilibria: the tempo and mode of evolution reconsidered. *Paleobiology* 3:115–151.

Greenberg, J. 1963. *Universals of language.* Cambridge, Mass.: MIT Press.

Greenewalt, C. A. 1968. *Bird song: acoustics and physiology.* Washington, D.C.: Smithsonian Institution Press.

Greenfield, P., and Smith, J. 1976. *The structure of communication in early language development.* New York: Academic Press.

Grosmangin, C. 1979. *Base du crane et pharynx dans leurs rapports avec l'appareil de langage articulé.* Mémoires du Laboratoire d'Anatomie de la Faculté de Médecine de Paris, no. 40-1979.

Gross, M. 1968. *Grammaire transformationnelle du français: syntaxe du verbe.* Paris: Larousse.

———— 1975. *Méthodes en syntaxe.* Paris: Hermann.

———— 1979. On the failure of generative grammar. *Language* 55:859–885.

Hadding-Koch, K. 1961. *Acoustico-phonetic studies in the intonation of southern Swedish.* Lund: C. W. K. Gleerup.

Haeckel, E. 1866. *Generelle Morphologie der Organismen: Allgemeine Grundzüge der organischen Formen-Wissenschaft, mechanisch begründet durch die von Charles Darwin reformirte Descendez-Theorie,* 2 vols. Berlin: Reimer.

Halle, M., and K. N. Stevens. 1959. Analysis by synthesis. In *Proceedings of seminar on speech compression and processing,* ed. W. Wathen-Dunn. Bedford, Mass.: Air Force Cambridge Research Center, AFCRC-TR-59-198.

Hamlet, S., M. Stone, and T. McCarty. 1976. Persistence of learned motor patterns in speech. *Journal of the Acoustical Society of America,* suppl. I, paper CC92.

Hammond, P. H. 1954. Involuntary activity in biceps following the sudden application of velocity to the abducted forearm. *Journal of Physiology* 127:23P.

Harris, C. M. 1953. A study of the building blocks of speech. *Journal of the Acoustical Society of America* 25:962–969.

Harris, K. S. 1974. Physiological aspects of articulatory behavior. In *Current trends in linguistics,* ed. T. Sebeok, vol. 12. The Hague: Mouton.

———— 1977. The study of articulatory organization: some negative progress. *Haskins Laboratories Status Report on Speech Research* 50:13–20.

Hayes, K. J., and C. Hayes. 1951. The intellectual development of a home-raised chimpanzee. *Proceedings of the American Philosophical Society* 95:105–109.

Head, H. 1926. *Aphasia and kindred disorders of speech.* London: Cambridge University Press.

Hebb, D. O. 1949. *The organization of behavior.* New York: Wiley.

Hediger, H. K. P. 1981. The Clever Hans phenomenon from an animal psychologist's point of view. In *The Clever Hans phenomenon: communication with horses, whales, apes, and people,* ed. T. A. Sebeok and R. Rosenthal. *Annals of the New York Academy of Sciences* 364:1–17.

Heffner, R., and H. Heffner. 1980. Hearing in the elephant *(Elephas maximus). Science* 208:518–520.

Heim, J. L. 1974. Les hommes fossils de la Ferrassie (Dordogne) et la problème de la définition des néandertaliens classiques. *L'Anthropologie* 78:6–377.

Hellwag, C. 1781. De formatione loquelae. Diss., Tubingen.

Helmholtz, H. L. 1863. *Die Tonempfindung.* Berlin.

Henke, W. L. 1966. Dynamic articulatory model of speech production using computer simulation. Ph.D. diss., Massachusetts Institute of Technology.

Hermann, L. 1894. Nachtrag zur Untersuchung der Vocalcurven. *Archiv für der geschichte des Physiologie* 58:264–279.

Hewes, G. W. 1973. Primate communication and the gestural origin of language. *Current Anthropology* 14:5–24.

Hirsch, I. J., and C. E. Sherrick. 1961. Perceived order in different sense modalities. *Journal of Experimental Psychology* 62:423–432.

Hixon, T., M. Goldman, and J. Mead. 1973. Kinematics of the chest wall during speech production: volume displacements of the rib cage, abdomen and lung. *Journal of Speech and Hearing Research* 16:78–115.

Hockett, C. F. 1960. Logical considerations in the study of animal communication. In *Animal sounds and communication,* ed. W. E. Lanyon and W. N. Tavolga, 392–430. Washington, D.C.: American Institute of Biological Sciences.

Hoffmeister, R. J., D. F. Moores, and R. L. Ellenberger. 1975. Some procedural guidelines for the study of the acquisition of sign languages. *Sign Language Studies* 7:121–137.

Holmes, J. N. 1979. Synthesis of natural-sounding speech using a formant synthesizer. In *Frontiers of speech communication research,* ed. B. Lindblom and S. Ohman, 275–285. London: Academic Press.

Hopkins, C. D., and A. H. Bass. 1981. Temporal coding of species recognition signals in an electric fish. *Science* 212:85–87.

Howell, F. C. 1951. The place of Neanderthal man in human evolution. *American Journal of Physical Anthropology* 9:379–416.

———— 1978. Hominidae. In *Evolution of African mammals,* ed. V. J. Maglio and H. B. S. Cooke, 154–248. Cambridge, Mass.: Harvard University Press.

Howells, W. W. 1970. Mount Carmel man: morphological relationships. In *Proceedings of the Eighth International Congress of Anthropological and Ethnological Sciences, Tokyo and Kyoto, 1968,* vol. 1, 269–272. The Hague: Mouton.

———— 1974. Neanderthals: names, hypotheses, and scientific method. *American Anthropologist* 76:24–38.

———— 1976. Neanderthal man: facts and figures. In *Proceedings of the Ninth International Congress of Anthropological and Ethnological Sciences, Chicago, 1973.* The Hague: Mouton.

———— 1980. *Homo erectus:* who, when and where: a survey. *Yearbook of Physical Anthropology* 23:1–23.

Hoy, R. R., and R. C. Paul. 1973. Genetic control of song specificity in crickets. *Science* 180:82–83.

Hubel, D. H., and T. N. Wiesel. 1962. Receptive fields, binocular interaction and functional architecture in the cat's visual cortex. *Journal of Physiology* 160:106–154.

———— 1970. The period of susceptibility to the physiological effects of unilateral eye closure in kittens. *Journal of Physiology* 206:419–436.

Hughes, G. W. 1961. *The recognition of speech by machine.* Research Laboratory of Electronics Technical Report 395. Cambridge, Mass.: Massachusetts Institute of Technology.

Humboldt, W. von. [1836] 1960. *Uber die Verschiedenheit des Menschlichen Sprachbaues.* Facsimile ed. Bonn: F. Dummlers Verlag.

Ianco-Worrall, A. D. 1972. Bilingualism and cognitive development. *Child Development* 43:1390–1400.

International Phonetic Association. 1949. *The principles of the International Phonetic Association: being a description of the International Phonetic Alphabet and the manner of using it.* London: Department of Phonetics, University College.

Irwin, O. C. 1948. Infant speech: development of vowel sounds. *Journal of Speech and Hearing Disorders* 13:31–34.

Jacob, F. 1977. Evolution and tinkering. *Science* 196:1161–1166.

Jakobson, R. 1940. Kindersprache, Aphasie und allgemeine Lautgesetze. In Jakobson, R., *Selected writings*. The Hague: Mouton.

———— G. M. Fant, and M. Halle. 1952. *Preliminaries to speech analysis*. Cambridge, Mass.: MIT Press.

Jerison, H. 1973. *Evolution of the brain and intelligence*. New York: Academic Press.

Jesperson, O. 1909. *A modern English grammar*. London: Allen and Unwin.

Johanson, D. C., and T. D. White. 1979. A systematic assessment of early African hominids. *Science* 202:321–330.

Jones, D. 1932. *An outline of English phonetics*. 3rd ed. New York: Dutton.

Joos, M. 1948. Acoustic phonetics. *Language*, suppl. 24:1–136.

Jordan, J. 1971. Studies on the organ of voice and vocalization in the chimpanzees, III. *Folia Morphologica* (Warsaw) 30:97–126, 222–248, 323–340.

Kahn, D. 1978. On the identifiability of isolated vowels. *UCLA Working Papers in Phonetics* 41:26–31.

Keating, P., and R. Buhr. 1978. Fundamental frequency in the speech of infants and children. *Journal of the Acoustical Society of America* 63:567–571.

Kellogg, R. H. 1964. Central chemical regulation of respiration. In W. O. Fenn and H. Ruhn, *Handbook of physiology: respiration*, vol. 1, 507–534. Washington, D.C.: American Physiological Society.

Kendon, A. 1975. Introduction to *Organization of behavior in face-to-face interaction*, ed. A. Kendon, R. M. Harris, and M. R. Key. The Hague: Mouton.

Kenyon, K. W. 1969. *The eastern Pacific Ocean*. Washington, D.C.: U.S. Government Printing Office.

Kimura, D. 1967. Functional asymmetry of the brain in dichotic listening. *Cortex* 3:163–178.

———— 1979. Neuromotor mechanisms in the evolution of human communication. In *Neurobiology of social communication in primates*, ed. H. D. Steklis and M. J. Raleigh. New York: Academic Press.

King, E. W. 1952. A roentgenographic study of pharyngeal growth. *Angle Orthodontist* 22:23–37.

King, A. P., and M. J. West. 1979. Species identification in the North American cowbird: appropriate responses to abnormal song. *Science* 195:1002–1004.

Klatt, D. H. 1976. Linguistic uses of segmental duration in English: acoustic and perceptual evidence. *Journal of the Acoustical Society of America* 59:1208–1221.

———— 1979. Speech perception: a model of acoustic-phonetic analysis and lexical access. *Journal of Phonetics* 7:279–312.

Klatt, D. H., and R. A. Stefanski. 1974. How does a mynah bird imitate human speech? *Journal of the Acoustical Society of America* 55:822–832.

Klatt, D. H., K. N. Stevens, and J. Mead. 1968. Studies of articulatory activity and airflow during speech. *Annals of the New York Academy of Sciences* 155:42–54.

Klein, R. G. 1973. Geological antiquity of Rhodesian man. *Nature* 244:311–312.

Köhler, W. 1927. *The mentality of apes.* 2nd ed. New York: Harcourt, Brace and World.

Kohonen, T. 1972. Correlation matrix memories. *IEEE Transactions on Computers* C-21:353–359.

———— 1977. *Associative memory: a system theoretical approach.* Berlin: Springer-Verlag.

Kohonen, T., P. Lehtio, J. Rovamo, J. Hyvarinen, K. Bry, and L. Vaino. 1977. A principle of neural associate memory. *Neuroscience* 2:1065–1076.

Kohonen, T., G. Nemeth, K. Bry, M. Jalanko, and H. Riittinen. 1979. A redundant hash addressing method adapted for the postprocessing and error-correction of computer-recognized speech. In *Proceedings of the 1979 International Conference on Acoustics, Speech, and Signal Processing,* 591–594. New York: Institute of Electronic and Electrical Engineers.

Kohonen, T., H. Riittinen, M. Jalanko, E. Reuhala, and S. Haltsonen. 1980. *A thousand-word recognition system based on the learning subspace method and redundant hash addressing.* Helsinki University of Technology report TKK-F-A412.

Kratzenstein, C. G. 1780. Sur la naissance de la formation des voyelles. *Journal of Physiology* 21 (1782):358–381. Trans. from *Acta Academie Petrograd.*

Kubaska, C. A., and P. A. Keating. 1981. Word duration in early child speech. *Journal of Speech and Hearing Research* 24:614–621.

Kucera, H. 1981. The abduction algorithm: a computer model of language acquisition. *Perspectives in Computing* 1:28–35.

Kuhl, P. K. 1979. The perception of speech in early infancy. In *Speech and language: research and theory,* ed. N. J. Lass. New York: Academic Press.

———— 1981. Discrimination of speech by nonhuman animals: basic auditory sensitivities conducive to the perception of speech-sound categories. *Journal of the Acoustical Society of America* 70:340–349.

Kuhl, P. K., and J. D. Miller. 1974. Discrimination of speech sounds by the chinchilla: /t/ vs. /d/ in CV syllables. *Journal of the Acoustical Society of America* 56, suppl. 2, 52A.

———— 1978. Speech perception by the chinchilla: identification functions for synthetic VOT stimuli. *Journal of the Acoustical Society of America* 63:905–916.

Labov, W. 1973. The boundaries of words and their meanings. In *New ways of analyzing variation in English,* ed. C.-J. Bailey and R. Shuy. Washington, D.C.: Georgetown University Press.

Ladefoged, P., and D. E. Broadbent. 1957. Information conveyed by vowels. *Journal of the Acoustical Society of America* 29:98–104.

Ladefoged, P., J. De Clerk, M. Lindau, and G. Papcun. 1972. An auditory-motor theory of speech production. *UCLA Working Papers in Phonetics* 22:48–76.

Laitman, J. T. 1983. The evolution of the hominid upper respiratory system and implications for the origins of speech. In *Proceedings of the Transdisciplinary Symposium on Glossogenetics, Paris, 1981*, ed. E. de Grolier. Paris: Harwood Academic Press.

Laitman, J. T., and E. S. Crelin. 1976. Postnatal development of the basicranium and vocal tract region in man. In *Symposium on Development of the Basicranium*, ed. J. F. Bosma, 206–219. Washington, D.C.: U.S. Government Printing Office.

Laitman, J. T., E. S. Crelin, and G. J. Conlogue. 1977. The function of the epiglottis in monkey and man. *Yale Journal of Biology and Medicine* 50:43–48.

Laitman, J. T., and R. C. Heimbuch. 1982. The basicranium of Plio-Pleistocene hominids as an indicator of their upper respiratory systems. *American Journal of Physical Anthropology* 59:323–344.

Laitman, J. T., R. C. Heimbuch, and E. S. Crelin. 1978. Developmental change in a basicranial line and its relationship to the upper respiratory system in living primates. *American Journal of Anatomy* 152:467–483.

——— 1979. The basicranium of fossil hominids as an indicator of their upper respiratory systems. *American Journal of Physical Anthropology* 51:15–34.

LaMettrie, J. O. [1747] 1960. *De l'homme machine*, ed. A. Vartanian. Princeton: Princeton University Press.

Landahl, K. 1981. Language-universal aspects of intonation in children's first sentences. *Journal of the Acoustical Society of America* 67:suppl. 63.

——— 1982. The onset of structural discourse: a developmental study of the acquisition of language. Ph.D. diss., Brown University.

Landahl, K., S. Peterson-Falzone, and P. Lieberman. 1978. Formant frequency patterns in anomalous supralaryngeal vocal tracts. Paper presented at the 1978 meeting of the American Speech and Hearing Association, San Francisco, November 18–21.

Lane, H. 1965. The motor theory of speech perception: a critical review. *Psychological Review* 72:275–309.

Langlois, A., R. J. Baken, and C. N. Wilder. 1980. Pre-speech respiratory behavior during the first year of life. In *Infant communication: cry and early speech*, ed. T. Murry and J. Murry. Houston: College-Hill Press.

Lashley, K. S. 1950. In search of the engram. In *Physiological mechanisms in animal behavior*, Symposia of the Society for Experimental Biology, no. 4. New York: Academic Press.

Leakey, M. D. 1979. Footprints in the ashes of time. *National Geographic* 155:446–457.

Leakey, R. E. F. 1973. Evidence for an advanced Plio-Pleistocene hominid from East Rudolf, Kenya. *Nature* 242:447–450.

Leibnitz, G. W. von. 1949. *Nouveaux essais sur l'entendement humain.* Trans. A. G. Langley. LaSalle, Ill.: Open Court Publishing.

LeMay, M. 1975. The language capability of Neanderthal man. *American Journal of Physical Anthropology* 42:9–14.

LeMay, M., and N. Geschwind. 1975. Hemispheric differences in the brains of the great apes. *Brain, Behavior and Evolution* 11:48–52.

Lenneberg, E. H. 1967. *Biological foundations of language.* New York: Wiley.

Lettvin, J. Y., H. R. Maturana, W. S. McCulloch, and W. H. Pitts. 1959. What the frog's eye tells the frog's brain. *Proceedings of the Institute of Radio Engineers* 47:1940–1951.

Lewis, M. M. 1936. *Infant speech: a study of the beginnings of language.* New York: Harcourt, Brace.

Liberman, A. M. 1970. Some characteristics of perception in the speech mode. *Perception and Its Disorders* 48:238–254.

Liberman, A. M., F. S. Cooper, D. P. Shankweiler, and M. Studdert-Kennedy. 1967. Perception of the speech code. *Psychological Review* 74:431–461.

Liberman, F. Z. 1979. Learning by neural nets. Ph.D. diss., Brown University.

Liberman, M. Y. 1978. *The intonational system of English.* Bloomington: Indiana University Linguistics Club.

Lieberman, M. R., and P. Lieberman. 1973. Olson's "projective verse" and the use of breath control as a structural element. *Language and Style* 5:287–298.

Lieberman, P. 1960. Some acoustic correlates of word stress in American-English. *Journal of the Acoustical Society of America* 33:451–454.

——— 1963. Some effects of semantic and grammatical context on the production and perception of speech. *Language and Speech* 6:172–187.

——— 1965. On the acoustic basis of the perception of intonation by linguists. *Word* 21:40–54.

——— 1967. *Intonation, perception and language.* Cambridge, Mass.: MIT Press.

——— 1968a. Primate vocalizations and human linguistic ability. *Journal of the Acoustical Society of America* 44:1574–1584.

——— 1968b. Direct comparison of subglottal and esophageal pressure during speech. *Journal of the Acoustical Society of America* 43:1157–1164.

——— 1970. Towards a unified phonetic theory. *Linguistic Inquiry* 1:307–322.

——— 1973. On the evolution of human language: a unified view. *Cognition* 2:59–94.

——— 1975a. *On the origins of language: an introduction to the evolution of human speech.* New York: Macmillan.

——— 1975b. More discussion of Neanderthal speech. *Linguistic Inquiry* 6:325–329.

——— 1976a. Interactive models for evolution: neural mechanisms, anatomy and behavior. *Annals of the New York Academy of Sciences* 280:660–672.

———— 1976b. Structural harmony and Neanderthal speech: a reply to LeMay. *American Journal of Physical Anthropology* 45:493–496.

———— 1976c. Phonetic features and physiology: a reappraisal. *Journal of Phonetics* 4:91–112.

———— 1977a. More on hominid evolution, speech, and language. *Current Anthropology* 18:550–551.

———— 1977b. *Speech physiology and acoustic phonetics.* New York: Macmillan.

———— 1978. A reply to Carlisle and Siegel's assessment of Neanderthal speech capabilities. *American Anthropologist* 80:676–681.

———— 1979a. Phonetics and physiology: some current issues. In *Current trends in linguistic theory: perspectives in experimental linguistics,* ed. G. D. Prideaux. Amsterdam: John Benjamins.

———— 1979b. Hominid evolution, supralaryngeal vocal tract physiology and the fossil evidence for reconstructions. *Brain and Language* 7:101–126.

———— 1980. On the development of vowel production in young children. In *Child phonology: perception and production,* ed. G. Yeni-Komshian and J. Kavanagh, 113–142. New York: Academic Press.

———— 1982a. On the evolution of human speech. In *The cognitive representation of speech,* ed. T. Myers, J. Laver, and J. Anderson, 271–280. Amsterdam: North-Holland.

———— 1982b. Can chimpanzees swallow or talk? A reply to Falk. *American Anthropologist* 84:148–152.

———— 1983. On the nature and evolution of the biological bases of human language. In *Proceedings of the Transdisciplinary Symposium on Glossogenetics, Paris, 1981,* ed. E. de Grolier. Paris: Harwood Academic Press.

———— In press. Genetically transmitted, discrete variations in the perception of speech. In *Variation and invariance and variability of speech processes,* ed. J. Perkell, G. Fant, and D. Klatt. New York: Academic Press.

Lieberman, P., and E. S. Crelin. 1971. On the speech of Neanderthal man. *Linguistic Inquiry* 2:203–222.

Lieberman, P., E. S. Crelin, and D. H. Klatt. 1972. Phonetic ability and related anatomy of the newborn, adult human, Neanderthal man, and the chimpanzee. *American Anthropologist* 74:287–307.

Lieberman, P., K. S. Harris, P. Wolff, and L. H. Russell. 1972. Newborn infant cry and nonhuman primate vocalizations. *Journal of Speech and Hearing Research* 14:718–727.

Lieberman, P., D. H. Klatt, and W. H. Wilson. 1969. Vocal tract limitations on the vowel repertoires of rhesus monkey and other nonhuman primates. *Science* 164:1185–1187.

Lieberman, P., R. Knudsen, and J. Mead. 1969. Determination of the rate of change of fundamental frequency with respect to subglottal air pressure during sustained phonation. *Journal of the Acoustical Society of America* 45:1537–1543.

Lieberman, P., K. Landahl, and J. Ryalls. 1982. Sentence intonation in British and American English. *Journal of the Acoustical Society of America* 71, suppl. 1:S112A.

Lieberman, P., and S. B. Michaels. 1962. Some aspects of fundmental fre-
quency, envelope amplitude, and the emotional content of speech. *Journal of the Acoustical Society of America* 34:922–927.
Lieberman, P., J. Ryalls, and S. Rabson. 1982. On the early imitation of
intonation and vowels. In *Handbook of the Seventh Annual Boston University
Conference on Language Development,* 34–35.
Lifshitz, S. 1933. Two integral laws of sound perception relating loudness
and apparent duration of sound impulses. *Journal of the Acoustical Society of
America* 7:213–219.
Lindblom, B., J. Lubker, and T. Gay. 1979. Formant frequencies of some
fixed-mandible vowels and a model of speech motor programming by
predictive simulation. *Journal of Phonetics* 7:147–161.
Lisker, L., and A. Abramson. 1964. A cross language study of voicing in
initial stops: acoustical measurements. *Word* 20:384–422.
Lock, A. 1980. *The guided reinvention of language.* London: Academic Press.
Lorber, J. 1980. Is your brain really necessary? Research news. *Science*
210:1232–1234.
Lukowiak, K., and C. Sahley. 1981. The in vitro classic conditioning of the
gill withdrawal reflex of *Aplysia californica. Science* 212:1516–1518.

Macchi, M. J. 1980. Identification of vowels spoken in isolation versus vowels
spoken in consonantal context. *Journal of the Acoustical Society of America*
68:1636–1642.
Maeda, S. 1976. A characterization of American English intonation. Ph.D.
diss., Massachusetts Institute of Technology.
Mandelker, A. 1982. New research in phonetic symbolism: the poetic context. Ph.D. diss., Brown University.
Manley, R. S., and L. C. Braley. 1950. Masticatory performance and efficiency. *Journal of Dental Research* 29:448–462.
Manley, R. S., and F. R. Shiere. 1950. The effect of dental efficiency on
mastication and food preference. *Oral Surgery, Oral Medicine and Oral
Pathology* 3:674–685.
Manley, R. S., and P. Vinton. 1951. A survey of the chewing ability of
denture wearers. *Journal of Dental Research* 30:314–321.
Marler, P. 1976. An ethological theory of the origin of vocal learning. *Annals
of the New York Academy of Sciences* 280:386–395.
Marler, P., and R. Tenaza. 1977. Signalling behavior of wild apes with special
reference to vocalization. In *How animals communicate,* ed. T. Sebeok.
Bloomington: Indiana University Press.
Marshack, A. 1972. *The roots of civilization: the cognitive beginnings of man's first
art, symbol, and notation.* New York: McGraw-Hill.
Mattingly, I. G., A. M. Liberman, A. K. Syrdal, and T. Halwes. 1971.
Discrimination in speech and nonspeech modes. *Cognitive Psychology*
2:131–157.
May, J. 1976. Vocal tract normalization for /s/ and /š/. *Haskins Laboratories
Status Report on Speech Research* 48:67–73.

Mayr, E. 1942. *Systematics and the origin of species.* New York: Columbia University Press.

——— 1964. Introduction to C. Darwin, *On the origin of species.* Facsimile ed. Cambridge, Mass.: Harvard University Press.

——— 1978. Evolution. *Scientific American* 239:47–55.

McIntire, M. L. 1977. The acquisition of American Sign Language hand configuration. *Sign Language Studies* 16:247–266.

McNeil, D. 1970. *The acquisition of language: the study of developmental psycholinguistics.* New York: Harper and Row.

Mead, J., A. Bouhuys, and D. F. Proctor. 1968. Mechanisms generating subglottic pressure. *Annals of the New York Academy of Sciences* 155:177–181.

Meltzoff, A. N., and M. K. Moore. 1977. Imitation of facial and manual gestures by human neonates. *Science* 198:75–78.

Metz, D. E., R. L. Whitehead, and J. J. Mahshie. 1982. Physiological correlates of the speech of the deaf: a preliminary view. In *A handbook of communication training for the severely hearing impaired,* ed. D. E. Metz. Baltimore: Williams and Wilkins.

Miles, F. A., and E. V. Evarts. 1979. Concepts of motor organization. *Annual Reviews of Psychology* 30:327–362.

Miles, H. L. 1976. Conversations with apes: the use of sign language by two chimpanzees. Ph.D. diss., University of Connecticut.

Miller, G. A. 1951. *Language and communication.* New York: McGraw-Hill.

——— 1956. The magical number seven, plus or minus two: some limits on our capacity for processing information. *Psychological Review* 63:81–97.

Miller, G. A., and P. E. Nicely. 1955. An analysis of perceptual confusions among some English consonants. *Journal of the Acoustical Society of America* 27:338–352.

Miller, J. L. 1981. Effects of speaking rate on segmental distinctions. *Perspectives on the study of speech,* ed. P. D. Eimas and J. L. Miller. Hillsdale, N.J.: Erlbaum Associates.

Miller, J. L., and P. D. Eimas. 1976. Studies on the selective tuning of feature detectors for speech. *Journal of Phonetics* 4:119–127.

Mitchell, D. E., R. D. Freeman, M. Millodot, and G. Haegerstrom. 1973. Meridional amblyopia: evidence for modification of the human visual system by early visual experience. *Vision Research* 13:535–558.

Mitchell, H. 1971. *The hammered dulcimer.* 3rd ed. Sharon, Conn.: Folk-Legacy Records.

Miyawaki, K., W. Strange, R. R. Verbrugge, A. M. Liberman, J. J. Jenkins, and O. Fujimura. 1975. An effect of linguistic experience: the discrimination of [r] and [l] by native speakers of Japanese and English. *Perception and Psychophysics* 18:331–340.

Montague, R. 1974. In *Formal philosophy: selected papers of Richard Montague,* ed. R. Thomason. New Haven: Yale University Press.

Morris, D. 1956. The function and causation of courtship ceremonies. In *L'instinct dans le comportement des animaux et de l'homme,* ed. M. Autori. Paris: Masson.

Morris, D. H. 1974. Neanderthal speech. *Linguistic Inquiry* 5:144–150.

Morse, P. A. 1974. Infant speech perception: a preliminary model and review of the literature. In *Language perspectives: acquisition, retardation, and intervention*, ed. R. L. Schiefelbusch and L. L. Lloyd, 19–54. Baltimore: University Park Press.

——— 1976. Speech perception in the human infant and rhesus monkey. *Annals of the New York Academy of Sciences* 280:694–707.

Morse, P. A., J. E. Kass, and R. Turkienicz. 1976. Selective adaption of vowels. *Perception and Psychophysics* 19:137–143.

Morse, P. A., and C. T. Snowden. 1975. An investigation of categorical speech discrimination by rhesus monkeys. *Perception and Psychophysics* 17:9–16.

Moslin, B. 1979. The role of phonetic input in the child's acquisition of the voiced-voiceless contrast in English stops: a voice-onset time analysis. Ph.D. diss., Brown University.

Müller, J. 1848. *The physiology of the senses, voice and muscular motion with the mental faculties.* Trans. W. Baly. London: Walton and Maberly.

Muller-Schwarze, D., B. Stagge, and C. Muller-Schwarze. 1982. Play behavior: persistence, decrease, and energetic compensation during food shortage in deer fawns. *Science* 215:85–87.

Murphey, P. K., and S. G. Matsumoto. 1975. Experience modifies the plastic properties of identified neurons. *Science* 191:564–566.

Nearey, T. 1978. *Phonetic features for vowels.* Bloomington: Indiana University Linguistics Club.

Neel, J. V., and R. H. Ward. 1970. Village and tribe genetic distance among American Indians and the possible implications for human evolution. *Proceedings of American Academy of Science* 65:323–330.

Negus, V. E. 1928. *The mechanism of the larynx.* London: Heinemann.

——— 1949. *The comparative anatomy and physiology of the larynx.* New York: Hafner.

Nelson, K. 1973. Structure and strategy in learning to talk. Monograph of the Society for Research in Child Development, 38 (1–2), serial no. 149.

Nissen, H. W., and T. L. McCullogh. 1936. Discrimination learning by chimpanzees. *Journal of Comparative Psychology* 22:377–381.

Oakley, K. P., B. G. Campbell, and T. I. Molleson, eds. 1971. *Catalogue of fossil hominids,* part II, *Europe.* London: Trustees of the British Museum (Natural History).

Ohala, J. 1970. Aspects of the control and production of speech. *UCLA Working Papers in Phonetics,* no. 15. Los Angeles: UCLA Phonetics Laboratory.

Ohman, S. E. G. 1966. Coarticulation in VCV utterances: spectrographic measurements. *Journal of the Acoustical Society of America* 39:151–168.

Oller, W. A., and C. Ross. 1976. Infant babbling and speech. *Journal of Child Language* 3:1–11.

Olmsted, D. L. 1971. *Out of the mouth of babes.* The Hague: Mouton.

Olson, C. 1959. *Projective verse.* New York: Totem Press.

Patterson, P. 1978. The gestures of a gorilla. *Brain and Language* 5:72–97.

Peal, E., and W. E. Lambert. 1962. The relation of bilingualism to intelligence. *Psychological Monographs: General and Applied* 76:1–23.

Perkell, J. S. 1969. *Physiology of speech production: results and implications of a quantitative cineradiographic study.* Cambridge, Mass.: MIT Press.

Peterson, G. E., and H. L. Barney. 1952. Control methods used in a study of the vowels. *Journal of the Acoustical Society of America* 24:175–184.

Peterson, G. E., W. S.-Y. Wang, and E. Sivertson. 1958. Segmentation techniques in speech synthesis. *Journal of the Acoustical Society of America* 30:739–742.

Peterson, M. R., M. D. Beecher, S. R. Zoloth, D. B. Moody, and W. C. Stebbins. 1978. Species-specific perceptual processing of vocal sounds by monkeys. *Science* 202:324–326.

Pfungst, O. 1907. *Das Pferd des Herrn von Osten (Der kluge Hans).* Leipzig: Joh. Ambrosius.

Piaget, J. 1980. In *Language and learning: the debate between Jean Piaget and Noam Chomsky,* ed. M. Piattelli-Palmarini, 23–34, 55–64. Cambridge, Mass.: Harvard University Press.

Pierce, C. S. 1955. *Philosophical writings of Pierce,* ed. J. Buchler. New York: Dover.

Pierrehumbert, J. 1979. The perception of fundamental frequency declination. *Journal of the Acoustical Society of America* 66:363–369.

——— 1981. Synthesizing intonation. *Journal of the Acoustical Society of America* 70:985–995.

Pike, K. L. 1945. *The intonation of American English.* Ann Arbor: University of Michigan Press.

Pilbeam, D. 1972. *The ascent of man: an introduction to human evolution.* New York: Macmillan.

Pinker, S. 1979. Formal models of language learning. *Cognition* 7:217–283.

Pisoni, D. B. 1971. On the nature of categorical perception of speech sounds. Ph.D. diss., University of Michigan.

——— 1977. Identification and discrimination of the relative onset time of two component tones: implications for voicing perception in stops. *Journal of the Acoustical Society of America* 61:1352–1361.

Pisoni, D. B., T. D. Carrell, and S. S. Simnick. 1979. Does a listener need to recover the dynamic vocal tract gestures of a talker to recognize his vowels? In *Speech communication papers,* ed. J. J. Wolf and D. H. Klatt. New York: Acoustical Society of America.

Polit, A., and E. Bizzi. 1978. Processes controlling arm movements in monkeys. *Science* 201:1235–1237.

Pollack, I. 1952. The information of elementary audio displays. *Journal of the Acoustical Society of America* 24:745–749.

Pollack, I., and J. M. Pickett. 1963. The intelligibility of excerpts from conversation. *Language and Speech* 6:165–171.

Port, D. K., and M. S. Preston. 1972. Early apical stop production: a voice onset time study. *Haskins Laboratories Status Report on Speech Research* 29/30:125–149.

Premack, D. 1972. Language in chimpanzee? *Science* 172:808–822.

———— 1976. *Intelligence in ape and man.* Hillsdale, N.J.: Erlbaum.

———— 1980. Interspecies comparisons of cognitive abilities. In *Language and learning: the debate between Jean Piaget and Noam Chomsky,* ed. M. Piattelli-Palmarini. Cambridge, Mass.: Harvard University Press.

———— 1981. Language and intelligence in chimpanzee. Lecture given at Brown University.

Premack, D., and F. Woodruff. 1978. Does the chimpanzee have a theory of mind? *Brain Behavior Sciences* 1:515–526.

Pribram, K. H. 1971. *Languages of the brain: experimental paradoxes and principles in neuropsychology.* Englewood Cliffs, N.J.: Prentice-Hall.

Pruzansky, S. 1973. Clinical investigations of the experiments of nature. In *Orofacial anomalies: clinical and research implications.* ASHA Report 8. Washington, D.C.: American Speech and Hearing Association.

Purkinje, K. 1836. *Badania w przedmiocie fizyologil mowy Ludzkiej.* Krakow.

Pysh, J. J., and G. M. Weiss. 1979. Exercise during development induces an increase in Purkinje cell dendritic tree size. *Science* 206:230–232.

Rabiner, L. R., and J. Shafter. 1979. *Digital processing of speech.* New York: McGraw-Hill.

Rand, T. C. 1971. Vocal tract size normalization in the perception of stop consonants. *Haskins Laboratories Status Report on Speech Research* 25/26:141–146.

Remez, R. E. 1979. Adaptation of the category boundary between speech and non-speech: a case against feature detectors. *Cognitive Psychology* 11:38–57.

Remez, R. E., P. E. Rubin, D. B. Pisoni, and T. O. Carrell. 1981. Speech perception without traditional speech cues. *Science* 212:947–950.

Remmers, J. E., and H. Gautier. 1972. Neural and mechanical mechanisms of feline purring. *Respiratory Physiology* 16(3):351–361.

Repp, B. H., A. M. Liberman, T. Eccardt, and D. Pesetsky. 1978. Perceptual integration of acoustic cues for stop, fricative, and affricate manner. *Journal of Experimental Psychology: Human Perception and Performance* 4:621–636.

Richman, B. 1976. Some vocal distinctive features used by gelada monkeys. *Journal of the Acoustical Society of America* 60:718–724.

Rightmire, G. P. 1979. Cranial remains of *Homo erectus* from Beds II and IV, Olduvai Gorge, Tanzania. *American Journal of Physical Anthropology* 51:99–116.

Rosenblatt, F. 1958. *The perceptron: a theory of statistical separability in cognitive systems (Project PARA).* Cornell Aeronautical Laboratory Report no. UG

1196-g-1. Washington, D.C.: U.S. Department of Commerce, Office of Technical Services.

Rozin, P. 1976. The evolution of intelligence and access to the cognitive unconscious. In *Progress in psychobiology and physiological psychology,* ed. L. Sprague and A. N. Epstein, vol. 6. New York: Academic Press.

Rozin, P., S. Poritsky, and R. Stosky. 1971. American children with reading problems can easily learn to read English represented by Chinese characters. *Science* 171:1264–1267.

Rumbaugh, D. M., T. V. Gill, and E. C. von Glasserfeld. 1973. Reading and sentence completion by a chimpanzee (Pan). *Science* 182:731–733.

Russell, B. R. 1967. *The autobiography of Bertrand Russell, 1872–1914.* Boston: Little, Brown.

Russell, G. O. 1928. *The vowel.* Columbus: Ohio State University Press.

Ryalls, J. H., and P. Lieberman. 1982. Fundamental frequency and vowel perception. *Journal of the Acoustical Society of America* 72:1631–1634.

Saban, R. 1980. Le système des veines méningées moyennes chez deux Néandertaliens: l'Homme de La Chapelle-aux-Saints et l'Homme de La Quina, d'après le moulage endocrânien. Comptes Rendu de l'Académie des Sciences, Paris, Iᵉʳ Semestre (T 290, no. 20), série D 1297–1300.

——— 1983. L'asymetrie du reseau des veines méningées moyennes chez les hommes fossiles et sa signification possible. In *Proceedings of the Transdisciplinary Symposium on Glossogenetics, Paris, 1981,* ed. E. de Grolier. Paris: Harwood Academic Press.

Sachs, M. B., and E. D. Young. 1979. Encoding of steady-state vowels in the auditory nerve: representation in terms of discharge rate. *Journal of the Acoustical Society of America* 66:470–479.

Sandner, G. W. 1981. Communication with a three-month-old baby. In *Proceedings of the Thirteenth Annual Child Language Research Forum.* Stanford, Calif.: Child Language Project, Stanford University.

Sarich, V. M. 1974. Just how old is the hominid line? In *Yearbook of physical anthropology, 1973.* Washington, D.C.: American Association of Physical Anthropologists.

Saussure, F. de. 1959. *Course in general linguistics.* Trans. W. Baskin. New York: McGraw-Hill.

Sawusch, J. R., and H. C. Nusbaum. 1979. Contextual effects in vowel perception I: anchor-induced contrast effects. *Perception and Psychophysics* 25:292–302.

Sawusch, J. R., H. C. Nusbaum, and E. C. Schwab. 1980. Contextual effects in vowel perception II: evidence for two processing mechanisms. *Perception and Psychophysics* 27:421–434.

Schlesinger, H. S., and K. P. Meadow. 1972. *Sound and sign: childhood deafness and mental health.* Berkeley: University of California Press.

Schrier, S. 1977. *Abduction algorithms for grammar discovery.* Department of the Navy Technical Report. Providence, R.I.: Division of Applied Mathematics, Brown University.

Schultz, A. H. 1968. The recent hominoid primates. In *Perspectives on human evolution*, ed. S. L. Washburn and P. C. Jay, vol. 1. New York: Rinehart and Winston.

Schupack, H., M. Chatillon, P. Lieberman, and R. Meskill. 1983. Some aspects of speech perception in normal and dyslexic populations. Presented at the April 17, 1983, meeting of the New England Child Language Association, Providence, R.I.

Sebeok, T. A. 1981. The ultimate enigma of "Clever Hans": the union of nature and culture. *Annals of the New York Academy of Sciences* 364:199–205.

Seidenberg, M., and L. Petitto. 1979. Signing behavior in apes: a critical review. *Cognition* 7:177–215.

———— 1981. Ape signing: problems of method and interpretation. *Annals of the New York Academy of Sciences* 364:115–129.

Senecail, B. 1979. *L'Os hyoide: introduction anatomique a l'étude de certains mechanismes de la phonation.* Mémoires du Laboratoire d'Anatomie de la Faculté de Médecine de Paris, no. 36-1979.

Shankweiler, D., and M. Studdert-Kennedy. 1967. Identification of consonants and vowels presented to the left and right ears. *Quarterly Journal of Experimental Psychology* 19:59–63.

Shelton, R. L., Jr., and J. F. Bosma. 1962. Maintenance of the pharyngeal airway. *Journal of Applied Physiology* 17:209–214.

Sherrington, C. S. 1948. *The integrative action of the nervous system.* New Haven: Yale University Press.

Shipp, T., E. T. Doherty, and T. Morrissey. 1979. Predicting vocal frequency from selected physiologic measures. *Journal of the Acoustical Society of America* 66:678–684.

Simon, H. J., and M. Studdert-Kennedy. 1978. Selective anchoring and adaptation of phonetic and nonphonetic continua. *Journal of the Acoustical Society of America* 64:1338–1357.

Simpson, G. G. 1944. *Tempo and mode in evolution.* New York: Columbia University Press.

———— 1966. The biological nature of man. *Science* 152:472–478.

Singh, J. A. L., and R. M. Zingg. 1942. *Wolf-children and feral man.* London: Archon Books.

Sinnott, J. M. 1974. A comparison of speech sound discrimination in humans and monkeys. Ph.D. diss., University of Michigan.

Siqueland, E. R., and C. A. DeLucia. 1969. Visual reinforcement of non-nutritive sucking in human infants. *Science* 165:1144–1146.

Smith, S. D., W. J. Kimberling, B. F. Pennington, and H. A. Lubs. 1983. Specific reading disability: identification of an inherited form through linkage analysis. *Science* 219:1345–1347.

Smith, W. J. 1977. *The behavior of communicating.* Cambridge, Mass.: Harvard University Press.

Snow, C. E. 1977. Mothers' speech research: from input to interaction. In *Talking to children: language input and acquisition,* ed. C. E. Snow and C. A. Ferguson. Cambridge: Cambridge University Press.

Solecki, R. S. 1972. *Shanidar: the first flower people.* New York: Knopf.

Sorenson, J. M., and W. E. Cooper. 1980. Syntactic coding of fundamental frequency in speech production. In *Perception and production of fluent speech,* ed. R. A. Cole, 399–440. Hillside, N.J.: Erlbaum.

Spencer, H. 1878. *The principles of psychology.* London: Appleton.

Spinelli, D. N., and F. E. Jensen. 1978. Plasticity: the mirror of experience. *Science* 203:75–78.

Spurzheim, J. K. 1815. *The physiognomical system of Gall and Spurzheim.* London.

––––––– 1826. *The anatomy of the human brain.* London.

Stampe, D. L. 1973. A dissertation on natural phonology. Ph.D. diss., University of Chicago.

Stark, R. E., S. N. Rose, and M. McLagen. 1975. Features of infant sounds: the first eight weeks of life. *Journal of Child Language* 2:202–221.

Stern, D. 1974. Mother and infant at play: the dyadic interaction involving facial, vocal and gaze behaviors. In *The effect of the infant on its caregiver,* ed. M. Lewis and L. A. Rosenblum. New York: Wiley.

Stetson, R. H. 1951. *Motor phonetics.* Amsterdam: North-Holland.

Stevens, K. N. 1972. Quantal nature of speech. In *Human communication: a unified view,* ed. E. E. David, Jr., and P. B. Denes. New York: McGraw-Hill.

Stevens, K. N., R. P. Bastide, and C. P. Smith. 1955. Electrical synthesizer of continuous speech. *Journal of the Acoustical Society of America* 27:207.

Stevens, K. N., and S. E. Blumstein. 1978. Invariant cues for place of articulation in stop consonants. *Journal of the Acoustical Society of America* 64:1358–1368.

Stevens, K. N., and A. S. House. 1955. Development of a quantitative description of vowel articulation. *Journal of the Acoustical Society of America* 27:484–493.

Stockard, C. R. 1941. *The genetic and endocrinic basis for differences in form and behavior.* Philadelphia: Wistar Institute of Anatomy and Biology.

Stockwell, R. P. 1961. In *Proceedings of 1st Texas Conference on Problems of Linguistic Analysis in English.* Austin: University of Texas Press.

Stokoe, W. 1978. Sign language versus spoken language. *Sign Language Studies* 18:69–90.

Strange, W., R. R. Verbrugge, D. P. Shankweiler, and T. R. Edman. 1976. Consonantal environment specifies vowel identity. *Journal of the Acoustical Society of America* 60:213–224.

Stratton, G. E., and G. W. Uetz. 1981. Acoustic communication and reproductive isolation in two species of wolf spiders. *Science* 214:575–577.

Straus, W. L., Jr., and A. J. E. Cave. 1957. Pathology and posture of Neanderthal man. *Quarterly Review of Biology* 32:348–363.

Streeter, L. A. 1976. Language perception of 2-month-old infants shows effects of both innate mechanism and experience. *Nature* 259:39–41.

––––––– 1978. Acoustic determinants of phrase boundary perception. *Journal of the Acoustical Society of America* 64:1582–1592.

Stringer, C. B., F. C. Howell, and J. K. Melentis. 1979. The significance of the fossil hominid skull from Petralona, Greece. *Journal of Archeological Science* 6:235–253.

Swaffield, J., J. N. Shearme, and J. N. Holmes. 1961. Some measurements on the vowel sounds of conversational speech. *Journal of the Acoustical Society of America* 33:1683A.

Swets, J. A., S. H. Millman, W. E. Fletcher, and D. M. Green. 1962. Learning to identify nonverbal sounds: an application of a computer as a teaching machine. *Journal of the Acoustical Society of America* 34:928–940.

Swift, J. [1726] 1970. *Gulliver's travels.* New York: Norton.

Takagi, Y. 1964. Human postnatal growth of the vomer in relation to base of the cranium. *Annals of Oto-Rhino Laryngology* 73:238–241.

Tallal, P., and M. Piercy. 1975. Developmental aphasia: the perception of brief vowels and extended stop consonants. *Neuropsychologia* 13:69–74.

Terrace, H. 1979a. *Nim.* New York: Knopf.

———— 1979b. How Nim Chimpsky changed my mind. *Psychology Today* 13:65–76.

Terrace, H., L. A. Petitto, and T. Bever. 1976. Project Nim: progress report. Manuscript. Department of Psychology, Columbia University.

Terrace, H., L. A. Petitto, R. J. Sanders, and T. Bever. 1979. Can an ape create a sentence? *Science* 206:891–902.

Timcke, R., H. von Leden, and P. Moore. 1958. Laryngeal vibrations, measurements of the glottic wave. *A.M.A. Archives of Otolaryngology* 68:1–19.

Tinbergen, N. 1953. *Social behavior in animals.* London: Methuen.

Trager, G. L., and H. L. Smith. 1951. *Outline of English structure.* Norman, Okla.: Battenburg.

Trinkaus, E., and W. W. Howells. 1979. The Neanderthals. *Scientific American* 241:118–133.

Truby, H. M., J. F. Bosma, and J. Lind. 1965. *Newborn infant cry.* Uppsala: Almquist and Wiksell.

Tseng, Chiu-Yu. 1979. The production and perception of Mandarin vowel i: in all four tones regarding duration. In *Speech communication papers,* ed. J. J. Wolf and D. H. Klatt. New York: Acoustical Society of America.

———— 1981. An acoustic phonetic study on tones in Mandarin Chinese. Ph.D. diss., Brown University.

Tuber, D. S., G. G. Berntson, D. S. Bachman, and J. N. Allen. 1980. Associative learning in premature hydroencephalic and normal twins. *Science* 210:1035–1037.

Tyson, E. 1699. *Orang-outang, sive homo sylvestris: or the anatomy of a pygmie compared with that of a monkey, an ape, and a man.* London: Thomas Bennet and Daniel Brown.

Van Cantfort, T. E., and J. B. Rimpau. 1982. Sign language studies with children and chimpanzees. *Sign Language Studies* 34:15–72.

Van den Berg, Jw. 1958. Myoelastic-aerodynamic theory of voice production. *Journal of Speech and Hearing Research* 1:227–244.

———— 1960. Vocal ligaments versus registers. *Current Problems in Phoniatrics and Logopedics* 1:19–34.

———— 1962. Modern research in experimental phoniatrics. *Folia Phoniatrica* 14:81–149.

Vanderslice, R., and P. Ladefoged. 1972. Binary suprasegmental features and transformational word-accentuated rules. *Language* 48(4):819–838.

Verbrugge, R., W. Strange, and D. Shankweiler. 1976. What information enables a listener to map a talker's vowel space? *Haskins Laboratories Status Report on Speech Research* 37/38:199–208.

Virchow, R. 1872. Untersuchung des Neanderthal-Schadels. *Zeitschrift für Ethnographie* 4:157–165.

von Kempelen, W. R. 1791. *Le Méchanisme de la parole suivi de la déscription d'une machine parlante.* Vienna: J. V. Degen.

Wall, R. 1972. *Introduction to mathematical linguistics.* Englewood Cliffs, N.J.: Prentice-Hall.

Walters, T., T. J. Carew, and E. R. Kandel. 1981. Associative learning in *Aplysia:* evidence for conditioned fear in an invertebrate. *Science* 211:404–506.

Wanner, E., and M. Maratsos. 1978. An ATN approach to comprehension. In *Linguistic theory and psychological reality,* ed. M. Halle, J. Bresnan, and G. A. Miller. Cambridge, Mass.: MIT Press.

Wanner, E., and S. Shiner. 1976. Measuring transient memory load. *Journal of Verbal Learning and Verbal Behavior* 15:159–167.

Waters, R. A., and W. A. Wilson, Jr. 1979. Speech perception by rhesus monkeys: the voicing distinction in synthesized labial and velar stop consonants. *Perception and Psychophysics* 19:285–289.

Whitehouse, P., A. Caramazza, and E. Zurif. 1978. Naming in aphasia: interacting effects of form and function. *Brain and Language* 6:63–74.

Whitfield, I. C. 1967. *The auditory pathway.* London: Arnold.

Whitfield, I. C., and E. F. Evans. 1965. Responses of auditory cortical neurons to stimuli of changing frequency. *Journal of Neurophysiology* 28:655–672.

Whorf, B. L. 1956. *Language, thought and reality,* ed. J. B. Carroll. Cambridge, Mass.: MIT Press.

Wiesel, T. N., and D. H. Hubel. 1965. Comparison of the effects of unilateral and bilateral eye closure on cortical unit responses in kittens. *Journal of Neurophysiology* 28:1029–1040.

Williams, E. S. 1981. Language acquisition, markedness, and phrase structure. In *Language acquisition and linguistic theory,* ed. S. L. Tavakolian. Cambridge, Mass.: MIT Press.

Williamson, P. E. 1981. Palaeontological documentation of speciation in Cenozoic molluscs from Turkana Basin. *Nature* 293:437–443.

Willis, R. 1828. On the vowel sounds, and on reed organ pipes. *Transactions of the Cambridge Philosophical Society* 3:10.

Wind, J. 1976. Phylogeny of the human vocal tract. *Annals of the New York Academy of Sciences* 280:612–630.

Witelson, S. F. 1977. Anatomic asymmetry in the temporal lobes: its documentation, phylogenesis, and relationship to functional asymmetry. In *Evolution and lateralization of the brain,* ed. S. J. Diamond and D. A. Blizard, 328–354. New York: New York Academy of Sciences.

Wollberg, Z., and J. D. Newman. 1972. Auditory cortex of squirrel monkey: response patterns of single cells to species-specific vocalizations. *Science* 173:1248–1251.

Yeni-Komshian, G. H., and D. A. Benson. 1976. Anatomical study of cerebral asymmetry in the temporal lobe of humans, chimpanzees, and rhesus monkeys. *Science* 192:387–389.

Young, E. D., and M. B. Sachs. 1979. Representation of steady-state vowels in the temporal aspects of the discharge patterns of populations of auditory-nerve fibers. *Journal of the Acoustical Society of America* 66:1381–1403.

Yunis, J. J., and O. Prakash. 1982. The origin of man: a chromosomal pictorial legacy. *Science* 215:1525–1530.

Zangwell, O. L. 1962. Dyslexia in relation to cerebral dominance. In *Reading disability,* ed. J. Money. Baltimore: Johns Hopkins University Press.

Zelazo, P. R., N. A. Zelazo, and S. Kolb. 1972. "Walking" in the newborn. *Science* 176:314–315.

Zinkin, N. I. 1968. *Mechanisms of speech.* The Hague: Mouton.

Zoloth, S. R., M. R. Peterson, M. D. Beecher, S. Green, P. Marler, D. B. Moody, and W. Stebbins. 1979. Species-specific perceptual processing of vocal sounds by monkeys. *Science* 204:870–873.

Zurif, E. B., and S. E. Blumstein. 1978. Language and the brain. In *Linguistic theory and psychological reality,* ed. M. Halle, J. Bresnan, and G. A. Miller. Cambridge, Mass.: MIT Press.

Zurif, E. B., and A. Caramazza. 1976. Psycholinguistic structures in aphasia: studies in syntax and semantics. In *Studies in neurolinguistics,* ed. H. Whitaker and H. A. Whitaker, vol. 1. New York: Academic Press.

Zurif, E. B., A. Caramazza, and R. Myerson. 1972. Grammatical judgments of agrammatic aphasics. *Neuropsychologia* 10:405–418.

NOTES

CHAPTER 2. DISTRIBUTED NEURAL COMPUTERS AND FEATURE DETECTORS

1. It is intriguing to pose the following questions: Are the basic primitives of human visual art structured by these elementary form classes? Do we respond to these shapes in a "stronger" mode than we do to other patterns? What makes a painting's composition appealing?

CHAPTER 3. AUTOMATIZATION AND SYNTAX

1. Rule-governed modes of behavior that take into account an entire derivation, or sequence of steps, typically structure social interaction. Phrase structure rules, for example, cannot describe the conventions of marriage. A man cannot marry his own sister; in some cultures the lineage of the bride and/or groom must be examined with great care before marriage is possible.

CHAPTER 4. SYNTAX, WORDS, AND MEANING

1. The animal may ignore a signal that is produced in an inappropriate context. Stickleback fish, for example, make use of sequential display patterns (Tinbergen, 1953; Morris, 1956) in their courtship routine; particular displays of the male elicit particular responses in the female and so on, until the completion of the ritual. The sequences are not completely rigid. A particular display by a male, for example, does not always elicit a given response by a female. However, the sequence as a whole has a simple fixed reference and is not like a word. It has elementary "phonetic" elements that must fit the "rules" of some fish "morphology" for the signal to be well formed, but the signal's reference is fixed.

2. Although ethological studies have not addressed the question of whether higher animals other than human beings make productive use of rule-governed sequences for communication, recent models of other aspects of animal behavior involve "syntactic" rules. Dawkins (1976) reviews a number of studies of animal behavior, pigeon courtship, grooming in flies, and mouse grooming and suggests several possible appropriate grammars. The evolutionary homologues of human syntactic behavior perhaps may be manifested in aspects of animal behavior other than communication.

364

CHAPTER 6. ELEPHANT EARS, FROGS, AND HUMAN SPEECH

1. The anatomy of respiration will be discussed in detail in Chapter 11 with regard to its ontogenetic development and probable evolution in hominids.

CHAPTER 7. SPEECH IS SPECIAL

1. The TASI system that has been in use since 1963 keeps track of the time in which you are not talking when you speak to someone. Every segment of time in which you do not speak is used to put another conversation through the same cable circuit. The system has to label and sort out each conversation at each end of the cable, but it works and saves lots of money on cables.

2. The acoustic correlates of the "distinctive feature" system proposed by Jakobson, Fant, and Halle (1952) often are misinterpreted to support the position that linguistic contrast can be derived from measurements on the actual "raw" acoustic spectrum. This is not the case. Jakobson's acoustic correlates constitute a set of hypothetical acoustic measures that can serve to differentiate phonetic or phonemic sound distinctions. Some of the acoustic correlates do relate directly to the acoustic signal—for example, the characteristics of the source, whether it is *voiced* or not, interrupted or continuous, and the like. Some of the acoustic correlates relate to the spectral properties of the speech signal, whether there is more high-frequency energy or low-frequency energy present, and so on. These acoustic correlates however, are defined in terms of the *formant frequency* patterns of the sounds. The energy balances discussed in the work of Jakobson, Fant, and Halle (1952) thus pertain to the derived filter function of the supralaryngeal filter. They are related to the actual acoustic spectrum in terms of the formant frequency patterns that must first be derived by the listener.

CHAPTER 8. LINGUISTIC DISTINCTIONS AND AUDITORY PROCESSES

1. Other adaptation experiments have claimed that the phenomenon has nothing to do with the perception of speech but instead follows from an "anchoring" effect (Simon and Studdert-Kennedy, 1978). However, the data that Simon and Studdert-Kennedy report do not support their conclusion. Remez (1979) derives adaptation data in which listeners were asked to differentiate between speechlike sounds and nonspeech sounds along a continuum that involves gradually increasing the band width of formant frequencies. Remez interprets his data as an argument against selective adaptation having anything to do with the perception of speech, since a nonspeech versus speech feature detector is most unlikely. The adaptation effects in Remez's experiment, however, could involve the listeners' response to the two phonetic categories of nonnasal versus nasal speech sounds, which differ among other acoustic cues in the band widths of formants (Fant, 1960).

Chapter 9. The Man on the Flying Trapeze

1.   Goldstein (1980), in her computer-implemented modeling study, claims
     that the newborn vocal tract can produce these vowels. The hypothetical
     newborn vocal tract on which Goldstein bases this claim, however, bears
     little relation to the supralaryngeal vocal tracts of newborn infants that
     have been described in a number of anatomic and radiographic studies
     (Negus, 1949; Lieberman and Crelin, 1971; Bosma, 1975; Laitman et
     al., 1977, 1978; George, 1978; Grosmangin, 1979). Goldstein did not
     base her study of the newborn vocal tract on data derived from newborn
     infants. The key parameters that she uses to estimate the shape of the
     tongue and the relation of the oral cavity to the pharynx are derived
     from King's (1952) data for 3-month-old infants. Her hypothetical new-
     born vocal tract is essentially that of a 3-month-old infant since she does
     not take account of the restructuring of the basicranium and mandible
     that occurs between birth and 3 months.
          Goldstein's objective was to devise a computer model that would (a)
     show a growth of the human supralaryngeal vocal tract from birth
     onward and (b) model the acoustic output of the supralaryngeal vocal
     tract at any age. Instead of using anatomical and x-ray data of the
     newborn vocal tract, though such data are available, Goldstein attempted
     to "project-back" dimensions derived from 3-month-old infants. She
     indeed notes that her hypothetical, projected-back version of the new-
     born vocal tract differs from anatomical data like those of Crelin and
     Lieberman (1971) and Bosma (1975), but she comes to the conclusion
     that the anatomical data are distorted. Goldstein calculates the length of
     the pharynx by subtracting the distance between the hard palate and roof
     of the nasopharynx from the distance between the roof of the nasophar-
     ynx and the hyoid bone. She derives these dimensions from King's
     (1952) x-ray study. King's data start with 3-month-old infants, so Gold-
     stein attempts to project-back these dimensions to age 0 by means of
     regression algorithms in which she essentially subtracts from each of
     these measures, SNHY and SNPNS, an offset that I will term D. The
     calculation is detailed in pages 108–110 of her dissertation, where she
     notes that subtracting these measurements will yield "a reasonably good
     approximation of the distance from the palatal line to the middle of the
     hyoid." It is worth running through these calculations. Figure 2-23 of
     Goldstein (1980), her plot of SNHY, yields an age 0 value of 48 mm.
     Figure 2-24, her plot of SNPNS, yields an age 0 value of 21 mm. The
     difference is 27 mm for the putative newborn. If Goldstein had checked
     this dimension against the actual data of King (1952), which formed her
     starting point, she would have seen that this dimension is approximately
     28 mm for a 3-month-old male infant. What Goldstein did in calculating
     this distance was to cancel out the offset term D, which was supposed to
     project-back to age 0, the dimensions derived from 3-month-old infants.
     If we use the notation $SNHY\ 0$ to signify the putative age newborn
     dimension and $SNHY\ 3$ to signify King's measured value for a 3-month-

old, it is easy to see the source of Goldstein's error. Going through the steps:

1   SNHY 0 = SNHY 3 − D
2   SNPNS 0 = SNPNS 3 − D

Thus:

3   SNHY 0 − SNPNS 0 = SNHY 3 − D − (SNPNS 3 − D)
4   SNHY 0 − SNPNS 0 = SNHY 3 − D − SNPNS 3 + D
5   SNHY 0 − SNPNS 0 = SNHY 3 − SNPNS 3

2.   Although the most dramatic change in the development of the human supralaryngeal vocal tract takes place between birth and age 3 months, the length of the pharynx does not become equal to that of the oral cavity until adolescence (George, 1978; Laitman et al., 1977, 1978; Grosmangin, 1979; Goldstein, 1980). In an [u], F_1 and F_2 each depend on the length of the oral and pharyngeal cavities (Fant, 1960). It thus is not possible to drive both F_1 and F_2 of the infant [u] as low in frequency as is the case for an adult [u].

3.   To keep the discussion from becoming confused in phonetic detail, the vowels will be grouped into two classes, one that includes the mother's and infant's [a]'s and [ae]'s and one that includes [u]-like vowels.

4.   As the discussion of Chapters 7 and 8 noted, the invariant units for speech perception may not all correspond to traditional phonetic segments or features. We may instead be equipped with neural devices that are equivalent to "fully specified syllable templates" in which the complex of integrated acoustic cues that specify syllables are stored in the brain. Syllable templates, of course, require much more storage space in the brain than do neural devices that instead analyze speech in terms of segmental phonemes or features. There, however, appears to be no lack of storage space in the brain (Anderson, 1972).

Chapter 10. Apes and Children

1.   Exponents of the theory of neoteny like Gould (1977) claim that one major element that changed the direction of human evolution from that of the apes is the "prolonged" childhood and adolescence of human beings, but chimpanzees are very similar in this regard.

2.   It is also apparent in listening to these tape recordings that another claim of Terrace and his colleagues (1979) and Seidenberg and Petitto (1979) is false. They claim that the utterances of chimpanzees contain many repetitions and that children do *not* repeat words. Their claim evidently is based on the data published by Bloom in which she *excluded* repetitions (Bloom, 1970, p. 261). Children continually repeat words and phrases.

        Terrace and Seidenberg and Petitto also build up a case against other investigators of chimpanzee signing by dwelling on the fact that they have not published a complete corpus. However, neither have

Terrace, Seidenberg, or Petitto published a complete corpus. The only complete one that has been published of chimpanzee conversations is that of Miles (1976), which Terrace appears to overlook. The studies of children's utterances that Terrace and colleagues cite, furthermore, do not contain any complete corpus. Van Cantfort and Rimpau (1982), in their review article, surveyed the *Journal of Psycholinguistic Research,* volumes 1-7 through 1978, and *Sign Language Studies.* No complete corpus was published. Small portions of a corpus occasionally were published. A larger corpus of children's speech derived from the tape recordings of the Brown University project was published by Landahl (1982). This corpus, like the tape recordings, shows many repetitions.

CHAPTER 11. THE EVOLUTION OF HUMAN SPEECH: COMPARATIVE STUDIES

1.   The situation is the reverse of the articulatory maneuver noted in connection with swallowing. The anterior digastrics in swallowing pull the hyoid upward and frontward—the mandible is stabilized and the hyoid relaxed so that it moves rather than the mandible.

CHAPTER 12. THE EVOLUTION OF HUMAN SPEECH: THE FOSSIL RECORD

1.   DuBrul (1977), in arguing that the classic Neanderthal hominids were similar to anatomically modern human beings, claims that Boule's (1911–1913) reconstruction of the La Chapelle-aux-Saints fossil is seriously deficient. DuBrul further claims that Heim's (1974) reconstruction of the La Ferrassie Neanderthal fossil shows that it, too, is similar to a modern human being with respect to the basicranium. Grosmangin, independently working from the original fossil material, refutes both of DuBrul's claims, though she was working in a neutral frame of reference since she was not aware of DuBrul's claims. She furthermore notes that some aspects of Heim's reconstruction, on which DuBrul places much value, are in error (Grosmangin, 1979, p. 189).

2.   Although Neanderthal and older archaic fossil hominids walked upright, their skeletal morphology is not as well adapted as ours for this posture. The recession of the mandible and palate that differentiates anatomically modern *Homo sapiens* from earlier hominids shortens the length of the palate, which is important in the development of the human supralaryngeal vocal tract. The human skull is also better balanced on the vertebral column because of these changes. Preadaptation for head balance thus may have been a factor in the evolution of the human supralaryngeal vocal tract (Lieberman, 1976a). The presence of hominid "experiments" like the Broken Hill fossil, in which the basicranium is flexed while retaining a somewhat longer palate than that of modern human beings, or the Saccopastore and Monte Circeo–I fossils, however, argues against upright posture and head balance being the only selective force that was involved in the evolution of the adult human skull.

3.   Dingwall (1979) and Falk (1980) cite an acoustic study by Jordan (1971) and claim that chimpanzees produce the vowels [i], [u], and [a]. Dingwall

and Falk appear to lack an elementary knowledge of the principles of acoustic analysis and standard phonetic notation. Jordan (1971) used a technique (an octave band analyzer) that is appropriate for the spectral analysis of industrial noise. He reports formant band widths in excess of 1 kHz (they should range between 60 and 300 Hz); the spectra that he publishes are furthermore not consistent with the claim that chimpanzees produce either [u] or [a]. Jordan, in fact, does not claim that they produce the vowel [i]; Dingwall and Falk have misinterpreted the phonetic symbol [y], which for Polish transcribes the vowel [I] (of the English word *bit*), for the vowel [i]. Jordan, moreover, qualifies his analysis and notes that the chimpanzee calls "sound like" the vowels of human speech but do not have the acoustic properties of human vowels (see Lieberman, 1982b).

4. As I noted in Chapter 9, the vocal tract modeling study of Goldstein (1980) confuses the issue by modeling the supralaryngeal vocal tract of a 3-month-old infant as that of a newborn. Goldstein has no data on newborn vocal tracts; she uses the radiographic data of King (1952) for 3-month-olds, which she assumes yield a vocal tract that is somewhat larger than that of the newborn. She does attempt to rescale the length of the pharynx to its newborn proportions, but she commits an arithmetic error in computing the length of the newborn pharynx. Goldstein's "newborn" vocal tract has a thick, round tongue and is not like any newborn supralaryngeal airway that has yet been described. For reasons that are not clear, Goldstein claims that the published descriptions of the newborn airway of Crelin (1969, 1973), Bosma (1975), Negus (1949), Lieberman and Crelin (1971), and George (1978) are all distorted, though she cites no anatomical or radiographic data that support this claim.

5. The specific objections to the reconstructions and the particular theory for the evolution of human speech that I have discussed include Morris (1974), Carlisle and Siegel (1974), LeMay (1975), DuBrul (1976, 1977), Wind (1976), Falk (1975), and Dingwall (1979). Responses to these criticisms have been noted earlier and may also be found in the works of Lieberman (1975a, 1975b, 1976a, 1976b, 1977b, 1979b, 1982a, 1982b, 1983).

6. An examination of marriage banns in a village like Saas-Fee in the Valais of Switzerland will establish this point.

Index